'Beard's cheerful scepticism makes her Pompeii more intriguing, more believable, than any version I have read' Christian Tyler, *Financial Times*

'This is ancient history as it should be written and the invaluable companion to any trip to Pompeii' Giles Foden, *Conde Nast Traveller*

'A forensic adventure through the back alleys and the mansions of a dead city, checking the beds, the looms, the loos, what time the carts rolled in the streets, what was for breakfast and the politics going down in the Forum ... a proper detective story ... a wonder', Michael Pye, *Scotsman*

'My advice? Buy this book before you go – all trips to Pompeii, armchair or actual, will be inordinately enhanced' Bettany Hughes, *Times*

'She makes the dead of Pompeii spring to life' Raymond Carr, *Spectator*

'This is a fascinating book' Alan Massie, *Literary Review*

'How exciting to have this perfect *vademecum* – another word for a guidebook, as all you Latin scholars will know, or literally, a "go-with-me"' Harry Mount, *Independent on Sunday*

'The book begins in darkness with desperate fugitives attempting to outrun the deadly flow. It ends with a practical guide to viewing the site, right down to tipping the lavatory attendants ... It is an odd juxtaposition, but an inspired one. Few could resist a visit having read Mary Beard's compelling account' Elizabeth Speller, *Independent*

'I'm tempted to say if you read one book of history this year it should be *Pompeii*. Not just because it is written with a rare mixture of scrupulous scholarship and a relaxed conversational narrative drive – Beard seems actually to like her readers, which is rare among serious scholars – but because Pompeii itself matters' Michael Bywater, *New Statesman*

'What Mary Beard , one of the most distinguished Roman historians in the English-speaking world, has given us here is a delightfully readable account ... She has the facility for bringing all the characters to life ... without sacrificing scholarly accuracy' John Dillon, *Irish Times*

MARY BEARD is one of the most original and best-known classicists working today. She has a chair of Classics at Cambridge where she is a Fellow of Newnham College, and she is Classics editor of the *Times Literary Supplement*. Her frequent broadcasts and her *Times* blog 'A Don's Life' have brought her a wide audience, like her books, which include *SPQR: A History of Ancient Rome*, *The Parthenon* and (with Keith Hopkins) *The Colosseum* (both Profile) and the acclaimed *The Roman Triumph* (Harvard University Press).

POMPEII

The Life of a Roman Town

MARY BEARD

P

PROFILE BOOKS

This paperback edition published in 2009
First published in 2008 by
PROFILE BOOKS LTD
3A Exmouth House
Pine Street
London ECIR OJH
www.profilebooks.com

9 10 8

Printed and bound by
CPI Group (UK) Ltd, Croydon, CRO 4YY

Typeset in Fournier by MacGuru Ltd
info@macguru.org.uk

A CIP catalogue record for this book is available from the British Library.

ISBN 978 1 86197 596 6

CONTENTS

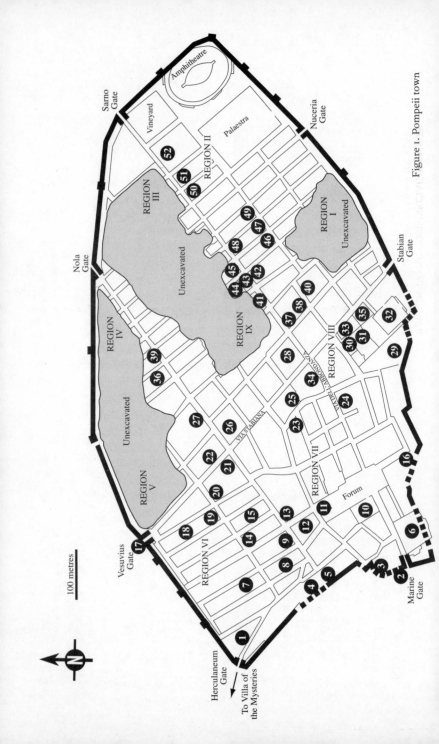

Figure 1. Pompeii town

KEY

HOUSES

House of Aramantus – see, Bar of Aramantus
22 House of Lucius Caecilius Jucundus (V.1.26)
37 House of Casca Longus (I.6.11)
38 House of the Ceii (I.6.15)
House of the Chaste Lovers – see, Bakery of the Chaste Lovers
24 House of the Doctor (VIII.5.24)
34 House of Epidius Rufus (IX.1.20)
7 House of the Etruscan Column (VI.5.17–18)
5 House of Fabius Rufus (VII.16[ins.occ.].22)
15 House of the Faun (VI.12.2)
4 House of the Golden Bracelet (VI.17[ins.occ.],42)
42 House of the Indian Statuette (I.8.5)
45 House of Julius Polybius (IX.12.1–3)
51 House of Marine Venus (III.3.3)
36 House of Marcus Lucretius Fronto (V.4a)
40 House of the Menander (I.10.4)
50 House of Octavius Quartio (III.2.2)
21 House of Orpheus (VI.14.20)
44 House of the Painters at Work (IX.12)
18 House of the Prince of Naples (VI.15.7–8)
9 House of the Tragic Poet (VI.18.3–5)
27 House of the Triclinium (V.2.4)
3 House of Umbricius Scaurus (VII.16 [ins.occ.],12–15)
48 House of Venus in a Bikini (I.11.6)
1 House of the Vestals (VI.1.7)
19 House of the Vettii (VI.15.1)
8 *Insula* Arriana Polliana (VI.6)
52 *Praedia* (Estate) of Julia Felix (II.4.2)

BARS, INNS AND COMMERCIAL PREMISES

43 Bakery of the Chaste Lovers (IX.12.6)
46 Bar of Amarantus (I.9.11–12)
41 Bar of Asellina etc. (IX.11.12)
47 Bar of Euxinus (I.XI.10–11)
14 Bar on the Via di Mercurio (VI.10.1)
20 Bar of Salvius (VI.14.36)
25 Bar of Sittius (VII.1.44–5)
23 Brothel (VII.12.18–20)
49 *Garum* Shop (I.12.8)

OTHER PUBLIC BUILDINGS ETC.

For buildings around the Forum, see *Figure 14*
35 Covered Theatre
31 Large Theatre
32+39 Lodging/barracks of gladiators
17 Water Castle

TEMPLES

10 Temple of Apollo
13 Temple of Fortuna Augusta
30 Temple of Isis
11 Temple of Jupiter, Juno and Minerva
29 Temple of Minerva and Hercules (Triangular Forum)
6 Temple of Venus
33 Temple of 'Jupiter Meilichios'

BATHS

26 Central Baths
12 Forum Baths
16 Sarno Baths
28 Stabian Baths
2 Suburban Baths

INTRODUCTION

Life interrupted

In the early hours of 25 August 79 CE, the rain of pumice falling on Pompeii was easing off. It seemed a good moment to leave the city and make a bid for safety. A straggling group of more than twenty fugitives, who had been taking shelter within the walls while the dreadful downpour had been at its worst, took a chance on one of the eastern gates of the city, hoping to find a way out of range of the volcanic bombardment.

A few others had tried this route some hours before. One couple had fled, carrying just a small key (they presumably hoped one day to return to whatever it locked – house, apartment, chest or strong box) and a single bronze lamp (Ill. 1). This can hardly have made much impact against the darkness of the night and the clouds of debris. But it was an expensive and fashionable object, moulded in the shape of a black African head – a hint of the (to us) disconcerting forms of ingenuity we shall often come across in Pompeii. The pair didn't make it. Overwhelmed by the pumice, they were found in 1907 where they had fallen, next to one of the grand tombs which lined this road, like others, out of the city. They collapsed, in fact, next to the lavish memorial to a woman who had died perhaps fifty years before, Aesquillia Polla, the wife of Numerius Herennius Celsus. Just twenty-two years old (as we can still read on the stone), she must have been less than half the age of her rich husband, a member of one of Pompeii's most prominent families, who had served as an officer in the Roman army and had twice been elected to the highest office in the city's local government.

The layers of pumice had built up to several feet by the time the other group

1. Small lamps in the shape of human heads (or feet) were fashionable in the first century CE. Here the oil was poured into the hole in his brow and the flame burned at his mouth. Including the petals which form the handle, it is just 12 centimetres long.

decided to risk escape in the same direction. Walking was slow and difficult. Most of these fugitives were young men, many carrying nothing with them, either because they had nothing to bring or because they could no longer get to their valuables. One man had taken the precaution of arming himself with a dagger, in an elegant sheath (he had another sheath with him too, empty, because he had perhaps lost or lent the weapon it had held). The few women in the group had rather more. One carried a little silver statuette of the goddess Fortuna, 'Good Fortune', sitting on a throne, plus a handful of gold and silver rings – one with a tiny silver phallus attached by a chain, as a lucky charm perhaps (and another object we shall often meet in the course of this book). Others had their own little store of precious trinkets: a silver medicine box, a tiny base to hold a (missing) statuette and a couple of keys, all stuffed into a cloth bag; a wooden jewellery case, with a necklace, ear-rings, silver spoon – and more keys. They had also brought what cash they could. For some just a bit of loose change; for others, whatever they had stashed away at home, or the takings of their shop. But it was not much. All in all, between the whole group there was barely 500 *sesterces* – which is in Pompeian terms about what it cost to buy a single mule.

Some of this group got a little further than the earlier couple. Fifteen or so had reached the next grand memorial, twenty metres further down the road, the tomb of Marcus Obellius Firmus, when what we now know as the 'pyroclastic surge' from Vesuvius wiped them out – a deadly, burning combination of gases, volcanic debris and molten rock travelling at huge speed, against which nothing could survive. Their bodies have been found, some mixed up with, even

2. The plaster casts made from the bodies of the victims are constant reminders of their humanity – that they were just like us. This memorable cast of a man dying, with his head in his hands, has been placed for safe-keeping in a site storeroom. He now seems to be lamenting his own imprisonment.

apparently still clutching, branches of wood. Maybe the more agile amongst them had taken to the trees which surrounded the tombs in a hopeless attempt to save themselves; more likely the surge which killed the fugitives also brought the trees crashing down on top of them.

The tomb of Obellius Firmus itself fared rather better. He was another Pompeian grandee, who had died a few decades earlier, and long enough ago for the sides of his monument to be used as a local message board. We can still read here the advertisement for some gladiatorial shows, and plenty of scrawlings by some tomb-side dawdlers: 'Hello Issa, from Habitus', 'Hello Occasus, from Scepsinianus', and so on (Habitus' friends apparently replied with a large phallus and testicles, and the message 'Hello Habitus from your mates everywhere'). Up above, the text of the formal epitaph of Obellius Firmus declared that his funeral had been paid for by the local council, to the cost of 5000 *sesterces* – with an extra 1000 *sesterces* being added by some other local officials for incense and 'a shield' (probably a portrait on a shield, a distinctive Roman type of memorial). These

3. Someone's precious possession? This squat little figurine made out of red amber from the Baltic was found with one of the unsuccessful fugitives. Just 8 centimetres tall, it was perhaps meant to represent one of the stock characters from Roman mime, popular entertainment in Pompeii (p. 256) .

funeral expenses were, in other words, well over ten times what the whole party of fugitives had managed to gather together for their flight to safety. Pompeii was a city of poor and rich.

We can trace many other stories of attempted flight. Almost 400 bodies have been discovered in the layers of pumice, and nearer 700 in the now solid remains of the pyroclastic flow – many of these recaptured vividly at the moment of their death by the clever technique, invented in the nineteenth century, of filling the space left by their decomposing flesh and clothes with plaster, to reveal the hitched-up tunics, the muffled faces, the grim expressions of the victims (Ill. 2). One group of four, found in a street near the Forum, was probably an entire family trying to make its escape. The father went in front, a burly man, with big bushy eyebrows (as the plaster cast reveals). He had pulled his cloak over his head, to protect himself from falling ash and debris, and carried with him some gold jewellery (a simple finger-ring and a few ear-rings), a couple of keys and, in this case, a reasonable amount of cash, at almost 400 *sesterces*. His two small daughters followed, while the mother brought up the rear. She had hitched up her dress to make the walking easier, and was carrying more household valuables in a little bag: the family silver (some spoons, a pair of goblets, a medallion with the figure of Fortuna, a mirror) and a small squat figurine of a little boy, wrapped up in a cloak, his bare feet peeking out at the bottom (Ill. 3). It is a crude piece of work, but it is made out of amber, which must have travelled many hundreds of kilometres from the nearest source of supply in the Baltic; hence its prize status.

Other finds tell of other lives. There was the medical man who fled clutching his box of instruments, only to be overwhelmed by the lethal surge as he crossed the *palaestra* (the large open space or exercise area) near the Amphitheatre, making for one of the southern gates in the city; the slave found in the garden of a large house in the centre of town, his movement surely hampered by the iron bands around his ankles; the priest of the goddess Isis (or maybe a temple servant) who had parcelled up some of the temple's valuables to take with him in his flight, but had not gone more than 50 metres before he too was killed. And then, of course, there was the richly jewelled lady found in one of the rooms in the gladiators' barracks. This has often been written up as a nice illustration of the penchant of upper-class Roman women for the brawny bodies of gladiators. Here, it seems, is one of them caught in the wrong place at the wrong time, her adultery exposed to the gaze of history. It is, in fact, a much more innocent scene than that. Almost certainly the woman was not on a date at all, but had taken refuge in the barracks, when the going got too rough on her flight out of the city. At least, if this *was* an assignation with her toy-boy, it was an assignation she shared with seventeen others and a couple of dogs – all of whose remains were found in the same small room.

The dead bodies of Pompeii have always been one of the most powerful images, and attractions, of the ruined city. In the early excavations during the eighteenth and nineteeth centuries, skeletons were conveniently 'discovered' in the presence of visiting royalty and other dignitaries (Ill. 4). Romantic travellers gushed at the thought of the cruel disaster that had afflicted the poor souls whose mortal remains they witnessed, not to mention the more general reflections on the perilous fragility of human existence that the whole experience prompted. Hester Lynch Piozzi – the English writer who owed her surname to her marriage to an Italian music teacher – captured (and lightly parodied) these reactions, after a visit to the site in 1786: 'How dreadful are the thoughts which such a sight suggests! How horrible the certainty that such a scene might be all acted over again tomorrow; and that, who today are spectators, may become spectacles to travellers of a succeeding century, who mistaking our bones for those of the Neapolitans, may carry them to their native country back again perhaps.'

4. Celebrity visitors to Pompeii had excavations re-staged for their benefit. Here, in 1769, the Emperor of Austria surveys a skeleton found in a house, now known after him as 'The House of Emperor Joseph II'. The lady of the party reacts with more obvious interest.

In fact, one of the most celebrated objects from the first years of digging was the imprint of a woman's breast found in a large house (the so-called Villa of Diomedes) just outside the city walls in the 1770s. Almost a century before the technique of making full plaster casts of the body cavities had been perfected, the solid debris here allowed the excavators to see the full form of the dead, their clothing, even their hair, moulded into the lava. The only part of this material they managed successfully to extract and preserve was that one breast, which was put on display in the nearby museum, and quickly became a tourist attraction. In due course it also became the inspiration for Théophile Gautier's famous novella of 1852, *Arria Marcella*. This features a young Frenchman who, infatuated with the breast that he has seen in the museum, returns to the ancient city (in an unsettling combination of time travel, wishful thinking and fantasy) to find, or to reinvent, his beloved – the woman of his dreams, one of the last Roman occupants of the Villa of Diomedes. Sadly the breast itself, despite all its celebrity, has simply disappeared, and a major hunt for it in the 1950s failed to reveal any hint of its fate. One theory is that the battery of invasive tests carried out by curious nineteenth-century scientists eventually caused it to disintegrate: ashes to ashes, as it were.

6

The power of the Pompeian dead has lasted into our own age too. Primo Levi's poem 'The Girl-Child of Pompei' uses the plaster cast of a little girl, found clutching her mother ('As though, when the noon sky turned black / You wanted to re-enter her'), to reflect on the fate of Anne Frank and an anonymous school-girl from Hiroshima – victims of manmade rather than natural disasters ('The torments heaven sends us are enough / Before your finger presses down, stop and consider'). Two casts even play a cameo role in Roberto Rossellini's 1953 film, *Voyage to Italy* – hailed as 'the first work of modern cinema', though a commercial disaster. Clinging to each other, lovers still in death, these victims of Vesuvius serve as a sharp and upsetting reminder to two modern tourists (Ingrid Bergman – then herself in a faltering marriage to Rossellini – and George Sanders) of just how distant and empty their own relationship has become. But it is not only human victims who are preserved in this way. One of the most famous, and evocative, casts is that of a guard dog found still tethered to his post in the house of a wealthy fuller (laundry-man-cum-cloth-worker). He died frantically trying to get free of his chain.

Voyeurism, pathos and ghoulish prurience certainly all contribute to the appeal of these casts. Even the most hard-nosed archaeologists can come up with lurid descriptions of their death agonies, or of the toll taken on the human body by the pyroclastic flow ('their brains would have boiled …'). For visitors to the site itself, where some of the casts are still on display near where they were found, they produce something like the 'Egyptian Mummy effect': small children press their noses against the glass cases with cries of horror, while adults resort to their cameras – though hardly disguising their similarly grim fascination with these remains of the dead.

But ghoulishness is not the whole story. For the impact of these victims (whether fully recast in plaster, or not) comes also from the sense of immediate contact with the ancient world that they offer, the human narratives they allow us to reconstruct, as well as the choices, decisions and hopes of real people with whom we can empathise across the millennia. We do not need to be archaeologists to imagine what it would be like to abandon our homes with only what we could carry. We can feel for the doctor who chose to take the tools of his trade with him, and almost share his regret at what he would have left behind. We can understand the vain optimism of those who slipped the front-door keys in their pockets before taking to the road. Even that nasty little amber figurine takes on special significance, when we know that it was someone's precious favourite, snatched up as they left home for the last time.

Modern science can add to these individual life stories. We can go one better than earlier generations in squeezing all kinds of personal information out of the surviving skeletons themselves: from such relatively simple calibrations as the height and stature of the population (ancient Pompeians were, if anything, slightly taller than modern Neapolitans) through tell-tale traces of childhood illnesses and broken bones, to hints of family relationships and ethnic origin that are beginning to be offered by DNA and other biological analysis. It is probably pushing the evidence too far to claim, as some archaeologists have done, that the particular development of one teenage boy's skeleton is enough to show that he had spent much of his short life as a fisherman and that the erosion of his teeth on the right hand side of his mouth was caused by biting on the line which held his catch. But elsewhere we are on firmer ground.

In two back rooms of one substantial house, for example, the remains of twelve people were discovered, the owner, presumably, with his family and slaves. Six children and six adults, they included a girl in her late teens, who had been nine months pregnant when she died, the bones of her foetus still lying in her abdomen. It may well have been her late pregnancy that encouraged all of them to take shelter inside, hoping for the best, rather than risk a hasty escape. The skeletons have been none too carefully preserved since their discovery in 1975 (the fact that, as one scientist has recently reported, 'the lower premolars [of one skull] had been erroneously glued into the sockets of the upper central incisors' is not evidence of ham-fisted ancient dentistry, but of ham-fisted modern restoration). Nonetheless, by piecing together various clues that remain – the relative ages of the victims, the rich jewels on the pregnant girl, the fact that she and a nine-year-old boy suffer from the same minor, genetic spinal disorder – we can begin to build up a picture of the family who lived in the house. An elderly couple, he in his sixties, she around fifty with clear signs of arthritis, were very likely the house owners, as well as the parents, or grandparents, of the pregnant girl. From the quantity of jewellery she was wearing we can be fairly sure that she was not a slave, and the shared spinal problem hints that she was a relative of the family by blood rather than marriage – the nine-year-old boy being her younger brother. If so, then she and her husband (probably a man in his twenties, whose head, so the skeleton suggests, had a pronounced, disfiguring and no doubt painful tilt to the right) either lived with her family, or had moved back to her home for the birth, or of course just happened to be visiting on the fatal day. The other adults, a man in his sixties and a woman in her thirties, may just as well have been slaves as relatives.

A close look at their teeth, reglued or not, adds further details. Most of them have a series of tell-tale rings in the enamel that come from repeated bouts of infectious diseases during childhood – a nice reminder of the perilous nature of infancy in the Roman world, when half those born would have died before they were ten. (The better news was that if you made it to ten, you could expect to live another forty years, or more.) The clear presence of tooth decay, even if below modern Western levels, points to a diet with plenty of sugar and starch. Of the adults, only the husband of the pregnant girl had no sign of decay. But he, again to judge from the state of his teeth, had fluoride poisoning, presumably having grown up outside Pompeii, in some area with unusually high levels of natural fluoride. Most striking of all, every single skeleton, even the children, had large build-ups – in some cases a couple of millimetres – of calculus. The reason for this is obvious. Toothpicks there may have been, even some clever concoctions for polishing and whitening the teeth (in a book of pharmacological recipes, the emperor Claudius' private doctor records the mixture which is said to have given the empress Messalina her nice smile: burnt antler-horn, with resin and rock-salt). But this was a world without toothbrushes. Pompeii must have been a town of very bad breath.

A city disrupted

Women about to give birth, dogs still tethered to their posts, and a decided whiff of halitosis … These are memorable images of normal, everyday life in a Roman town suddenly interrupted in midstream. There are plenty more: the loaves of bread found in the oven, abandoned as they baked; the team of painters who scarpered in the middle of redecorating a room, leaving behind their pots of paint and a bucketful of fresh plaster high up on a scaffold – when the scaffold collapsed in the eruption, the contents of the bucket splashed right across the neatly prepared wall, leaving a thick crust still visible today (see pp. 120–24). But scratch the surface, and you find that the story of Pompeii is more complicated, and intriguing. In many ways Pompeii is not the ancient equivalent of the *Marie Céleste*, the nineteenth-century ship mysteriously abandoned, the boiled eggs still (so it was said) on the breakfast table. It is not a Roman town simply frozen in midflow.

For a start, the people of Pompeii had seen the warning signs, hours if not days before. The only eyewitness account of the eruption we have is a couple of letters written a quarter of a century after the event to the historian Tacitus by his friend Pliny, who had been staying on the Bay of Naples when the disaster struck. No doubt composed with the benefit of hindsight and imagination, these make it clear that escape was still possible even after the cloud 'like an umbrella pine' had appeared from the crater of Vesuvius. Pliny's uncle, the most famous victim of the eruption, only died because he was asthmatic and because he bravely, or stupidly, decided that he needed to take a closer look at what was going on, in the interests of science. And if, as many archaeologists now think, there had been a series of tremors and small earthquakes in the days or months leading up to the final disaster, those too would have encouraged people to quit the area. For it was not only Pompeii itself that was threatened and eventually engulfed, but a wide swathe of land to the south of Vesuvius, including the towns of Herculaneum and Stabiae.

Many did leave, as the tally of bodies found in the city confirms. Around 1100 have been unearthed in the excavations. We need to make allowance for those that still lie in the unexcavated part of the town (about a quarter of ancient Pompeii is as yet unexplored), and for those human remains missed in earlier excavations (children's bones can easily be mistaken for those of animals, and discarded). Even so, it seems unlikely that more than 2000 of the inhabitants would have lost their lives in the disaster. Whatever the total population – and estimates vary from about 6400 to 30,000 (depending on how tightly packed we imagine these people to have lived, or on what modern comparisons we choose) – this was a small, or very small, proportion.

People fleeing in the rain of pumice may have taken with them only what they could grab and carry. Those with more time will have taken more of their possessions. We must imagine a mass exodus from the city with donkeys, carts and barrows, as the majority of the population left, loading up as many of their household effects as they reasonably could. Some made the wrong decision, locking away their most precious possessions, intending to return when the danger had passed. This is what accounts for some of the magnificent treasures – stunning collections of silver, for example (see p. 220), found in houses in and near Pompeii. But for the most part what has been left for archaeologists to discover is a city *after* its inhabitants had hurriedly packed up and left. This may help to explain why the houses of Pompeii seem so sparsely furnished, and so uncluttered. It may not be that the prevailing aesthetic of the first century CE was a kind of modernist minimalism. Much of the household bric-a-brac had very likely been carted off by its loving owners, by the wagonload.

This speedy decampment may also explain some of the oddities of what we do find in the city's houses. If, for example, a pile of gardening tools comes to light in what appears to be a rich dining room, it may be that – surprising as it may seem to us – that was where they were regularly kept. It may also be that in the flurry of departure, as possessions were gathered together and choices were made about what to take and what not, this is where the shovel, hoe and barrow happened to end up. Even if some of the population carried on their daily business as if tomorrow would surely come, this was not a normal city, going about its normal business. It was a city in flight.

In the weeks and months after the eruption many survivors also came back for what they had left behind, or to salvage (or loot) reusable material, such as bronze, lead or marble, from the buried city. It may not have been quite so unwise as it now seems to have locked away your valuables in the hope of getting them back later. For in many parts of Pompeii there are clear signs of successful re-entry, through the volcanic debris. Whether the rightful proprietors, robbers or treasure hunters taking a chance, they tunnelled through into rich houses, sometimes leaving a little trail of holes in the walls, as they went from one blocked-up room to the next. A nice glimpse of their activities is found in two words scratched by the main door of one grand house, which was found to be almost empty when uncovered by nineteenth-century excavators. It reads: 'House tunnelled', words hardly likely to have been written by an owner, so presumably a message from one looter to the rest of his gang, to tell them that this one had been 'done'.

We know almost nothing about who these tunnellers were (but the fact that the message, though written in Latin, was in Greek characters is a pretty clear sign that they were bilingual, part of the Greco-Roman community of South Italy which we shall explore in Chapter 1). Nor do we know exactly when they made their raid: post-eruption Roman coins have been found in the ruins of Pompeii, dating from the end of the first century CE to the beginning of the fourth. But whenever, and for whatever reason, later Romans decided to dig down to the buried town, it was a phenomenally dangerous activity, driven by the hopes of recovering substantial quantities of the family wealth, or coming away with a prize haul of loot. The tunnels must have been perilous, dingy and narrow, and in places – if the size of the holes in some of the walls is anything to go by – only accessible by children. Even where it was possible to walk more freely, in pockets unfilled by the volcanic debris, the walls and ceilings would have been in danger of imminent collapse.

The irony is that some of the skeletons that have been found are almost certainly not the remains of the victims of the eruption, but of those risking a return

5. The engraving of one of a pair of sculptured panels, almost a metre long, depicting the earthquake of 62 CE. On the left, the Temple of Jupiter, Juno and Minerva in the Forum visibly totters. On the right, a sacrifice is in progress. A bull is being brought up to the altar, while around the scene are dotted various instruments of sacrifice – a knife, bowls and offering dishes.

to the city in the months, years or centuries that followed. So, for example, in a smart room off the garden courtyard of the House of the Menander – a modern name, taken from the painting of the Greek dramatist Menander found there (Ill. 44) – the remains of a little party of three have been discovered, two adults and child, equipped with a pick and a hoe. Were these, as some archaeologists believe, a group of residents, maybe slaves, trying to batter a way *out* of the house as it became engulfed, and losing their lives in the attempt? Or was it, as others imagine, a party of looters, battering their way *in*, killed perhaps as their fragile tunnel collapsed on top of them?

This picture of a disrupted city is made even more complicated by an earlier natural disaster. Seventeen years before the eruption of Vesuvius, in 62 CE the town had been badly damaged by an earthquake. According to the historian Tacitus, 'a large part of Pompeii collapsed'. And the event is almost certainly depicted in a pair of sculptured panels found in the house of a Pompeian banker, Lucius Caecilius Jucundus. These show two areas of the city rocked by the quake: the Forum, and the area around the northern gate of the city facing towards Vesuvius. In one the Temple of Jupiter, Juno and Minerva leans alarmingly to the left; the equestrian statues on either side of the temple seem almost to come alive, the riders unseated from their mounts (Ill. 5). In the other the Vesuvian Gate takes an ominous lurch to the right, parting company with the large water reservoir on its left. This disaster raises some of the trickiest questions in the history of Pompeii. What was its effect on life in the town? How long did it take the city to recover? In fact, did it ever recover? Or were the Pompeians in 79 CE still living in the wreckage – the Forum, temples and baths, not to mention many private houses, not yet restored?

There have been theories aplenty. One idea is that a social revolution struck

Pompeii after the earthquake. Many of the traditional aristocracy decided to leave town once and for all, no doubt to family properties elsewhere. Their departure not only left the way open for the rise of ex-slaves and other nouveaux riches, but it also started the 'decline' of some of Pompeii's more elegant houses, hastily converted into fulleries, bakeries, inns and other commercial or industrial uses. In fact, that pile of gardening tools in the dining room could itself be a sign of just such a change of use: a once upmarket residence dragged dramatically downward by new occupants who had turned it into the base for a market gardening business.

Maybe so. And we may have here yet another reason to see the state of the city as anything but 'normal' when it was overwhelmed in 79. Yet we cannot be certain that all these changes were a direct result of the earthquake. Some of the industrial conversions probably happened before the disaster anyway. Some – if not many – were almost certainly part of the regular pattern of shifts in wealth, use and prestige that marks the history of any town, ancient or modern. Not to mention the hint of 'officer class' prejudices in many modern archaeologists who have so confidently equated social mobility and the rise of new money with revolution or decline.

Another big claim is that in 79 Pompeii had still not finished the long process of repair. So far as we can tell from the archaeological evidence, Tacitus' assertion that 'a large part of Pompeii collapsed' was something of an exaggeration. But the state of many of the public buildings (only one set of public baths, for example, were in fully working order in 79) and the fact that, as we shall see, so many private houses had the decorators in at the time of the eruption seems to suggest not only that the damage had been considerable, but that it had not yet been put right. For a Roman city to pass seventeen years with most of its public baths out of action, several of its main temples unusable and its private houses in disarray points either to a serious shortage of cash or to an alarming degree of institutional dysfunction, or both. What on earth was the town council doing for nearly two decades? Sitting back and watching the place crumble?

But here too everything is not as it may at first seem. Can we be certain that all the repairs going on when the eruption struck were in response to the earthquake? Leaving aside the obvious point that there is almost always a lot of building work under way in any town (the repair and construction industry is at the centre of urban life, ancient or modern), there is the 'one earthquake or more?' question which has fiercely divided archaeologists who study Pompeii. Some still stick firmly to the view that there was just one single devastating earthquake in

6. The Temple of Isis was one of the high-spots for early tourists and it inspired writers and musicians from the young Mozart to Edward Bulwer-Lytton, author of *The Last Days of Pompeii*. This engraving shows the main temple building in the centre and, on the left, the small, walled enclosure for a pool containing water used in the rituals of Isis.

62 and – yes – the city was in such a shambles that many repairs were still unfinished years later. More now emphasise the series of tremors that there must have been in the days, and perhaps months, leading up to the eruption. That is what you would expect before a major volcanic explosion, vulcanologists assure us, and it is, in any case, exactly what Pliny described: 'For many days previously,' he wrote, 'there had been earth tremors.' If there was a flurry of decorating going on, so this argument runs, then it was much more likely to be patching up the damage that had just occurred, not a belated and ill-timed attempt finally to clear up the mess of seventeen years.

As for the state of the town more generally, and especially the public buildings, here again the issue of later looting turns out to be a complicating factor. It is quite clear that in 79 some public buildings were in ruins. One huge temple overlooking the sea, and usually assumed to have been dedicated to the goddess Venus, was still a building site – though it seems as if the restoration was intended to be on an even grander scale than what it replaced. Others were very much back in working order. It was business as usual in the Temple of Isis, for example, which had been reconstructed and richly redecorated with what are now some of the most famous paintings from the city (Ill. 6).

The condition of the Forum, however, at the time of the eruption is much more of a puzzle. One view is that it was a half-abandoned wreck, hardly restored at all. If so, it would be at the very least an indication that the priorities of the Pompeians had, to put it politely, shifted away from communal life. At worst, it would signal the complete breakdown of civic institutions, a state of affairs which (as we shall see) doesn't fit at all well with other evidence from the city. More recently an accusing finger has been pointed at post-eruption recovery parties or looters. Much of the Forum, this view holds, had been made good and indeed improved. But knowing of all the expensive marble facing that had recently been installed, the locals dug down to retrieve it soon after the city was buried, hacking it off the walls – which were left looking for all the world as if they were unfinished or simply dilapidated. The salvagers would also, of course, have been after the many expensive bronze statues which adorned this piazza.

These debates and disagreements continue to fuel archaeological conferences. They are the stuff of scholarly warfare and student essays. But however they are eventually resolved (if ever they are), one thing is absolutely clear: 'our' Pompeii is not a Roman city going about its everyday business, then simply 'frozen in time', as so many guidebooks and tourist brochures claim. It is a much more challenging and intriguing place. Disrupted and disturbed, evacuated and pillaged, it bears the marks (and the scars) of all kinds of different histories, which will be part of the story of this book, and which underlie what we might call the 'Pompeii paradox': that we simultaneously know a huge amount and very little about ancient life there.

It is true that the city offers us more vivid glimpses of real people and their real lives than almost anywhere else in the Roman world. We meet unlucky lovers ('Successus the weaver's in love with a barmaid called Iris and she doesn't give a toss' as one scrawled graffito runs) and shameless bed-wetters ('I've pissed in bed, I messed up, I haven't lied / But, dear landlord, there was no chamber pot supplied,' boasts the rhyme on a lodging house bedroom wall). We can follow the traces of Pompeii's children, from the toddler who must have had great fun sticking a couple of coins into the fresh plaster of the main hall, or atrium, of one smart house, leaving more than seventy impressions just above floor level (and so also inadvertently leaving a nice piece of dating evidence for the decoration) to the bored kids who scratched a series of stickmen at child height in the

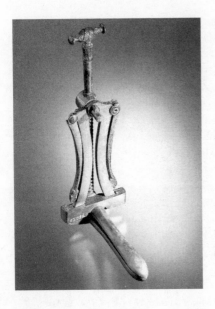

7. There is something uncannily familiar between our own gynaecological *specula* and this ancient version from Pompeii. Though some parts of it are missing, it is clear that the 'arms' of the instrument were opened by turning the T-shaped handle.

entranceway to a suite of baths, doodling as they waited maybe for their mothers to finish steaming. Not to mention the horses' harnesses with their jangling bells, the gruesome medical instruments (Ill. 7), the curious kitchen equipment, from egg poachers to mousse moulds, if that's what they are (Ill. 78), or those irritating intestinal parasites whose traces can still be found on a lavatory rim after 2000 years – all of which help to recapture the sights, sounds and senses of Pompeian life.

Yet while details like this are wonderfully evocative, the bigger picture and many of the more basic questions about the town remain very murky indeed. The total number of inhabitants is not the only puzzle we face. The relationship of the town to the sea is another. Everyone agrees that the sea came much nearer to Pompeii in antiquity than it does today (when it is 2 kilometres away). But, despite the skills of modern geologists, exactly how much nearer is still uncertain. Particularly puzzling is that just next to the western gate of the city, the main modern visitor entrance, is a stretch of wall with what look like very obvious mooring rings for boats, as if the sea lapped almost right up to the city at that point (Ill. 8). The only trouble is that Roman structures have been discovered further west, that is towards the sea, and they could hardly have been built under water. The best way to explain this returns again to on-going seismic activity. Here – as at the

8. These look like obvious mooring rings for boats on the wall near the Marine Gate. Almost certainly the coastline changed over the last hundred years of the town's life, leaving these rings high and dry.

nearby town of Herculaneum, where the movement can be documented very clearly – the coastline and the sea-level must have changed dramatically over the last few hundred years of the town's history.

Even more surprisingly, there is debate too about the basic dates – not only the date of the big earthquake (which might just as well have taken place in 63 as 62), but also of the eruption itself. I shall be using the traditional dating of 24 and 25 August 79 throughout this book, which is what we now read in Pliny's account. But there is good reason to think that the disaster happened later in the year, during the autumn or winter. For a start, if you go back to the different medieval manuscripts of Pliny's *Letters*, you find that they give all kinds of different dates for the eruption (for Roman dates and numerals were always liable to be miscopied by medieval scribes). It is also the case that a suspiciously large quantity of autumnal fruits are in evidence in the remains and that many of the victims appear to be wearing heavy-duty, woollen clothes, hardly suitable garments for a hot Italian summer – although what people choose to put on as they make their escape through the debris of a volcanic eruption may not be a good indicator of the seasonal

9. Allied bombing in 1943 did terrible damage to Pompeii, destroying many major buildings. This shows the condition of the House of Trebius Valens after the raids. Many of the bombed buildings were so expertly rebuilt after the war that you would never guess that they had been, to all intents and purposes, destroyed again.

10. An excavation of the 1930s. Pompeian houses do not emerge from the ground in a pristine state. In fact, the force of the eruption means that they look rather as if they had been bombed. Here the painted plaster of the upper floor has collapsed into the rooms below.

weather. More clinching evidence comes in the shape of a Roman coin, found in Pompeii in a context where it could not have been dropped by looters. Specialists think that the earliest this coin could have been minted was September 79.

The fact is that we know both a lot more and a lot less about Pompeii than we think.

The two lives of Pompeii

There is an old archaeological joke that Pompeii has died twice: first, the sudden death caused by the eruption; second the slow death that the city has suffered since it began to be uncovered in the mid eighteenth century. Any visit to the site will show exactly what that second death means. Despite the heroic efforts of the Pompeian archaeological service, the city is disintegrating, weeds overgrow many of the areas that are off-limits to visitors, some of the once brilliantly coloured paintings left in place on the walls have faded to almost nothing. It is a gradual process of dilapidation, aggravated by earthquakes and mass tourism, and given an extra helping hand by the rough methods of the early excavators (though, to be honest, many of the fine wall paintings that they hacked out and deposited in the museum have fared better than those left in their original context); by Allied bombing campaigns in 1943 (Ill. 9) which wrecked several areas of the town (most visitors have no clue that considerable parts of the Large Theatre, for example, and of the Forum, as well as of some of the most celebrated houses, were almost entirely rebuilt after the war, or that the on-site restaurant was planted on one area of particularly devastating bomb damage); and by thieves and vandals, for whom the archaeological site, large and hard to police, is an enticing target (in 2003 a couple of newly excavated frescoes were prised off their wall, to be found three days later at a nearby builder's yard).

But equally the city has had two *lives*: one, in the ancient world itself; the other, the modern re-creation of ancient Pompeii that we now visit. This tourist site still tries to preserve the myth of an ancient town 'frozen in time', one into which we can walk as if it was only yesterday. It is, in fact, striking that, although Roman Pompeii lies many feet below modern ground level, the entrances to the site are laid out so that we get little sense that we are going *down* to it; the world of the ancients merges almost seamlessly with our own. Yet, look a little harder, and we find that it exists in that strange no-man's land between ruin and reconstruction, antiquity and the present day. For a start, much of it is heavily restored, and not just after the wartime bomb damage. It comes as quite a shock to look at photographs of the buildings as they were excavated (Ill. 10), and to see in what a poor state most of them were found. Some, it is true, have been left just like that. But others have been smartened up, their walls patched and rebuilt, to hold new roofs – primarily to protect the structure and decoration, but often taken by visitors for miraculous survivals from the Roman period.

More than that, the city has been given a new geography. We now navigate Pompeii using a series of modern street names: amongst them, Via dell'Abbondanza (the main east–west thoroughfare leading directly to the Forum, named after the figure of the goddess Abundance carved on one of the street fountains), Via Stabiana (intersecting Abbondanza and leading south towards the town of Stabia), and Vicolo Storto (Twisty Lane, so-called for obvious reasons). We have almost no idea what these streets were called in the Roman world. One surviving inscription seems to suggest that what we call the Via Stabiana was then the Via Pompeiana, while referring also to two other streets (Via Jovia, that is Jupiter Street; Via Dequviaris, perhaps connected with the town council or *decuriones*) which cannot be pinpointed. But it may well be that many did not have specific names in the modern way. Certainly there were no street signs, and no system of using street name and house number to give an address. Instead people used local landmarks: one landlord, for example, had his jars of wine delivered (as we can still read round the top of one): 'To Euxinus [which translates roughly as 'Mr Hospitality'], the innkeeper, at Pompeii, near the Amphitheatre'.

We have likewise given modern names to the town gates, calling them after the place or direction they faced: the Nola Gate, the Herculaneum Gate, the Vesuvius Gate, the Marine Gate (towards the sea) and so on. In this case, we have a rather clearer idea of what the ancient names might have been. What we call Herculaneum Gate, for example, was to the Roman inhabitants the Porta Saliniensis or Porta Salis, that is 'Salt Gate' (after the nearby saltworks). Our Marine Gate may well have been called the Forum Gate, or so a few scraps of ancient evidence combined with some plausible modern deduction suggest; after all, it not only faced the sea, but it was also the closest gate to the Forum.

In the absence of ancient addresses, modern gazetteers to the city use a late nineteenth-century system for referring to individual buildings. The same archaeologist who perfected the technique of casting the corpses, Giuseppe Fiorelli (one-time revolutionary politician, and the most influential director of the Pompeian excavations ever), divided Pompeii into nine separate areas or *regiones*; he then numbered each block of houses within these areas, and went on to give every doorway onto the street its own individual number. So, in other words, according to this now standard archaeological shorthand, 'VI.xv.1' would mean the first doorway of the fifteenth block of region six, which lies at the north-west of the city.

To most people, however, VI.xv.1 is better known as the House of the Vettii. For, in addition to that bare modern numeration, most of the larger houses at least, as well as the inns and bars, have gained more evocative titles. Some of these go back to the circumstances of their first excavation: the House of the Centenary, for example, was uncovered exactly 1800 years after the destruction of the city, in 1879; the House of the Silver Wedding, excavated in 1893, was named in honour of the twenty-fifth wedding anniversary of King Umberto of Italy, celebrated in that same year – the house, ironically, being now better known than the royal marriage. Other names reflect particularly memorable finds: the House of the Menander is one; the House of the Faun another, named after the famous bronze dancing satyr, or 'faun', found there (Ill. 12), (its earlier name, the House of Goethe, went back to the son of the famous Johann Wolfgang von Goethe, who witnessed part of the excavation in 1830 very shortly before he died – but his sad story proved rather less memorable than the spritely sculpture). Very many, however, like the House of the Vettii, have been named after their Roman occupants, as part of that much bigger project of repopulating the ancient town, and of matching up the material remains to the real people who once owned them, used them or lived in them.

This is an exciting, if sometimes dodgy, procedure. There are cases where we can be sure that we have made the right match. The house of the banker Lucius Caecilius Jucundus, for example, is almost certainly identified by his banking archives, which had been stored in the attic. Aulus Umbricius Scaurus, the most successful local manufacturer of *garum* (that characteristically Roman concoction of decomposing marine life, euphemistically translated as 'fish sauce'), left his mark and his name on his own elegant property – with a series of mosaics, featuring jars of the stuff labelled with such slogans as 'Fish sauce, grade one, from Scaurus' manufactory' (Ill. 57). The House of the Vettii, with its exquisite frescoes, has been confidently assigned to a pair of (probably) ex-slaves, Aulus Vettius Conviva and Aulus Vettius Restitutus. This is on the basis of two seal stamps and a signet ring with those names found in the front hall, plus a couple of election posters, or at least their ancient equivalent, painted up on the outside of the house ('Restitutus is canvassing for ... Sabinus to be aedile') – and on the assumption that another seal stamp found in another part of the house, this time naming Publius Crustius Faustus, belonged to some tenant living on the upper floor.

In many cases the evidence is far flimsier, relying on perhaps a single signet ring (which, after all, could just as easily have been dropped by a visitor as the owner), a name painted on a wine jar, or a couple of graffiti signed by the same person, as if graffiti artists always chose to write on their own home walls. One particularly desperate deduction has come up with the name of the man who owned the brothel in the town, and the high-spot for many modern as no doubt ancient visitors: it is Africanus. This is an argument based largely on a sad message scratched, by a client most likely, on the wall of one of the girls' booths. 'Africanus is dead' (or literally 'is dying'), it reads. 'Signed young Rusticus, his school mate, grieving for Africanus'. Africanus, to be sure, may have been a local resident: or so we might guess from the fact that on a wall close-by someone of that name pledged their support in the local elections to Sabinus (the same candidate who had won Restitutus' vote). But there is no reason at all to imagine that young Rusticus' expression of post-coital misery, if that is what it was, was making any reference at all to the owner of the brothel.

The end result of this and other such over-optimistic attempts to track down the ancient Pompeians and put them back into their houses, bars and brothels is obvious: in the modern imagination, an awful lot of Pompeians have ended up in the wrong place. Or, to put it more generally, there is a large gap between 'our' ancient city and the city destroyed in 79 CE. In this book, I shall consistently be using the landmarks, finding aids and terminology of 'our' Pompeii. It would be confusing and irritating to give the Herculaneum Gate its ancient name of 'Porta Salis'. The numeration invented by Fiorelli allows us quickly to pinpoint a location on a plan, and I shall be using it in the reference sections. And, incorrect as some of them may be, the famous names – House of the Vettii, House of the Faun, and so on – are much the easiest way of bringing a particular house or location to mind. Yet, I shall also be exploring that gap in more detail, thinking about how the ancient city has been turned into 'our' Pompeii, and reflecting on the processes by which we make sense of the remains that have been uncovered.

In stressing those processes, I am being both up to the minute and, in a sense, returning to a more nineteenth-century experience of Pompeii. Of course, nineteenth-century visitors to the city, like their twenty-first-century counterparts, enjoyed the illusion of stepping back in time. But they were also intrigued by the ways in which the past was revealed to them: the 'how' as well as the 'what' we know of Roman Pompeii. We can see this in the conventions of their favourite guidebooks to the site, above all Murray's *Handbook for Travellers in Southern Italy*, first published in 1853 to cater for the beginning of mass tourism (rather than Grand Tourists) to the site. The railway line had opened in 1839 and became the favoured method of transport for visitors, and they were serviced by a tavern near the station where they could take lunch after their exertions among the ruins. This was a place of fluctuating fortunes (in 1853 it supposedly had 'a very civil and obliging landlord', by 1865 readers were recommended not to tuck in without coming to 'an agreement as to the charge beforehand with mine host'). But it was the germ of the vast industry of snacks, fruit and, especially, bottled water that now dominates the outskirts of the site.

Murray's *Handbook* repeatedly engaged these Victorian visitors with the problems of interpretation, sharing the various competing theories about what some of the major public buildings that had been discovered were for. Was the building we call the *macellum* (market), in the Forum, really a market? Or was it a temple? Or was it a combination of a shrine and a café? (As we shall see, many such questions of function have not yet been resolved, but modern guidebooks tend to deprive their readers of – they would say spare them – the problems and controversies.) They are even careful to note, along with the description of each ancient building, the date and circumstances of its rediscovery. It is as if those early visitors were supposed to keep two chronologies running in their heads at the same time: on the one hand, the chronology of the ancient city itself and its development; on the other, the history of Pompeii's gradual re-emergence into the modern world.

We might even imagine that the famous stunts in which dead bodies or other notable finds were conveniently 'discovered', just as visiting dignitaries happened to be passing, were another aspect of the same preoccupations. We tend now to laugh at the crudeness of these charades and the gullibility of the audience (could visiting royalty have been so naive as to imagine that such wondrous discoveries just happened to be made at the very moment of their own arrival?). But, as often, the tricks of the tourist trade reveal the hopes and aspirations of the visitors as much as they expose the guile of the locals. Here the visitors wanted to witness not just the finds themselves, but the processes of excavation that brought the past to light.

These are some of the issues that I wish to bring back into the frame.

A city of surprises

Pompeii is full of surprises. It makes even the most hard-nosed and well-informed specialists rethink their assumptions about life in Roman Italy. A large pottery jar

11. This Indian ivory statuette offers a glimpse of the wide multicultural links of Pompeii. Depicted nearly naked apart from her lavish jewels, is she (as is usually thought) Lakshmi, the goddess of fertility and beauty? Or is she just a dancer?

with a painted label advertising its contents as 'Kosher *Garum*' reminds us that men like Umbricius Scaurus might be looking to serve the niche market of the local Jewish community (with a guarantee of no shellfish among the now unrecognisable ingredients of that rotten concoction). A wonderful Indian ivory statuette, found in 1938 in a house now called after it 'The House of the Indian Statuette', encourages us to think again about Rome's connections with the Far East (Ill. 11). Did it come via a Pompeian trader, a souvenir of his travels? Or maybe via the trading community of Nabataeans (from modern Jordan) who lived at nearby Puteoli? Almost equally unexpected was the recent discovery of a monkey's skeleton scattered, unrecognised by earlier excavators, among the bones in the storerooms on the site. An exotic pet perhaps – or, more likely, a performing animal, in street-theatre or circus, trained to amuse.

It is a city of the unexpected, simultaneously very familiar to us and very strange indeed. A town in provincial Italy, with horizons no further than

Vesuvius, it was at the same time part of an empire that stretched from Spain to Syria, with all the cultural and religious diversity that empires so often bring. The famous words 'Sodom' and 'Gomora' written in large letters on the walls of the dining room of a relatively modest house on the Via dell'Abbondanza (assuming that they are not the gloomy observation of some later looter) give us more than an eyewitness comment – or joke – on the morality of Pompeian social life. They remind us that this was a place in which the words of the Book of Genesis ('Then the Lord rained upon Sodom and Gomorrah brimstone and fire from the Lord out of heaven') as well as the works of Virgil must have rung a bell with at least some inhabitants.

A small-town community with – once we leave the women, children and slaves out of the equation – a citizen body of just a few thousand men, no bigger than a village or the student union of a small university, it nonetheless has a more forceful impact on the mainline narrative of Roman history than we tend to imagine. As we shall see in Chapter 1.

CHAPTER ONE

LIVING IN AN OLD CITY

Glimpses of the past

Down a quiet back street in Pompeii, not far from the city walls to the north and just a few minutes' walk from the Herculaneum Gate, is a small and unprepossessing house now known as the House of the Etruscan Column. Unremarkable from the outside and off the beaten track both in the ancient world and now, it conceals, as its modern name hints, a puzzling curiosity within. For lodged in the wall between two of its main rooms is an ancient column, its appearance reminiscent of the architecture of the Etruscans – who were a major power in Italy through the sixth and fifth centuries BCE, before the rise of Rome itself, with influence and settlements extending far beyond their homeland in north Italy to the area around Pompeii. The column almost certainly dates from the sixth century BCE, several hundred years before the house was built.

Careful digging under the house has thrown some light on this puzzle. It turns out that the column is in its original position and the house has been built around it. Part of a sixth-century BCE religious sanctuary, it was not a support for a building, but freestanding, possibly next to an altar and once carrying a statue (an arrangement known in other early religious sites in Italy). Sixth-century Greek pottery, presumably from offerings and dedications, was found in the area round about, as was evidence (in the form of seeds and pollen) for a significant number of beech trees. These were not likely to be natural woodland; for beech trees, it is argued, do not grow naturally on low ground in southern Italy. The speculation is, therefore, that this venerable old sanctuary had originally been surrounded by another of those characteristic features of early Italian religion: a sacred

12. The House of the Faun was one of the grandest, and by the first century CE most old-fashioned, houses of the town, though it is now sadly dilapidated. Here we look through its front door into the main atrium, with the dancing satyr (or Faun). Beyond lay two large peristyle gardens and the famous Alexander Mosaic (Ill. 13).

grove, here specially planted in beech. And by way of confirmation (rather weak confirmation, in my view) we are asked to compare a similarly ancient sanctuary of the god Jupiter in Rome, set in its own sacred beech grove: the 'Fagutal' as it was called, from *fagus* meaning beech tree.

However we imagine the column in its original setting, with beech trees few or many, woodland or artificial grove, the main lines of its story are clear enough. When the early shrine was eventually covered by housing, probably in the third century BCE, the standing column was preserved intact within the later structures, out of respect – or so we may guess – for its religious status. Centuries later, in 79 CE, it was still visible in the house that then stood on the plot: whether even at that date it retained some trace of special sanctity, or had simply become an interesting talking point for its owners in an otherwise nondescript house, we do not know.

The little story of this column is a reminder of a much bigger point: that by the time it was finally destroyed Pompeii was an old city, and visibly so. Although,

13. The most intricate ancient mosaic ever discovered, the Alexander Mosaic covered the floor of one of the main display rooms of the House of the Faun. This engraving shows the complete design. Alexander the Great (on the left) is fighting Darius the King of Persia. As his horses tell us (for they have already turned) Darius is about to flee in the face of the onslaught of the young Macedonian. There are all kinds of virtuoso artistic touches here – such as the horse in centre stage seen as if from behind. (See also Plate 15.)

to most modern eyes, the ruins appear homogeneously Roman, indistinguishable in date and style, they are in fact nothing of the sort. For a start, as we shall soon see, in 79 CE Pompeii had strictly speaking been a 'Roman' town for less than 200 years. But also, like most cities, ancient or modern, it was a sometimes messy amalgam of spanking-new building, esteemed antiques and artful restorations – as well as of the quaintly old-fashioned and the quietly dilapidated. Its residents would no doubt have been well aware of these differences and of the mixture of old and new that made up their town.

The most extraordinary example of a 'museum piece' is one of the most famous, and now most visited, of all Pompeian houses: the House of the Faun. This house is vast, the biggest in the city, and at some 3000 square metres is of positively regal dimensions (approaching the scale, for example, of the palaces of the kings of Macedon at Pella in northern Greece). It is now known not only for its bronze statue of the dancing 'faun' but also for its stunning suite of decorated floor mosaics. Prime amongst these is the so-called 'Alexander mosaic' (Ill. 13), one of the star exhibits of the National Museum in Naples, and painstakingly constructed from a countless number of tiny stones or *tesserae*: estimates have

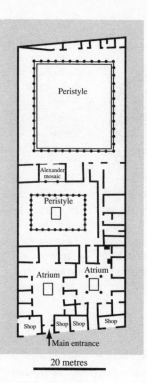

Figure 2. The House of the Faun. Though vastly over-blown (covering a whole city block), the House of the Faun still shows many characteristic features of more ordinary Pompeian houses. The street frontage, for example, is occupied by a series of shops. This version of the standard plan takes the visitor through a narrow entrance way into one of two atria. Beyond lie two peristyle gardens.

20 metres

varied from 1.5 million to 5 million, no one ever having had the patience to count them one by one. When first excavated in the 1830s, its epic proportions and confused mêlée of fighting prompted the ingenious idea that it depicted a battle scene from Homer's *Iliad*. We are now convinced that it shows the defeat of the Persian king Darius (in his chariot, on the right; Plate 15) by the youthful Alexander the Great (on horseback, on the left) – perhaps, as is usually assumed, a virtuoso copy in mosaic of a lost masterpiece in painting, or perhaps an original creation.

Few modern visitors, who marvel at its size or admire its exquisite mosaics (there are nine others in the Naples Museum), realise quite how old-fashioned the House of the Faun would have seemed by the time of the eruption. The house was given its final form in the late second century BCE, when the mosaics were installed and many of its walls were grandly painted in the characteristic style of the time, and it remained more or less the same for the next 200 years. New paintings and restorations were done carefully to match. Who the rich owners of this

14. One of a series of terracotta reliefs (60 centimetres high) found re-used in the garden wall of the House of the Golden Bracelet – originally having adorned some sacred building, possibly the Temple of Apollo in the Forum. On this panel, the goddess Diana (Greek Artemis) stands on the right, and a figure of Victory on the left.

house were we do not know (though one nice suggestion is that they were a long-standing local family, called Satrius – in which case that bronze faun or 'satyr' is a visual pun on their name). Still less do we know what encouraged (or forced) them to keep it unchanged over the centuries. What *is* clear is that the experience in 79 of visiting the House of the Faun would have been not so far different from our own experience of visiting a historic house or stately home. Passing through its portals – stepping over another mosaic, this time blazoning the Latin word *HAVE*, meaning 'greetings' (though the entirely unintended English pun on possession seems appropriate for this vast mansion) – you would have found yourself back in the second century.

The House of the Faun is an extreme case. But all over the town the old was mixed up with the new. Distinctly old-fashioned styles of interior decor, for example, were lovingly preserved, or left to peel, next to the newest decorative fashions. The sundial in the exercise area of one of the main public baths, allowing busy bathers or exercisers to keep an eye on the time, was not only two centuries old by the time of the eruption, but it carried a commemorative inscription written in the native, pre-Roman language of the area – Oscan. By 79 probably only a few of Pompeii's inhabitants could have deciphered that it had been paid for by the local council, using money they had accrued from fines.

We can also glimpse other stories of preservation and reuse to rival that of the Etruscan column. One recent discovery has revealed the ultimate fate of a series of terracotta sculptures which (to judge from their subject matter and shape) must once have adorned a temple in Pompeii itself or its surrounding countryside, possibly even the temple of the god Apollo in the Forum (Ill. 14). Crafted sometime in the second century BCE, and decommissioned perhaps after the earthquake of 62 CE, they ended up built into the garden wall of a rich multi-storey house (the House of the Golden Bracelet) which overlooked the sea – with what must have been stunning views – on the western edge of the town. A nice piece of architectural salvage maybe, though a far cry from the religious sanctity of their original location.

Before Rome

Pompeii was an even older city than its visible remains suggest. In 79, there was no building in use – public or private – that was earlier than the third century BCE. But at least two of the main temples of the city, even if repeatedly restored, rebuilt and brought up to date, had a history stretching back to the sixth century. The Temple of Apollo, in the Forum, was one, as was the Temple of Minerva and Hercules nearby. This seems to have been in ruins at the time of the eruption, and had possibly been abandoned once and for all, but excavations have brought to light some of the decorative sculpture from its earlier phases, pottery from the sixth century BCE and hundreds of offerings – many of them little terracotta figurines, some clearly representing the goddess Minerva (Greek Athena) herself. Besides, as the explorations around the Etruscan column show, digging down under the surviving structures elsewhere in the city can also produce evidence of much earlier occupation of the site.

One of the boom industries in the current archaeology of Pompeii is, in fact, the story of the town's early history. The fashionable question for specialists has shifted from 'What was Pompeii like in 79 CE?' to 'When did the city originate and how did it develop?'. This has launched a whole series of excavations deep under the first-century CE surface to discover what was on the site before the structures that we can still see. It is a fiendishly difficult process, not least because hardly anyone is keen to destroy the surviving remains simply to find out what they replaced. So most of the work has been 'key-hole archaeology', digging down in small areas, where it can be done with minimum damage to what lies above – and to the attractiveness of Pompeii for visitors. For most of us, let's face

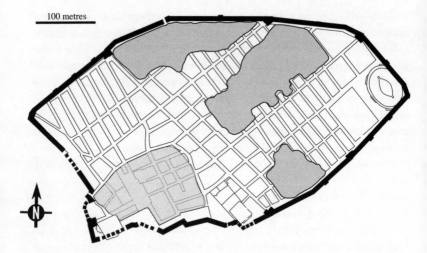

Figure 3. The development of the city plan. The chronology of the city's growth appears to be visible in the street plan. The 'Old Town' at bottom left (shaded) has an irregular street pattern. Other blocks of streets follow different alignments.

it, come to see the impressive ruins of the city overwhelmed by Vesuvius, not the faint traces of some archaic settlement.

The challenge is to match up these isolated pockets of evidence both to each other and to the hints of the history of urban development given by the city's ground plan. For it has long been recognised that the pattern of streets, with different areas having differently shaped 'blocks' and subtly different alignments, almost certainly reflects in some way the story of the city's growth (Fig. 3). The other key fact is that the circuit of the town walls on their present line dates back to the sixth century BCE – meaning that (surprising as this may seem) the ultimate extent of the town was established from this early period.

Given the tricky evidence, there is an unusual amount of agreement about the main lines of the history it reveals. Most people accept that, as the city's plan suggests, the original nucleus of the settlement was in the south-west corner, where the irregular pattern of streets points to something that archaeologists have rather grandly called the 'Old Town'. But, beyond that, the number of early finds, both pottery and the evidence of buildings, from all over the town has made it increasingly clear that Pompeii was already a relatively widespread community within the walls in the sixth century BCE. In fact there is hardly anywhere in the city where deep digging under the existing structures has not produced some traces of sixth-century material, albeit in tiny fragments and sometimes the product of especially keen searching (one story being that Amadeo Maiuri, the 'Great Survivor', who directed the excavations on the site from 1924, through fascism and the Second World War, up until 1961, used to give his workmen a bonus if they found early pottery where he hoped – an archaeological tactic that usually produces results). It is also clear that there is a dramatic falling off in finds through the fifth century, a gradual build-up again through the fourth, until the third century marks the start of the recognisable urban development as we now see it.

There is much less agreement about exactly how old the original nucleus is, and whether the occasional finds of material on and near the site from the seventh, eighth or even ninth centuries BCE represent a settled community as such. And there are sharp differences of opinion about how the area within the walls was used in the sixth century BCE. One view holds that it was mostly enclosed farmland, and that our finds come from isolated agricultural buildings or cottages or rural sanctuaries. This is not implausible, except for the unconvincingly large number of 'sanctuaries' that this view seems to produce – some of them much less obviously religious sites than the 'Etruscan column'.

A more recent and rival position sees a much more developed urban framework, even at this early date. The main argument for this is that, so far as we can tell from the now scanty traces, all the early structures outside the 'Old Town' were built following the later, developed alignment of the streets. This does not mean that sixth-century Pompeii was a densely occupied town in our sense. In fact, even in 79 CE there was plenty of open, cultivated land within the circuit of the walls. But it does imply that the street grid was already established, at least in some rudimentary form. On this interpretation Pompeii was at that point a city already 'waiting to happen' – even if there was an uncomfortably long three centuries before that 'happening' was to come about

Equally debated is the question of who these early Pompeians were. It is not only the town's latest phases that have a decidedly multicultural tinge, with their Greek art, Jewish dietary rules, Indian bric-a-brac, Egyptian religion and so forth. Even in the sixth century BCE Pompeii stood at the heart of a region – known, then and now, as Campania – where, long before the Romans came to dominate, indigenous peoples speaking the native Oscan language rubbed shoulders with Greek settlers. There had, for example, been a substantial Greek town at Cumae, fifty kilometres away across the Bay of Naples, since the eighth century BCE. Etruscans too were a significant presence. They had settled in the region

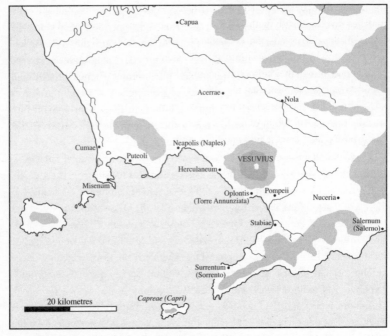

Figure 4. Map of area surrounding Pompeii

from the middle of the seventh century, and for 150 years or so rivalled the Greek communities for control of the area. Which of these groups was the driving force behind the early development of Pompeii is frankly anyone's guess, and archaeology does not provide the answer: a fragment of an Etruscan pot, for example, almost certainly shows contact between the inhabitants of the town and the Etruscan communities of the area, but it does not demonstrate (despite some confident assertions to the contrary) that Pompeii was an Etruscan town.

What is more, ancient writers seem to have been no more certain than we are about how to disentangle the city's earliest history. Some relied on marvellously inventive etymologies, deriving the name 'Pompeii' from the 'triumphal procession' (*pompa*) of Hercules, who was supposed to have passed this way after his victory over the monster Geryon in Spain, or from the Oscan word for 'five' (*pumpe*), so inferring that the town had been formed out of five villages. More soberly, the Greek writer Strabo, first-century-BCE author of a multi-volume

34

treatise on *Geography*, offered a list of the town's inhabitants. At first sight this matches up reassuringly with some of our own theories: 'Oscans used to occupy Pompeii, then Etruscans and Pelasgians [i.e. Greeks]'. But whether Strabo had access to good chronological information, as more optimistic modern scholars have hoped, or whether he was just hedging his bets in the face of uncertainty, as I tend to feel, we simply cannot be sure.

Strabo did not, however, stop with the Pelasgians. 'After that,' he wrote, 'it was the turn of the Samnites. But they too were ejected.' Here he was referring to the period between the fifth and third centuries BCE, when Pompeii began to take its familiar form. These Samnites were another group of Oscan-speakers, tribes from the heartlands of Italy, who feature in later Roman stereotypes – not entirely unfairly – as a tough race of mountain warriors, hard-nosed and frugal. In the shifting geopolitics of pre-Roman Italy, they moved into Campania and managed to establish control of the region, decisively defeating the Greeks at Cumae in 420 BCE, only fifty years after the Greeks themselves had managed to get rid of the Etruscans.

It is perhaps this series of conflicts that accounts for the apparent change in Pompeii's fortunes in the fifth century. In fact some archaeologists have concluded from the more or less complete absence of finds on the site at that point that the town was abandoned for a time. But only for a time. By the fourth century BCE, Pompeii was probably – though firm evidence for this, beyond Strabo himself, is virtually nil – part of what is now grandly known as a 'Samnite Confederacy'. At least, in a key position on the coast and at the mouth of the river Sarno (whose precise ancient course is hardly better known to us than the shoreline), it acted as the port for the settlements upstream. As Strabo noted, hinting at yet another derivation of the town's name, it was located near a river which served to 'take cargoes in and *send them out* (Greek: *ekpempein*)'.

'But the Samnites too were ejected'? Strabo had no need to explain who was behind the ejection. For this was the period of Rome's expansion through Italy, and of its transformation from a small central Italian town with control over its immediate neighbours to the dominant power in the entire peninsula and increasingly in the Mediterranean as a whole. In the second half of the fourth century BCE Campania was just one of the fields of operation in a series of Roman wars against the Samnites. Pompeii had its own cameo role in these, when in 310 BCE a Roman fleet landed there and disembarked its troops, who proceeded to ravage and plunder the countryside up the Sarno valley.

These wars involved many of the old power bases of Italy: not just Rome and various tribes of Samnites, but Greeks now concentrated in Naples (Neapolis) and, to the north, Etruscans and Gauls. And they were not a walkover for Rome. It was at the hands of the Samnites, in 321 BCE, that the Roman army sustained one of its most humiliating defeats ever, holed up in a mountain pass known as the 'Caudine Forks'. Even the Pompeians put up a good fight against the plunderers from the Roman fleet. According to the Roman historian Livy, as the soldiers laden with their loot had almost made it back to the ships, the locals fell upon them, grabbed the plunder and killed a few. One small victory for Pompeii against Rome.

But the Romans – as was always the way – won in the end. By the early third century BCE, Pompeii and its neighbours in Campania had been turned, like it or not, into allies of Rome. These allies retained more or less complete independence in their own local government. There was no concerted attempt to impose on them Roman-style institutions, nor to demand the use of Latin rather than their native Italic language. The main language of Pompeii continued to be Oscan, as it had been under the Samnites. But they were obliged to provide manpower for the Roman armies and to toe the Roman line in matters of war, peace, alliances and the rest of what we might anachronistically call 'foreign policy'.

In many ways Pompeii did very well out of this dependent status. From the end of the third century, the population of the town increased dramatically, or so we conclude from the tremendous expansion of housing. In the second, an array of new public buildings were erected (baths, gymnasium, temples, theatre, law courts), while the House of the Faun is only the largest of a number of grand private mansions that made their permanent mark on the urban scene at this period. It was now that Pompeii, for the first time, began to look like what we would call 'a town'. Why?

One answer may be Hannibal's invasion of Italy at the end of the third century. As the Carthaginians pressed south from their famous crossing of the Alps, Campania became once again a major arena of fighting – some communities remaining loyal to Rome, others defecting to the enemy. Capua to the north was one of those which defected, and it was in turn besieged by the Romans and dreadfully punished. Nuceria, on the other hand, just a few kilometres from Pompeii, remained loyal and was destroyed by Hannibal. Even if it can hardly have remained entirely unscathed in the middle of this war zone, Pompeii was not directly hit and must have been a likely refuge for many of those displaced and dispossessed in the conflict. This may well account for some of the striking growth in housing at this period, and the spurt in urban development. The town, in other words, was an unexpected beneficiary of one of Rome's darkest hours.

Another answer is the onward expansion of Roman imperialism in the east and the wealth that came with it. Even if the allies were not free agents in Rome's wars of conquest, they certainly took some share in the profits. These came partly from the spoils and booty of the battlefield, but also from the trading links increasingly opened up with the eastern Mediterranean and the new avenues of contact with the skills and artistic and literary traditions of the Greek world (beyond those offered by the Greek communities that still remained in the local area).

At least one plundered showpiece, captured when the Romans and their allies sacked the fabulously rich Greek city of Corinth in 146 BCE, seems to have been on display outside the temple of Apollo in Pompeii. What exactly it was we do not know (a statue, perhaps, or luxury metalwork), but the inscription in Oscan recording its gift by the Roman commander, Mummius, on that occasion still survives. Further afield, family names found at Pompeii are recorded also in the great Greek trading centres, such as the island of Delos. It is impossible to be absolutely certain that any of the individuals concerned were actually native Pompeians. Nonetheless, the impact of trading contacts like these is clear to see – right down to the daily bread and butter of (at least) the Pompeian elite. Carefully collecting seeds and the microscopic traces of spices and other foodstuffs, archaeologists exploring a group of houses near the Herculaneum Gate have suggested that, from the second century on, the inhabitants were enjoying a more varied diet, drawn from further afield, including a good sprinkling of pepper and cumin. And even if the House of the Faun was hardly a typical Pompeian residence, its array of mosaics – especially the *tour de force* that was the Alexander mosaic – attest to the high level of Greek artistic culture that could be found in the city.

In short, second-century BCE Pompeii was an expanding and thriving community, doing very nicely out of its relations with Rome. But, though allies, the Pompeians were not Roman citizens. For the privileges of that status, and to become a truly Roman town, they had to resort to war.

Becoming Roman

The so-called 'Social War' broke out in 91 BCE, when a group of Italian allies (or *socii*, hence the name) went to war with Rome. Pompeii was one of them. It now seems a peculiar kind of rebellion. For, although the allied motives have been endlessly debated, it is most likely that they resorted to violence, not because they wished to turn their back on the Roman world and escape its domination, but because they resented not being full members of Rome's club. They wanted, in other words, Roman citizenship, and the protection, power, influence and the right to vote at Rome itself which went with it. It was a conflict notorious for its savagery, and in effect – given that Romans and allies had become used to fighting side by side – a civil war. Predictably enough, the vastly superior force of Romans was victorious in one sense, but the allies were in another: for they got what they wanted. Some of the rebel communities were bought off instantly by the offer of citizenship. But even those who held out were enfranchised once they had been defeated in battle. From then on, for the first time, more or less the whole of the peninsula of Italy became Roman in the strict sense of the word.

During this war, Pompeii itself was besieged in 89 by the famous general Lucius Cornelius Sulla, who was later to become – albeit briefly – a murderous dictator in the city of Rome itself (between 82 and 81 he put a price on the head of more than 500 of his wealthy opponents, who were brutally hunted down if they didn't manage to kill themselves first). And in the ranks of Sulla's army, so we are told by his biographer, Plutarch, was the young Marcus Tullius Cicero, then in his late teens, and years away from the oratorical triumphs in the Roman law courts that would launch his political career and become the 'set-books' for budding orators and students of Latin ever after.

Sulla's handiwork is still visible at Pompeii, in the shape of numerous lead bullets and ballista balls (the Roman equivalent of cannon shot) found on the site, and a smattering of small holes in the city walls where shots that had presumably been aimed to clear the defences fell short and left their tell-tale mark. Inside the city, houses close to the walls at the north came off particularly badly. The House of the Vestals – so called because of a fanciful eighteenth-century notion that it was the residence of a group of virgin priestesses, the 'Vestal Virgins' – suffered serious damage, even if its wealthy owners managed to turn the chaos and destruction to their own advantage. In the aftermath of the war it seems that they got their hands on some of the neighbouring property, rebuilding their house on a much larger scale. By an uncanny coincidence, the House of the Vestals was again a victim of warfare almost 2000 years later, when it was hit by Allied bombs in September 1943. Excavations now turn up pieces of modern shrapnel alongside the Roman sling bullets.

How vigorously or how long the Pompeians resisted the Roman fire we do not know. A series of notices in Oscan, painted up at street corners, may give us some hint of their preparation in the face of attack. These are usually thought to go back to the time of the siege, preserved under layers of later plaster, which has since fallen off to reveal them. The translation is by no means certain, but they very likely give instructions to the defending troops on where exactly they should muster ('between the twelfth tower and the Salt Gate'), and under whose command ('where Matrius, son of Vibius, is in charge'). If so, they suggest a fair degree of organisation, as well as a community literate enough to make use of written instructions in an emergency. There was also help for Pompeii from the outside. One ancient account of the Social War describes how a rebel general, Lucius Cluentius, came to relieve the town. In the first skirmish, he actually came out ahead, but Sulla returned to the fight and decisively defeated him and chased his army off to the nearby rebel stronghold of Nola, killing more than 20,000 of them, according to (not necessarily reliable) ancient estimates. Pompeii must have fallen soon after.

It did not suffer the violent treatment meted out to some other allied towns in their defeat. But less than a decade after the war had ended and the Pompeians had been granted citizenship of Rome, Sulla got his revenge in another way. Needing places to settle his veteran soldiers, brought home after long wars in Greece, he chose to plant some of them – at a conservative estimate a couple of thousand, plus their families – at Pompeii. This was a substantial and sudden addition to the population, perhaps increasing the number of inhabitants by almost 50 per cent. But the impact was even bigger than that. The town was formally converted into a Roman 'colony' and its local government was reformed accordingly. Its annual elected officials were given new names and, no doubt, new duties. The old Oscan chief magistrate, the *meddix tuticus*, was replaced by a pair known as *duoviri iure dicundo*, literally 'two men for pronouncing the law'.

The name of the town was also changed to reflect its new status. Pompeii was now officially known as *Colonia Cornelia Veneria Pompeiana*: *Cornelia* from Sulla's family name, Cornelius; *Veneria* from his patron goddess, Venus. It became, in other words, 'The Cornelian Colony of Pompeii, under the divine protection of Venus' (a mouthful in Latin as well as in English). As that title hints, the official public language of the town now became Latin, even though in private contexts Oscan continued to be used by some of the locals – an ever-dwindling minority no doubt – up until 79 CE. It was these few who would have been able to decipher those ancient Oscan inscriptions still on view. And in the final years of the city one of them, a client presumably, left his name scratched on the wall of the brothel – in the distinctive letters of the Oscan alphabet.

These 'colonists', as they are now often called, changed the face of Pompeii. A large new suite of public baths was erected near the Forum, and improvements were made to others – including a new sauna – funded by two of the early *duoviri*. Most dramatically of all, existing housing was demolished and an Amphitheatre was erected in the south-east corner of the town, the earliest surviving stone Amphitheatre anywhere in the world. This was put up, as the inscriptions displayed above its main entrances declared, thanks to the generosity of another pair of prominent newcomers, who also sponsored – though did not pay for out of their own pockets – the construction of a brand-new Covered Theatre (or 'Odeon', as it is sometimes now called). There is good reason to think that one of these grandees, Caius Quinctius Valgus, was a man also known to us from his walk-on part in Latin literature: 'Valgus', the father-in-law of one Publius Servilius Rullus, whose attempt to redistribute land to the Roman poor was the target of Cicero's invective in his three speeches *Against Rullus*. If so, and if we can trust half of what Cicero says about him, then the man who bankrolled the Pompeian Amphitheatre was not (or not only) an altruistic benefactor of his local community, but a nasty piece of work who had made a considerable financial killing out of Sulla's reign of terror in Rome.

It is not so clear where this influx of new inhabitants lived. In the absence of any signs of an obvious 'colonists' quarter' inside the city, one recent idea is that they largely had their property and land, smallholdings or grander villas, in the surrounding countryside. This is a convenient solution to a nagging problem, but only a partial one. Some of the colonists must have lived within the walls. Good candidates for the property of the richest among them, though certainly not the rank and file, are the range of houses built on the coastal side of the city (the House of the Golden Bracelet and its neighbours). These were sited directly over the city wall – no longer a strategic necessity once Pompeii was part of a supposedly peaceful, Roman Italy – multi-storey structures, built onto land sharply sloping down to sea-level, with a total floor area sometimes not far short of the House of the Faun. Magnificent entertainment suites, with large windows and terraces, opened onto what must once have been a spectacular beach and sea view (Ill. 15). Sadly these houses are not regularly open to visitors. For, with their many levels, their labyrinthine corridors and stairways, not to mention the panoramic vistas (whoever said Romans did not care for scenery?), they offer a dramatic alternative to the standard image of a Roman house. They must have been some of the most fashionable pieces of real estate in the town.

In some ways, the arrival of the colony simply speeded up a process

15. Located on the western edge of the city, above the old city wall, the House of Fabius Rufus enjoyed a enviable view over the sea. It was designed to make the most of this, with large windows and terraces.

of 'Romanisation' that was already underway in the town. After all, unless that particular mosaic is a later insertion, the owner of the House of the Faun had chosen to greet his visitors in Latin (*HAVE*) as early as the second century BCE. And some of the wave of early first-century public buildings may actually have predated the arrival of the colonists, rather than (as is often assumed) being their initiative. The truth is that, unless there is firm evidence in an inscription, it is very hard to be precise about the date of these buildings, one side or the other of the foundation of the colony. The argument for making many of them the work of the colonists is almost entirely circular, even if not necessarily wrong (the colonists were avid builders; all buildings of the early first-century BCE are therefore the work of the colonists; this in turn proves that the colonists were avid builders). It is still disputed, for example, whether the temple of Jupiter, Juno and Minerva which dominates one end of the Forum was a colonial foundation (one archaeologist has recently claimed that its unit of measurement appears to be the 'Roman foot', suggesting a Roman construction), or whether it was an earlier temple already dedicated to Jupiter alone, later adapted to that characteristically Roman

41

divine triad. There was, unsurprisingly given Rome's growing influence, a good deal of 'self-Romanisation' going on in 'pre-Roman' Pompeii.

Yet, true as it is, that picture tends to underestimate the degree of conflict which existed in the first years of the colony between the Roman newcomers and the Oscan inhabitants. This was partly a cultural clash, no doubt; though I suspect that the view, held by some modern historians, that the sophisticated, theatre-loving Pompeians found the brutish Amphitheatre-loving veterans a bit hard to take, is as unfair to the veterans as it is over-generous to the Pompeians. More to the point, the incomers seem, for a time at least, to have seized day-to-day political control of the town, to the exclusion of its old residents.

There are signs of this exclusion on the site itself. The names of the town's elected officials that survive from the first decades of the colony include none of the traditional Oscan family names, but are solidly Roman. And the inscription commemorating the building of the new Amphitheatre declares that Valgus and his co-benefactor donated it 'to the colonists'. Of course, 'to the colonists' would in a technical sense include all the inhabitants of what was now formally known as the *Colonia Cornelia Veneria Pompeiana*. But, technically correct though it may have been, it is hard to imagine that this formulation would have sounded inclusive to the old families of the town. And, in fact, the idea that in popular talk 'the colonists' and 'the Pompeians' were treated as separate and rival groups in the town is confirmed by a speech of Cicero's delivered at Rome in 62 BCE.

Cicero was defending Publius Sulla, the nephew of the dictator, against the accusation that he had been an accomplice of Lucius Sergius Catilina, an indebted aristocrat and luckless revolutionary, who had died earlier in the year in a botched attempt to overthrow the Roman government. Twenty years earlier, this young Sulla had been the man on the ground in charge of establishing the colony at Pompeii. At one point – in answer to the, not wholly implausible, allegation that Sulla had driven the Pompeians into Catilina's plots – Cicero treats his Roman audience to a discussion of local Pompeian politics. It is a suspiciously tortuous defence, focusing on the disputes in the town between the 'colonists' and the 'Pompeians'. These are now over, he claims, thanks in part (believe it, or not) to the interventions of Sulla himself; and both groups – still operating separately, we should note – have sent delegations to Rome in Sulla's support. But what had the disputes been about? Cicero talks vaguely about Pompeian grievances over 'their votes' and over *ambulatio*, a Latin word which can mean anything from 'walking' to a place in which to walk, i.e. 'a portico'.

It is easy enough to see what the arguments about 'votes' might have been. Put this hint together with the absence of local names from the first magistrates of the colony, and it seems certain that the new political arrangements somehow disadvantaged the old inhabitants. Some modern scholars have even imagined that they were completely debarred from voting – though other less extreme forms of disadvantage are possible, and more plausible. But an enormous amount of ingenuity has been deployed in trying to work out what the dispute about *ambulatio* could have been. Had, for example, restrictions been placed on the Pompeians' right of movement about the city (*ambulatio* in the sense of 'walking')? Was there a particular portico that was out of bounds to them, which caused offence? Or was Cicero not talking about *ambulatio* at all, but (as one manuscript of the speech has it) about *ambitio*, i.e. 'bribery' or 'corrupt practices' – which might again refer back to a problem with the voting system?

There is, frankly, something of a mystery here. But whichever solution we find least implausible, one thing is clear. Temporary though the troubles were (within a couple of decades, those absent Oscan names start to reappear in the local government), the first years of Pompeii's life as a fully Roman town cannot have been happy ones for its old population.

Pompeii in the Roman world

There is a well-established myth that Pompeii was an insignificant backwater in the Roman world. Its main claim to fame was its production of fish sauce (*garum*). Praised, in passing, by the elder Pliny ('... Pompeii too has a good reputation for its *garum*'), the Pompeian version of this delicacy clearly enjoyed brisk sales throughout Campania, to judge from all its distinctive pottery jars which so often turn up in excavations. It has even been found in Gaul. But the isolated discovery of a Pompeian jar may not necessarily indicate a thriving international export market, so much as culinary supplies, or even a gift, taken on his travels by a wandering Pompeian. Next to its fish sauce came its wine – admittedly a mixed bag. There were some distinguished labels, but Pliny warned that the local plonk was liable to give you a hangover until midday the next day.

The usual idea is that the people of Pompeii went on with their lives, untroubled, as the big events of Roman history unfurled; first as the free quasi-democratic Republic of Rome collapsed into dictatorship and bouts of civil war, until Augustus (31 BCE–14 CE) established the one-man rule of the Roman empire; then later as one emperor succeeded the next, some like Augustus himself or Vespasian (who came to the throne, after another bout of civil war, in 69 CE) gaining a reputation for probity and benevolent autocracy, others like Caligula (37–41 CE) or Nero (54–68 CE) decried as mad despots. For the most part the centre of action remained a long way from Pompeii, though occasionally it came a little too close for comfort. In the late 70s BCE, for example, not long after the foundation of the colony, the slave rebels under Spartacus temporarily made their encampment in the crater of Vesuvius, just a few kilometres to the north of the town. This is an incident perhaps immortalised in a rough painting discovered in a house at Pompeii under layers of later decoration which shows a scene of combat including a man on horseback labelled, in Oscan, 'Spartaks'. It is a nice idea. But more likely the painting shows some kind of gladiatorial fight.

Very occasionally, too, Pompeii itself made an impact on the capital and on Roman literature, whether because of some natural disaster, or because of what happened in 59 CE. In that year some gladiatorial games got out of hand, a murderous fight ensued between the local inhabitants and the 'away supporters' from nearby Nuceria, and the wounded and bereaved ended up taking their complaints to the emperor Nero himself. By and large, however, the usual line is that life in Pompeii went on its sleepy way, without making much of a dent on life and literature at Rome – or, vice versa, without being much affected by international geopolitics and the machinations of the elite in the capital.

In fact, Cicero could even joke about the doziness of local Pompeian politics. On one occasion, he was attacking the way that Julius Caesar would appoint anyone of his favourites to the senate, without the usual processes of election. In a quip reminiscent of all those modern disparaging references to Tunbridge Wells or South Bend, Indiana, he is supposed to have said that while it was easy enough to get into the senate at Rome, 'at Pompeii it is difficult'. Eager students of Pompeian local government have sometimes seized on this to argue that the political life of the town really was buzzing with competition, even more so than Rome itself. But they have missed the heavy irony. Cicero's point is along the lines of 'It's easier to get into the House of Lords than to be mayor of Tunbridge Wells' – in other words, it is even easier than the easiest thing you can think of.

Archaeologists have greeted the insignificance of Pompeii in two ways. Most have, openly or privately, lamented the fact that the single town in the Roman world to have been preserved at this level of detail should be one so far from the mainstream of Roman life, history and politics. Others, by contrast, have celebrated the fact that the city is so unremarkable, seeing it as a bonus that we here get a glimpse of those inhabitants of the ancient world who are usually unnoticed by history. No deceptive Hollywood-style glamour here.

But Pompeii was by no means the forgotten backwater that it is usually painted. True, it was not Rome; and, to follow Cicero, its political life (as we shall see in Chapter 6) can hardly have been as cut-throat as that in the capital. It was in many ways a very *ordinary* place. But it is a feature of ordinary places in Roman Italy that they had close bonds to Rome itself. They were often linked by ties of patronage, support and protection to the highest echelons of the Roman elite. We know, for example, from an inscription that once adorned his statue in the town, that the emperor Augustus' favourite nephew and would-be heir, Marcellus, at one point held the semi-official position of 'patron' of Pompeii. The histories of communities like this were bound up with that of Rome. They provided a stage on which the political dramas of the capital could be replayed. Their successes, problems and crises were capable of making an impact well beyond the immediate locality, in the capital itself. To put it in the jargon of modern politics, Roman Italy was a 'joined up' community.

Pompeii lay just 240 kilometres south of Rome, linked to it by good roads. An urgent message – provided the messenger had enough changes of mount – could reach Pompeii from the capital in a day. For ordinary travel, you would allow three days, a week at dawdling pace. But it was not just that, in ancient terms, Pompeii was easily accessible from the capital. The Roman elite, and their entourages, had good reason to make the journey. For the Bay of Naples, then as (in parts) still now, was a popular area of relaxation, holiday-making and often luxurious 'second homes' in the lush countryside or, best of all, overlooking the sea. The town of Baiae, across the Bay from Pompeii, had become by the first century BCE a byword for an upmarket, hedonistic resort – more or less the ancient equivalent of St Tropez. We have already spotted the young Cicero, serving as a raw recruit in the siege of Pompeii during the Social War. Twenty-five years later, he acquired – for slightly more than he could afford – a country residence 'in the Pompeii area', which he used as a bolt-hole away from Rome and, while he vacillated in the run-up to the Civil War between Julius Caesar and Pompey the Great in 49 BCE, as a convenient place from which to plan his getaway by sea. Eighteenth-century scholars were convinced that they had identified the very building, in a substantial property just outside Pompeii's Herculaneum Gate (and since covered over again) (Plate 1). Based on a minute analysis of all Cicero's references to his 'Pompeianum' and combined with a good deal of wishful thinking, their identification is – sadly – almost certainly wrong.

Their twentieth-century followers became almost equally excited about pinpointing the property of another grandee in the area near the city: this time,

Nero's second wife, Poppaea, the celebrity beauty for whom the emperor killed both his mother and his first wife, Octavia, and who was herself eventually to die at her husband's hands, inadvertently (he kicked her in the stomach while she was pregnant, but had not meant to kill her). As with Cicero, we have clear evidence that she was a local proprietor. In this case, some legal documents discovered in the nearby town of Herculaneum record 'the empress Poppaea' as owner of some brick- or tile-works 'in the Pompeii area'. Her family may have come from Pompeii itself, and it has even been suggested that they were the owners of the large House of the Menander. Although it is nowhere directly stated in any of the ancient discussions of Poppaea's (bad) character and background, the brickworks, combined with plenty of evidence in the town for a prominent local family of 'Poppaei', makes her Pompeian origin quite likely.

That is enough on its own to illustrate again the strong connections between this area and the world of the Roman elite, but the temptation to find the remains of Poppaea's local residence has proved just too strong, even for hard-headed modern archaeologists. The prime candidate is the vast villa at Oplontis (modern Torre Annunziata, some eight kilometres from Pompeii). Perhaps it was hers; for it is a very large property, on an imperial scale. But, despite the fact that it is now regularly called the 'Villa of Poppaea' as if that were certain, the evidence is extremely flimsy, hardly going beyond a couple of ambiguous graffiti, which do not necessarily have any link with Poppaea or Nero at all. Take the name of 'Beryllos', for example, scratched on one of the villa walls. That may, but just as easily may not, refer to the Beryllos who is known from one reference in the Jewish historian Josephus to have been one of the slaves of Nero. Beryllos was a common Greek name.

Connections of a different kind between Pompeii and Rome are seen in the account of what is for us the second most famous appearance of Pompeii (after the eruption itself) in the narrative of Roman history: that riot in the Amphitheatre in 59, as described by the Roman historian Tacitus:

About the same time, there was a minor skirmish between the men of Pompeii and Nuceria, both Roman colonies, which turned into a ghastly massacre. It happened at a gladiatorial show given by Livineius Regulus, whose expulsion from the senate I discussed above. In the unruly way of these inter-town rivalries, they moved from abuse, to pelting each other with stones, until they finally drew swords. The Pompeians had the advantage, because it was in their town that the show was being put on. So many Nucerians were taken off to Rome, with their terrible injuries and mutilations, and there were also many who lamented the

16. This painting shows the riot in the Amphitheatre in 59 CE in full swing. The Amphitheatre itself on the left is carefully depicted, with its steep external staircase, the awning over the arena and a variety of stalls set up outside. On the right the fighting is spreading to the next door exercise ground or *palaestra*.

deaths of their children or parents in the affray. The emperor instructed the senate to clear the matter up; the senate referred it to the consuls. When it came back to the senate again, the Pompeians were forbidden from holding any public gathering of that kind for ten years, and their illegal clubs were disbanded. Livineius and the others who had stirred up the trouble were punished with exile.

Amongst those exiled with Livineius, were the serving *duoviri* of Pompeii; or that at least is a reasonable inference from the fact that the names of *two* pairs of these officials are known for this year.

This story is made even more memorable because a painting survives from the town, in which for some reason – jingoistic lack of repentance, perhaps? – the artist has chosen (or been instructed) to illustrate the notorious event (Ill. 16). What might at first sight appear to be gladiators fighting inside the arena are presumably the rioting Pompeians and Nucerians, who are also doing battle around the outside of the building.

Modern, as much as Roman, obsession with gladiatorial culture has put this incident centre-stage. But there is more to Tacitus' account than a vivid glimpse of a gladiatorial display gone wrong. He notes, for example, that the Pompeian show in question was given by a disgraced Roman senator, who had been expelled from the senate some years earlier (frustratingly, the portion of the narrative where Tacitus discusses this 'above' no longer survives). It is hard, however, to resist the conclusion that a rich man, out of favour in Rome itself, was looking to Pompeii as a place where he could play the part of benefactor and grandee. More than that, it is hard not to wonder whether there was some connection between the shady, and perhaps controversial, sponsor of the show and the violence that it sparked. Tacitus also hints here at the ways in which the local communities might be able to foster interest in their own problems at Rome. For it is clear that the Nucerians (though in other circumstances it might have been the Pompeians) could go off to the capital and get the emperor himself to take notice and initiate a practical response. How they met him (if they did) is not stated. But this is where a Roman 'patron' of a town (like Marcellus at Pompeii) would come in, either arranging for his 'clients' an audience with the emperor or with one of his officials, or perhaps more likely taking up the case on their behalf. The rule was that local Italian issues did matter at Rome; the imperial palace was, in principle at least, open to their delegations.

This kind of delegation to Rome may lie behind a later intervention by an emperor into the affairs of Pompeii. A series of inscriptions have been found outside the gates of the city, recording the work of an agent of Vespasian, an army officer by the name of Titus Suedius Clemens, who 'made an inquiry into the public land appropriated by private individuals, carried out a survey and restored them to the town of Pompeii'. What lies behind this is a common cause of dispute in the Roman world: state-owned land illegally occupied by private owners, followed by the efforts of the state (whether Rome or a local community) to recover it. In this case, some historians have suspected a spontaneous intervention by the new emperor Vespasian, who seems to have played the part of a new broom in the matter of imperial finances. More likely the local council of Pompeii had approached the emperor, as the Nucerians had earlier, asking for his help in recovering their state property and this Clemens had been dispatched. A long-serving army professional, he had played an inglorious part in the civil wars that ushered in Vespasian's rule, written up by Tacitus as a trigger-happy NCO, ready to trade in proper standards of military discipline in return for popularity with his men. Whether he was a reformed character by the time he arrived to sort out

Pompeii's land disputes, we can only hope. But he certainly interfered (by request or not) rather more extensively in the town's affairs. A number of notices survive in which his public support is paraded for one of the candidates in the forthcoming elections: 'Please elect Marcus Epidius Sabinus as *duumvir* with judicial power, backed by Suedius Clemens.' How long he was active in the city, again we do not know, but he seems to have escaped the eruption. In November of 79 CE we find him carving his name on the so-called 'singing statue of Memnon' (in fact a colossal statue of a pharaoh, which produced a strange sound at daybreak), a Roman tourist hot-spot deep in Egypt.

The fact is that Pompeii existed very much in the penumbra of the city of Rome, and the history, literature, culture and people of the capital were embedded in the life and fabric of the small town, in sometimes surprising ways. If part of Mummius' booty from the sack of Corinth ended up in the town, so too did at least one part of the property of one of the assassins of Julius Caesar. Discovered in the garden of a small house is a magnificent marble table support, with sculpted lions' heads, inscribed as being the property of Publius Casca Longus (Ill. 17). This is almost certainly the man who was the first to put his dagger into the dictator, and it may be that the house was owned by one of his descendants. But it is much more likely (particularly given the house's small size) that this was not an heirloom, but part of the property of Longus and the other guilty parties, auctioned off by the future emperor Augustus, who was Caesar's great-nephew, adopted son and heir, after the assassination. However it found its way to Pompeii, it was presumably – like the Etruscan column – a curious historical talking point for the house's visitors.

More generally, people from Rome came to Pompeii for business or pleasure. A group of four tombstones commemorating soldiers from the praetorian guard has recently been found in one of the Pompeian cemeteries, adding to half a dozen praetorians known from the 'signatures' they left in graffiti on the walls. Some were in relatively senior ranks; one of the dead was a young recruit, who at the age of twenty had served just two years. We can only guess at what they were doing in Pompeii – perhaps, like Clemens, on missions from the emperor, perhaps taking time off from guard duty on members of the imperial family staying in the area, perhaps even accompanying the emperor on a 'royal visit' to Pompeii itself.

In fact much scholarly energy has recently gone into re-creating the details of a visit by Nero and Poppaea in 64 CE, soon after the major earthquake and when Nero is known to have performed on the stage at Naples. It is, of course, possible that the imperial couple did make a visit, but the evidence for it is predictably

17. What is the connection between Pompeii and the assassination of Julius Caesar in 44 BCE? The name of one of Caesar's killers is inscribed on this table support, found in a small house in the town. The most likely explanation is that it ended up in Pompeii when the possessions of the guilty parties were auctioned off in Rome.

much less firm than is usually admitted. The strongest indication is a couple of scrawled pieces of graffiti from inside one of the large houses in the town. Not easy to decipher or interpret, they *may* refer to gifts of jewels and gold to Venus by the imperial couple, and possibly a visit to Venus' temple by 'Caesar' (that is, Nero) – even though, inconveniently for this interpretation, the temple of Venus, if we have identified it correctly, was in ruins at this point. All the same, this is much better evidence for Nero's links with Pompeii than the paintings discovered in a building with an elaborate series of dining rooms, recently discovered at Moregine just outside Pompeii. Starting from the observation that a painting of Apollo on its walls looks distinctly like the emperor himself (Plate 3), archaeologists have claimed that this was the staging post, or temporary imperial residence, where Nero stayed on his visit to the town. This is a fantasy worthy of the most inventive eighteenth-century antiquarian.

Just how canny we have to be in interpreting this kind of evidence is illustrated by another graffito. It reads, in Latin: *Cucuta a rationibus Neronis*. The position of *a rationibus* is roughly the equivalent of the English 'accountant' or 'bookkeeper'. So this has been seen as a simple signature of 'Cucuta Nero's accountant', writing his name on a wall, perhaps while accompanying his master on the visit to Pompeii. But this might be to miss the joke. For *cucuta* (or more regularly *cicuta*) is the Latin word for 'poison'. This is much more plausibly a satirical squib at Nero's expense than the autograph of a man with a slightly odd name. 'Poison is

18. On the outside wall of a Pompeian fullery were paintings of two of the founders of Rome. Here Romulus, carrying his defeated enemy's suit of armour, matched another which depicted Aeneas carrying his father out of Troy. Both were based on sculptures which stood in the Pompeian Forum – which were in turn based on sculptures in Rome itself.

Nero's accountant' looks like a joking allusion to those accusations which claimed that, in his financial difficulties, Nero put people to death to get his hands on their money. Someone in Pompeii was up with this kind of imperial gossip.

But for a visitor in 79 CE, the most striking aspect of the connections between Rome and Pompeii would have been the various ways in which the fabric of the town, its buildings and art, replicated or reflected the concerns or even the very architecture of the capital. These ranged from the layout of the Forum, with its temple of Jupiter, Juno and Minerva standing at one end as a symbol of 'Romanness', through a couple of sacred buildings dedicated to the religious cult of the emperors, to self-conscious copying of celebrated Roman monuments. Outside one of the largest buildings in the Forum, the Building of Eumachia (so-called after the woman who sponsored it in the first years of the first century CE), are two particularly striking 'quotations' from the capital. The function of this vast structure remains disputed (suggestions have included a guildhall for cloth workers and, recently, a slave market), but in its façade, under the portico which lined the Forum, two large inscriptions were set into the wall, beneath niches which must once have displayed statues. One inscription gave a detailed, if mythical, account of the achievements of Aeneas (the hero of Virgil's epic poem, who escaped from the fall of Troy to found the city of Rome as a new Troy). The other expounded the deeds of Romulus, another of Rome's mythical founders. Both of these texts were derived from similar inscriptions, lauding the achievements of hundreds of Rome's heroes, Aeneas and Romulus included, that once stood in the Forum of Augustus in Rome, the showpiece monument of the first emperor. A visitor from the capital would have felt at home.

Such a visitor to Pompeii would have spotted less-formal resonances to this famous monument too. Decorating the façade of a fullery (a cloth-working shop, plus laundry) along the main street, which we now call Via dell'Abbondanza, were two striking paintings. One showed Romulus, carrying a trophy of victory (Ill. 18), the other Aeneas, carrying his elderly father away from the burning city of Troy. Some wit in Pompeii not only recognised that this second image was a scene described by Virgil but also scrawled underneath a parody of the first line of the *Aeneid* ('Arms and the man, I sing …'): 'I don't sing of arms and the man, but of the fullers …'. But these paintings must have been recognisable in a more specific sense too. For, to judge from the surviving descriptions of the decoration of the Forum of Augustus in Rome, the images on the fuller's shop front were based on two famous statuary groups – one of Aeneas and one of Romulus – which took pride of place there. There is no reason to suppose that the painter had copied them directly from the Forum in Rome itself. The best guess is that he had based them on the statues that once stood above the inscriptions outside the Building of Eumachia – presumably Aeneas and Romulus, which in all likelihood (just as the inscriptions) were themselves copies of the famous Roman models.

Here the little town of Pompeii has the last laugh. For the original statues from the Forum of Augustus are lost too. These paintings, copies of copies, decorating a shop wall in a small town, are now the best evidence we have for a major imperial commission and decorative scheme in Rome itself. It is a good illustration of the complex and inextricable links there are, even now, between Rome and Pompeii.

CHAPTER TWO

STREET LIFE

Beneath your feet

Every modern visitor to Pompeii remembers the streets: their shiny surfaces pieced together out of large blocks of black volcanic rock; the deep ruts formed by years of cart traffic (and perilous to twenty-first-century ankles, as they must surely have been to first-century ones); the high pavements, occasionally as much as a metre above street-level; and the stepping stones carefully placed to allow pedestrians to cross the road without an inconvenient jump down, while being just far enough apart to let ancient wheeled transport through the gaps.

It is the sense of immediacy that makes the Pompeian street scene so memorable. The ruts are almost the equivalent of an ancient footprint, the indelible mark of human movement and of the passage of carts that once went about their daily business down these very streets. And when we hop across the stones, from pavement to pavement, part of the fun is knowing that we are treading in the very same path as thousands of Roman pedestrians before us. Or at least, it is part of the fun for most of us ordinary visitors. When Pope Pius IX made a celebrity visit to the site in 1849, it was thought best 'to save His Holiness from a long walk in the ruins', so a number of the stepping stones were removed to allow his cart – which obviously had a different wheel span from its Roman ancestors – to pass through. Some were never put back.

This chapter will take a close look at the streets and pavements of the ancient city. As so often in Pompeii, the tiniest traces preserved beneath our feet, often unnoticed by most of those who now wander through the town, can be pressed into service to reveal all kinds of intriguing and unexpected aspects of Roman

19. A characteristic Pompeian scene. This street leads to the Vesuvius Gate and the *castellum aquae* ('water castle'), just visible at the end. Regular series of stepping stones cross the street between the high pavements.

life: a picture that is simultaneously familiar and deeply alien. We shall find pedestrianised areas, one-way streets, traffic-calming, roadworks, loiterers and litter; and some sharp detective work will give us a glimpse of the private enterprise involved in the upkeep of the city and its highways. Yet we shall also find all kinds of surprising things going on in Pompeii's streets and squares (including a very nasty bit of corporal punishment meted out to an unfortunate schoolboy), not to mention the disconcerting presence of water wherever we go. In fact, Pompeii was rather more like Venice than most of us realise.

Much of the evidence for this comes from the very building blocks of the city's fabric, the ancient traffic bollards, the marks made by generations of carts hitting the kerb, or by generations of hands pressing on the street fountains. But we can also draw on an extraordinary series of paintings which offer an image of street life under the colonnades of the Pompeian Forum.

What were streets for?

The first question is one that we often forget to ask, as we jump across the stepping stones from pavement to pavement. Why were the sidewalks in the town so high? There are two answers to that question. Both open up a vision of the Pompeian streets strikingly at odds with their condition today, regularly cleaned, neat and tidy – sullied only by the occasional discarded water bottle or lost site plan.

The first is *filth*. Historians are divided about quite how dirty we should imagine the average Roman city to have been, largely because – as usual – the evidence we find in ancient writers cuts two ways. On the one hand, we have the complaints of the poet Juvenal, a Roman satirist who made a profession out of indignation and directed his bile towards, among other things, the condition of the streets of the capital itself. He offers a vivid rant on the dangers of a night-time walk, between the high-rise apartments on either side:

> There are various other nocturnal perils to be considered:
> it's a long way up to the rooftops, and a falling tile
> can brain you. Think of all those cracked or leaky vessels
> tossed out of windows – the way they smash, their weight,
> the damage they do to the side-walk! You'll be thought most improvident,
> a catastrophe-happy fool, if you don't make your will before
> venturing out to dinner. Each upper casement
> along your route at night may prove a death-trap:
> so pray and hope (poor you!) that the local housewives
> drop nothing worse on your head than a pailful of slops.

Even less savoury is the story told by the biographer Suetonius about an incident early in the career of the emperor Vespasian, who died just a few months before the eruption of Vesuvius. Vespasian, it was said, was sitting one day having his breakfast, when a stray dog ran into the house and dropped under the breakfast table a human hand which it had picked up from the nearby crossroads. This was not, for Suetonius, an indictment of the state of the neighbourhood, but an omen of Vespasian's future rise to greatness (for the Latin for 'hand', *manus*, also meant 'power').

But for those who would resist the lurid picture of Roman streets as filled with stray dogs, excrement dumped out of flying chamber pots, and human body parts mixed into the detritus, there is other, conflicting, evidence that can be pressed into service. Just a few lines after his tale of the human hand, Suetonius tells of another incident in Vespasian's early life. He was just thirty and had been elected to the office of aedile (*aedilis*), which had responsibility for the upkeep of the city of Rome, from public buildings and temples to brothels and streets. The story goes that Vespasian had sorely neglected the cleaning of the streets, and as punishment the emperor Caligula exacted appropriate punishment: he had him covered in mud, dressed in his official toga. Suetonius, unconvincingly, sees another omen here. But presage of power or not, it assumes some considerable interest on the part of the highest authorities in the cleanliness of the city.

We can also point to occasional hints from local communities in the Roman empire of ingenious improvisation in the daunting task of rubbish disposal. Some three centuries after the destruction of Pompeii, in Antioch (in Syria), we hear of a clever scheme by which the country people who had brought their produce into the city to sell at market were forced, on their return journey, to use their animals to carry building rubble out of the city. It didn't work. The farmers objected to this imposition and their complaints reached the emperor.

Where the streets of Pompeii stood on this spectrum between dirt and cleanliness, we do not know. No archaeologist has ever systematically examined the material that was lying on the surface of the street when the pumice fell. And, although we assume that the aediles at Pompeii had some of the same functions as those officials at Rome, we have no idea whether street hygiene was top of their agenda, nor whether they would have had the will, let alone the necessary resources, to keep the town clean. There are reasons, as we shall see, for imagining that householders took some responsibility for the pavements bordering on their property. But my guess is that the roadways themselves were much messier than most wholesome modern reconstructions of Pompeii tend to suggest.

For this was not a community with regular municipal rubbish collections. Even if huge quantities of commercial or domestic waste were not dumped in the street (though, presumably, some of it was), the horses, asses and mules that were the main means of transport would have dropped plenty of their own refuse. And it is hard to believe that all those Pompeians who lived in a single room above their shop, with not always adequate lavatory facilities, never found it convenient simply to piss into the streets. Some proportion of the human faeces and urine produced in the city (6,500,000 kilos of it a year on a very crude estimate) presumably ended up in the public highway. It was certainly enough of a problem for the occasional warning notice to be posted up: 'Shitter – make sure you keep it in till you've passed this spot'. Stepping down onto the road surface risked more than a twisted ankle; it most likely involved treading into a smelly mixture of animal dung (each horse producing up to 10 kilos a day), rotting vegetables and human excrement – which was, just to complete the picture, no doubt covered in flies.

Filth, however, cannot be the only answer to the question of those high walkways. If it were, we would be faced with the unlikely conclusion that the burghers of nearby Herculaneum (where we do not find stepping stones or particularly high pavements) were a cleaner and neater lot than their neighbours at Pompeii. In fact, anyone who has visited the city during a rainstorm will have seen an overriding reason for the Pompeian arrangement: that is *water*. When it pours with rain, the streets turn into torrents. For the city is built on land which slopes, in places quite steeply, from north-west to south-east (the Stabian Gate is 35 metres lower than the Vesuvius Gate); and unlike Herculaneum, it has few underground drains. It was the function of the streets to collect the rainwater and channel it out of the city through the walls, or towards such internal drains as there were, mostly around the Forum. Even when it was not raining, water – supplied, for the last hundred years or so of the city's existence, by aqueduct – spewed into the roadways from the incessant street fountains, and as the overspill from houses and baths.

The streets, in other words, doubled as water channels, as well as refuse dumps. One thing that can be said in favour of this arrangement is that the occasional downpour, and the rush of water that it caused, must have helped flush away all that decaying rubbish.

Boulevards and back alleys

Most ancient Pompeians, like most modern visitors, would have spent a lot of time on their city's streets. This was not simply a consequence of the warm weather or some laid-back 'Mediterranean lifestyle'. Many of the inhabitants of ancient Pompeii had little choice but to live outdoors. They had nowhere else to go. True, the super-rich families had plenty of space in their large houses and palaces: quiet retiring rooms, shady gardens, showy dining rooms, even private bath suites. Others who were not in that league lived comfortably enough in houses of half a dozen rooms. Further down the scale of wealth, many of the town's inhabitants lived in a single small room above their shop, bar or workshop, with no 'mains' water supply, and often no means of heating or cooking – except perhaps for a small brazier (which must have doubled as a serious fire hazard).

20. The ubiquity of the phallus. Here a phallus is carved into the paving stones of the street. But does it really point, as some claim, to the nearest brothel?

Compact quarters for a single occupant, this kind of apartment would have been little more than a cramped dormitory for a family of three or four. For almost all their basic needs they would have gone outside: for water to the street fountains, for a meal – beyond bread, fruit and cheese, and whatever simple concoction could be brewed up on the brazier – to one of the many bars and cafés which opened directly onto the pavements (Plate 4). Pompeii offers a striking reversal of our own social norms. For us, it is the rich who visit restaurants, the poor who cook economically at home. At Pompeii, it was the poor who ate out.

The streets of Pompeii came, as you would expect, in many shapes and sizes. Some of the back lanes were not even paved at all, but remained dirt trails or unprepossessing alleyways between blocks of housing; and earlier in the town's history many more would have been muddy or dusty tracks, rather than solid, carefully engineered highways. Some of them, particularly the main routes across the town, were comparatively wide, others could not take a single cart. That said, all the streets were narrow in our terms, most less than three metres across. To judge from the size of the cart found in the House of the Menander – or, more strictly, the iron wheel trims and fittings found, combined with impressions of the wood in the volcanic debris – only a few roads would have been wide enough to let two vehicles pass each other. And, when the buildings were standing to their full height, often with upper storeys, even the wider streets would have felt much more cramped and confined than they do now.

They were also much brighter, gaudier and more 'in your face'. Crude paintings marked out local religious shrines, often where streets intersected. Phalluses

21. The woolworkers' trade. On the left a man is busy combing the wool at a low table. In the centre, four men are engaged in the messy business of making felt from a mixture of wool and animal hair, held together with a sticky binder. (This gave the Romans their equivalent of a 'water-proof'.) On the far right, past another comber, the finished product is displayed by a man named in small letters underneath Verecundus. The large letters above are part of an electoral poster.

decorated the walls, moulded on terracotta plaques or, in one case, carved into the street surface itself. (Modern explanations for this range feebly from 'an expression of good luck' to 'protection against the evil eye'; the line spun by the tourist guides that the phallus on the street is a directional sign to the local brothel is certainly wrong.) Many of the houses were originally richly coloured – in reds, yellows and blues – and provided a convenient surface for electoral slogans (often one on top of another), 'For Rent' notices, advertisements for gladiatorial games, or just the scribbles of Pompeii's graffiti artists. 'I am amazed that you haven't fallen down, O wall / Loaded as you are with all this scrawl', as one popular piece of Pompeian doggerel ran – scratched up in at least three places in the town, and so adding to the phenomenon it deplored.

Shops and bars often used their street façades for painted signs, advertising their business, blazoning their name (rather like an English pub sign) and normally parading some usefully protective deities. The pictures of Romulus and Aeneas that we saw in the last chapter enlivened the outside of a fullery. Just a couple of blocks away, what we assume to have been an establishment of cloth-makers and cloth-sellers made an even bigger splash (*assume*, because the building has not been excavated further back than the frontage, so we cannot be certain what went on inside). On one side of the doorway Venus, the city's patron goddess, rode in a chariot pulled by elephants; on the other Mercury, the divine protector of commerce, stood in his temple grasping a fat bag of coins. Under Venus was a scene of workers busy combing the wool and making felt (with the boss himself, presumably, showing off a finished product on the right); under Mercury, the lady of the house, or perhaps an employee, is busy selling her wares (which appear now to be largely shoes).

Sadly, one of the most striking examples of this type of painting – and one which captured the imagination of nineteenth-century visitors – has now disappeared completely, a victim of the elements. Decorating the front wall of a bar, near the town gate leading to the sea, was a large picture of an elephant with a pygmy or two – and a painted sign saying 'Sittius restored the Elephant'. Sittius was probably the last landlord, and he had restored either the painting or maybe the whole place ('The Elephant Bar'). If so, he had a good name for a barman, so good one suspects that it may have been a 'trade-name'. For the best English translation of 'Sittius' would be 'Mr Thirsty'.

Different streets – and different stretches of the same streets – had noticeably different characters. Part of this is a difference between the main roads on the one hand, lined with shops, bars and the front doors of private houses great and small, and on the other the back streets, narrow, little-trod and interrupted only by the occasional service entrance. One of these, running between two city blocks that face onto the Via dell'Abbondanza, carried so little traffic that it could be partially blocked with a water tower and then effectively 'privatised' by the owner of the large adjacent house – and the only one with a door opening directly into it. Whether with permission from the town council, or simply with the self-confidence that went with wealth then as now, he walled off each end of the street, so creating a private annexe (storage area, animal pen or cart park) accessed from his service basement.

But there are also noticeable clusters of activity that characterise particular areas. Entering the city from the north, for example, just inside the Herculaneum Gate, you would have found a street dominated by the hospitality business – an array of roadside bars and inns, all trying to persuade the passing travellers to part with their cash in return for a drink and a bite to eat. And there is a similar pattern at the other northern entrance, the Vesuvius Gate, and at the Stabian Gate to the south. Not so at the other city gates, which suggests that the routes from north and south carried the majority of traffic in and out of the city: for bars tend to follow the crowds rather than vice versa. Or, to put in another way, only a Pompeian fool would have set up a retail outlet where there was little passing trade.

Enterprising archaeologists have even tried to work out what direction the bar owners expected their customers to be coming from – on the basis of the exact position of the counter, and from where the potential client would get the best view of the food and drink on offer. Whether this is one step too far in trying to second-guess the behaviour of the Romans, I am not sure. But the conclusion was that the establishments around these two gates aimed primarily at those coming *into* the city, catering to hungry travellers who had just arrived. The couple of bars, however, on the road leading from the Forum to the Marine Gate to the west had their eye (according to this logic) on people leaving the city, or at least coming away from the Forum.

There are also notable absences from the street scene which signal the different character of different areas. To continue the theme of bars, there are relatively few in the area of the Forum itself (though not quite as few as it now appears: ironically three once stood a few metres from the Forum on the site of the modern tourist refreshment centre). Walking away from there along the Via dell'Abbondanza to the east, there are perhaps two at the most until you reach the intersection with the Via Stabiana. At that point, they start to appear again in significant numbers (in fact more than twenty food and drink outlets in 600 metres have been identified), giving that eastern stretch of the Via dell'Abbondanza a very different 'feel'. This has led to all kinds of speculation, including the idea that the Pompeian authorities actively prevented the opening of such establishments with their discreditable associations in the main formal and ceremonial areas of the city.

Maybe. But what *is* certain is that the Forum of Pompeii, with its public buildings – temples, shrines, markets and so on – was not like the central square of modern Italian towns, with a café at each corner, designed for pleasure and relaxation as much as for business. It was, no doubt, this image of modern Italy that persuaded Sir William Gell, *bon viveur* and one of the leading authorities on Pompeii in the early nineteenth century, that the building in the Forum that we know as the market or *macellum* functioned partly as a restaurant – the booths down one side being intended for semi-private dining. After all, how could you have a central piazza without a place to get a meal?

More significant, though, than the differences between the various areas of Pompeii are the overall similarities of the urban landscape across the town. In this respect Pompeii is quite unlike many modern Western cities, where what social geographers call 'zoning' tends to be the rule. That is to say, particular activities (whether commercial, industrial or residential) tend now to be concentrated in different parts of the urban area, and the character of the streets changes accordingly: the roads of a suburban residential area are recognisably different, not just in their size, but in their planning and their relationship to the adjacent buildings, from those in the commercial centre. There also tend to be definite divisions within this arrangement between the rich and the poor, and sometimes between different races. By and large, even in relatively small conurbations (country villages are another matter) those with money live separately from those without. High-rise tenement blocks do not rub shoulders with the detached mansions of the wealthy; they are in a different part of town.

Valiant attempts have been made to detect some kind of 'zoning' in Pompeii. Archaeologists have pointed to the 'entertainment areas' for example (though that hardly means much more than Amphitheatre and the theatres, nothing remotely like a 'Broadway' or 'West End'). They have argued, not implausibly but not conclusively, that the north-western sector of the city contains more than its fair share of large, rich houses, as does also the far western strip with its marvellous sea views. And they have attempted to pinpoint, if not a red-light district in the modern sense, then at least areas associated with various forms of 'deviant behaviour', from commercial sex to dice games (a project complicated by long-running modern controversies on how many brothels there were in the city, and how we can now identify them; (below, pp. 232–3; 236–8).

But the simple truth is that Pompeii was a city without the zoning we have come to expect, and without significant distinction between elite and non-elite residential areas. In fact, it is not just that the richest domestic properties existed side by side with much more humble establishments. The elegant House of the Vestals, for example, had its main entrance in the midst of all the bars near the Herculaneum Gate and was, in fact, almost next door to a couple of noisy black-smiths' workshops. More than that, it was the standard pattern in the city for even the grandest residences to have small commercial units built into their street façade – an integral part of the main property, although usually no doubt managed not by the proprietor but by his dependants or tenants. So visitors to the palatial House of the Faun would have found its two main entranceways leading back from the street, between a row of four shops. This is not unlike the pattern in early modern cities. In eighteenth-century London the mansions of the rich in Piccadilly rubbed shoulders with chemists, shoemakers, hair-dressers and uphol-sterers. And, despite our general assumptions about zoning, it is what you find even today in Naples. The Neapolitan workshops and stores occupying small units on the ground floor of grand mansions are the closest we can get to an impression of ancient Pompeii.

How such striking juxtapositions of function and wealth were experienced by the town's inhabitants, we can only guess. But my suspicion is that the rich

22. At this crossroads we find both a street fountain and one of the dozen or so water towers in the town. The water from the 'water castle' was fed into a tank at the top of each tower, and then distributed to nearby properties. The point of this was to reduce the pressure of the water, which otherwise came down from the *castellum* with much too great force.

occupants of the House of the Vestals would have found it easier to ignore the constant hammering of the blacksmiths and the noise of the late-night clientèle at the bars, than the poor shopkeepers would have found it to ignore the vast wealth and opulence of those living on the other side of their shop walls. Divisive as it may seem, zoning has its advantages: at least the poor do not always have their noses rubbed in the privileges of their rich neighbours.

Water features

The stories of the Pompeian streets – glimpses of how they were used and by whom – can still be recovered from the traces that remain on the ground. Sometimes these are clear for all to see. We have already noted the stepping stones across the water and mire; these were strategically placed at junctions, other popular crossing points, and occasionally leading directly to the portals of the largest houses, for the convenience of the rich owners and their guests. Almost as memorable features of the street scene for most modern visitors are the water towers and, especially, the street fountains – more than forty of them surviving – that were spread all over the city, to be within easy reach of everyone; it has been calculated that very few Pompeians lived more than 80 metres from a fountain.

Both towers and fountains were elements in a complex system, supplying piped water through the town, from a 'water castle' or *castellum aquae* (itself fed by an aqueduct from the nearby mountains) just inside the city walls, next to the Vesuvius Gate – an innovation replacing an earlier system of supply which relied on deep wells and rainwater. This new service (immortalised more or less accurately in Robert Harris's best-seller *Pompeii*) has usually been dated to the 20s BCE, and the reign of the first emperor Augustus. But recent work has suggested that the first Pompeians to benefit from a piped public water supply of some sort, even if it was improved under Augustus, were the Sullan colonists some sixty years earlier.

The water towers, a dozen or so built of concrete faced with local stone or brick, up to six metres tall, and holding a lead tank at the top, were sub-stations in the system, distributing water by lead pipes which ran under the pavements to the public fountains and to nearby private residences, whose owners must have paid a fee for the privilege. Something must have gone wrong with this system of supply on the eve of the eruption. For it is clear from the empty trenches filled with volcanic debris that, at the time of its destruction, the pavements in various places in the city had been dug up and the water pipes removed. Most likely this was an instant attempt to investigate and repair the damage done to the water system by earthquakes that occurred in the run-up to the final eruption.

Archaeologists have speculated that similar problems might explain why, down one back alley (running beside the House of the Chaste Lovers and the House of the Painters at Work), the cess pits filled by the domestic latrines had been dug up and their contents left piled up unsalubriously in the pathway when the disaster struck. Though why seismic movements should affect the operation of cesspits is less clear. Perhaps this is more of an indication of the regular state of a Pompeian backstreet.

Beyond simple distribution points, the water towers fulfilled a more technical hydraulic function too, offering a nice example of Roman engineering expertise. The steep gradient down from the water castle, which was built at the highest point in the town, meant that the water pressure was, if anything, *too* strong, especially in the low-lying areas to the south. The towers, by collecting the water in the tank at the top, and letting it down again, acted to reduce the pressure. They also added to the water in the streets: the deposits of lime still visible on the outside of some of the towers suggest that they not infrequently overflowed.

Fountains are an even commoner feature than towers. Most of them followed the same general plan: a large spout, with constantly running water; a tank beneath, to catch some of the flow, made out of four large blocks of volcanic rock. Usually placed at junctions and crossroads, some jutted out from the kerb-side into the line of traffic; so, to protect them from damage by passing carts and trucks, sturdy upright stones were set in the ground next to them, the ancient equivalent of traffic bollards. No one with a private supply of water at home would rely on this public service, but the less wealthy did – in large numbers, to judge from the heavily worn surfaces of the stone, on either side of the spout. One of the tricks of the local guides in Pompeii today is to demonstrate just how that distinctive pattern of wear must have been formed, as Pompeian after Pompeian over a century or more came up behind the spout, rested one hand on one side of it and held the bucket under the stream of water with the other.

Whether or not they became the centre of organised neighbourhood associations, as some modern scholars have suspected (see pp. 211, 299), these fountains were certainly informal meeting places for the more humble local residents. In fact, on one occasion, we get a glimpse of a nearby house owner taking advantage of the throngs that such a facility was expected to attract. When a new fountain was erected so close to his little house that part had to be demolished to accommodate it, the owner responded by turning his front room into a shop.

One-way streets

Scratch the surface of the streets below the stepping stones and the fountains, look more carefully at the layout of the city's network of routes and thoroughfares, and there are other, even more intriguing stories to be reconstructed of street life in a Roman town. The tiniest hints on the surface of pavement or road open up some of the most fascinating pieces of history.

In many ways the schematic plan of the Pompeian street system, so often reproduced, is misleading. For, just as today many motorists find that a simple map of an unfamiliar town may fail to warn them of the pedestrianised precincts or the one-way streets, so this plan tends to conceal the actual pattern of movement around ancient Pompeii. The picture of free circulation implied by the diagram is contradicted by the evidence on the ground. Here too we find traffic-

23. Traffic barriers old and new. These three stone blocks emphasize the ban on traffic travelling between the Forum, which lies behind us, and the Via dell'Abbondanza, which stretches into the distance. On the left, the modern site authorities use plastic fencing to keep visitors from buildings under restoration.

free zones and, it seems, some control of the direction of traffic flow. Recent work – looking very carefully again at the ruts and stepping stones – has even suggested that we can begin to reconstruct the Pompeian one-way street system.

The streets of Pompeii could be closed to wheeled transport by simple devices: by large stone bollards fixed in the roadway, by the placing of fountains or other obstructions across the traffic path, or by steps or other changes of level that were impassable to carts. Every one of these was used to ensure that, at least in its final phases, the Pompeian Forum was a pedestrian area. We should put out of our minds any fanciful reconstruction of the central piazza criss-crossed by chariots and carts. Each entry point to the Forum was blocked to wheeled traffic: at the Via dell'Abbondanza by three bollards and a high kerb, at the south-east entrance by a strategically positioned water fountain, and so on. Interestingly, it was not only wheeled transport whose access to the Forum could be controlled. At every entrance point, fittings for some form of barrier or gate can still be made out, closing the area off even to those on foot. The precise purpose of these gates is unknown. Perhaps they were to close the area at night (though they would have to have been formidable barriers to put off a determined vandal). Perhaps, as one recent suggestion has it, they were used when elections were taking place in the Forum, as a means of controlling entrance to the elections and of excluding those without the right to vote.

A pedestrianised central square is one thing. But the Pompeian traffic schemes went beyond that. For the Via dell'Abbondanza is also blocked to wheeled transport almost 300 metres further along, at its junction with the Via Stabiana, where an abrupt drop of more than 30 centimetres makes it impassable to even the most sturdy cart. This stretch of the street between the Forum and Via Stabiana was not completely traffic-free, as it could be accessed from some of the intersections to north and south. But it obviously did not provide the easy through-route across the town that the map at first sight suggests. Its comparatively shallow cart ruts also indicate that it did not carry a large volume of traffic (although one sceptic has argued that the relative absence of ruts is equally well explained by the road having been repaved not long before 79). There are other signs too that this piece of road was in some way special. Part of it, the section in front of the Stabian Baths, is unusually wide: in effect it forms a small triangular piazza at the entrance to the Baths. And it was, of course, this stretch of road where, unlike the section to the east, we noted the almost complete absence of bars and taverns.

Exactly what was 'special' about it is harder to say. But one good guess is that it has something to do with the position of this stretch of the Via dell'Abbondanza between the theatres and ancient Temple of Minerva and Hercules to the south and the main Forum, with its temples and other public buildings. Little-used for day-to-day traffic, and not the main transport artery that most people now imagine, perhaps it formed part of a processional route from one civic centre to the other, from Forum to Theatre, or from Theatre to Temple of Jupiter? Processions were a staple of public and religious life in the Roman world: a means of celebrating the gods, parading divine images and sacred symbols before the people, honouring the city and its leaders. The details and calendar of these ceremonies at Pompeii are lost to us, but we maybe have the traces of one favoured route.

There are, however, still more road blockings along the Via dell'Abbondanza. Moving from the Via Stabiana towards the eastern gate (the Sarno Gate, so called after the river which flows on this side of the town), most of the road intersections to the south and some to the north are either completely impassable to carts or steeply ramped but still – as the ruts running over them make clear – accessible to wheeled transport. Part of the purpose of this must have been traffic control, but the other part was, once again, the control of water. The Via dell'Abbondanza runs across the town about two thirds of the way down the slope on which the city rests: the streets below it must have been particularly liable to nuisance and damage by the torrents flowing down from above. Hence these ramps and block-ings, which would have prevented much of that water flowing into the lower region of the town, directing it instead into the Via dell'Abbondanza and chan-nelling it out at the Sarno Gate. Part of this street may have been a 'processional way'; another part was certainly a major drain.

Pompeian traffic was then reduced or, in modern terms, 'calmed' by the crea-tion of cul-de-sacs, and other kinds of road block. But there remains the more general problem of narrow streets and what would happen if two carts should meet in those many roads which were wide enough only for one. Needless to say, reversing a cart drawn by a pair of mules, down a road impeded by stepping stones, would have been an impossible feat. So how did the ancient Pompeians avoid repeated stand-offs, between carts meeting head-to-head? How did they prevent a narrow street being reduced to an impasse?

One possible answer is a combination of loudly ringing bells, shouts and boys sent ahead to ensure the path was clear. The horse trappings found with the cart in the House of the Menander certainly included some harness bells which would have made a distinct jingle to warn of approaching traffic. But there are signs that a system of one-way streets was in operation in the town, to keep the carts moving freely. The evidence for this comes from some of the most painstaking efforts in Pompeian archaeology over the last decade or so, and from the clever idea that the precise pattern of the street ruts, and the exact position of the marks produced by carts colliding with the stepping stones, or grazing the kerb at corners, could tell you which way the ancient traffic was moving along a particular stretch of road.

One of the most convincing examples of this occurs in the north-west part of the town, on the way from the Herculaneum Gate to the Forum, where the road we now know as the Via Consolare meets the narrow Vico di Mercurio (Fig. 5). Here the combination of the collision marks on the south-west side of the step-ping stone in the middle of the Vico di Mercurio and the precise pattern of grind-ing on the kerbstone to the north indicates that traffic was coming along the Vico di Mercurio from the east and mostly turning north when it met the two-way Via Consolare at the junction. The Vico di Mercurio was, in other words, a one-way

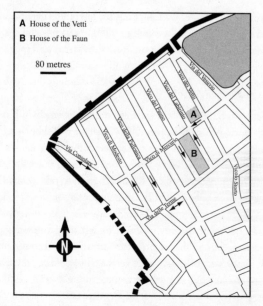

Figure 5. The road system in the north-west of Pompeii: the conjectural lay-out of one-way streets.

street, running east to west. Traffic coming down the Via Consolare, wanting to take a left turn towards the east, would have to wait until it reached the broad Via delle Terme – which was a two-way street. Similar evidence has been taken to suggest that there are clear distinctions on the north–south streets in the area too: the Vico di Modesto and Vico del Labirinto carrying northbound traffic, the Vico della Fullonica and Vico del Fauno southbound.

Whether the degree of systematisation is quite so rigid as the most enthusiastic modern archaeologists would have us believe, I am rather doubtful. When they write, on the basis of apparently conflicting evidence in some places, that the Vico di Mercurio had originally carried traffic in the other direction and that it 'underwent a reversal from an eastbound to a westbound route', it is hard to imagine how such a reversal would have been brought about. Who decided? And how would they have enforced the decision? Ancient cities had no traffic police or transport department. Nor have we found any trace of traffic signs, in a town where there are plenty of other kinds of public notices. Nonetheless, there seems little doubt that there was a pattern of traffic direction generally observed, even if only enforced by common usage. By following the agreed routes, the cart drivers of Pompeii had a better chance of avoiding a complete jam than if they merely rang their bells loudly and hoped that nothing was coming round the corner.

Pavements: public and private

The pavement was the borderland between the public world of the street and the more private world behind the thresholds of houses and shops – a 'liminal zone', as anthropologists would call it, between outside and inside. At busy taverns, facing onto the street, the pavement provided overspill space for customers who 'propped up the bar', or waited for food and drink to take away. For drivers of animals, making deliveries or simply taking a break, and for visitors arriving on horseback at large houses, it also offered convenient tethering posts, or rather tethering *holes*. All over the city, in front of bakeries, workshops, taverns and stores, as well as at the entrance to private residences, you can still find small holes drilled through the very edge of the pavement, hundreds of them altogether.

Puzzling to archaeologists, these were once thought to be the fixing points for sun blinds to provide shade for the open premises behind – an idea drawn in part from the practice in historical Naples of draping awnings over shop fronts. If this were the case, it would have turned the pavements, on sunny days at least, into a forest of fabric, and dark, makeshift tunnels between shop and kerbside. Maybe that is how it was. But a much simpler idea, and one that fits better with the distribution of these holes, is to think of them as places to tie up animals (and if not here, then where else?). Even this would hint at another awkward picture of Pompeian street life: the delivery man's donkeys, tethered to the edge of the narrow street, being forced to join the pedestrians on the pavement in order to clear the way for a cart squeezing its way through.

Awnings or not, the sun must sometimes have made the city's pavements unpleasantly hot, even if two-storey houses on both sides of the road (especially where the upper storeys were built out at an overhang) did offer more shade than weary visitors find in the ruined streets today. Unsurprisingly some householders took remedial action. Across the frontage of some of the larger residences canopies once jutted out from the façade, providing extra shade not only for those entering the property, but for any passer-by. Stone benches were sometimes added on either side of the front door, also taking advantage of the shade provided. Exactly who we are to imagine sitting on these depends on our view of the mentality of the Pompeian elite. They may have been installed, partly at least, as an act of generosity to the local community: a resting place for one and all. They may, however, have been intended solely for visitors waiting to be admitted to the house itself. In fact, it's not at all difficult to picture the porter emerging from behind those vast front doors to chase off the riff-raff who had chosen to sit down there uninvited.

Walking around the town today, we can spot all kinds of other examples of private property, and its amenities, encroaching onto the pavement. Some owners turned the pavement in front of their houses into a ramp, to allow carts easy access inside. That, at least, was how the landlord of one of the inns or lodging houses near the Herculaneum Gate catered for the needs of his guests – allowing them easily to bring their carts, belongings and merchandise into the security of the inner court. Others used it to construct themselves even more monumental entrances than usual. One large property at the far east end of the Via dell'Abbondanza, now known as the Estate (*Praedia*) of Julia Felix, after the woman who once owned it, was given a pretentious stepped walkway, built right over the pavement. Further up the same street towards the Forum, the front door of the House of Epidius Rufus opened onto an extra terrace, more than a metre high, which was set on top of the already elevated pavement – giving the house a lofty remoteness from the life of the street beneath. With a more practical aim in view, the owners of the House of the Vettii inserted a series of bollards into the street along the side wall of their mansion. The roadway was narrow and there was no pavement to act as a barrier between house and road. They must have been worried about the damage that might be done by passing carts, carelessly driven.

Some of these encroachments may have received permission from the town council or the local aediles. A handful of painted notices found on the outside of the Amphitheatre suggest that it was the aediles who authorised the street vendors plying their trade underneath the monument's arches, and assigned their pitches: 'By permission of the aediles. Licensed to Caius Aninius Fortunatus' etc., as the faint and fragmentary Latin seems to say. Maybe the better-off made a similar application to the authorities. Or maybe they simply assumed the right to do much as they pleased with the pavements in front of their houses.

The householders might have had good reason to make that assumption – to judge from some tell-tale traces in the pavements themselves. Most city pavements, ancient or modern, are much less homogeneous than the casual passer-by tends to recognise. Their surfaces have been laid at different periods; they have been repaired in patches, often with not much care to make a match with the surrounding material. This is as true of Pompeii as it is of modern London or New

York. Yet in Pompeii a closer look reveals rather more systematic discrepancies. In some streets the pavements seem originally to have been laid in different materials (volcanic rock, limestone, tufa) – and in stretches corresponding to the frontages of houses. In places there are even blocks set into the pavement marking the division between one property (and its pavement) and the next.

The conclusion is obvious. Even though they must have been planned by some central city authority, their width and height fixed to an agreed standard, some of these pavements were paid for on a private basis, by an individual householder, or by a group of them clubbing together – the choice of material to be used left up to those who were footing the bill. It is logical to imagine that their upkeep was similarly privatised. That idea is supported by a surviving Roman law (inscribed on bronze and found in the far south of Italy) which gives the regulations for, amongst other things, the upkeep of roads and pavements in the city of Rome itself. The basic principle was that each householder was responsible for the pavement frontage of his own property, and if he did not maintain it properly the aediles could themselves contract the maintenance work out and then recover the cost from the defaulter. Interestingly, an additional obligation on the householder at Rome was to make sure that water did not collect so as to inconvenience people in the street. It was not only Pompeii that had trouble with overspills.

The people in the streets

So far the people in the Pompeian streets have been rather shadowy figures. We have spotted the traces they left behind them: the scrawls on the walls, the hands on the fountains, the scratches and scrapes left by the carts on the kerbsides. But we have not seen the men, women and children face to face; we have not caught them at their daily business.

We can in fact get one step closer to them, thanks to an extraordinary series of paintings found in the Estate of Julia Felix. At the time of the eruption this large property, with its imposing entrance that we have already noted, covered the whole of what had once been two city blocks not far from the Amphitheatre. It included a number of different units: a privately run, commercial bathing establishment, a number of rental apartments, shops, bars and dining rooms, a large orchard and a medium-sized private house. One large room in this establishment (an inner courtyard or atrium, just over 9 metres by 6) was decorated with a painted frieze, two and a half metres above the ground, apparently showing scenes of life in the Pompeian Forum. This was uncovered by eighteenth-century

24. This eighteenth-century engraving preserves details of the now faded painted scenes of life in the Forum. Behind the traders it is interesting to see how the bare columns of the Forum colonnade might have appeared in the ancient world itself: decorated with hanging festoons and used to support temporary partitions and gates.

excavators who removed to the museum about 11 metres of it, in small, broken sections, leaving just a couple of fragments on the wall. What happened to the rest, or even how much more there was (it's only an assumption that it once extended around the whole room), we do not know. But it is a likely guess that much of it fell victim to the robust excavation techniques of the time.

The paintings are now badly faded. Even so, they offer as vivid a picture as we could hope for of life on the Pompeian streets – particularly when combined with engravings of them made soon after they were found which help to throw light on some of the murkier sections. They are not, of course, strictly realistic. The background architecture is a rather rough-and-ready version of the two-storey Forum colonnade (though the position of the statues and their relationship to the columns matches up quite closely to the remains on the ground). The intense bustle of activity at every point almost certainly goes well beyond what would be found even on the busiest market day. This is not daily life, but an imaginative re-creation of it. It is a Pompeian street scene in the mind's eye of a Pompeian painter: beggars, hucksters, schoolkids, fast food, ladies out shopping ...

In one of the most detailed sections (Ill. 24) we get a glimpse of a couple of street traders at work, with varying degrees of enterprise. On the left of the scene is a dozy ironmonger. His table is set out with what look like hammers and

25. Buying and selling. On the left a couple of women are negotiating for the sale of some cloth. On the right a man, who has come shopping with his son, is buying a pan.

26. While a lady gives a handout to a scruffy beggar (plus dog), in the background a pair of children play peek-a-boo around a column. In the foreground is one of the many statues that stood around the Forum.

27. Methods of transport. On the right a donkey or mule is laden with a heavy saddle (note there are no stirrups). On the left is the kind of cart that once trundled the streets of the town.

28. A couple of men sitting on a bench under the Forum colonnade are perhaps adjudicating some legal case. Three men behind watch the proceedings with some care, but in the background is a more domestic scene: a Pompeian toddler asks his mother or carer to pick him up.

pincers, which he has brought to his stall in the baskets lined up at the front (or are they metal jars for sale?). He has a couple of customers: a young boy with an older man, shopping basket on his arm. A sale is in the offing. But it looks as if the ironmonger has nodded off, and needs a wake-up call from the man behind him. On the right, a shoemaker in a bright red tunic is doing much more active trade, pitching his wares to a group of four ladies and a baby, who sit on the benches he has provided for his customers. Behind him, his range of shoes are on show in a way that baffled our eighteenth-century copyist (who depicts them floating in mid-air) and is now impossible to make out on the original. Most likely he has fixed up some display stands, propped against the columns behind. These run all along the back of the scene, festoons hanging between them. On the right, behind a couple of diminutive statues of men on horseback (in this position, probably local bigwigs – emperors would be given a more prominent setting), the space between two columns is closed by a gate. All of this is a good antidote to the austere, uncluttered, lifeless appearance of the colonnade today.

We are given plenty of other vignettes of buying and selling. In one section (Ill. 25), women negotiate with salesmen over pieces of cloth; a man (one of the relatively few characters here to be dressed in a toga – although it is red rather than white) chooses a metal saucepan, while his young son carries the shopping basket; and a baker serves a pair of men with what appears to be a basket of rolls. Elsewhere, in the shadow of an arch, a greengrocer has a magnificent collection of figs for sale, while a food vendor has rigged up a brazier and is busy selling hot drinks or snacks. But it is not only commercial activities that the painter has shown.

There is a touch of low life (Ill. 26): an elegant lady, plus slave or child, appears to be helping the homeless, by offering cash to a very ragged beggar with a dog. And there are several glimpses of the Pompeian traffic in the shape of mules and carts (Ill. 27). Given that, as we have seen, the Forum was a pedestrianised area, is the cart artistic licence? Or were there ways – ramps over the steps perhaps – of allowing wheeled transport into the area on some occasions, or at certain times?

Local politics too plays a significant part in this vision of Pompeian life. In one scene (Plate 7), some men are reading a long public notice, written on a board or scroll, which has been fixed across the bases of three more equestrian statues (this time, perhaps members of the imperial house, shown as military heroes). Elsewhere it looks as if some kind of legal case is going on (Ill. 28). A couple of men, dressed in togas, are seated, concentrating hard as they are addressed by a standing figure – often identified as a woman, but the traces are too ambiguous to be sure of the sex. He, or she, is making a particular point, gesturing to a tablet held by a young girl who stands in front. Whether, as some have thought, this girl is meant to be the subject of the case (an issue of guardianship perhaps), or whether she is merely a convenient prop for the evidence in question, it is impossible to tell. Behind looms another of those ubiquitous equestrian statues.

But the most arresting section of all depicts a scene from a Pompeian classroom (Ill. 29). One of the puzzles in the archaeology of the city has been how and where the children were educated. We have plenty of evidence of writing and literacy (even practice alphabets scratched onto walls at child height), but – despite all kinds of implausible and over-optimistic identifications – there is no trace of a school as such. That is because Roman schoolmasters did not regularly operate in purpose-built premises, but would sit down with their class in any convenient location where there was some space and shade. One such location in Pompeii was very likely the large open space or exercise ground (*palaestra*) near the Amphitheatre, For it was here, on a column of its colonnade, that a schoolmaster inscribed his gratitude for payment, and by implication his frustration at the still outstanding bills: 'May those who have paid me their school fees get what they want from the gods'. Some archaeologists have even guessed that the list of names and sums of money scratched up on the same column was a list of the poor man's receipts.

The paintings from the Estate of Julia Felix depict a lesson going on under the colonnade of the Forum. A man, dressed in a cloak, sporting a pointed beard, appears to be supervising three pupils who are studying tablets on their knees. Other pupils or the children's minders watch what is going on from under the

29. Rough justice in the Pompeian classroom. One schoolboy miscreant gets a hiding, while the rest of the class get on with their work, keeping their eyes carefully on their tablets.

colonnade. What none seem to be observing is the nasty scene to the right. One boy has had his tunic lifted to reveal his bare buttocks (or has even been stripped down to a waistband – the painting itself is not clear). Suspended on the back of another, while his feet are held tight, he is being given a good lashing. It seems a peculiarly brutal form of punishment, even by the toughest standards of the recent past, and the awkward, helpless position of the boy only serves to accentuate the cruelty. Yet interestingly, this may well have been the normal style of schoolboy beating in the ancient world. A light-hearted poem by Herodas, a Greek poet of the third century BCE, describes a mother's attempt to reform her no-good son, Kottalos, who has been neglecting his studies in favour of gambling. She arranges for the schoolmaster to give him a hiding – and the description of the other boys lifting the unfortunate Kottalos onto their shoulders is strikingly reminiscent of what we see here.

The frieze, fragmentary and faded as it now is, offers all kinds of precious hints about how we might begin to repopulate the Pompeian cityscape: and not just with men in white togas (indeed there are rather few of those). It prompts us to imagine children at their lessons, beggars plying for cash, traders and hucksters of all kinds, or local officials at their business. Women are prominent too, out on the streets on their own, or with their children, haggling, chatting, buying, even distributing the occasional largesse to those less fortunate than themselves. But more than that, the paintings hint at the colour, clutter and bric-a-brac of urban life that tends to get forgotten when we stare at the now bare ruins: the bright clothing, the portable tables and braziers, the wicker baskets, the garlands and all those statues. One estimate has it that in early imperial Rome live human beings outnumbered statues by a factor of only two to one – which would make a total of some half a million statues in a human population of a million. There was nothing like that concentration of sculpture in Pompeii. But, nonetheless, life in the Forum here unfolds under the watchful eyes of men in bronze (or marble), emperors alive or dead, imperial princelings and local notables.

The city that never sleeps

In 6 BCE, the emperor Augustus was called upon to adjudicate a tricky case from the Greek city of Cnidus. A couple of residents, Eubulus and Tryphera, had been troubled night after night by a group of local thugs who 'laid siege' to their house. Finally, their patience at an end, they told one of their slaves to get rid of them by throwing the contents of a chamber pot on their heads. But things went from bad to worse: for the slave lost his grip on the pot, it fell and killed one of the assailants. The Cnidian authorities were minded to accuse Eubulus and Tryphera of unlawful killing, but the emperor came down on the side of the couple – long-suffering victims, as he saw it, of anti-social behaviour. His judgement was inscribed publicly in a nearby town: hence our knowledge of the affair.

Whatever the rights and wrongs of the case (and some scholars have suspected that Eubulus and Tryphera might not have been quite as innocent as the emperor found them), it is one of the very few glimpses we get, leaving aside Juvenal's poetic hyperbole about Rome itself, of how an 'ordinary' ancient town might have appeared at night: dark, unpoliced, slightly scary. How like that were the streets of Pompeii when the sun had gone down?

One image of night-time Pompeii would see even the main streets as almost pitch black. Although Romans went to enormous trouble to bring light to their world in the hours of darkness (as the thousands of bronze and pottery oil lamps found in Pompeii demonstrate), the results were patchy at best. Most people had to live their lives by the rhythms of daylight, sunrise to sunset. The inns and bars kept serving into the evening hours, illuminated in part by lamps hanging over their open doorways, their fixings in some cases still visible. In fact, one electoral poster – a satiric piece of 'anti-propaganda' or not – offers the support of 'the late drinkers' to one particular candidate for public office: 'All the late drinkers are canvassing for Marcus Cerrinius Vatia to be aedile'. But the big houses would have shut their doors and presented a solid, uninviting blank wall to the outside world, punctured only by the occasional tiny window. The shops and workshops would have closed too, secured with the shutters whose slots are still visible in

30. Shut up shop? The wide openings of the shops could be closed by heavy wooden shutters. This plaster cast of a set of shutters on the Via dell'Abbondanza shows how the section on the right could operate as a small door to give access when the shop was shut.

their thresholds, as well as occasionally the impression of the wood itself. Without street lighting, and with uneven pavements, irregular stepping stones and a good deal of filth, pedestrians – equipped only with the light of a portable lantern, and whatever the moon provided – would have ventured about at their peril.

But there was life in the streets at night too, and a good deal more noise and hustle and bustle about the town than the gloomy darkness would suggest. In addition to the barking of the dogs and the braying of the donkeys, men might be at work. It is certain, for example, that on some occasions the signwriters putting up the advertisements for the next gladiatorial display in the Amphitheatre, or the electoral posters urging support for this or that candidate for local office, plied their trade by night. One such writer, Aemilius Celer, who posted an advertisement for thirty pairs of gladiators fighting over five days, carefully signed his work: 'Aemilius Celer wrote this on his own by the light of the moon'. Such solitary activity was probably not the norm. One notice posted high up on a wall, urging support for Caius Julius Polybius in the forthcoming elections, includes a joke from the signwriter to his mate: 'Lantern carrier, steady the ladder'. Why did they choose to work after dark? Perhaps because they were sometimes putting up notices without permission, where they should not have been (but not always – else why sign their names?). Perhaps it was more convenient to be painting when there were fewer people about to disturb the work, or rock the ladder.

There may well have also been a good deal more traffic trundling down the streets than we would at first imagine. In the same document as the regulations for the upkeep of pavements in Rome were listed are also found the rules for the entry of wheeled traffic into the city of Rome. Although all kinds of exceptions are noted (carts used for building work on temples, to remove rubble from public demolition sites, or those used in connection with important rituals), the basic principle was that wheeled transport was excluded from the city from sunrise until the tenth hour of the day – that is, given that the hours of daylight were divided into twelve, until the late afternoon or early evening. The hours of darkness, in other words, were the time when you were most likely to find carts on the streets of the capital. Indeed, in addition to his complaints about falling objects and muggers, Juvenal has some sharp words about the noise of the night-time traffic.

We cannot be certain if these regulations applied, in exactly these terms, to Pompeii; though it is a fair assumption that they did, more or less. Nor can we be certain how rigorously they would have been enforced. A law is one thing, having the will or the resources to police it, quite another. (And remember that a cart appeared in the Forum frieze in a scene that was clearly not intended to be night-time ...) Nevertheless, there is a reasonable chance that a good proportion of the wheeled traffic whose management and control we have explored in this chapter would have been out in the street after dark. As well as the howling dogs, the carousing of the 'late drinkers', the whistling and joking of the signpainters at their jobs, we have to imagine the sounds of the rumbling carts, the jingling of the bells, the scraping of iron-clad wheels against the kerb or the stepping stones. Literally, a city that never slept – and was never quiet.

CHAPTER THREE

HOUSE AND HOME

The House of the Tragic Poet

In *The Last Days of Pompeii*, Edward Bulwer-Lytton's classic disaster novel first published in 1834, a pair of lovers, Glaucus and Ione, manage to escape from the doomed city. As the volcanic debris falls, they are led to safety by a blind slave girl who is used to navigating her way around Pompeii in darkness. Tragically – but conveniently for the plot, since she too is in love with Glaucus – the slave girl drowns herself, after stealing a single kiss from her beloved. Glaucus and Ione meanwhile relocate to Athens, where they live happily ever after, as Christian converts.

The appeal of *The Last Days*, one of the best-selling books of the nineteenth century, was partly its colourful romance: the volcano was only one of the lovers' problems – in the days leading up to the eruption they faced any number of impediments, from a malevolent Egyptian priest to wrongful imprisonment. It was partly too its moral message, pointing up the depravity of the pagan world, from which Glaucus and Ione escaped. But a significant part of its appeal was also the vivid, and carefully researched, archaeological backdrop, from Amphitheatre to baths, Forum to private houses. Bulwer-Lytton had drawn heavily on Sir William Gell's *Pompeiana*, the first comprehensive guide to Pompeii in English, and had even dedicated the novel to Gell.

The house of the hero Glaucus himself was based on the House of the Tragic Poet, a small but exquisitely decorated property uncovered in 1824 (Fig. 6). This quickly became famous as an ideal vision of Pompeian domestic life and was described in great detail in *Pompeiana*. A few years later – partly, no doubt, thanks

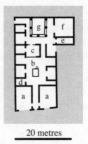

Figure 6. The House of the Tragic Poet. Visitors entered this house between two shops (a), down a narrow passageway to the atrium (b), with its porter's cubby-hole (d). Beyond the *tablinum* (c) with its mosaic of actors preparing (Plate 17), was the garden (g). Opening onto it was a *triclinium* (f) and kitchen (e).

20 metres

to the extra celebrity bestowed on it by *The Last Days* – it even provided the model for the 'Pompeian Court' at the Crystal Palace, that vast entertainment venue, combining commercial showcase with museum, which opened just outside London, at Sydenham, in 1854. It was a strange afterlife for a house that had been overwhelmed by Vesuvius almost two millennia earlier. The House of the Tragic Poet was more or less faithfully reconstructed within the Palace, and at first intended – appropriately enough, given its domestic image – to act as a tearoom for visitors. In the event plans changed, and the only visitor ever officially to sit down to tea there was Queen Victoria. In France it had a more socially exclusive nineteenth-century imitator. The interior design of the mansion in the rue Montaigne in Paris, where Prince Jérôme Napoléon and his aristocratic friends enjoyed dressing up in togas and pretending to be Romans, was also based on the House of the Tragic Poet.

The original remains of this house are to be found in the north-west corner of Pompeii, between the Herculaneum Gate and the Forum – directly across the street from one of the main sets of public baths, and a near neighbour, just two small blocks away, of the vast House of the Faun. Named, when it was excavated, after one of its wall paintings – then believed to depict a tragic poet reciting his work to a group of listeners (now re-identified as the mythical scene in which Admetus and Alcestis listen to the reading of an oracle) – the house was built in its present form towards the end of the first century BCE. The surviving decoration, including a striking series of wall paintings which featured scenes from Greek myth and literature, is somewhat later, the result of a makeover in the decade or so before the eruption. A few years after they were discovered, most of the figured scenes were cut out and taken to the museum in Naples, creating unattractive scars on the walls of the house. What was left in place – the surrounding patterns and the general wall colouring – is now dreadfully faded,

31. A reconstruction of the outside of the House of the Tragic Poet. With one of the shops shut, and only a few windows on the upper storey, the appearance is rather forbidding. The overhanging balcony at the side was a more common feature of Pompeian architecture than we would now imagine; made of wood, few have survived.

despite the fact that it was roofed over in the 1930s to protect it from the elements. The impact is obviously much less breathtaking than when it was first discovered. That said, we can still fairly confidently reconstruct its ancient appearance and organisation, as well as glimpse something of the tremendous impression it made on visitors in the nineteenth century.

The façade of the house onto the main street (Ill. 31) is dominated by a pair of shops, in a good position to attract customers from the public baths opposite (in fact there is a strategically placed set of stepping stones across the road at this point). What they sold we do not know. In the one to the left some precious pieces of jewellery were discovered, gold and pearl ear-rings, bracelets, necklaces and finger-rings. But there was not enough to prove, as some archaeologists have suggested, that it was a high-class jewellery outlet (these things might, after all, have been the contents of a jewellery box that was never rescued). There were few windows, and those that there were, small and on the upper storey, well above eye-level. But between the shops was the grand entrance to the house, more than three metres high, fitted (as we can tell from the pivot holes on either side of the threshold) with double doors. Just to the left of this some signpainters had been busy, painting on the door pier a notice of support for Marcus Holconius, who was standing for the office of aedile, and for Caius Gavinius. Presumably this had been done with the owner's encouragement or, at least, permission; if not, it was extremely cheeky use of someone's doorpost.

32. At the front entrance of the House of the Tragic Poet, marked here by the round fixings for the door, was this mosaic of a guard dog, and underneath the words *CAVE CANEM*. The round hole below in the centre is a drainage hole – water conscious as the Pompeians always were.

Here the doors themselves have not survived, but in other houses it has occasionally been possible to make a cast of them by the same technique as has been used for the bodies of the victims – filling with plaster the hole left by their decay. From these we get a stark, and more than slightly forbidding, impression of a great barrier of wood, with metal fittings and studded with bronze, dividing the house from the outside world. There can have been no practical necessity for portals of quite this size, strength and splendour. They were there to make a visual impact on visitors and passers-by: as much a symbolic boast, as a physical barrier.

Not that the doors were always closed, of course. At night, they surely did shut off the house and its activities from the world of the street. In the daytime, they may often have been open, allowing a view into the interior. If that was not the case, then the point of one of the House of the Tragic Poet's most iconic images would have been lost. For directly on the other side of the threshold, and just past the small drainage hole for overflow water that must sometimes have flowed down the front hall from inside the house, is a memorable image in mosaic of a dog, teeth bared and ready to pounce were he not chained up (Ill. 32). In case you missed the point, he is accompanied by the words *CAVE CANEM* ('beware of the dog'). This would only have been visible if the front doors were ajar.

There are other such warning signs in Pompeii, in paint as well as mosaic, not to mention the plaster cast of the real-life dog which died still tethered to his post. One is actually described by Petronius in his novel, the *Satyrica*, written during the reign of the emperor Nero. Much of the book has been lost or survives only in snatches, but the most famous and best-preserved section is set in a town somewhere near the Bay of Naples and features a dinner party given by an ex-slave called Trimalchio – a man of staggering riches, but of sometimes frankly grotesque taste. When the novel's narrator and his friends arrive at Trimalchio's front door, the first thing they see is a notice pinned right next to it: 'No slave to leave the premises without permission from the master. Penalty 100 lashes' (a nice touch from one who had once been a slave himself). Then they come across the porter, flamboyantly dressed in green with a cherry-red belt, who is keeping watch over the doorway while shelling peas into a silver bowl; and, hanging over the threshold, a magpie in a golden cage sings a greeting to the visitors. But the real shock comes next: 'I almost fell flat on my back and broke a leg,' explains the narrator, 'because on the left as we went in, not far from the porter's cubby-hole, was a huge dog, tethered by a chain ... painted on the wall. And written above him in capital letters it said *CAVE CANEM*, BEWARE OF THE DOG.' Just for a minute, he has taken the picture of the dog for the real thing – only the first of many occasions at Trimalchio's dinner party when the guests will not quite know whether to believe their eyes.

It would be dangerous to take Petronius' fantastic novel too literally as a guide to daily life in ancient Pompeii. But it does offer a hint here of how we might reconstruct the scene at the entrance of the House of the Tragic Poet. The door was very likely open for much of the daytime. But the security would not have been left to the mosaic guard dog, however fearsome or lifelike it might have been, or even to the actual dog signalled by the image (like the one which Trimalchio later brings into his dinner party, with predictably disruptive results). Almost certainly a porter, albeit more modestly dressed than Trimalchio's, would have kept an eye on who was coming and going. In fact a small room just inside the house, under the stairs, with a rough floor, has been tentatively identified as the porter's cubby-hole.

Visitors who stepped over the threshold found themselves in a corridor, once brightly painted, though precious little colour now survives. A narrow door from each of the shops opens onto this, suggesting that whoever owned the house was closely connected with these two commercial establishments; even if he did not service them himself, he was probably their proprietor and reaped the profits. Or that at least is the modern view. Earlier observers were more puzzled by this layout. In the absence of any obvious fixtures and fittings, despite the wide openings characteristic of shops, Gell wondered if they were not shops at all but quarters for the servants. Bulwer-Lytton trailed a different idea. They were, he suggested, 'for the reception of visitors who neither by rank nor familiarity were entitled to admission' into the inside of the house. Bright ideas, but certainly wrong.

At the end of the corridor you came into the house proper, arranged around two open courts (Plate 8). The first, the atrium, was again lavishly decorated – including six large wall paintings of scenes from Greek mythology. At its centre the roof was open to the skies, and underneath the opening a pool collected the rainwater, which drained into a deep well. On the well-head, you can still see the deep grooves made by the ropes which brought the buckets up, full of water from below. A number of mostly rather small rooms, some brightly painted, opened directly onto the atrium, while stairways ran up on either side to whatever lay on the upper floor. Beyond the atrium was a garden, lined on three sides by a shady colonnade (an arrangement known as a 'peristyle' – meaning 'surrounded by columns'), with more rooms, including a kitchen and latrine, opening off it. One of these columns has the name 'Aninius' scratched on it twice: the owner of the house, some archaeologists have suggested; but equally well, a friend, relative, bored guest with time on his hands, or the name of someone's heartthrob lovingly inscribed. The back wall of the peristyle supported a small shrine, and continued the garden theme, being covered with illusionistic paintings (now completely vanished) of trelliswork and foliage (Plate 9). In the very back corner, another door led out into the lane which ran up the side of the house.

We do not know how this particular garden was planted and stocked (though the shell of what was probably the household's pet tortoise was found there). But new techniques developed long after 1824, such as the analysis of seeds and pollen, or the careful excavation, and plaster-casting, of the root cavities, have allowed archaeologists to reconstruct in vivid detail gardens in other houses. In one, the House of Julius Polybius (where the remains of the pregnant girl were found; see p. 8), the garden – about twice the size of this one – turned out to have been more of an orchard-cum-wilderness than the display of elegant, formal flowerbeds we often imagine. In a space of some 10 by 10 metres there were five large trees, including a fig (to judge from the large number of carbonised figs discovered), an olive and a variety of fruit trees, apple, cherry or pear. Some were so large that they needed stakes to hold up their branches. They were tall too: the imprint of a ladder, eight metres in length, which must have been used for picking the fruit, was detected by the excavators on the ground surface. But, even so, the owners of the house had packed more in. In the shade of the branches, other small trees, shrubs and bushes were growing, and there were eight more trees espaliered (or so the pattern of nail holes hint) to the west wall of the garden. Fragments of terracotta around the roots of these show that they had been started out in large pots, then replanted. Perhaps they were more exotic species needing more careful early tending, such as lemon. Overall it must have been a dark and shady area. It was certainly dark and shady enough to make a comfortable environment for the ferns whose spores were found in large quantities at the garden's edge.

Other house gardens were much more formal and decorative. Just a few doors away from the House of Julius Polybius, a peristyle garden has recently been uncovered, with carefully arranged geometric flowerbeds, and footpaths running between them. The beds were bordered by fences, made of reed, and were planted with a regular and colourful scheme of cypress bushes and roses, with other ornamental and flowering plants along the edges of the beds (including, to judge from the pollen remains, artemisia and pinks). The boundary wall of the garden was covered with a vine, and there were plenty of ferns along the open drains which caught the rainwater from the roof – not to mention the presence of nettles and sorrel, familiar weeds then as now. The numerous cockle shells also found in the garden have encouraged the charming idea that the occupants of the house might have wandered round the garden while eating cockles; but it might simply have been a convenient place to throw waste shells, garden perambulations or not.

Whatever the style of the garden in the House of the Tragic Poet (apart from the turtle and some fixtures on the columns, suggesting that – on one side at least – it was fenced off, we know nothing), Bulwer Lytton saw the property in terms of a nineteenth-century bachelor's residence, and therefore suitable for the unmarried Glaucus. He had some doubts, in general, about the refinement of Pompeian wall painting: 'The purity of the taste of the Pompeians in decoration is questionable,' he carped. But the fine paintings in this house he reckoned 'would scarcely disgrace a Rafaele'. Overall, he judged it as 'a model ... for the house of "a single man in Mayfair"': not just for its decor, but for also for its entertainment facilities. One of the first scenes of the novel, in fact, features a dinner party hosted by Glaucus, in his dining room off the peristyle: a stereotypically Roman banquet, 'figs, fresh herbs strewed with snow, anchovies and eggs', followed by a nice tender, roast kid, swilled down with a good vintage from Chios. The kid had not been his first choice. '"I had hoped," said Glaucus, in a melancholy tone, "to have procured you some oysters from Britain; but the winds that were so cruel to Caesar have forbid us the oysters."'

In creating this image of a sophisticated, nineteenth-century bachelor pad, Bulwer-Lytton fails to point out to his readers that the kitchen of the House of the Tragic Poet was, like that of the majority of houses, even the grandest, in Pompeii, tiny and could hardly have been adequate for the preparation of a lavish banquet. Nor does he mention that the single latrine in the house was located in – or, at best, you might say, 'just off' – the kitchen itself. This was again a typical arrangement, which enabled the latrine to be used for the disposal of kitchen waste, even if it upsets twenty-first-century ideas of hygiene (though perhaps not so shocking to Bulwer-Lytton, as the juxtaposition of lavatory and kitchen was not uncommon in nineteenth-century Britain). He is also silent on the fact that just over the back wall of the garden, which he imagines blooming 'with the rarest flowers placed in vases of white marble, that were supported on pedestals', was a cloth-processing workshop, or fullery. Fulling was a messy business, its main ingredient being human urine; hence the emperor Vespasian's famous tax on urine, which was presumably a levy on the fulling industry. The work was noisy and smelly. In the background to Glaucus' elegant dinner party there must have been a distinctly nasty odour.

The art of reconstruction

Houses built around an atrium, sometimes with the additional peristyle, make up almost half the housing stock surviving in Pompeii – originally (including a rough estimate about what remains unexcavated) perhaps 500 or so properties out of a total of 1200–1300 'habitable units' in the town. They range from small properties with just four rooms opening onto an atrium to such overblown palaces as the House of the Faun, with its two atria and two peristyles. But their various arrangements are similar enough to be taken broadly as a single type. That is to say, for all their differences in size, wealth and detail, there is a certain predictability to their layout. This is much as we find in modern domestic properties: whatever their idiosyncrasies of design, you *expect* to walk from the street into a hallway rather than a bathroom; when a house is on two floors, you expect to find the bedrooms on the upper floor.

Bulwer-Lytton emphasised the familiar modernity of the House of the Tragic

Poet. Underneath the colourful Roman idiosyncrasies of painting, design and diet, he found a society and an architecture which was not so far away from his own, elite nineteenth-century London. Most modern archaeologists would stress exactly the opposite: the huge gap not only between the appearance of the ruined Pompeian houses now and how they would have appeared to a visitor in the first century CE, but also between the ancient idea of a 'house and home' and ours. One of the biggest archaeological projects of recent years at Pompeii has been to try to understand what these houses once looked like and, at a very basic level, what they were *for*. Almost inevitably this work has tended to concentrate on the larger and more affluent properties, where their usually better state of preservation, as well as the greater range of finds and their more complex design, produce both bigger puzzles and better hope of an answer.

Those who walk into one of the grander Pompeian houses today would be forgiven for imagining that the wealthy inhabitants of first-century CE Pompeii espoused an austere modernist aesthetic, uncluttered, even uncomfortably empty. But, as with the streetscape, what we see (or rather don't see) now is misleading. For a start, almost all the furniture that there once was has disappeared, much of it without a trace. A lot of the most valuable material, which might well have included precious furnishings, was removed by the Pompeians themselves, whether by those in flight in the days just before the final disaster or by salvagers and looters afterwards. Besides, unlike at the nearby town of Herculaneum, where the different composition of the volcanic material, and the pattern of its flow, preserved all kinds of charred wooden furniture, only small fragments of carbonised wood have survived at Pompeii. All the same, we can still get some idea of what went where, and what it looked like – beyond the occasional marble table that has remained in place.

This is partly from what has been found at Herculaneum, which can hardly be very different from what was once at Pompeii: ranging from tables to beds (Ill. 33), and in one case a wooden screen, which could be opened or closed, stretching right across the back of the atrium. It is partly from the paintings of furniture in the scenes on Pompeian walls. The chair on which the Greek poet Menander sits in the famous picture which gives its name to the House of the Menander cannot be much different from those once used in the house itself (Ill. 44). But it has also sometimes been possible to reconstruct wooden objects from Pompeii by the familiar technique of moulding the impressions they left in the hardened debris. This is how we know, for example, that five cupboards lined one wall of the colonnade in the House of Julius Polybius, containing all kinds of domestic articles,

33. This child's wooden cradle from nearby Herculaneum gives some idea of the furniture than must once have filled the houses of Pompeii – where the volcanic material destroyed most of the wood, leaving only hinges and fittings to help us to reconstruct the cupboards, chairs, and beds, etc.

from food in jars (one cupboard was effectively a pantry) to the household glass-ware, lamps, a bronze seal, some bronze chains and a tooth.

In other cases we can reconstruct the presence of furniture from yet fainter traces. You can still see, for example, the fixings for shelves on walls – as in one of the rooms off the atrium in the House of the Tragic Poet, which must have been converted into a storeroom after it had been elegantly painted for some grander use. It has also been possible to re-create chests and cupboards from the remaining tell-tale bone hinges and bronze fittings or locks. The truth is that these were often missed or ignored by early excavators; and even when they were collected, the rough-and-ready approach to archaeological record keeping that prevailed until very recently means that it can be hard now to find out exactly where they were found (the same is true for very many 'minor', and not so minor, objects). But we have enough evidence to be able to say that the atrium, grand and lofty as it might appear, also doubled as a major storage area.

In the atrium of the House of Venus in a Bikini, a relatively small house, named after a statuette of Venus found there, thirty-two bone hinges were dis-covered in one corner – all that was left of a large wooden cupboard, fronted with doors. Still surviving were its contents, a range of very ordinary, and mixed, household equipment and other bric-a-brac: bronze jugs and plates, a bronze basin and a cake mould, small glass bottles and jars, a bronze lantern, inkwell and compass, a mirror, a couple of bronze signet rings, some other assorted pieces of jewellery, a coloured marble egg, nine dice and other bits of gaming equipment, some metalwork which has been (rightly or wrongly) identified as leg irons, plus some gold, silver and bronze coins. In another corner, more bone hinges and bronze fittings indicated another cupboard, this time containing a range of rather more prized possessions: the statuette of Venus, a glass swan, a terracotta Cupid, plus some rock-crystal jewellery, a broken horse bit, a couple of strigils (used for 'scraping down' after exercise) and various bits and pieces of bone and bronze, including two lamp-stands. Some of this might be the result of a hasty departure by the house's occupants, and the speedy stashing away of valuables in the hope perhaps of return. But, in general, the impression is of a pair of regular domestic store cupboards, with that mixture familiar from our own cupboards, of household essentials in everyday use, broken bits and pieces which really should have been thrown away, and a couple of valuables put out of harm's way.

We find much the same in the atria of other houses. One had a cupboard loaded with pottery and glassware, including some food in glass jars (to judge from the fishbones). Another had a couple of chests holding some candelabra, as well as more mundane domestic equipment and clothing (or so a buckle would suggest), while a tall upright cupboard had been used to store the best tableware, in bronze, silver and glass as well as pottery. But it was not just a question of storage. In any house not directly connected to the aqueduct supply, the atrium also usually contained the main well; so we could expect to see the buckets and tackle for drawing water. What is more, the loom weights (used in weaving to keep the vertical strands of thread taut) commonly found in atria or in the rooms opening off them make it almost certain that the atrium was a normal place for the household loom, or looms, to be placed. Unsurprisingly perhaps, since cloth production required a considerable amount of space, which in all but the largest houses you would find only in the atrium or peristyle.

Weaving also needed good lighting, which the atrium could also reliably provide. One of the hardest things to recapture is the combination of gaudy brightness and dingy gloom that characterised Pompeian houses of this type. The vast majority were originally painted in vivid colours, which have in many cases now faded to, literally, pale imitations of what they once were: deep reds to washed-out pinks, bright yellows to creamy pastel. And it was not just a matter of coloured walls. Though the original ceilings rarely survive, where they have been reconstructed (by piecing together the fallen plasterwork found on the floor) they also are sometimes ornately decorated and coloured in rich hues. Columns too would have been decorated. They were regularly painted plain red at least part-way up their shaft, but inside one house, just outside the Herculaneum Gate, some of the columns were completely covered in glittering mosaic – a flamboyant gesture even by Pompeian standards, and one which has given the modern name to the property, 'The Villa of the Mosaic Columns'. Like the Pompeian street, many a Pompeian house would have been, in our terms, an assault on the visual senses.

That assault was perhaps mitigated by the general darkness. For while the sunlight would have streamed into the atrium through the open roof, and into the peristyle garden, many other rooms had little or no direct access to light – except what they could borrow from those internal sources. There were, it is true, those vast multi-storey houses on the west of the town that made the most of their sea view with huge picture windows, but mostly – as we saw from the street – external windows were few and small. Within these constraints the Pompeians went to some trouble to bring as much light as they could into dark places. Walking round the ruined houses you can still spot small light wells, or holes in walls above doors, designed to shed light inside a room even when the door was closed.

And there were literally thousands of lamps, in pottery or bronze, plain and ornate, with single or multiple flames, hanging, on tall stands, or simply made to rest on the floor or table. In general they ran on oil; though recent chemical analysis has pointed to an unexpected refinement. Oil mixed with tallow was regularly burned in bronze lamps, pure oil in the unglazed pottery. Is that because, being porous, the pottery would quickly have absorbed an unpleasant smell from the tallow? These objects were household staples, most of the pottery versions being produced by local industry (a small but thriving lamp workshop has been found not far from the Amphitheatre). There are now ranks and ranks of them of all sorts in the museum in Naples, including one in bronze in the shape of a sandalled foot (the flame coming out of the big toe), and at least one more like the African head dropped by that unsuccessful pair of refugees whose escape attempt we tracked in the Introduction. In the House of Julius Polybius alone more than seventy pottery lamps were found, and one bronze example. Even so, it is hard to imagine that the side rooms were ever well lit by modern standards, or that by night the whole house was anything other than blanketed in darkness – brightened only by moon and stars, a couple of braziers (which would give heat too), and the rather feeble twinkling of any number of little lamps.

Adjustments to lighting – and to privacy – could also be made with the various doors, shutters and curtains that were once attached to almost every opening. The open-plan atmosphere of most Pompeian houses today is not entirely misleading. As we shall see, part of their design intentionally emphasised the open vistas through the property. But, at the same time, there is hardly a doorway or other opening in these houses that could not also be shut or curtained off if the inhabitants so wished. It is easy to spot, once you have been alerted, the grooves and holes that held the fittings for doors in the rooms round the atrium and peristyle, or the tell-tale traces of the fixtures for – no doubt brightly coloured

– curtains, which would have added to the gaudy razzmatazz. Where there were no doors as such, or curtains, we might imagine free-standing screens, like the one preserved at Herculaneum. There might even once have been fences, as in the House of the Tragic Poet, between the columns of what is now an open colonnade. Many of the rooms that now look stark and open could have been made private, cosy nooks. Though privacy would have come at a price: darkness.

So far, so good. But the nagging question remains of *what happened where?* in one of these Pompeian houses. We have already glimpsed the atrium with its store cupboards, weavers and slaves drawing the water. But suppose we had walked in through the front door, what would we have found going on in other rooms? Or to put it the other way round, where did the people who lived here eat, cook, sleep, or shit? And who were 'people who lived here' and how many?

Some activities are easily enough located – or striking by their absence. Apart from a few private bath suites in the grandest properties, there were, for example, no designated bathrooms or washrooms in these houses. However often people might have rinsed their hands in a fountain or washed their face (or hair) in a bowl of water, bathing as such was a public activity, which took place in the city baths. Even in houses that were directly connected to the aqueduct supply, very little water overall went to sanitary or domestic use. Most of what came through the pipes was used for fountains and garden features – the triumphs of Roman engineering giving the wealthy a chance to demonstrate their control of the elements rather than encouraging them to take a more robust attitude to hygiene.

By contrast lavatories are a common feature of Pompeian houses and easy to spot. One archaeologist, a dedicated toilet specialist, has recently examined 195 of these, a total which does not include those that have collapsed since excavation or those which are apparently still used by visitors 'caught short'. Almost always only one per house (we must imagine that all kinds of pots, as well as the garden bushes, served the same function), these were commonly found, as in the House of the Tragic Poet, in kitchens. They were partly screened off from the surrounding area, but in this case usually without any sign of a door – an indication, like the multi-seater public latrines found in Pompeii and elsewhere, that Romans did not share our own obsession with total privacy in this sphere of life. The arrangement was simple: a wooden seat over a drain, leading usually to a cesspit. As they remained unconnected to the mains water supply, presumably a bucket or two of water was thrown down the drain every now and then to speed the detritus on its way.

This picture of a rather makeshift (and distinctly smelly) facility is usually completed in the modern imagination with a pot carrying the sponge on a stick with which, we are always told, Romans wiped their bottoms. No doubt sometimes they did. But the evidence for this is flimsier than it is often presented (and does not stretch very far beyond the gruesome anecdote told by the emperor Nero's tutor, the philosopher Seneca, about the German prisoner who killed himself by stuffing the lavatory sponge down his throat rather than face the beasts in the arena). Pompeians may have improvised with any number of materials for this task. One nice suggestion is that in a house converted in the last years of the city into a *garum* depot, the large leaves of an adjacent fig tree might well have served instead of a sponge. New evidence from a large cesspit at nearby Herculaneum suggests that they may also have used strips of cloth.

It is also easy enough to identify kitchens and dining rooms. Or so it is in the richer houses, at least. Medium-sized and poorer houses were much more likely to have a latrine than any area specially designed for cooking, still less for eating. But with food and food preparation we begin to get the clear sense that in these Pompeian houses function did not match up to rooms as precisely as we might imagine.

You can tell a kitchen from its cooking hearth, with occasionally a fixed water basin too, and even more rarely still a connection to the mains water supply. Normally, as in the House of the Tragic Poet, they were rather poky little affairs (Ill. 34). Certainly some cooking took place in them, and perhaps some food preparation as well (especially if we imagine that the adjacent lavatory doubled for waste disposal). But only a few were big enough to accommodate all the preparations necessary for a large dinner. We must also imagine meat roasting on portable braziers in the peristyle, with peeling, gutting and all the rest going on wherever there was space – just as Trimalchio's porter was doubling as a pea-sheller by the front door. As for the washing up, one of the main tasks of the modern kitchen, it is a matter of guesswork how and where the dishes, glasses, knives and spoons (they had no forks, which were a medieval invention) were cleaned and dried in a Pompeian house.

Eating and dining also spread all around the house. It is true that unlike kitchens – which are often so unimpressive that they can be entirely missed by modern visitors – dining rooms can be eye-catching and some of the most exquisitely crafted and decorated rooms in the city. The Latin word for dining room, *triclinium* means literally 'three couches', reflecting the common pattern of formal dinners in the Roman world, which involved the participants reclining, three to a couch on three separate couches. In Pompeii, *triclinia* came in various forms and

34. The hearth of a typically poky kitchen in the House of the Vettii. The pots and pans have been placed there for effect – they were not found in this position.

locations within the house. Some were equipped with movable wooden couches (of which nothing or only faint traces of the fixtures may remain), others were designed with fixed masonry couches. Some were inside, others in garden areas in the semi-open air (so-called 'summer *triclinia*' – on the assumption that they were used for dining on balmy Mediterranean evenings during the summer months).

None was more elegant than the partly open-air installation that looked out onto the garden of the House of the Golden Bracelet (Ill. 35). This had just two fixed couches, faced in white marble, on opposite sides of the room. For where, at the end of the room, a third couch might have been fitted to make the characteristic 'U'-shaped arrangement of the Roman *triclinium*, there was a striking water feature, or *nymphaeum*. This was a flight of twelve steps, set in a niche covered in mosaics made out of glass and sea shell, down which a stream of water, brought from the mains supply, cascaded – or, more realistically perhaps, trickled. From the base of the steps, the water was channelled into a bowl that stood between the couches, and then on into another pool and fountain along the garden edge of the room. This is an arrangement found elsewhere in Pompeii, not to mention other, grander, places in the Roman world, and it must have come close to the Roman idea of 'dining heaven'. For them, it seems, nothing could beat the pleasure of eating against a background of softly splashing water, set off by the twinkling of light catching the mosaic. In the House of the Golden Bracelet, the whole effect might have been enhanced, in the evening darkness, by an array of lamps placed in the line of tiny niches that ran all along the front of the couches (though those would also have provided a convenient place for resting nibbles between mouthfuls).

But not all dining was formal. We have no idea how often dinners would have

35. A *triclinium* to die for. The diners reclined on either side of the water, which flowed down from the niche at the end into the pool between the couches. Imagine the scene in the evening, as the diners could look out from here on to the garden, to the sound of babbling water – and lamps twinkled perhaps in those little holes beneath the couches.

been eaten in this style. Modern scholars often imply that this was a regular Roman fixture: 'the main meal of the Roman day, *cena* or "dinner" was taken in the *triclinium* in the late afternoon ...', as you can find stated in many modern handbooks to the ancient world. In fact, as with so much of what we now read about social life in Rome, this is wild over-generalisation based on a few isolated references in Latin writers, of different periods, stitched together as if it was the norm. The truth is that the majority of the inhabitants of Pompeii only rarely, if ever, dined formally on couches; most houses did not have a *triclinium*. Even for the richest, with not just one but a choice of *triclinia* at home, it still might have been an unusual event. We certainly should not imagine other meals being taken in this way: whatever the Pompeians ate when they got out of bed in the morning, there is no reason at all to suppose that they ate it reclining on a *triclinium*.

Food must have been consumed in all kinds of other locations about the house. In the smaller houses there would hardly have been much choice: you ate where you could. In larger houses slaves perhaps ate what they managed to pick up on the job, or out of sight in the service quarters; the porter presumably quaffed in his cubby-hole. Other people too maybe grabbed what food was to hand, or sat on a bench in the peristyle, or pulled a chair up to a table in the atrium. That is certainly what the pattern of finds suggests. Even bearing in mind all the likely disturbance before and after the eruption, plates, drinking cups and other stand-ard pieces of tableware are found all through Pompeian houses. The impression is one of people eating 'on the wing'.

There is then a piquant contradiction built into these rich Pompeian houses. They blazon a culture of leisured dining, with its own special locations, fixtures and equipment. Yet we also find, side by side, a culture that is much closer to that of the modern barbecue or fast-food. To put it another way, despite some rooms designed with a particular function in mind, there was much less differentiation of space and activity in the Pompeian house than in our own – with our clearly demarcated 'bed-rooms', 'living rooms', 'bathrooms' and so on. As in many domestic arrangements before the modern era, most of the Pompeian house was multi-purpose.

Upstairs, downstairs

This becomes even more clear if we broach two other related questions. Where did people sleep? And what happened upstairs? The upper floors are one of the most intriguing mysteries when we try to figure out what these houses would have originally looked like, and how they would have been used. We know that many properties had an upper floor. Sometimes this was accessed directly from the street, and in all likelihood consisted in a flat for rental. In Roman law owner-ship went with the ground, so any separate living units on the upper floor could not have been 'owner-occupied'. Elsewhere stairs led up directly from inside. That is the case, for example, in the House of the Tragic Poet, though Bulwer-Lytton ducks the issue: his characters don't go upstairs.

What would they have found there? That question is particularly hard to answer because relatively little of the upper structure survives anywhere in the town (where it appears to be intact, it is often in large part modern restoration). Sometimes objects found in the rooms below have been thought to have come from the quarters above, falling through the floor in the destruction. That is almost certainly the case with the famous wax record tablets of the Pompeian banker Lucius Caecilius Jucundus, which suggests that in his house part of the loft was being used as an overspill filing cabinet for out-of-date documents. How usual that arrangement was, we are not sure.

The obvious answer, based on our own experience, that the upper floors were designed for sleeping is probably only partially right. The principal occupants of the house would have slept downstairs. We often find the traces of a fitted bed or couch still visible in those small rooms off the atrium or peristyle and others would have had similar, but movable furniture – though even these were not necessarily 'bedrooms' in our narrow sense of the word, but rooms where the couch could do duty as both sofa and bed, used by day and night. The upper floor was perhaps more likely to be used by the household slaves for sleeping, if they did not just lie down on the floor in the kitchen, at the master's door or at the foot of his bed, or sometimes, of course, *in it*, given the sexual duties that ancient slaves might be expected to perform. Another view would see here more rooms for the ancient equivalent of lodgers, who would have accessed their quarters upstairs from inside the house itself, perhaps not using the grand front door from the main street, but one of the back doors that most houses had. In truth, we are probably dealing with a mixture of all three uses: attic storage, bedrooms, and rooms or apartments to let.

In one relatively small house (the House of the Prince of Naples, named after the local aristocrat who witnessed its excavation in the 1890s), there are no fewer than three staircases leading to rooms on the upper floor. One leads up from the street outside, to – presumably – a separate rented apartment. Another leads up from the atrium to what were at best a few dingy rooms. The most recent archaeologist to study this house thought these were most likely sleeping quarters for a handful of slaves. They could equally well have been attic storerooms. Another stairway went up from the kitchen, to rather brighter accommodation which overlooked the garden. Perhaps this was another rented apartment (but accessed from the kitchen?), or more quarters for domestic slaves, or maybe for the children of the house with their slave carers. This last option would be one solution to another little Pompeian problem: where did the children sleep? Apart from a single wooden cot found at Herculaneum (Ill. 33), we have no evidence at all of any special provision for sleeping infants. They must simply have bedded down with adults, either their parents or much more likely slaves.

The even bigger question that the upper storeys raise is how many people would have lived in one of these houses, and – leaving aside the apartments with their own independent street access – what kind of relationship would they have had to one another. Pompeian houses were not usually occupied by just one married couple, their children and a couple of faithful retainers. Anyone who once studied Latin using the *Cambridge Latin Course* and its (partly) imaginary

Pompeian family should put the idea of Caecilius and Metella, their son Quintus, with slaves Clemens and Grumio, the cook, right out of their minds.

Well-off Romans lived in an extended family. This was not the loose mixture of cohabiting grandparents, aunts, uncles and a variety of cousins which we usually mean by that term (a mixture that is anyway more nostalgic fiction than historical reality). It was rather an extended *household* – or *houseful* as one scholar has more aptly put it – consisting of a more or less 'nuclear family' and a wide array of dependants and hangers-on. These included not just slaves (and there may have been very many of these in the richest households), but ex-slaves too.

In Rome, unlike the Greek world, domestic slaves were often granted their freedom after long years of service: an act of apparent generosity on the part of the master, which sprang from a mixture of humanitarian fellow-feeling and economic self-interest – for it got rid of the expense of feeding and supporting those no longer fit for much work, while also acting as an incentive to the others to remain obedient and hardworking. The fictional Trimalchio was very much an exception among this class. Most ex-slaves remained in various ways attached and obligated to their old master and his family, running their shops and other commercial enterprises, even still living on the premises – perhaps now with their own wives and children. In fact, the Latin word *familia* does not mean 'family' in our sense, but the wider household *including* the slaves and ex-slaves.

So adding together the nuclear family of the house owner, the slaves and ex-slaves, and the lodgers, how many people would have been resident in a house like the House of the Tragic Poet? The truth is we can only guess. One idea has been that the number of beds might help the calculation. But even when we find a clear trace of one, we cannot be certain that it was actually used for sleeping, or, if it was, how many people it would have contained. (Recognisably 'double beds' are not found at Pompeii or Herculaneum, though many do seem large enough to hold more than one occupant, adult or child.) And the number of people we pack in upstairs or imagine sleeping curled up on the floor is quite imponderable. One recent estimate for the House of the Tragic Poet gives a figure around forty. In my view, this is much too large. It involves housing no fewer than twenty-eight sleepers upstairs, and, if multiplied across the whole city, would give an implausible total of 34,000 inhabitants. Nonetheless, even if you halve it, it offers an image of a relatively crowded lifestyle, a very long way from Bulwer-Lytton's idea of the sophisticated bachelor pad – and with considerable pressure on that single lavatory.

But reconstructing the houses of Pompeii demands more than filling in the gaps of what has been lost, satisfying as it is to restock those bare atria with their cupboards, looms, screens and curtains, not to mention the odd sleeping slave. There are also bigger issues of what these Pompeian houses were for. To reflect on these, we must look at how the one surviving Roman discussion of domestic architecture presents the purpose of the house and how that can help us understand what remains at Pompeii.

Show houses

An important guide to the social function of the Roman house is Vitruvius' treatise *On Architecture*, probably written in the reign of the emperor Augustus. Vitruvius is largely concerned with methods of construction, public monuments and city planning, but in his sixth book he discusses the *domus* or 'private house'. It is at once clear that, for him, it was not 'private' in the sense that we usually mean. For us, 'home' is firmly separated from the world of business or politics; it is where you go in order to escape the constraints and obligations of public life. In Vitruvius' discussion, by contrast, the *domus* is treated as part of the public image of its owner, and it provides the backdrop against which he conducts at least some of his public life. Roman history provides telling examples of just that kind of identification between a public figure and his residence: when Cicero is forced into exile, his adversary pointedly demolishes his house (which Cicero rebuilds on his return); shortly before the assassination of Julius Caesar, his wife had a dream in which the gable of their house collapses.

Vitruvius recognises that different areas of the house have different functions. But the distinctions he suggests are unexpected. He does not, for example, suggest that the house be divided into men's and women's areas (as it regularly was in classical Athens). Nor does he suggest a division by age: there are no 'nursery wings' in Vitruvius' ideal house plan. Instead he draws a distinction between those 'common' parts of the house which visitors may enter uninvited, and the 'exclusive' parts into which guests would only venture if they were invited. The 'common' parts include atria, vestibules and peristyles; the 'exclusive' parts include *cubicula* ('chambers', despite its old-fashioned ring, is a better translation than the more usual 'bedrooms'), *triclinia* ('dining rooms') and bath suites. This is almost, but not quite, a distinction between public and private areas. Not quite, because – as other Roman writers make clear – all kinds of public business might be conducted *intra cubiculum*, from recitations and dining to (in the case of emperors) judicial trials. It was not, like a modern bedroom, a room from which visitors are almost completely excluded, still less was it used principally for sleeping. It was one to which access was restricted *by invitation*.

He also emphasises a social hierarchy in the design of a house. The Roman elite, those holding public and political office, needed the grand 'common' areas of a house. Those lower down the social spectrum could do without a grand vestibule, atrium or *tablinum* (the name given to the relatively large room often found, as in the House of the Tragic Poet, between atrium and peristyle – and used, we guess, by the master of the house). Of course they could do without them. For they did not have a public civic role, with subordinates, dependants and clients to entertain. Quite the reverse: it was they who frequented the vestibules, atria and *tablina* of others.

This theorizing of Vitruvius does not exactly match the evidence from Pompeii. For example, atria are not restricted, as he seems to imply, to the grand display houses, but are found in many very small establishments too. And it can often prove hard to pin the names that Vitruvius uses for individual rooms to the remains we find on the ground (although modern plans tend to be littered with his Latin terminology). Vitruvius was offering an ideal of Roman architecture at its highest and most abstract level, and certainly did not have the houses of a small southern Italian town in mind. Nonetheless, his overall view of the public purpose of the *domus* can help us get a better understanding of at least the more showy houses at Pompeii.

Whether or not the porter actually allowed you access (walking in completely 'uninvited' is, I am sure, a more theoretical than real proposition), the interiors of houses were made *to be seen*. Of course, they were closed up and forbidding by night, and even by day the view towards the heart of the house might sometimes have been blocked by screens, internal doors and curtains. But this does not detract from the underlying logic of their plan: that the open front door should offer a carefully designed vista into the interior space. Peering into the House of the Tragic Poet, for example, your eye was drawn first to the large show room between the atrium and the peristyle (Vitruvius' *tablinum*), then through the peristyle directly on to the shrine on the back wall of the garden. Out of vision were the more 'exclusive' areas, such as the large room that was probably a dining room off the peristyle, as well as the service areas and kitchen.

In the House of the Vettii, more imaginative effects were contrived, on a 'priapic' theme which has often captured the interest of modern visitors. In the vestibule of this house is one of the most photographed and reproduced images to have been found at Pompeii: a painting of the god Priapus, divine protector of

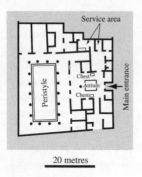

Figure 7. The House of the Vettii. A large peristyle garden dominates the House of the Vettii, and the most lavishly decorated rooms open onto it. Visitors entering the house looked through to this, past the chests that symbolised (and, no doubt, literally contained) the owners' wealth.

the household, weighing his huge phallus against a bag of money (Ill. 36). There was a more learned point here than might first meet the eye, for as well as showing off a boastful erection, the image also cleverly visualises a pun on the words *penis* and *pendere*, 'to weigh'. But he was not the only such figure in the house. In the ancient visitor's line of vision this Priapus was most likely linked to another priapic image. Looking ahead from the front door, through the atrium, to the peristyle and garden (there was no *tablinum* in the House of the Vettii) the eye was drawn to a large marble fountain statue of Priapus, rhyming with the figure in the entranceway – though in this case the joke was that a stream of water spurted out of his erect penis. The implied message of power and prosperity was reinforced by the layout of the atrium itself. On either side large bronze chests – to hold the kind of riches that the Priapus at the doorway is weighing out – were on prominent display. Out of direct vision, were the more 'exclusive' zones and the service quarters.

Again taking their cue from Vitruvius, who related the design of the house to the hierarchies of Roman society (and especially to the relations between men of the elite and their various dependants), archaeologists have re-imagined how one characteristic Roman social ritual might have taken place in this Pompeian setting. That ritual is the early morning *salutatio*, at which 'clients' of all sorts would call on their rich patrons, to receive favours or cash in return for their votes, or for providing more symbolic services (escort duty, or simply applause) to enhance the patron's prestige. From Rome itself, we have plenty of complaints about this from the client's point of view in the poetry of Juvenal and Martial, who – as relatively well-heeled dependants – predictably enough made the most noise about the indignities they had to suffer in return for a modest handout. 'You promise me three *denarii*,' moans Martial at one point, 'and tell me to be on duty in your atria, dressed up in my toga. Then I'm supposed to stick by your side, walk in front of your chair, while you go visiting ten widows, plus or minus ...' In Pompeii, it is easy to imagine how such a social ritual might have taken place within the *domus*: the clients lined up outside on those stone benches, then – when the house doors were opened first thing in the morning – they made their way through the narrow entrance passage, into the atrium, to wait their turn to speak to their patron proudly sitting in his *tablinum*, dispensing favours, or not, as the mood took him.

In all likelihood, that image is rather too grand and formal for what would actually have happened in Pompeii. Even if in Rome itself the ritual of morning *salutatio* was as regular and structured as the poets imply (and I have my doubts about that), it could not possibly have been so in a small town. Besides, we have to remember that in Pompeii the ritual would have taken place in a space which was also the house's main storage area and may well have included a loom or two as well. Rather than imagining the *salutatio* interrupted by the clattering of the women weaving and the slaves rushing to and from the cupboards, some archaeologists have suggested a kind of temporal zoning. On this model, the atrium was the master's territory early in the morning, to be taken over by family and slaves only once he had left home for the Forum and other public business. But here again I have my doubts that it all really was so neatly arranged.

We are also in danger of over-simplifying the social dynamics of the relationships involved, whether in Rome or Pompeii. The anxieties and humiliations of those waiting to be admitted to the presence of their patron are one thing. We can all imagine what it must have been like waiting to put one's case to some bigwig who could choose whether to help you or not (with a job for your son, a loan, or a blind eye to the unpaid rent). There must have been anxieties on the other side too. For, in this world of status and show, patrons needed clients almost as much as clients needed patrons. Imagine the anxiety and humiliation on the other side, for a patron installed in his *tablinum* waiting for clients – and not a single one shows up.

Nonetheless, these rituals of power, dependence and patronage do help to reveal the logic of the Roman house and its arrangements. These were houses meant for show – and that idea trickled down, albeit in diluted form, even to those properties which consisted of just a few rooms around an atrium.

36. An image of plenty. Just past the front door of the House of the Vettii, the god Priapus greets the visitor – weighing his large phallus against a money bag.

Plate 1. Mosaic of musicians, probably intended to depict a scene from a comedy by the fourth-century Greek dramatist, Menander (pp. 253–4). It comes from the so called Villa of Cicero, just outside the Herculaneum Gate.

Plate 2. The whole of the garden wall of one house carried this striking scene of Orpheus charming the animals with his music (p. 128).

Plate 3. Is this the emperor Nero? This painting from a luxurious dining room in a building just outside Pompeii has been identified as Nero in the guise of the god Apollo. So, it has been suggested, this may have been where he stayed on his visit to Pompeii – if he really did visit Pompeii, that is (p. 50).

Plate 4. Reconstruction of a typically colourful façade on the Via dell'Abbondanza. On the far right a crossroads shrine, then an open bar or shop counter. Election notices are painted on the next door house. Above, wooden overhangs shade the street and entrance ways.

Plate 5. The carpenters display their craft in a procession. At the far left was a statue of their patron deity Minerva, though little more than her distinctive shield survives. In the middle is a model of their carpentry work (pp. 294–5).

Plate 6. The gaming table, from a painting in the Bar on the Via di Mercurio (p. 230–31). The brightly coloured, casual clothing contrasts with our image of white toga-clad Romans.

Plate 7. One of the best preserved of the scenes of Forum life from the Estate of Julia Felix. A group of men consult a written notice that has been displayed across the bases of the statues in front of the colonnade (p. 76).

Plate 8. This model of the House of the Tragic Poet shows a cross section of the house from the front door to the rear peristyle (see Fig. 6). In the central atrium, the well sinks down below the floor. The front part of the house has substantial rooms on the upper floor.

Plate 9. Model of the peristyle garden of the House of the Tragic Poet. The back wall is painted with a garden scene. Under the colonnade is the famous painting of the sacrifice of Iphigeneia (Ill. 55).

Plate 10. Painting from the wall of the large dining room in the Chaste Lovers bakery (p. 218). At first sight an elegant scene, with comfortable cushions and drapes, and glass vessels set out neatly on the table. But the woman behind is already so drunk she can hardly stand up and just visible between the two reclining couples a man has passed out.

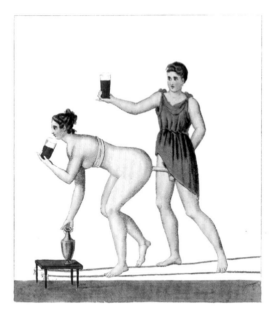

Plate 11. Balancing act. A nineteenth-century copy of a lost painting from the Bar on the Via di Mercurio. The tightropes are probably a figment of the modern artist's imagination (pp. 231–2).

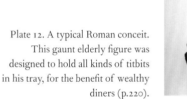

Plate 12. A typical Roman conceit. This gaunt elderly figure was designed to hold all kinds of titbits in his tray, for the benefit of wealthy diners (p.220).

For richer for poorer: not 'the Pompeian house'

These houses built around an atrium and, often, a peristyle garden have come to stand for the domestic world of Pompeii. They have long caught the popular imagination, partly because of books such as the *Last Days of Pompeii*, and they are now commonly known in shorthand simply as '*the* Pompeian house', as if they were the only form of domestic architecture in the city. In fact they are just one amongst many. That itself is significant. The very variety of housing at Pompeii, in size, type and grandeur, points to huge disparities in wealth in the town. This is in marked contrast to the relatively homogeneous housing stock in some ancient Greek cities that have been excavated, where the differences between rich and poor were at least masked by houses that were all more or less of the same size and type. In Pompeii there was a very big gap between the smallest and largest atrium house, but even the smallest would have been beyond the means of many hundreds of the free inhabitants of the city. Ironically a good many slaves, even if consigned to dingy attics, lived in conditions and surroundings that would have been the envy of some of the free poor.

So where did the poor live? That depends a bit on what we mean by 'poor' – and *how* poor. One particularly bleak view is that, if by 'poverty' we mean 'destitution', then there were very few poor in the ancient world: for the simple reason that destitution was the first step on a fast track to death. The 'poor' had to have a reasonably secure means of support simply to survive, whether a trade or craft, or connections with the extended households of the rich. Those with no means did not survive; end of story.

We have already noted the cramped living and sleeping quarters attached to shops and workshops. These probably accounted for as many living units in Pompeii as the atrium house, though they obviously housed far fewer people in total. Below that, the beggar pictured in the scenes of the Forum gives a hint of life on the very margins of destitution. We can only guess where he might have laid his head at night. But given the anxiety of the Roman law codes about those who desecrate large tombs by squatting in them ('Anyone who so wishes may prosecute a person who lives or makes his dwelling in a tomb', as later Roman legal opinion had it), the impressive family mausolea along the roads leading out of the town seem very likely candidates. But there were plenty of other options, from the arches of the Amphitheatre to colonnades of temples.

Almost as close to the edge were those who occupied the single rooms squeezed in among the houses and shops, opening onto the street but with no fittings other than a masonry bed (Ill. 37). These are usually identified as prostitutes' booths, and

37. An overgrown single room dwelling, fitted out with just a masonry bed. A prostitute's booth? Or the cheapest form of Pompeian bedsit?

indeed several of them do have a prominent phallus above the entrance. But they could equally well be the tiny, austere quarters of the poor – the phallus an optimistic symbol of good luck, rather than an advertisement for sexual services. Or, of course, they might be both. For prostitution was in the Roman world, as so often, the last resort of the disadvantaged. It could be the last hope of survival for those without the usual support networks: from the runaway slave to orphan or widow.

Higher up the spectrum of wealth there are other varieties of housing. In the south-east corner of the city there is a distinctive group of what we would call small *terraced* houses. Narrow single-storey dwellings, with an open central court, but no atrium, these were all built in a row, to the same design, on the same scale (roughly the size of a small atrium house), at the same time towards the end of the third century BCE. Presumably part of a planned development to receive an influx of new people (perhaps those displaced in the war against Hannibal), they were still in use at the time of the eruption, although by that time many had had an atrium and upper floor added.

Different again is the range of rented apartments or flats. We have already seen

38. A bath block with a river view: the Sarno Baths. The bathing establishment was on the lower floors. Residential apartments occupied the upper levels.

the clear signs of rented accommodation on the upper floors of atrium houses. There is also vivid evidence for a rather more systematic, large-scale and purpose-built rental market. So, for example, a mixture of substantial flats and atrium apartments occupy the three upper floors of a rather flashy multi-storey building which clings to the slope on the south side of the city, overlooking the river valley. The lower levels of the block were used by one of the privately run commercial bathhouses in the city, now called, after its river view, the Sarno Baths (it is here that the graffiti of the waiting children were discovered; see pp. 15–16). The only such building in the town, its overall style is reminiscent of some of the more expensive blocks of apartments found at Ostia. Many of the rooms are light and airy, with large windows and terraces offering great vistas – quite unlike the inward-looking atrium house. They can hardly have been the accommodation of the really poor. Were these more like Bulwer-Lytton's bachelor pads?

There were downsides here, however. Although a good number of upper floor apartments in other houses did have lavatories (a wooden seat over a chute in the wall), these – so far as we can tell – did not. And the proximity of the baths could have been an irritant to those who valued peace and quiet. At least, that is the

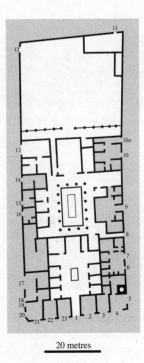

Figure 8. *Insula* Arriana Polliana. This whole property was divided between an elite residence (unshaded), with atrium and peristyle, accessed by entrance 1, and various smaller units around the edge of the property – shops and apartments – that were available for rent. Stairways gave access to apartments on the upper floor.

20 metres

implication of the complaints of the philosopher Seneca who once lived in a similar situation in Rome.

> I live over some baths. Imagine the assortment of sounds, which make me hate the very power of hearing. When the muscle boys are exercising and pumping the lead weights, when they are working out, or pretending to, I hear their grunt … Finally imagine the hair-plucker with his strident, shrill voice, never holding it in, except when he's plucking someone's armpit and making his client yelp instead.

Seneca could be a bit of a killjoy, but in this case we can sympathise.

In another large property, five minutes' walk north of the Forum, a lucky find gives us a glimpse of the organisation of the rental market, and the various kinds of properties that were available. Just near a street corner, a notice was once visible (though it has now vanished):

To let from 1 July. In the *insula* Arriana Polliana, property of Cnaius Alleius Nigidius Maius, commerical/residential units with mezzanines [*tabernae cum pergulis suis*], quality upper floor apartments [*cenacula equestria*] and houses [*domus*]. Agent: Primus, slave of Cnaius Alleius Nigidius Maius.

Three kinds of accommodation were on offer via the owner's slave agent, each of which we can match up to different parts of the large property on which the notice was painted (Fig. 8).

In the centre of the whole block – the *insula* Arriana Polliana – is a substantial atrium house, with a peristyle and (at least in its final form) a further garden beyond. This house used to be called, by a misidentification, the House of Pansa, but it must actually have belonged to Cnaius Alleius Nigidius Maius, a member of one of the region's old families and active in the local government of the town in the 50s and 60s CE, who was looking for tenants for his *tabernae*, *cenacula* and *domus*. *Tabernae* are usually translated 'shops' or 'workshops', and that is what we find along the main road, in the units with their characteristic wide-open fronts (numbers 21–3, 2–4); the mezzanine floors, where the shopkeeper and his family would have had their living quarters, have disappeared, but in places the holes for the cross-beams are still visible. Down the side street, numbers 14–16, without the distinctive shop front, may have been purely residential: hence my translation 'commercial/residential units'.

The upper-floor apartments, *cenacula*, were accessed through stairways from the street at numbers 18, 19, 6, 8 and 10a. The description *equestria* refers literally to the Roman elite class of 'knights' (or 'equestrians'), a wealthy group who would expect to live in rather grander circumstances than this. Here the adjective is probably used as a promise (or an expectation) of some social respectability, as in the old phrase '*gentleman's* outfitter'. The houses (*domus*) were most likely the ground floor apartments, numbers 7, 9 and 10, unless the atrium house in the centre was also up to rent, Nigidius Maius himself having moved elsewhere.

It is hard to know exactly where on the social spectrum of the town's popula-tion to place the occupants of these various units, though various remarks in Petronius' *Satyrica* confirm the relative ranking of prestige implied by the mate-rial remains. At one point, in the middle of a marital row, Trimalchio takes a barbed potshot at his wife's lowly origins: 'if you're borne on a mezzanine, you don't sleep in a house.' Elsewhere, the social rise of one of Trimalchio's guests is marked by the fact that he is subletting his *cenaculum* ('from the 1 July', interest-ingly the same date as Nigidius Maius' contracts began) because he has bought a *domus.* Nor can we be certain about the length of these leases, and so about the security of tenure enjoyed by the tenants. But another rental notice in the town, referring to accommodation in the Estate of Julia Felix, advertises 'an elegant bath suite for prestige clients, *tabernae*, mezzanine lodgings [*pergulae*] and upper-floor apartments [*cenacula*] on a five year contract'.

What is clear, however, is that the *insula* Arriana Polliana nicely captures in a single block the varieties of housing available in the city. We can only now pity the poor *pergula* dwellers, constantly faced with the comparatively palatial expanses of the atrium house next door.

But it was not only the poorer Pompeians who lived in different kinds of accommodation. Not all the wealthier inhabitants of the town lived in the 'stand-ard' Pompeian atrium house. There are some houses, for example, which in the last phases of the city's history – while retaining some of the basic elements that we have already seen – have garden areas so developed and expanded that the whole focus and the character of the property seems completely altered.

A classic case of this is the House of Octavius Quartio (so called after the name on a signet ring found in one of the shops there), which was being reno-vated at the time of the eruption. As the plan shows (Fig. 9), the house buildings themselves were not particularly spacious, but the focus of attention was on the large garden, and its elaborate decorations and water features (exploiting the mains water supply). Along the garden front of the house stretched a long pergola, covering a narrow course of water, crossed by a bridge and originally lined with statues. At one end was an outdoor dining room, at the other an orna-mental 'shrine', which once held an image of the goddess Diana or Isis (the sur-viving paintings here include Diana bathing and a priest of Isis). At a lower level, another narrow waterway stretched some 50 metres down the length of the garden, spanned by bridges and arches, with elaborate fountains at one end and in the middle, and paintings decorating almost all possible surfaces. The garden on either side was planted with walkways of shrubs and trees, as well as more pergolas. The water itself doubled as ornamental pool and fish farm (Ill. 39).

The influence behind many of these features is the architecture of the out-of-town Roman house, or 'villa'. Characteristic elements of the villa garden were ornamental watercourses, shrines and walkways between flowers and trees. Cicero on one occasion mocked the shamelessly aggrandising titles given to their garden canals by the Roman elite: 'Nile' or 'Euripus' (after the stretch of water between the island of Euboea and the Greek mainland). But he was, nonetheless, very keen on a Euripus in one of his brother Quintus' country properties, and at

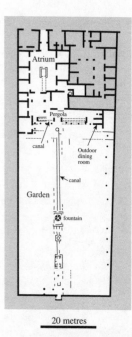

Figure 9. House of Octavius Quartio. A relatively small site, and even so the ornamental garden in this house vastly outstrips the small area of the building itself. The shaded portions are parts of different properties.

one stage he had it in mind to build himself a shrine to the obscure goddess Amalthea, in imitation of an elegant feature in his friend Atticus' villa garden. Later the emperor Hadrian was to install a very flashy 'Canopus' (another Egyptian waterway), which still survives, in his rural palace at Tivoli. Also the mark of a villa garden was the combination of productivity and ornament that we find in this particular pool/fishpond. For the Roman proprietor, part of the pleasure of his country estate was the way productive farming might be integrated into its decorative scheme: a meeting of agriculture and elegance.

This design, then, brings the style of the out-of-town property into the city itself. It is very successful with modern visitors to the site, who love wandering along the waterways and under the pergolas, just as the ancient residents must have done. Some archaeologists, however, have been rather sniffy about it. There is too much, they argue, crammed into too small a space ('two people cannot walk next to each other under the pergola without running up against a fountain, little bridge, pillar, or post at every turn, or tripping over the statuettes in the grass'). This is a 'Walt Disney world', in which an owner with little taste has tried to imitate the

39. The view down the long garden of the House of Octavius Quartio. An elegant series of pools and pergolas – in a jewel-like miniature design? Or is this a scheme completely out of scale to the site, a classic case of *nouveau riche* pretensions going wrong? Archaeologists are divided on the question.

leisured country world of his betters, consistently choosing quantity over quality.

It is right to face the fact that ancient art and design can be decidedly second-rate. And some of the paintings in this house are 'of modest quality', to put it politely. Yet it is hard not to suspect that in finding the house 'tasteless', we are – albeit unconsciously – sharing the prejudices of many elite Romans, who were ready to scoff at palatial schemes brought down to an ordinary domestic scale. After all, Trimalchio, the ex-slave may have been horribly vulgar. But part of the joke of Petronius' novel is that he is aping the culture of the aristocratic elite all too well. In laughing at him, we find we are laughing at them (or at ourselves) too.

No one has ever been sniffy in that way about the group of houses on the western edge of the city, built directly over the old city wall in the early years of the Roman colony (after 80 BCE, perhaps by some of the original colonists) – and in their final form dramatically dropping down the slope towards the sea, in up to four or five storeys (Ill. 15). These are now, in many ways, the most impressive properties in all of Pompeii, partly because to walk around them on their different levels, up and down their surviving staircases, gives a feeling of being *right inside* an ancient house that you rarely get elsewhere.

They are also one of the saddest stories of the modern excavations. Bombed in 1943, they were excavated in the 1960s but have never been properly published and even the unpublished records and notebooks are often skeletal. This means that we have little idea of the history of their development or of some of the details of their internal layout. It is hard in places to work out where the divisions between the houses fall, or how many living units there were in all. They are also not open to the public (although you can get a good view of them from the main entrance to the site at the Marine Gate). The result of all this is that, although they are a fondly remembered highlight of the site for those who have been lucky enough to get permission to visit them, they have not often made much of an impact in guidebooks, general histories of the town or even student courses. They have not affected our view of Pompeian houses as much as they should have done.

The best way of understanding these large, multi-layered properties is to think of them as atrium houses organised along Vitruvius' principles, but vertically rather than horizontally, and facing the view over the sea rather than turned in on themselves. In the very grandest of these, the House of Fabius Rufus (named after a man whose name appears in several graffiti in the house), you enter from the ground level on the city side, into a relatively modest atrium for an establishment of this size. But instead of moving on through the house to the 'exclusive' areas, you move downstairs to two further levels where on the sea side there is a series of lavish entertainment suites with large windows and in places

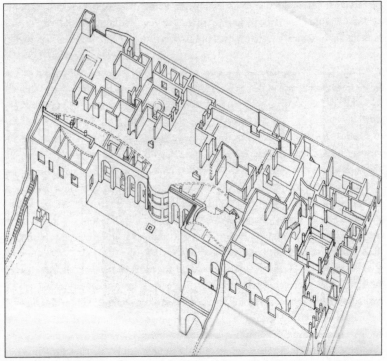

40. The House of Fabius Rufus. This axionometric reconstruction gives an idea of the complexity of this multi-level design. The show rooms look over the sea. The service quarters are tucked behind in the hillside, dark and gloomy as usual.

terraces outside. The service areas seem to be in dark quarters, set back into the hillside, with no view and precious little natural light (Ill. 40).

For the owners and the favoured invited guests, this was a place to enjoy the light, the air and the vista. A graffiti artist, at work on a stairway within the house, got the point. Amidst the scrawlings of one Epaphroditus, who has scratched his name several times, plus his girlfriend ('Epaphroditus and Thalia'), and just under a lover's rhyme that was enough of a cliché to be found written up several times across the town ('I wish I could be a ring on your finger for an hour, no more ...'), someone has inscribed the first three words of the second book of Lucretius' philosophical poem *On the Nature of Things*: '*Suave mari magno*' – 'Pleasant it is, when on the wide sea ...' This continues, as our scribbler presumably knew, '… the winds stir up the waters, to gaze from dry land at the great troubles of another.'

Pleasant indeed it must have been to gaze out to sea from the House of Fabius Rufus.

Names and addresses

At the doorway of a small house in the south of the city, most of which behind the entrance still remains unexcavated, a small bronze plaque was found. It reads: 'Lucius Satrius Rufus, imperial secretary (retired)'. If it is, as seems plausible, the name plaque from the door, then it is the only such marker so far known in the city. Here lived a man who was a member of, or at least connected to, one of the oldest families in Pompeii. His exact geneaology is uncertain because ex-slaves and their descendants took the family name of their masters, so a Satrius might be one of this local line of notables, or might trace his ancestry back to one of their slaves. In this case, given the apparent size of the house and the nature of his job, we might suspect the latter. But whichever is the case, it looks as if we are dealing with a local man, who worked in the administration of the imperial palace in Rome, retired to his home city. There he proudly boasted on his doorplate of his employment in the emperor's service.

We know the names of thousands of people of Pompeii, from the grand families of the Satrii or the Holconii Rufi to the single names or nicknames of those who scrawled, or were scrawled about, on the walls (who were not necessarily, of course, any less grand – graffiti writing not being a habit restricted to the underclass): 'Hello my Prima wherever you are. From Secundus. Please love me darling', 'Ladicula's a thief', 'Atimetus got me pregnant'. We can even occasionally put faces to names, even if some of the formal statues of local notables that still survive do tend to flatter their subjects beyond credibility. Standing on his plinth in the plaza outside the Stabian Baths on the Via dell'Abbondanza, Marcus Holconius Rufus, city bigwig of the Augustan period, was dressed up to look more like a conquering Roman emperor than a small-town official (Ill. 71). More realistic perhaps – or at least funnier – is the caricature of one 'Rufus', complete with his Roman nose (Ill. 41).

What has proved particularly tricky is matching houses to names or families, and this becomes an even trickier process if we try to think in terms of the 'housefuls' of people and dependants that might have lived together in a single establishment. As we saw earlier, very many of the identifications are not much more

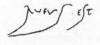

41. 'This is Rufus' – '*Rufus est*' as the original Latin reads. The subject (or victim) of this caricature is shown with a laurel wreath, pointy chin and magnificent 'Roman' nose.

than guesswork, based on groupings of election posters which are taken to indicate either that the candidate concerned, or the canvasser, lived close by – or on signet rings and seal stones. It is not too much of an exaggeration to say that wherever the poor refugees from the city had the misfortune to drop their signet rings on their dash out of town, that is the place where they have been deemed by archaeologists to have lived.

Occasionally the guesses prove right, or at least half right. It was suggested decades ago that the proprietor of a small bar, standing one block south of the Via dell'Abbondanza, was a man called Amarantus – on the basis of an election notice outside in which one 'Amarantus Pompeianus' (that is 'Amarantus the Pompeian') urges his fellow townspeople to elect his own particular candidate. At the same time, on the basis of a signet ring, it was decided that the small house next door was owned by Quintus Mestrius Maximus.

These properties have recently been re-excavated. This new work has shown that in the last years of the city the two houses were joined and that they were in a very run-down state. The bar counter was ruined, the garden overgrown (pollen analysis produced some tell-tale bracken spores), and the combined property was being used as a warehouse for wine jars (*amphorae*). The skeleton of the mule which had been used to transport these was found there, along with a (guard) dog by its feet. On two of the wine jars was the name 'Sextus Pompeius Amarantus', or just 'Sextus Pompeius'. The business, such as it was, must indeed have been in the hands of this Amarantus, whose name also crops up in a couple of graffiti found elsewhere in the neighbourhood. Indeed, it may not be too

42. 'Hello Amarantus hello' (or, in the hard to decipher Latin, *'Amarantho sal(utem) sal(utem)'*). Presumably one of these men is meant to be the Amarantus who owned the bar where the graffito was found.

fanciful to imagine that the big-nosed chap (or alternatively the man with the beard) pictured next to a scrawled 'Hello Amarantus, hello' is a picture of the man himself (Ill. 42). And Quintus Mestrius Maximus? He might have been his partner, or simply the owner of a lost ring.

The truth is that we can very occasionally be certain about the identity of the occupants of a house. One example would be the house of Lucius Caecilius Jucundus, whose banking records were found fallen from the attic. A little more often we can be reasonably confident about who they were. Despite the odd nagging doubt, the balance of probability must be that the House of the Vettii was the property of one, or both, of the brothers Aulus Vettius Conviva and Aulus Vettius Restitutus (though one sceptical archaeologist has recently come up with the idea that they were a couple of dependants, charged with stamping goods in and out of the house). The House of Julius Polybius takes its modern name from a man who appears as both candidate and canvasser on election notices on its façade and inside the house itself. But it is also strongly connected with a Caius Julius Philippus, probably a relation, whose signet ring was found inside one of the house's cupboards – and not therefore casually dropped – and who is also mentioned in writing inside the house.

But when we know the identity of the occupants, what extra does that tell us? With Amarantus, it gives us nothing more than the satisfaction of being able to put a name to a house. But in other cases, further information we have about the people concerned, or even just the name itself, can point in interesting directions. The fact that one of the Vettii brothers was a member of the local *Augustales* (part social club, part priesthood, part political office, see pp. 212–13) is a powerful hint that they were themselves ex-slaves, since the *Augustales* were almost entirely made up of that rank of Roman society. In the case of Julius Philippus and Julius Polybius, whatever the precise relationship between them, their name alone suggests that – however lofty their status in the political elite of Pompeii by the middle of the first century CE – they too may trace their descent to freed slaves; for the name Julius often indicates a slave freed by one of the early emperors whose family name was Julius. These are all nice indications of the permeable boundary between slave and free in Roman society.

79 CE: all change

It is almost inevitable that we know most about the houses in Pompeii and about their occupants as they were in the last years before the eruption. But we can still see something of the redesigns, extensions and change of function that marked their history. Like any town, Pompeii was always on the move. House owners grabbed more space by buying parts of the neighbouring property and knocking a door through. The boundaries of the House of the Menander expanded and contracted, as its owners either bought up or sold off again parts of the next-door houses. The House of the Vettii was formed by joining together, and adapting, two smaller properties. Shops opened up and closed down. What had been residential units were converted to all kinds of other uses: bars, fulleries and workshops. Or vice versa.

There is an obvious temptation to blame any apparent shift downmarket on the effects of the earthquake of 62 CE. In fact, where there is no other evidence, it has always been convenient to date industrial conversions to 'post-62'. But beware. It is clear that these kinds of change had a much longer history in the town than that. One careful study of three fulleries which are usually assumed to have 'taken over' private houses after the earthquake has shown that all three of them co-existed with the residential function of the houses (despite the dreadful smell). At least one of the conversions was definitely to be dated before 62.

Yet, there *was* an enormous amount of construction work and decorating going on at the time the eruption came, more than seems easily compatible with the usual processes of change and renovation. And there is some evidence, beyond that, for decommissioning and downgrading. To take examples only from houses we have met so far: in the House of the Prince of Naples, what had been a grand entertainment room appears to have been in use for storage; so too in the House of Julius Polybius (where some of the rooms were also empty, and jars of lime were found, suggesting ongoing restoration); in the House of Venus in a Bikini, redecoration had been started and shelved; it was still going on, it seems in the House of Fabius Rufus and the House of the Vestals; in the House of the Menander, the private bath suite was largely out of commission, having collapsed or been dismantled; in the little House of Amarantus building materials were also found, but there was no sign of active work (plans may have been abandoned).

It seems implausible that all this activity had been caused either by the general need for running repairs, or by the earthquake as long ago as 62 (in fact some of the work was clearly repatching the repairs already carried out 'post-62'). Almost certainly, much of what we see is the response to the damage caused by pre-eruption tremors, over the weeks or months before the final eruption itself. It was not business as usual for householders in Pompeii in the summer of 79 CE. For the optimists among them, it must have been a series of annoying cracks in the paintwork which needed fixing. For the pessimists (and those with the leisure to worry about their future), it must have been a time to reflect on quite what was going to happen next.

It is to the reaction of one family of optimists, living in the House of the Painters at Work, that we turn next.

CHAPTER FOUR

PAINTING AND DECORATING

Beware: painters at work

On the morning of 24 August 79 CE a team of painters, perhaps three or four altogether, had turned up at a large house almost next door to the House of Julius Polybius to continue a job they had started a couple of weeks earlier. Exactly how large, or grand, this house was we do not yet know, for it has not been completely uncovered. What we have so far is only the rear portion of the property: a peristyle garden (described on p. 87), the rooms around it, and a small entrance onto a side alley (Fig. 10). Between the back wall of the garden and the Via dell'Abbondanza there stood – in one of those characteristic Pompeian juxtapositions between upmarket residence and the economic infrastructure – a shop and a commercial bakery (which we shall visit in the next chapter). The main front door of this house, now known for obvious reasons as the House of the Painters at Work, must have opened onto a street to the north.

Major redecoration works were obviously going on. Piles of lime were found in the colonnades of the peristyle, as well as sand and mosaic *tesserae* and other flooring material in a dump near the kitchen. The painters were in the middle of their work in the most impressive room of this part of the house, some 50 square metres, opening onto the garden. They must have taken to their heels sometime around midday, leaving their equipment and paints behind almost in mid-brush-stroke. Compasses, traces of scaffolding, jars of plaster, mixing bowls have all been found there, as well as more than fifty little pots of paint (including some – mostly empty ones – stacked in a wicker basket in one of the rooms to the north

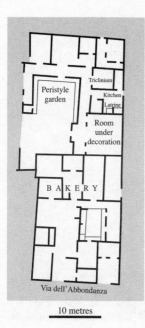

Figure 10. The House of the Painters at Work. This house has still not been fully excavated. Its rear portions abut onto the Bakery of the Chaste Lovers. The front entrance must be somewhere to the north (above).

of the peristyle, which was obviously being used as a store during the building works).

Thanks to the sudden interruption we get a rare glimpse of their handiwork before it was quite complete, and from that we can begin to reconstruct how they worked, in what order, how quickly and how many of them there were. One basic principle is – and it is not much more than common sense – that they started at the top and worked down. Although the uppermost levels of the room are now almost completely destroyed, it is clear that the very top sections of the wall had been finished and painted. So too, to judge from fragments found fallen to the floor, had the coffered ceiling. The very bottom level of the wall, below the 'dado', had not been given its final coat of plaster.

The painters were working, as the eruption began, on the large middle zone of decoration. They were using true fresco technique. That is to say, the paint was being applied to the plaster while it was still wet, which – as the paint bonds with the plaster – produces a much more stable colour, which does not flake off at a single knock. But it also means that they had to work very quickly, to be certain that the paint was on before the plaster had dried. Painters in the

43. A half-finished wall, abandoned by the painters when the eruption came. At first sight this is not much to look at, but it is possible to reconstruct some of the painters' methods. The central and right-hand panel had already been given their wash of colour – except for the central figured scene for which the design had been merely sketched out. The left hand section (just visible) was still covered in bare plaster. At the bottom of the central panel painted cupids are enjoying a perilous chariot race.

Renaissance had the exactly same problem and sometimes hung damp cloths over the plaster to keep it moist. Keen eyes have occasionally spotted what might be such cloth marks in other houses in Pompeii, but not here. So too, on other paintings, it is possible to detect the pressure marks, where the painter has pressed down on the plaster to try to bring the remaining moisture to the surface.

A closer look at the north wall gives a good idea of exactly the stage they had reached (Ill. 43). Two of the main panels, one black and one red, had already been completed. They were mostly plain, but enlivened by several groups of tiny figures: including what looks like an amorous god making off with a nymph, and some sporting cupids, racing their chariots pulled by goats (with a nasty accident to the leading pair). Separating these panels of colour were narrower sections, where fantastic architecture and impossibly attenuated columns were intertwined with flowers, foliage and precariously balanced birds. On the left, a whole section remained to be painted: the final layer of fine plaster was still wet and would presumably have been coloured in matching black by the end of the day – had disaster not struck.

Also in the final stages was the main picture that was to have been the focal point in the very centre of the wall. Here a rough drawing, in yellow ochre, had been made in the wet plaster to plan out the design and guide the painter in what would have to be speedy work on the final image. All that we can tell now is that it would have included a number of figures (someone seated on the left, and a several standing on the right) and that the upper portion, where some paint had already been applied, was to be blue: presumably, as many other surviving examples make almost certain, it would have been a scene drawn from the repertoire of mythology. In this panel, the under-drawing was relatively detailed, with some careful modelling of the anatomy.

The same was not true for those delicate architectural images. On the east wall of the room, these are still unfinished – but here the sketch in the plaster amounts to no more than some schematic straight lines, geometric curves (hence the compasses) and the occasional diagram of a tricky shape, such as urns. It is as if these elegant and apparently whimsical designs were so much the stock-in-trade of the painters that they could fill in the detail – the birds and the foliage, the architectural extravaganzas – from only the most skeletal outline.

We cannot be more certain about the planned subject of that central panel of the north wall for the simple reason that most of its under-drawing has been covered by a rough layer of irregular dripping plaster. But this turns out to give us another glimpse into how the painters were working. For this pattern of plaster can only have been caused by a bucketful of the stuff falling against the wall from a ladder or scaffolding, knocked over when the painters made their escape or when the eruption came. Underneath the central panel, the two holes at either side, with a line running between them, suggest that a temporary shelf had been rigged up here, to hold the paint pots of the man painting the main scene.

Chemical analysis of the surviving paints yields further hints. They were using seven basic colours (black, white, blue, yellow, red, green and orange), made up in different shades from fifteen different pigments. Some must have been easy to get hold of locally: soot, for example, gave them their black, and various forms of chalk or limestone produced white paints. But they were also using more distant or sophisticated ingredients: celadonite, perhaps from Cyprus, for green; haematite for red, also probably imported; and so-called 'Egyptian blue' made commercially by heating together sand, copper and some form of calcium carbonate (according to Pliny, this was at least four times as expensive as a basic yellow ochre). These paints came in two significantly different types. The first included an organic 'binder' (probably egg). The second had no such binder but had been mixed with water. This points to two different painting techniques. The binder was needed in the paint used for the finishing touches (extra twirls on the architectural designs, or even those racing cupids) which were applied secco, that is onto plaster or paintwork that was already dry. It was not used in the paint applied directly onto the wet plaster (fresco).

Putting all this evidence together, we can get a rough outline of the team which was doing this work, and of its division of labour. It must have involved at least three workers. On the morning of 24 August, one was busy on the central panel of the north wall. One was working next to him, charged with the less skilled task of putting on the plain wash of black paint (perhaps it was his bucket of plaster that fell). Another was painting the as yet unfinished architectural decoration on the east wall (the central panel there had not yet been plastered, so was due to be painted on a later day). Another may have been at work on the secco details. But as there was no time pressure with these (unlike the fresco), they would more likely have been added by the other painters when their fresco work was finished. A small business then: with an apprentice, son or slave supporting the work of a couple of more experienced craftsmen.

Who exactly they were, how they were hired, what they charged or how the wall designs they were creating were chosen, we can only guess. Only two possible signatures have ever been found on paintings at Pompeii, and we have no local evidence of prices for such work. The best we have, in fact, comes from much later, in a set of imperial regulations about maximum prices issued in the early fourth century. In this a 'figure painter' (who may be the equivalent of those here who painted the central panels) could earn twice as much per day as a 'wall painter', and three times as much as a baker or a blacksmith. If the 'figure painter' is the equivalent of those who worked here on the central panels (rather than, as some scholars believe, a portrait artist), then such decoration must have been pricey, but hardly a luxury affordable only by the very rich. The negotiations between client and painter were probably not all that different from those we know today. A lot of money will buy you anything you choose. Otherwise it is a trade-off between the wishes and whims of the clients and the preferences of the painter, his competence and his established repertoire.

44. The painting that gave its name to the House of the Menander. The fourth-century BCE comic playwright Menander is here seen relaxing with a scroll of his own work.

What is certain is that the distinctive painting of Pompeian houses, their vivid decorative schemes, the colourful assault they make on the visual senses were almost all the product of the kind of working methods and small-scale business we glimpse in the House of the Painters at Work. A small property, down a back street just two doors away from Amarantus' bar, was most likely the home base of one such painting business, or at least of a family which made part of its living in that way. Near the front door, a wooden cupboard originally stood, containing more than a hundred pots of paint, as well as other tools, such as plumb-bob and compasses, spoons and spatulas, and grinding equipment for turning the pigments into fine powder ready for mixing. Taking account of itinerant labour or even special commissions from prestige firms outside the area, a small number of workshops like this must have been responsible for the majority of the painted houses in Pompeii, and so there must be plenty of examples of the same painter's work in different properties.

Spotting the work of the same 'hand', where there is no written evidence to help, is a seductive but dangerous business. One very distinguished archaeologist has even managed to convince himself that he can spot the very same painter at work at Fishbourne in England, in the so-called 'Royal Palace' of Togidubnus, and at Stabiae, just south of Pompeii. In Pompeii itself, all kinds of – sometimes wild – theories of 'who painted what' have been floated. So, for example, the work of the painter responsible for several of the main figured scenes in the House of the Tragic Poet has also been identified in more than twenty other houses in the town, from the famous painting of Menander in the House of the Menander (Ill. 44) to a matter-of-fact picture of a man relieving himself that decorates a corridor on the way to the latrine in a small house plus shop. Maybe – or maybe not. But, to indulge in the same game myself for a moment, the tiny vignette of the cupids in the chariot accident on the painted border of that north wall we have been looking at is so similar to a scene with cupids in the House of the Vettii (Plate 21) that it is hard to imagine that they are not by the same painter or painters.

Pompeian colours

If the painters had not been interrupted, the finished product in the House of the Painters at Work would have been something very close to the 'Pompeian painting' of modern imagination. For the rediscovery of Pompeii in the eighteenth century launched a widespread European fashion for 'Roman' interior design. Travellers who had paid a visit to the ruins, or those who had merely enjoyed some of the lavish early publications of the decorations found there, began to reinvent the walls of Pompeii in their own houses, whether in city-centre Paris or the English countryside. Anyone with the money could re-create the ambience of a Roman room by following a simple formula: walls painted in panels of that deep red colour now known as 'Pompeian red' (or in an almost equally characteristic yellow), decorated with fantasy architecture, floating nymphs and scenes drawn from classical myth. For us, this has become the stereotype of Pompeian domestic style.

It was not, of course, simply an invention. Indeed, this 'Pompeian style' reflects the commonest format of domestic decoration in the ancient town. That deep red was one of the Roman colours of choice, along with black, white and yellow (though we should not forget that the heat of the volcanic debris may have produced more red than there once was, by discolouring what was originally painted yellow). Many designs combine mythological scenes, ranging from such sultry subjects as Narcissus admiring his own reflection in the pool to the menace of Medea about to draw her sword on her children, with exuberant versions of architectural form. These are sometimes precariously spindly, sometimes so successful a *trompe l'oeil*, revealing vistas extending far into the distance, that the

45. The walls of Pompeian houses often used painted columns, pediments and dadoes to create a vision of fantastical architecture. The effect of these two paintings is very different, but the standard division of the painting into three zones is clear in both.

solid surface of the wall itself seems almost to disappear. Another distinctive feature, as we saw in the unfinished room and as is carefully replicated in modern imitations, is the three-fold division of the design into three vertical registers: a broad central section carrying the main figured scenes, with dado below and an upper zone carrying more decoration above the cornice (Ill. 45).

Nonetheless, the imagination of the Pompeian painter and his patron was much more fertile than this. Looking around Pompeian houses, you would have spotted on their walls a range of subjects, themes and styles far wider than that modern stereotype suggests. Delicate landscapes were tucked away among the architectural fantasies, as well as touching portraits (Ill. 46) and still-lifes, not to mention stunted dwarfs, scenes of sex and fearsome wild beasts, both in miniature and on a grand scale. There were also styles of decoration much more like modern wallpaper than you would ever have predicted. Many householders painted long tracts of their corridors and service quarters with a black and white design, known for obvious reasons as 'zebra stripe', which would not have looked wholly out of place in the 1960s. Even a prestige room might be decorated in

46. A striking image of a young woman with a stylus pressed against her lips, a detail less than 10 centimetres tall in the original. Modern imaginations have fancied – for no good reason – that she might be a portrait of the Greek poetess Sappho.

swathes of repeating geometric and floral patterns utterly unlike what we would think of as 'Pompeian' (Ill. 47). And all this variety was before you looked down at the floor, where, in the wealthier houses at least, almost anything that might be painted on the wall could also be turned into an image in mosaic, from guard dogs to the occasional full-scale battle. The 'home decorating' of Pompeii springs all kinds of surprises.

Particularly memorable are the large paintings that often plaster the whole back walls of garden areas. We saw the traces of painted foliage and other garden features on the wall of the House of the Tragic Poet, merging the real and imaginary garden. Other houses opted for something more exotic. Visitors to one relatively modest property (known as the House of Orpheus) would have been able to see straight through its front door to the peristyle garden at the rear – and to a well-over life-size figure of a naked Orpheus painted on the wall, sitting on a rock in a country landscape and strumming his lyre to the delight of a motley collection of beasts (Plate 2). On another garden wall, a colossal Venus emerges

47. Some of the wall decoration of Pompeii looks surprisingly modern. This patterned design from the House of the Gilded Cupids, believed to imitate fabric hangings, could almost pass for wallpaper.

from the sea, sprawled out somewhat uncomfortably in her shell (Ill. 97). On another, a fantastic landscape, with palm trees in the foreground and grand villas in the distance, is the setting for a (painted) shrine of a trio of Egyptian deities, Isis, Sarapis and the child Harpocrates, the symbol of the rising sun.

Hunting scenes were also favourites (Plate 19). Even the small garden of the House of Ceii (named after its possible owners) offered visitors the thrill of the chase. The back wall of this space, not much more than 6 by 5 metres, is dominated by a dramatic hunt, with lions, tigers and other varieties of more or less fierce creatures (Ill. 48). But then turn to left or right, and the side walls are covered with images of the Nile and its inhabitants – pygmies hunting a hippo, sphinxes, shrines, shepherds muffled in cloaks, palm trees, sailing boats and barges (one loaded with *amphorae*). It is slightly clumsy workmanship. But the idea presumably was that to enter this tiny space should be to enter another world, part wild-animal park, part exotic foreign territory.

A whole variety of other themes was on display in sometimes elaborate painted friezes – and in sometimes surprising locations. We have already explored the surviving sections of the frieze from the Estate of Julia Felix, with its images of Forum life. But this was only one among many. All around the entrance hall of the private suite of baths in the House of the Menander ran a series of caricatures of the exploits of gods and heroes, humorous parodies of famous myths: Theseus, in the guise of a barrel-chested dwarf, killing the minotaur; a middle-aged and none too lovely Venus busy telling little Cupid where to fire his arrow (Ill. 51). In the same house, painting spilled onto the cramped surface of the low wall which ran between the columns of the peristyle: here herons pranced among some

48. The garden wall of the House of the Ceii, covered with an animal hunt. The painting is crude and patchy in its survival. But it still vividly brings the wild countryside into the tiny urban garden.

luscious plants, while a motley collection of wild animals were on the chase, hound after deer, boar sniffing after a lion.

In a much more modest property close to the Forum on the Via dell'Abbondanza, now called the House of the Doctor (after some medical instruments found there), the wall between the columns of the small peristyle was covered with a frieze of pygmies. These were pictured getting up to all kinds of adventures, and into all kinds of scrapes: some attempting to catch a crocodile (Plate 22), one being eaten by a hippopotamus (while a friend vainly tries to pull him out of the creature's mouth), a couple having sex in front of an admiring throng of pygmy revellers. But the most striking image is the scene which appears to depict a pygmy parody of the Judgement of Solomon, or some story on very much the same lines. Here a soldier is already wielding a large hatchet above the disputed baby, ready to cut it in half, while one of the claimant women, presumably its true mother, is pleading with three officials watching the scene from their raised dais (Ill. 49). If pygmies are not an unusual presence in various decorative schemes in the town (they have been found, for example, painted on the sides of the stone couches in one lavish outdoor *triclinium*, as well as in the House of the Ceii), the scene with the baby has no parallel elsewhere in Pompeii.

49. In this painting pygmies play out the story of the Judgement of Solomon (or some very similar tale). The disputed baby lies on the table, ready to be cut in two. On the right, one of its competing 'mothers' pleads in front of a group of judges seated on a raised dais.

Even so, for visual impact and intriguing subject matter, pride of place among friezes must go to the even more extraordinary series of paintings found in the Villa of the Mysteries (part working farm, part lavish domestic property), just over 400 metres outside the Herculaneum Gate. These now rival the Vettii's Priapus as the iconic symbol of Pompeian art. They are reproduced on the same range of modern souvenirs, from ashtrays to fridge magnets – and have the added advantage that you don't have to be quite so careful about who you give them to.

Life-size figures, set against a rich red background, running around all four walls of a large room, almost enclosing the viewer in the painting, they are a stunning example of 'saturation viewing' (Ill. 50). At one end, the god Dionysus lounges in the lap of Ariadne, whom he rescued after she had been abandoned by the hero Theseus – itself a favourite theme of Pompeian painting. Around the other walls, we are faced with a curious array of humans, gods and animals: a naked boy reading from a papyrus roll (Plate 14); a woman bringing in a loaded tray turns to catch our eye; an elderly satyr plays a lyre; a female version of the god Pan (a 'Panisca') suckles a goat; a winged 'demon' whips a naked girl; another naked woman dances to castanets; a woman has her hair braided, while a winged Cupid holds up the mirror. And that is to pick out only about half of what is going on.

To be honest, this is all completely baffling, and no amount of modern scholarship has ever managed to unravel the meaning – or, at least, not wholly convincingly. Some have argued that the images refer specifically to initiation into

50. The mysterious frieze of the Villa of the Mysteries. At the far end of the room the god Dionysus slumps in the lap of his lover Ariadne. On the left, opposite the large window, some of the figures that make up the procession are visible: a child reads from a scroll watched over by a seated woman, perhaps his mother. (See also Plate 14)

the religious cult of Dionysus. Note, for example, the flagellation, and the revelation of what might be a phallus on the end wall next to the divine couple. If so, then the room itself might have been some kind of sacred precinct within the house. This is not impossible, but it is certainly in no sense hidden away, as you might expect an esoteric cult room to be. In fact, it opens onto a shady portico, with a lovely view of the sea beyond; while on another side it has a large window looking onto the mountains in the distance. Others have seen the paintings as a rather extravagant allegory on marriage, and the young woman admiring herself in Cupid's mirror as the bride. In which case, we are dealing with nothing specifically religious – but a perfectly plausible, if somewhat idiosyncratic, set of decorations for a major entertaining room. The house has been called the Villa of the *Mysteries*, after the Dionysiac 'mysteries' of initiation, following the strictly religious reading of the frieze. The truth is that these paintings are *mysterious* in the popular modern sense of the word too.

Most Pompeian houses have now lost their sparkle – their interior decoration, as we have already noted, sadly faded, or worse. Only tantalising fragments survive of those caricatures in the baths of the House of the Menander (Ill. 51).

51. Parodies of the gods in the baths of the House of the Menander. This drawing of a now very faded painting shows a nasty little Cupid taking aim, under the instruction of a decidedly frumpish goddess of love.

We will never be able to recapture that Egyptian garden landscape in all its gaudy freshness, for – thanks to the combination of rain, sun, frost and an earthquake or two – it has simply disappeared since it was first uncovered in the early nineteenth century. Go to visit the house now, and you will find hardly any plaster left on the wall, and on what does remain it takes the eye of faith to make out more than a few vague blotches. All that we have comes courtesy of the energetic artists who worked in Pompeii in the years after its discovery, copying paintings for armchair archaeologists and aesthetes. It had already gone, it seems, by the 1860s.

But there are nasty shocks of a different sort too. What makes the frieze in the Villa of the Mysteries so memorable is not just its curious subject matter. It is the completeness of the images that surround you, the luscious red background behind the figures and the glistening sheen of the paintwork. Here is one of the few places in the city where the full ancient experience of the painted walls seems to have been preserved.

Sadly not. The fact is that this is no miraculous preservation, but the product of aggressive restoration after its excavation in April 1909. To be fair, what we now see may give roughly the right impression of the original. But the paintings were not in this perfect state when they were dug out of the ground, in a private-enterprise dig, by the local hotel keeper, and they were further damaged by the various strategies of conservation that followed. In the months after the discovery, these famous images were exposed to the elements, protected only by hanging cloths, which did nothing to prevent damage to the area above Dionysus in an earthquake in June 1909.

A worse problem was the rising damp. From the moment they were exposed, salts rose from the ground and leached through the paintings, leaving nasty white patches. Starting only days after the discovery, these were removed with a mixture of wax and petroleum which was repeatedly applied to the surface. Hence not only that impressive sheen, which (even though some wax might have been applied in antiquity) is not itself ancient at all, but also the deep hue. A recent 'excavation' back to the Roman paintwork has revealed a distinctly lighter background colour. More radically, though it was standard practice at the time, stretches of the original walls of the room were demolished and replaced with damp-proof versions, the paintings being first detached from their original surface then reset into the new. All this had happened before a German team arrived in the autumn of 1909 to restore the frescoes, and to return them so far as possible to their pristine state.

The Villa of the Mysteries is one house in Pompeii which does have a sparkle. But, despite its iconic status, that sparkle is not an ancient one. It is in large part the work of modern restorers.

What went where

When Cicero was buying sculpture to decorate his various houses and villas, he was very choosy about what went where. On one occasion in the 40s BCE, he wrote a cross letter to one of his friends who was acting as his agent. The unfortunate Marcus Fabius Gallus had, amongst other purchases, acquired a set of marble 'Bacchantes' – the female followers of the god Dionysus (or Bacchus), and a well-known symbol in the ancient world of wildness, intoxication and lack of restraint. They were, as Cicero admitted, 'pretty little things'. But they were completely unsuitable for a (sober) library. A set of Muses, on the other hand, would have been just the ticket. And that was not the end of his complaints. Gallus had also come up with a statue of Mars, the god of war. 'What good is that to me, the champion of peace,' moaned the ungrateful Cicero.

The logic of Cicero's schemes for interior decoration is clear enough. The subject has to fit the function of the room, or the image he wants to present. Can we trace that, or some other, logic behind the decorative choices made in the houses of Pompeii? Amidst all the variety, can we begin to explain why any particular painting was chosen for any particular room?

There must have been some element of personal whim involved. Whatever the precise meaning of the frieze in the Villa of the Mysteries (whether the sacred rites of Dionysus, an allegory of marriage, or any of the other bright ideas that scholars have come up with over the years), the whole ensemble is so lavish and distinctive that it points to a patron with strong views of what he wanted on the walls of this room, and the cash to pay for it. The same is true for the Alexander mosaic in the House of the Faun, a fabulously expensive installation, whether it was purpose-made for the spot, with its millions of tiny stone *tesserae*, or imported from the East. Someone very much wanted it to be there – though why, we cannot now hope to know. But decoration is not only a matter of personal whim. As we take for granted in our own world, there are cultural 'rules' which govern how houses are painted and decorated. Can we reconstruct those rules for Pompeii? And what do they tell us about life in the Roman town?

These questions have exercised archaeologists for generations. One of the favourite suggested answers, first floated in the nineteenth century, is that fashion or changing taste lie at the root of the many different styles we see on the walls of the city. To put it another way, there is a chronological development in painting, with different styles indicating a different date for the decoration. It is especially the stereotypical 'Pompeian' manner of painting, with its broad washes of colour, its mythological scenes and architectural frames and fantasies, that has been scrutinised in this way. Archaeologists have tracked down various clues to the precise dating of individual paintings – whether hints offered by Vitruvius or those coin impressions made while the job was still wet (p. 15) – to reconstruct a complete design chronology. What looks to the untutored eye like a fairly homogeneous series of paintings can, so this argument goes, be divided into four distinct chronological styles, one succeeding the next in a fashion-conscious city. These are what are known in archaeological jargon (which regularly spills into guidebooks and museum labels) simply as the 'Four Styles', found not only in Pompeii but throughout Roman Italy.

These styles are characterised by their different techniques of illusion, from the imitation blocks of coloured marble in the First Style to the sometimes baroque architectural confections of the Fourth. In between came the more solid architectural *trompe l'oeil* of the Second Style (often assumed to have been introduced to the town with the Roman colonists) and the delicate, decorative ornamentalism of the Third, which reduced columns to mere stalks, pediments to twirls of foliage. Vitruvius, writing in the reign of the emperor Augustus, had no time at all for the then new-fangled Third Style, seeing it not just as unrealistic, but almost immoral: 'How can a reed really support a roof or a candelabrum support gable ornaments? How can such a thin and pliant stalk carry a seated figure, or how can both flowers and half-length statues emerge from roots and

Figure 11. Four Styles of wall decoration. Top left, (a) The First Style. Second century BCE. Top right, (b) The Second Style. In Pompeii this is usually dated to after the arrival of the Roman colonists in 80 BCE. Bottom left, (c)The Third Style. From the Augustan period (*c.* 15 BCE) to the mid first century CE. Bottom right, (d) The Fourth Style. The style of the final years of Pompeii, from the mid first century CE on.

shoots? Yet the people who look at these lies find no fault with them. On the contrary they like it, and they don't pay any attention to whether any of it could actually exist … No paintings should be sanctioned except those that obey the principles of authenticity.' Had he lived to see it, the Fourth Style would have hardly appealed to him either. Ranging from relatively restrained compositions in white and red to breathtaking and sometimes frankly garish extravaganzas, it hardly displayed much concern for 'authenticity'.

There is a lot to be said in favour of this model of chronological development in the house decoration of Pompeii. It is, after all, entirely plausible that Pompeian taste in interior design did change over time. Any modern builder who is used to working in old houses knows exactly what style of wallpaper to expect as he peels back the layers of the decoration that have been applied with each new fashion of the twentieth and nineteenth centuries. Why not the same sort of changes in Pompeii? In fact, there is plenty of evidence on the site that fits neatly with the idea of a progression of Four Styles. The vast majority – some 80 per cent – of the painted walls in Pompeii are done in Fourth Style, as you would expect for the latest in the chronological sequence. Besides, tentative as the dating of Pompeian structures and paintings often has to be, there is no evidence that a Fourth Style scheme was ever applied to a house wall before the middle of the first century CE.

All the same, the fixation of some modern archaeologists with the Four Styles is much too rigid. True, any visitor to Pompeii in 79 CE would have found painting in the Fourth Style dominating the domestic landscape. But it goes without saying (because they are still there for us to see) that all the other styles were on show too. One house, known for obvious reasons as the House of the Four Styles, sported decoration from each of the Four Styles, perhaps the result of piecemeal decoration at different periods. The House of the Faun, as we have already seen, had preserved a large stretch of First Style decoration, in its strangely old-fashioned, almost museum-style environment, and had even applied it afresh on rebuilt walls. And there were a number of other splendid examples of First Style painting which had been carefully preserved, and no doubt retouched and repainted, right up to the end of the city's life. It even seems that in public buildings (such as the Basilica in the Forum, a multi-purpose legal, political and commercial building) First Style decoration was in regular use long after it was the popular choice for domestic property. Pompeian decoration, both inside and outside the home, was a combination of old and new.

What is more, as so often with such rigid schemes, the distinction between one style and the next is not quite so clear on the ground as the usual 'type examples' selected by most books (this one included) would suggest. Although a small band of archaeologists continue to work at refining the chronology and the stylistic categories, inventing more and more micro-subdivisions (Third Style Phase 1A, B, C, 2A etc.), the untutored eye may not be entirely wrong in suggesting that there are more similarities than differences in these styles. Generations of students have made their first visit to Pompeii, armed with book-learning about these stylistic divisions, only to discover, as I did myself years ago, that – distinctive though the First Style is – it is in most cases much harder to pinpoint the Second, Third and Fourth Styles than they had ever imagined. Even the specialists occasionally gesture at this problem, when they refer to the Fourth Style as 'eclectic', or 'taking elements from what went before and putting them together in new and often unexpected ways'. One goes so far as to admit that the Fourth Style is 'scarcely distinguishable from the Third' – which leaves only the relatively few examples of First and Second as clearly distinctive.

But the bigger problem is that the theory of the Four Styles pays almost no attention to the possibility of a link between the function of a room and the type of decoration on its wall. In the modern house, this is a powerful factor in design choice. Walk into an empty property today and there is fair chance that, even without the beds or wardrobe, you will be able to tell the main bedroom from the sitting room or the children's room, relying only on the colour and patterns on the walls. And Cicero suggested that a similar concern with function might dictate a rich Roman's choice of statuary. Does the same thing apply in Pompeii, where – as we have already seen – household activities were rather less precisely tied to particular rooms or areas of the house than in our own domestic environment?

Yes – or, at least, up to a point. The zebra stripe design is very obviously associated with the service quarters. It is true that there are one or two more upmarket rooms in the town decorated in this style, but by and large this was the cheap wall decoration slapped onto latrines, slave rooms, utility areas and corridors (the ancient equivalent of a quick coat of white emulsion). We have also seen that the walls of a garden would often be decorated with themes which picked up the idea of verdant foliage, and hinted at an imaginary wilderness (populated by beasts, pygmies and other exotic figures) stretching in the mind's eye far beyond the confines of the house. It is significant too that those parodies of well-known myths, treated with all due seriousness in most other paintings in Pompeii, are found in a private bath suite. For baths were a place of pleasure where social norms were relaxed, as is signalled in the House of the Menander by the mosaic on the floor at the entrance to the 'hot room': a dashing and scantily clad black slave, garland on his head, carrying two water flasks which rhyme in colour and shape with his (large) penis; underneath an arrangement of four strigils (oil scrapers) and a jar on a chain which is also decidedly phallic (Ill. 52).

But we can trace a few more-general links between the use of different areas of the house and the decoration on its walls, its colours and themes. In the modern Western home, pastel colours regularly signal bedrooms or bathrooms. In Pompeii, the householder often seems to have chosen black background paint for his grandest rooms, cheap though the basic ingredient of that paint could be (Pliny, interestingly, refers to various more-expensive black pigments, including one imported from India). Yellow and red were relatively high-status alternatives.

52. The mosaic floor at the entrance to the hot room in the House of the Menander. An almost naked black slave displays his large penis, while underneath the strigils used by bathers for scraping off the sweat and grease are arranged in a matching phallic pattern. What message was this for the naked bathers?

To judge from the cost and from the comments of Roman writers, one very special red pigment, cinnabar or vermilion ('mercury sulphide' to a scientist), which was mined in Spain, was the very height of luxury. This was so sought after that, according to Pliny, a maximum price was set by law (just over twice the price of Egyptian blue), to keep it 'within limits'. He also notes that it was one of a small number of expensive colours which were usually paid for by the patron separately, over and above the standard contract price for the job. It's not hard to imagine how those negotiations might have gone: '... well, of course, I *could* do it in cinnabar, sir, but it'd cost you. It'd have to come as an extra. You'd probably be better getting hold of some yourself ...' Negotiations between client and builder may not have changed very much over the centuries.

Not only a very desirable shade of red, cinnabar was also tricky to handle (no doubt part of its allure). For in certain conditions, particularly in the open air, it rapidly discoloured, turning a mottled black, unless a special coating of oil or wax was applied. As if to drive the point home, Vitruvius tells the story of a lowly but rich 'scribe' in Rome who had his peristyle painted with cinnabar and it had changed colour within a month. It served him right for not being better informed was the moral. The work being done in the House of the Painters at Work was not in the cinnabar range. But that pigment has been discovered in two of the obviously most prestige decorative schemes in Pompeii: the Villa of the Mysteries frieze and one of the rooms off the peristyle in the House of the Vettii.

Different decorative styles also pointed to different functions or different levels of exclusivity with the house. The fact that the First Style is most often preserved in domestic atria and that it continued in use in public buildings in the town is probably no coincidence. Within the domestic sphere it came to signal public areas of the house. Likewise (though this argument is perhaps rather too circular for comfort) you can often spot rooms, large or small, that were intended to impress the invited guest by their concentration of mythological paintings, almost as if in an art gallery, and by their extravagant architectural vistas. One scholar has even suggested a simple rule of thumb, which works well enough for Second and Fourth Styles at least: 'the greater the depth suggested by the perspective effects, the higher the prestige of the room.'

So decorative choices for the Pompeian householder came down to a trade-off between fashion and function. This was true right across the social spectrum. For, as we saw with the overall architecture of the house, there is no sign of any particular difference in taste, or in the underlying logic of their decor, between the properties of the rich and those of modest means, or between those of the old elite families and rich ex-slaves. Even if the houses of the poor had no public role, the householders followed the same cultural norms of decoration so far as they could afford it. And, despite many attempts by modern archaeologists to sniff out the vulgarity of the Trimalchio-style nouveaux riches, it has usually been more a projection of their own class prejudices than anything else. In the end, the differences between the paintings in rich and poor houses come down to not much more than this: the poor had fewer figured scenes, fewer dramatic extravaganzas of design and no cinnabar, and (notwithstanding a few second-rate daubings in elite properties) the quality of painting in their houses was generally much cruder. Pompeii was a town where you got what you paid for.

Myths do furnish a room

When the eighteenth-century excavators first discovered the paintings of Pompeii, it was the figured scenes in the centre of many of the Third and Fourth Style walls, not the extravagant or whimsical architectural fantasies, that caught their imagination. For these were the first visual representations of ancient myth ever to be discovered in such quantity. What is more, they offered a first glimpse of the lost tradition of painting which Pliny and other ancient writers hyped as one of the highlights of ancient art. True, Pliny was usually referring to masterpieces of easel painting by famous Greek artists of the fifth and fourth centuries BCE, prize possessions of temples and monarchs; and these were panels painted directly onto the wet wall plaster of domestic housing in a small Roman town. But, in the absence of the original works by Apelles, Nicias, Polygnotus and the others, they were the best evidence available. Many of the most striking examples were cut out of the wall on which they were found and taken to the nearby museum – where, of course, they came to resemble 'gallery art' even more closely.

The range of myths chosen by the painters and their patrons is very wide. There are, it is true, some puzzling absences. Why, for example, so few traces of the myth of Oedipus in Pompeii? But some of the themes of Pompeian painting are old favourites for us too: Daedalus and Icarus, Actaeon accidentally (but disastrously) catching sight of the goddess Diana at her bath, Perseus rescuing Andromeda from her rock, the self-regarding Narcissus, and a variety of familiar scenes from the story of the Trojan War (the Judgement of Paris, the Trojan Horse and so on).

Others, though obviously favourites in Pompeii, are to us rather more arcane. No fewer than nine similar paintings have been discovered depicting a tale which came to be told as a 'prequel' to the Trojan War: Achilles on the island of Skyros. At first sight their subject looks like any other heroic brawl. But there is a curious

53. A tale of cross-dressing – and a favourite theme of Pompeian painting. Achilles, in the centre, is in hiding from the Trojan War, dressed as a woman and living among the daughters of the king of Skyros. But he is 'outed' by Odysseus, who grabs him from the right, to take him back to do his duty as a warrior.

back story. The Greek hero has been hidden away by his mother Thetis to keep him out of the conflict; he is disguised as a woman and lodged with the daughters of Lycomedes, the king of the island. Knowing that Troy can only be taken with Achilles' help, Odysseus arrives disguised as a pedlar and succeeds in 'outing' him with a cunning ruse. When he lays out his wares – trinkets, ornaments and an assortment of weapons – the 'real' girls go for the ornaments, while Achilles reveals his manhood by choosing the weapons. Odysseus, as we see here (Ill. 53), takes that as his opportunity to pounce on the renegade.

An even stranger story appears in at least four paintings, plus a couple of terracotta statuettes (Ill. 54). It is the image of one of the most extreme forms of filial piety imaginable. An old man, Micon, has been imprisoned with no food and risks dying of starvation. He is visited, so the legend goes, by his daughter, who has recently had a baby. To keep her father alive, she feeds him with the milk of her breast. In one version, in the House of Marcus Lucretius Fronto (so called after the likely owner), the scene is explained and the message is underlined by some lines of poetry, painted next to the figures: 'Look how in his poor neck the veins of the old man now pulse with the flow of the milk. Pero herself caresses Micon, face to face. It is a sad combination of modesty [*pudor*] and a daughter's love [*pietas*]'. A

54. A devoted daughter feeds her imprisoned father. This myth of filial piety caught the imagination of the Pompeians. Here it is represented in a terracotta figurine. Elsewhere it provides the subject for paintings.

superfluous explanation perhaps. For paintings of this story were notorious at Rome for their visual impact: 'Men's eyes stare in amazement when they see what is happening', in the words of one roughly contemporary Roman writer.

Why so many versions of the same scene? Almost certainly, in some cases, because they were inspired by the same famous old master of Greek art. The archaeologists of the eighteenth century were not entirely wrong when they imagined that the paintings in Pompeii might give a glimpse of lost Greek masterpieces, faint as it might be. Occasionally, in fact, there are tantalising similarities between the images on these walls and the descriptions of much earlier paintings given by Pliny and others.

One of the best-known panels from the House of the Tragic Poet, for example, shows the sacrifice of the young Iphigeneia by her father Agamemnon before the Greek fleet sailed for the Trojan War – an offering to the goddess Artemis in return for fair winds (Ill. 55). The almost naked girl is being carried to the altar while her father, distraught at his own deed, covers his head in sorrow. This is exactly how both Pliny and Cicero describe a painting of the sacrifice of Iphigeneia by the fourth-century BCE Greek painter Timanthes: 'the painter ... felt that Agamemnon's head must be veiled, because his intense grief could not be

55. King Agamemnon, on the left, cannot bear to look as his daughter Iphigeneia is taken off to be sacrificed to the goddess Artemis, who is appearing in the heavens. This drawing (like Ill. 53) is from the famous nineteenth-century guide book to the site, *Pompeiana* by Sir William Gell.

represented with the paint brush.' But, as a whole, what we see at Pompeii was nowhere near an exact copy of Timanthes' masterpiece, in which Odysseus and the girl's uncle Menelaus also featured, and Iphigeneia, rather than being carried as she is here, stood calmly by the altar awaiting her fate. There seems a fair chance too that some of the scenes of Achilles among the women of Skyros go back ultimately to a famous easel painting by one Athenion: 'Achilles concealed in girls' clothes when Ulysses [i.e. Odysseus] finds him out', as Pliny briefly describes it; though the differences in detail from one Pompeian version to the next suggest again that they are variations on the theme, not exact copies of the original.

In all likelihood the Pompeian painters were working from a range of well-known and 'quotable' masterpieces which had entered their own artistic reper-toire. There is no reason at all to suppose that they had ever seen the original paintings or even that they had pattern books or exact templates to copy. These famous images were as much part of the common artistic currency as the *Mona Lisa* or Van Gogh's *Sunflowers* are in the West today. As such they could be adapted to new locations at will, riffed and improvised, made to *evoke* the original rather than to *reproduce* it exactly. And not only in paint. Achilles on Skyros turns up in mosaic too, and one popular theory has it that the Alexander mosaic in the House of the Faun is a version of a painting by a Greek artist, Philoxenus of Eretria, mentioned by Pliny.

The big question, though, is what the Pompeian residents made of all these myths decorating their walls. Was it the ancient equivalent of wallpaper,

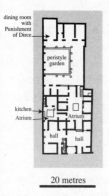

dining room with Punishment of Dirce

peristyle garden

kitchen
Atrium

Atrium

hall   hall

20 metres

Figure 12. The House of Julius Polybius. This has an unusual arrangement of large entrance halls, as well as the standard atrium. It was in this house that the twelve victims of the eruption were discovered (p. 8), in rooms off the peristyle.

occasionally glanced at and admired maybe, but always in the background? Would, in fact, many of the Pompeians have found it as difficult as we do to explain exactly what was going on in many of these images? Or were they carefully studied, loaded with meaning, and intended to convey a particular message to the viewer? And if so, then what message?

Archaeologists divide on the question. Some see little more than attractive decoration in most of these images. Others like to detect complex, even mystical significance in the painted plaster. Of course, the paintings no doubt spoke differently to different people, and some observers were more observant than others. But there are a number of hints that viewers on occasion took notice of the images that surrounded them, or at least were expected to. Even if the most ingenious modern theories – which would see the interior decoration of many Pompeian houses as an elaborate mythological 'code' – are decidedly unconvincing, some painters and patrons astutely planned their content and arrangement.

Ancient writers tell vivid stories of the impact a mythological painting could make on a viewer. A Roman lady, about to part from her own husband, was once reduced to tears, it was said, at the sight of Hector, the Trojan hero, saying his final farewell to his wife Andromache (he was going off to battle, one from which he would never return). There are no tears at Pompeii. But one person who had a very good idea of what he was looking at, and took the time to reflect on it, has left a record of his reflections – and it probably was *his* – scrawled on a wall in the House of Julius Polybius (Fig. 12). In the grandest room off its peristyle garden is a large painting of another favourite scene in the repertoire of Pompeian myths: the punishment of Dirce – a gory tale, in which (to cut a very long story short) her victims take revenge on Dirce, the Queen of Thebes, by tying her to the horns of a wild bull, and so inflicting a slow, painful and bloody death. In Pompeian terms, there is nothing particularly remarkable about the painting, one of eight on the same theme discovered in houses of the city. But this particular version made enough of an impression on our writer that he advertised it, in a one-line graffito, found in one of the service areas of the property: 'Look. There's not only those Theban women, but Dionysus and the royal maenad too.'

Unearthed before the painting had been found, this message at first puzzled the archaeologists who were excavating the house in the 1970s. What was some scribbler doing in the kitchen, rambling on about Theban women? It only fell into place when it was put together with the nearby image. For, as well as the final punishment of Dirce with the bull, the painting also depicts the scene of her capture dressed as a follower of Dionysus (the 'royal maenad' of the graffito), as well as a shrine of the god and, in the foreground, a larger group of maenads ('those Theban women'). Whoever wrote the graffito had not only paid careful attention to the painting, but knew enough of the story to identify the scene as Thebes, and Dirce (as written versions of the myth insist) as a follower of Dionysus. Exactly what prompted him to write, who knows? But whatever it was, he would no doubt have been amazed to discover that his words have become, 2000 years on, rare and clinching proof that some people in the city certainly cast an intelligent eye on the pictures on their walls.

On other occasions a particular subject in a particular location clearly implies some calculated choices on the part of painter or patron. Whoever decided to decorate the wall above one of the couches of the outdoor dining installation in the House of Octavius Quartio with a painting of the mythical Narcissus gazing at his own reflection in the pool must have thought that the diners would enjoy the joke. For this was one of those upmarket installations (as in the House of the Golden Bracelet, p. 95), with a gleaming channel of water between the pair of couches on which the company reclined. Presumably as you gazed at your reflection in the water, you were supposed to enjoy a wry smile at the overlap between myth and real life, while reflecting, perhaps, on the myth's lesson about the tragic consequences of falling in love with that image of yourself.

There may be a similar pointed reference lying behind the painting of Micon and Pero in the House of Lucretius Fronto, with its verses underlining the combined virtues of modesty or a sense of decency (*pudor*) and piety (*pietas*) which the story celebrates. Though some archaeologists have thought this an apt decoration for a child's bedroom (a strange choice, if you ask me), there may be a more specific political resonance to the image. Is it just a coincidence that, in a couple of lines of poetry painted on the outside of this house as an electoral jingle, it is the *pudor* of Marcus Lucretius Fronto which is given pride of place?

> If decency [*pudor*] is thought to help a man get on in life at all
> To our Lucretius Fronto that high office which he seeks should fall

If Marcus Lucretius Fronto really was the occupant of this house (and the combination of graffiti inside and outside makes that very likely), then it looks as if the painting was meant to reflect one of his trademark public virtues.

But, even more often, the *combination* of subjects chosen to decorate a room seems to be significant. The removal of figured panels from their original setting to the safety of the museum certainly did much to preserve their colour and detail. Yet it also makes it hard to see them in their original context and the relationship between them in their original position. In the House of the Tragic Poet, for example, many of the paintings, now displayed in the Naples Museum as if they were individual examples of gallery art, once combined to make a connected cycle of themes from the Trojan War: Helen leaving for Troy with Paris; the sacrifice of Iphigeneia; his prized captive and concubine Briseis being removed from Achilles – the cause of his quarrel with Agamemnon which launches Homer's *Iliad* and which was depicted in another panel in the house. There was more to this than a simple coherence of theme. In their original locations, all kinds of questions must have been raised in the clever visual juxtapositions and in the 'provocative correspondences' between individual paintings and their subjects.

Originally, it seems, the scenes of Helen and Briseis stood in adjacent panels in the atrium (Plate 23). These were two vignettes of women's desertion, each one a linch-pin in the story of the Trojan War, and the parallels are underlined by the similar dress of each woman, her bowed head and the surrounding cast of soldiers. Yet, for anyone familiar with the Trojan story, the comparison must have prompted reflection on the differences between the two scenes as much as on the similarities. For Helen, the Greek queen, was leaving her husband Menelaus and embarking on an adulterous journey of her own free will – and in so doing would be the catalyst to the whole catastrophic war between Greeks and Trojans. Briseis, the Trojan prisoner of war, was leaving Achilles to be handed over to King Agamemnon, against her will – and Achilles' anger at his loss would

56. A little cupid stands at the doorway as Paris and Helen decide to elope, so launching the Trojan War. But this painting from the House of Jason is more loaded than it might seem at first sight. For here Paris is sitting down as if taking the female role, while Helen stands – and the architectural background is reminiscent of Pompeii itself, suggesting that the myth of adultery, elopement and domestic disruption was relevant to 'real life' too.

lead directly, as Homer's epic tells, to the death of his friend Patroclus and of Hector, prince of Troy. Virtue, blame, status, sex, motivation and the causes of suffering are all at issue in this pairing. Whoever designed this series of images certainly knew their Trojan myths and must have expected the audience to do so likewise.

An unsettling undertone can be detected in another series of paintings, which also features Helen's adultery with Paris. Three panels decorate a small room in the House of Jason, so called after a painting of the Greek hero Jason in another room. Each one depicts a moment of calm before tragedy strikes: Medea watches her children play, before killing them, to take revenge on the husband who has abandoned her; Phaedra talks to her nurse before killing herself in unrequited love for her stepson Hippolytus, accusing the innocent young man of incest in the process; while Helen entertains Paris at her marital home before their elopement – which is already signalled by the little cupid at the door (Ill. 56).

As with the series in the House of the Tragic Poet, visual rhymes between the paintings prompt the viewer to compare and contrast the different versions of domestic disaster on show. For example, both Medea and Phaedra are seated, as you would expect of a respectable Roman matron; but in the other scene it is Helen who stands, while her effeminate 'Oriental' lover takes the women's place. But the architectural background adds a disturbing dimension. Its similiarity in each scene does not just bind the three stories together; the style of the architecture and those big heavy doors bear more than a passing resemblance to the style of upmarket domestic architecture in Pompeii itself. It is almost as if the paintings have a point to make about the relevance of the myth to contemporary Roman life, in exposing the tragic dysfunction – from adultery to infanticide – that can creep up on any family, anywhere.

A room with a view?

The decoration of Pompeian houses has kept scholars busy for centuries, figuring out the chronology, the aesthetic and functional choices made, the meaning of the myths on the walls. Fascinating details continue to be discovered on everything from the logic of the designs to the technical procedures of the painters who carried them out (the House of the Painters at Work only began to be unearthed in the late 1980s, and the excavations are still incomplete). But there is an important and obvious point about the domestic style of this Roman town which often gets lost among the detail.

To judge from their plans and the surviving remains, many if not most Pompeian houses would count as claustrophobic places. Only a few of the very richest exploited any kind of view onto the outside world; the vast majority were inward-looking, with hardly more than a couple of tiny windows, to bring in light, onto the street outside. Most of the rooms were small and dark. And although some (the wealthiest again) were endowed with lofty atria and with extensive internal gardens and walkways, in many even the atrium must have felt relatively cramped (especially when filled with all those cupboards and looms) and the garden was not much more than pocket-handkerchief size, more a light-well than a place of pleasure and relaxation.

Yet the painted decoration tells another story. The clever tricks of illusion suggest vistas that do extend beyond the confines of the house. In the most extravagant cases the internal walls seem to dissolve into a vision of competing perspectives, glimpses beyond the horizon and distant views. Around the borders of the tiny gardens, it must sometimes have been hard to decide at a glance where the domestic plants stopped and the wild landscapes or the river Nile started. Even in the more austere First Style, the viewer is confronted with the puzzle of what the wall they are looking at really consists in: is it painted plaster and stucco or the marble blocks that it pretends to be?

This sense of something beyond the house is powerfully reinforced by the subjects of the wall paintings. Pompeii was, after all, a small town in southern Italy. Yet it is striking how far its cultural and visual reference points extend: across the Mediterranean, through the repertoire of ancient literature and art, to more exotic shores beyond. The imaginary world of decoration was not claustrophobic in the slightest. It embraced a galaxy of Greco-Roman myth and literature, from the Homeric epics on; it evoked and adapted the masterpieces of classical Greek painting; it exploited the cultural highlights of Egypt, from sphinxes and the goddess Isis, to satires and burlesques on its inhabitants and their weird customs. This is not, of course, all benign multiculturalism. The stereotyped pygmies chasing crocodiles or having riotous sex are portrayed with a mixture of aggressive humour and xenophobia. But the crucial fact is that these distant horizons were portrayed at all. On top of its mixed cultural roots in southern Italy, Pompeii was part of the global Roman empire – and it shows.

It shows also in the other forms of ornament and bric-a-brac that have been found in these houses. The Indian statuette of Lakshmi (Ill. 11) may be an extreme and unusual case of cultural 'reach'. But there is plenty of other material to suggest how outward-looking the world of the Pompeian house could be, at least for those with enough cash to spare for decoration. There are, for example, columns, floor tiles and tabletops made from expensive coloured marbles, imported from far-off parts of the empire – from the Peloponnese and the Greek islands, from Egypt, Numidia and Tunisia in Africa, from the coastlands of modern Turkey. Overall Greece, and its history, was in the forefront: a rough-and-ready terracotta statuette identified on its base as 'Pittacus of Mytilene' (a sixth-century BCE Greek sage and moralist) and found in the Estate of Julia Felix; an elegant mosaic with a group of Greek philosophers chatting under a tree with what looks like the Athenian Acropolis in the background, unearthed in a villa just outside the city; and of course the Alexander mosaic.

One of the most striking discoveries is from the House of Julius Polybius. Packed away with other valuables at the time of the eruption, in the grand room with the painting of Dirce, was a fifth-century BCE Greek bronze jug. It had originally been, as an inscription on it declares, part of the prizes at the games held in honour of the goddess Hera at Argos, in the Peloponnese. After a chequered career in which it lost its handles (one suggestion is that it was used in a burial) and had a tap added, it ended up in Pompeii. Whether a prize purchase or a family heirloom, it was a nice reminder of a world and a history outside Pompeii.

How the painters in the House of the Painters at Work had intended to fill the large, as yet blank, panels we shall never know. Nor can we know if they took to their heels in time to escape to safety. But there's little doubt that their job had been to create, in paint, 'a room with a view'.

CHAPTER FIVE

EARNING A LIVING: BAKER, BANKER AND *GARUM* MAKER

Profit margins

Just along the street from the House of Fabius Rufus, in that row of grand mansions with views over the sea, stood a house occupied in the last years of the city by Aulus Umbricius Scaurus, a man who had made his money in the fish sauce (*garum*) business. He was, in fact, the biggest *garum* dealer in town. To judge from the painted labels on *garum* jars found in the area, he and his associates and subsidiaries controlled almost a third of the local supply of this staple of Roman food preparation. The house itself is a vast sprawling affair, made by knocking together at least two earlier, separate properties. It is now in a sadly dilapidated state, partly as the result of the bombing in 1943, which hit this part of town very badly. But in its final form it clearly had not just two, but three atria, as well as one or more peristyles (one with an ornamental fishpond), plus a bath suite on a lower floor.

We know that it was owned by Umbricius Scaurus because the mosaic decoration on the floor of the third atrium once featured at each of its four corners a jar for fish sauce (Ill. 57). Now removed for safe-keeping, these were made out of white *tesserae* on a black background, and each one carried an inscription referring to different varieties of fish sauce sold by Umbricius Scaurus: 'Scaurus' best *garum*, mackerel-based, from Scaurus' manufactory', 'Best fish sauce', 'Scaurus' best *garum*, mackerel-based', 'Fish sauce, grade one, from Scaurus' manufactory'. Unless we are to imagine that some satisfied customer chose to decorate his atrium floor with versions of his favourite sauce jars, then this must be the house of Scaurus himself. Here interior decoration was a form of self-advertisement and product promotion.

57. In the atrium of the House of Umbricius Scaurus, four jars of fish sauce in mosaic proclaim the family's source of wealth. Here the jar proclaims 'Best fish sauce' – in Latin '*Liqua(minis) flos*', literally 'Flower of *liquamen*'. *Liquamen* was a variety of the (to us) better known *garum*.

Umbricius Scaurus was not the only resident of Pompeii explicitly to celebrate his business success on the floor of his house. At one of the main street entrances of another huge property, the visitor was greeted by a slogan picked out in mosaic: 'Welcome, profit!' The sheer size of this house is enough to suggest that the wish had been amply fulfilled. But elsewhere such words must have been more an expression of vain hope. On the atrium floor of a tiny house, we can still see the catchphrase 'Profit is pleasure'. There is little sign here that this went beyond wishful thinking.

The Roman economy

Historians have argued for generations about the economic life of the Roman empire, about its trades and industries, its financial institutions, credit systems and profit margins. On the one hand, are those who see the ancient economy in very modern terms. The Roman empire was effectively a vast single market. There were fortunes to be made from the demand for goods and services, which also drove up productivity and stimulated trade to levels never seen before. A favourite illustration of this comes – unlikely as it may seem – from deep in the

Greenland ice-cap, where it is still possible to find the residue of the pollution from Roman metal-working, not equalled again until the Industrial Revolution. Underwater archaeology tells much the same story. Many more shipwrecks have been discovered at the bottom of the Mediterranean, from between the second century BCE and the second century CE, than from any period until the sixteenth century. This is not an indication of the poor quality of either boat-building or seamanship in the Roman period, but of the high volume of sea-borne traffic.

On the other hand, there are those who argue that Roman economic life was utterly different from our own, in fact decidedly 'primitive'. Wealth combined with social prestige remained rooted in the land and the main aim of any community was to feed itself, not to exploit its resources for profit or investment. Long-distance transport of goods was risky by sea (witness all those shipwrecks) and prohibitively expensive by land. Trade was only a very thin icing on the economic cake, small-scale and not particularly respectable. Inscriptions on mosaic floors may celebrate healthy profit margins, but there are few Roman authors, elite class that they are, with a good word to say for trade or traders. By and large, trade was vulgar and traders untrustworthy. In fact, from the end of the third century BCE, the highest echelons of Roman society, senators and their sons, were expressly forbidden from owning 'ocean-going ships', defined as those that would hold 300 *amphorae* or more.

Besides, Rome developed none of the financial institutions needed to support a sophisticated economy. There was limited 'banking', as we shall see, in Pompeii. It is not even clear if there were such things as credit notes, or if you wheeled around a load of coins in a wheelbarrow to make large purchases, such as houses. And, while Roman metal-working may have polluted Greenland, there is very little trace of the kind of technological innovation that went hand in hand with the eighteenth-century Industrial Revolution. The biggest invention of the Roman period was probably the water-mill, and that – so this side of the argument goes –is not saying very much. But why bother with new technologies, when you have vast quantities of slave power to stoke the fires, man the levers or turn the wheels?

Country life and country produce

Most historians now come down judiciously somewhere between these two extremes. And Pompeii itself has features of both the 'primitive' and the 'modern' model of the economy. It is almost certain that the basis of most wealth in the city was the land in the surrounding area, and that the families which owned the largest houses there would also have had other properties and substantial holdings in the region round about. 'Pompeii' as an economic and political unit would have consisted of the urban centre plus its hinterland. The area beyond the city itself probably covered some 200 square kilometres – or, at least, that is a good, if slightly generous, guess, since we have no hard evidence at all where the boundaries lay between what counted as Pompeian land and that of neighbouring towns. It has not been very thoroughly explored by archaeologists, most of their interest being concentrated on the town. In fact, locating villas, farmsteads and other rural settlements under several metres of volcanic debris has been chancy.

Altogether the remains of almost 150 properties have been discovered in the hinterland of the city, but our knowledge of what kind of establishments they were or who owned them is very hazy, for only rarely have they been systematically excavated. Some were certainly pleasure villas for the rich, even those from as far away as Rome: it was not only Cicero who had his 'Pompeian place'. Some were working farms. Others were a combination of the two. Almost certainly there is a bias, in what we have discovered, towards more substantial remains, rather than the huts and sheds of the poorer peasant farmers. If, as some archaeologists have half suspected, there were the ancient equivalent of shanty towns or squatter settlements of poor labourers in the countryside outside the walls, we have found no trace of them.

There is one case where we can pin down a country property of a leading Pompeian family. In the 1990s, excavation at Scafati, a few kilometres east of Pompeii, turned up a family burial ground, with eight memorials to various Lucretii Valentes in the first century CE, most of the men carrying exactly the same name, Decimus Lucretius Valens. They ranged from tiny children, like the toddler who died when he was just two years old, to a distinguished young man, who had been buried elsewhere at public expense, but was given a memorial plaque here alongside the rest of his relations, where he was celebrated for sponsoring, together with his father, a gladiatorial show consisting of thirty-five pairs of fighters. That was about as generous as a Pompeian benefactor could be.

In Pompeii itself this family has been associated with a group of houses at the far end of the Via dell'Abbondanza, near the Amphitheatre, including the House of Marine Venus, with its sprawling goddess on the garden wall. In fact, some graffiti in one of these properties refer not only to a Decimus Lucretius Valens, but also to a couple of the more distinctively named women known from the burial ground, Iusta and Valentina – clinching the association between the family and the house. But why the group of family memorials in this particular out-of-town location? Presumably because the the Lucretii Valentes had a country house here, in all likelihood the very one that has been partly uncovered, just adjacent to the burial ground.

The Lucretii Valentes, like most of the local Pompeian aristocracy, owed their wealth to the products of their land, even if they did not work it themselves. Some of their holdings would have been farmed by tenants. Some they would have controlled more directly. Often, as in the Villa of the Mysteries and in the house at Scafati no doubt, prestige entertaining rooms for the owner and his family were combined with a working agricultural establishment, operated by a farm manager, using hired labourers and slaves. Vivid evidence for the use of a slave workforce on these farms comes from a distinctive type of metal contraption, almost certainly stocks, or leg irons (one big enough to shackle fourteen people) found at a number of out-of-town properties. In the Villa of the Mosaic Columns just outside the walls, human leg-bones were unearthed still held in iron chains. The idea of slaves and prisoners meeting a horrible end because they were unable to break free of their bonds is a powerful myth of disaster stories, from the destruction of Pompeii to the film *Titanic*, and many early guidebooks to the buried city point to several (quite fictitious) instances of this horror. In this case, the story seems to be confirmed by photographs of the bones as they were discovered, still fused to the metal – though whether the slave concerned was a farm worker or a domestic we have no idea.

Part of this country territory around Pompeii was certainly used for the grazing of sheep, which would have provided both milk and wool. Indeed Seneca hints that some of this husbandry might have been on a relatively large scale, when he claims that a flock of no fewer than 600 perished in the earthquake of 62 CE. For the rest, we should imagine an agricultural landscape of very fertile volcanic soil supporting cereals, grapes and olives. These were the staples of ancient Mediterranean life, essential for basic subsistence and light (from olive oil), and most of them were consumed locally. Exactly how much of the available land was given over to which crop is a tricky question. Roman writers tend to stress the vines and wines of the region, and excavated farms often preserve clear traces of wine production, in the shape of vats and presses. But this may overestimate the importance of vines. The literary emphasis may partly be a reflection of the fact that elite Romans were generally more interested in the varieties of grape than in the varieties of grain, and the archaeological prominence may partly be due to the fact that the paraphernalia of wine-making are so instantly recognisable.

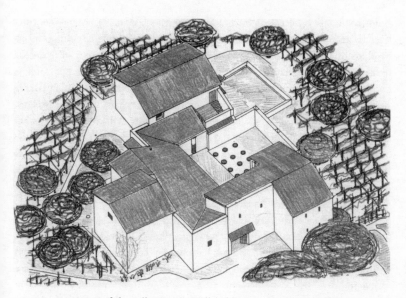

58. A reconstruction of the Villa Regina small-holding near Pompeii. It was an unpretentious property surrounded by vineyards. In the central courtyard, the *dolia*, or storage jars, set in the ground are visible.

One smallholding that has recently been thoroughly excavated, the Villa Regina (known from the modern place name) near Boscoreale, to the north of Pompeii, shows how diverse the cultivation may have been even when a vineyard dominated (Ill. 58). First discovered in the 1970s, this is a relatively humble house with just ten rooms on its ground floor, set around a courtyard. It is a long way from the grand style of the country properties of the wealthy. Most of those rooms were connected with farm work, only two had painted decoration. Presumably the property was owned by a farmer of modest means, though one who, like many in the city, was busy with renovations at the time of the eruption. The lintel of one doorway had had to be propped up, foundations were being underpinned, pavements had been removed, and the kitchen and painted dining room were not in use.

Much of the surviving agricultural equipment was connected with wine-making, including a press and eighteen huge storage jars, or *dolia*, set in the ground, enough to hold 10,000 litres of wine. Unless Roman domestic life was lived through a drunken haze, such a large quantity must have been for more than home consumption. Even so it would have needed less than 2 hectares of vine-yard to produce (a small villa nearby had seventy-two wine *dolia* to hold the produce of its, obviously much larger, estate). Part of this vineyard has been excavated, the root cavities filled with plaster and the remains of seeds and pollen analysed. What has emerged are not only the traces of vines trained on poles, but other plants being grown in between and alongside them – olives, apricots, peaches, almonds, walnuts and figs, to name just a few of the more than eighty species that have been identified.

The physical remains of the house also point to a range of cultivation extending beyond vines. There is what appears to be a threshing floor, suggesting that cereal crops were also being grown, and a hay store, for animal bedding and feed. The animals on the farm certainly included whatever mules, donkeys or horses drew the large cart whose iron wheels and fittings have been found. Pigs were kept too, for meat, as the plaster cast of a splendid young porker found in one of the rooms under repair shows. It must have fled here during the eruption from its pen or sty elsewhere. In the vineyard itself, excavators unearthed the skull of a guard dog.

Wine production on this scale was for the local market rather than for the export trade, perhaps delivered to customers in the town in the kind of trans-porter pictured on the walls of one inn in Pompeii: a vast leather wine skin on a cart, from which the contents were decanted directly into wine jars (Ill. 59). From what we know of the prices of wine on sale in the town (written up, as they some-times were, for customers in bars) and from the usual mark-up that Roman writers suggest between the point of final sale and the farmgate price, this 10,000 litres of wine might have brought in between 5000 and 7500 *sesterces* for the pro-prietor of this farm. But when all the production and equipment costs have been taken into account (in Pompeii, a single mule could set you back more than 500 *sesterces*), the actual profit would have been much less, even if more cash came in from selling some of the other fruit, crops or animals found there. This was not breadline living. It is usually reckoned that 500 *sesterces* would have kept a family of four at absolute minimum subsistence, alive but hungry, for a year; while the basic annual pay of a legionary soldier was 900 *sesterces*. But it was not lavish either. It was enough, presumably, to support, feed, clothe and shelter a house-hold – slaves included – of somewhere between five and ten, with some cash to spare for the occasional little luxury, such as smartening up a few rooms with a coat of decorative paint.

Could the hinterland of Pompeii, thanks to farms like this and other larger

59. Wine was brought to local traders and innkeepers in large wineskins drawn on carts. In this nineteenth-century drawing of a now very faded painting from a Pompeian bar, the men are about to decant it into jars, or *amphorae*.

estates, have supported the population of the area, in basic staples, without the need for mass imports? This has been the subject of intense modern debate and little agreement. Part of the problem is that we can only guess at some of the figures that would be vital for any accurate calculation: not only the total size of population, but also the kind of yield the Romans would have extracted from this land, and the levels of consumption we should expect (is a quarter-litre of wine per day for every man, woman and child in the right order of magnitude or not?).

To try out one line of speculation: suppose we assume that the city in 79 CE was home to roughly 12,000 people, and some 24,000 more lived in the surrounding country (a shot in the dark, based partly on the later population figures). It would then be a reasonable guess, given the fertility of this soil and the climate, that if 120–130 square kilometres out of the 200 were sown with grain, that would have provided the necessary quantities to feed this total of 36,000. And it is almost certain that you could produce enough wine for everyone to have a quarter of a litre per day in less than 2 square kilometres of vineyard. As for olive oil, if we reckon that each person would have consumed (or burnt) 10 litres a year, that could have been produced in less than 4 square kilometres of olive groves all told. Not that we should imagine continuous fields of a single crop, as these calculations might imply. The planting at the Villa Regina, with olives and fruit trees amidst the vines, shows just how mixed this ancient farming could be.

Of course, change any one of these rough estimates – increase the population by 50 per cent, for example, or decrease the amount of available land – and the overall picture can change dramatically. Even on these optimistic calculations, there will also have been years of shortage, drought or crop failure which would have left the Pompeians looking elsewhere for their staples. All the same, it looks very much as if they would usually have had enough to be exporting their surplus, and that is borne out by other evidence. Ancient writers certainly associated the area round Vesuvius with well-known varieties of grape, one even known as *Pompeiana*. This celebrity suggests that the wines reached well beyond the local area. In fact, Pliny's sniffy remarks about the inferiority of some of the Pompeian plonk (p. 43) may suggest not that it was merely a rustic brew made for local consumption only, but, as one historian has recently proposed, that they were over-stretching production to meet a larger market ('the old story of the sacrifice of quality to quantity'). Nor was it just the wine from Pompeii that had gained a reputation outside the area. Columella, a first-century writer on agriculture, particularly recommended the Pompeian onion, and Pliny described in some detail the Pompeian cabbage, warning those who might try to grow it that it cannot survive cold weather.

Archaeology, both on land and under water, can occasionally help us trace the produce of Pompeii around the Mediterranean and beyond – the pottery wine jars at least, which are virtually indestructible after 2000 years, even if not the cabbages. As early as the beginning of the first century BCE, probably before the foundation of the colony at Pompeii, wine was going from the Bay of Naples to southern France. So much is clear from one cargo boat that did not make it, but was wrecked off Anthéor, not far from Cannes. This was carrying wine jars with stoppers stamped, in Oscan script (hence the dating of the wreck), with a very rare name: Lassius. The only other Lassii we know in the Roman world are from Pompeii and nearby Surrentum (Sorrento), including a Pompeian priestess of the goddess Ceres, Lassia, whose tombstone has been discovered outside the city walls. The chances are that this wine was from Pompeii or thereabouts.

Other cargoes made it safely to their destination. These included Pompeian wine jars that ended up in Carthage in North Africa. Some of these were stamped with the name L. Eumachius. Whether he was the producer of the wine or merely the maker of the jars (the stamp could indicate either), he was very likely the father of another Pompeian priestess, Eumachia, who is best known for sponsoring one of the large public buildings in the Forum which now takes her name, the Building of Eumachia. Other Pompeian wine jars, some stamped by the same Eumachius, have turned up in France and Spain, as well as in other parts of Italy. One has even been found in Stanmore in Middlesex. But before we leap to the appealing conclusion that there was a brisk market for Pompeian wine in Roman Britain, we should remember that one solitary *amphora* does not necessarily indicate a major trade route. In any case, these jars were too good and sturdy for single use, and they were often reused over years, if not decades. The jar found at Stanmore might have originally been made in Pompeii, but not necessarily its final contents.

There was plenty of trade in the other direction too. If Pompeii could in theory have supplied its needs entirely from the surrounding territory, it certainly did not choose to do so – or, at least, not by its later years. The pottery jars for wine and other foodstuffs tell a clear story of imports on a relatively large scale. Many of these came from not so distant parts of Italy. Richer Pompeians, for example, enjoyed Falernian wine, one of the classiest *premier crus* of the Roman world, produced some 80 kilometres to the north of the city. But there were imports from further afield too. In the House of the Menander some seventy *amphorae* and other jars were discovered, many still bearing indications of their contents and place of origin. True, there were some very local products: a couple bore Eumachius' stamp, another couple had contained wine from Surrentum and one, much smaller, local honey. But some had brought olive oil or fish sauce from Spain, others were from Crete, and at least one came from Rhodes and was billed as containing *passum*, a special variety of sweet wine made out of raisins, rather than fresh grapes. Roughly the same picture emerges from the store of *amphorae*, some full, some empty, in the run-down House of Amarantus. Probably a mixture of first-, second-, or third-hand containers, they included a substantial number that had originated in Crete (thirty, apparently full, which must have been a recent shipment), a couple from Greece, and one – a rare specimen – from the city of Gaza which, in a poignant contrast to its present state, was to become one of the most celebrated and profitable centres of wine production in the early Middle Ages.

The import business dealt in more than the contents of *amphorae* and other jars, whether wine, olive oil or *garum*. We have seen how microscopic analysis has brought to light the remains of exotic herbs and spices (see p. 37). But other sorts of relatively indestructible materials, such as fancy Egyptian glassware and coloured marble, are even easier to trace. Ordinary ceramic tableware could also come from well outside the local area. In fact, one packing case containing some ninety new Gallic bowls and almost forty pottery lamps was found intact, presumably having arrived in the town too close to the eruption ever to have been unpacked. In this case, if archaeologists are right to say that the lamps were made not in Gaul, but in northern Italy, we must imagine that some kind of 'middleman' had been involved, packaging up a mixed consignment.

All in all, there can hardly be any doubt that, wherever exactly it was, and however small by comparison with the great trading centres of Puteoli or Rome, Pompeii's port must have been a thriving, international and multilingual little place.

City trades

Agriculture was not only an activity for the countryside outside the city. Current estimates are that within the city walls as much as 10 per cent of the land, even in the years leading up to the eruption, was in agricultural use; in earlier periods it would have been even more. Some of this was the home to animals, an underestimated part of the Pompeian population, largely because earlier generations of archaeologists tended to overlook animal bones. But even they did not miss the skeletons of two cows which were in the House of the Faun when the eruption came, and we shall be looking at another yet more dramatic discovery later in this chapter. There was plenty of cultivation too. We have already glimpsed a small 'kitchen garden' in the House of Julius Polybius, with a fig tree, and olive, lemon and other fruit trees. There were other cases of city cultivation on a much larger, more commercial scale.

On one piece of open ground near the Amphitheatre, once thought to be the burial ground for dead gladiators, or alternatively a cattle market, careful excavations in the 1960s revealed a closely planted vineyard (Fig. 13), with olive and other trees growing among the vines, and possibly vegetables too (or so it has been deduced from the discovery of a single carbonised bean). The vineyard covered about half a hectare, and the wine – several thousand litres of it – was not only produced on the spot (as the wine press and large *dolia* show), but was also retailed from a bar facing onto the Via dell'Abbondanza or served to customers dining at one of the two outdoor *triclinia* built at the edge of the property.

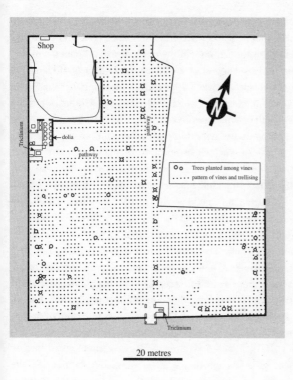

Figure 13. Plan of an excavated vineyard. Painstaking modern excavation has revealed the planting of this commercial vineyard (plus dining establishments) within the walls of the town. It was well positioned for different types of trade. On the north it faced onto the Via dell'Abbondanza; to the south, it would have been convenient for customers from the Amphitheatre.

And there were many other, smaller vineyards, orchards and vegetable gardens (stocked with those famous cabbages and onions, perhaps), all identified from the traces of root cavities, carbonised seeds, pollen and carefully laid-out beds and irrigation systems. In one garden, with a particularly elaborate watering arrangement, it seems as if flowers were being grown commercially – maybe, it has been argued from the quantity of glass jars and phials in the adjacent house, for the production of perfume. Some very recent work has found evidence of 'nurseries' which probably supplied the local gardeners with their herbaceous plants.

It should be no surprise, then, that so many pieces of agricultural equipment have been found in the city's houses: forks, hoes, spades, rakes and so on. Some of these were no doubt used by those who lived in the town but went out, day by day, to work on fields outside the walls. But others would have been for use on city-centre plots of land.

The overall impression, however, of a walk through Pompeii was not of a world of peaceful gardening or other pastoral pursuits. This was a bustling, commercial, market town. True, land and agriculture almost certainly remained the most significant basis of wealth throughout the city's history. Pompeii was not, as some modern fantasies have suggested, an ancient equivalent of Renaissance Florence, where economic success was built on manufacturing industries and political power was vested in the guilds which controlled those industries and in the financial wheeler-dealers who invested in them. The fullers and textile workers of ancient Pompeii were no driving force of economic power. The 'banker' Lucius Caecilius Jucundus, whose business we shall shortly be exploring, was no Cosimo de' Medici. That said, Pompeii provided a whole range of services, from laundry to lamp-making, and acted as a centre of exchange for a community of probably more than 30,000 people, country dwellers included.

This meant an infrastructure for buying and selling. The local council took care to regulate the standard of weights and measures used by traders. The official gauge had already been set up in the Forum in the second century BCE, following Oscan standards of measurement (Ill. 60). These standards were adjusted, as an inscription on it declares, at the end of the first century, to bring it into line with the Roman system – a change which, whatever the council's rulings, may have been as patchy, contested and politically loaded as the British change at the end of the last century from imperial measures (pounds and ounces) to metric (kilos and grams).

But the involvement of local government in the commercial life of the city went further than this. We have already seen the aediles assigning sales pitches to traders (p. 71). They may also have regulated the dates of markets. A very messy graffito on the outside of a large shop ('Lees of *garum* for sale, by the jar') lists a seven-day cycle of markets, based on days of the week much like our own: 'Saturn's day at Pompeii and Nuceria, Sun's day at Atella and Nola, Moon's day at Cumae ... etc.' This may reflect an official and regular commercial calendar, rather than just a one-off, one-week timetable. That, at least, is what most archaeologists have assumed, glossing over the fact that another graffito appears to put Cumae's market day on Sun's day and Pompeii's on Mercury's day. Either way, this seems evidence for some degree of official planning and attempted coordination.

It is likely too that the local council had control over the city's major communal, commercial buildings. These have been harder to identify than you might imagine. In fact, the question of what many of the large buildings that surrounded the Forum were actually used for is, despite many confident claims, one

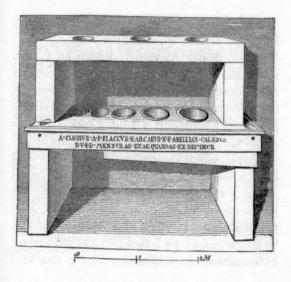

60. Cheats beware. An official gauge of measurements was established in the Forum. Originally it followed the old Oscan standard, but as the inscription on it declares, it was adjusted to conform to Roman standards in the first century BCE.

of the biggest puzzles of Pompeian archaeology. According to the currently favoured guesses, the long narrow building in the north-west corner of the Forum (half of which is modern reconstruction after the Allied *Blitzkrieg*) is some kind of market, perhaps for cereals. Opposite, at the north-east corner, stood the meat and fish market. For the first of these identifications there is no evidence whatsoever, apart from the fact that the official weight gauge is nearby. The second may be correct. But it depends on taking very seriously the fish scales found in the central area and playing down the possibly religious elements and the painted decoration which seems rather too elegant for a market (Ill. 61). Some archaeologists have preferred to see it as a shrine or temple – or (in the case of William Gell) a shrine-cum-restaurant.

Whatever the official involvement in local commerce, particularly striking is the sheer variety of trades and businesses carried on in the town. Today, just wandering through the streets, it is easy to spot the sturdy stone mills and the large bread ovens used by the bakers, or the vats and troughs used by the fullers in their textile processing. Meanwhile the cabinets of the Naples Museum are full of the tools and instruments of all kinds of crafts found in the excavation: from heavy-duty hatchets and saws, through scales to balances, plumb-bobs and pliers, to fine-tuned doctors' equipment (some of it, like the gynaecological *speculum* (Ill. 7), uncannily modern).

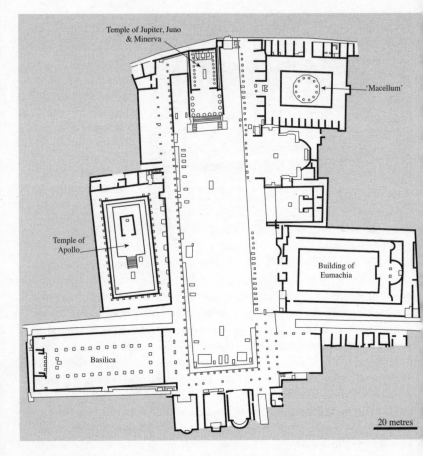

Figure 14. Plan of the Forum. The civic centre of Pompeii, but to this day the title and function of many buildings around the Forum remain unclear.

These can sometimes be neatly matched up with surviving trade or shop signs. One rough-and-ready plaque, for example, once attached to the outside of a workshop, seems to advertise the skills of 'Diogenes the builder' with images of his tools (plumb-bob, trowel, chisel, mallet), plus a phallus thrown in for good luck. They even occasionally turn up on tombstones, celebrating the dead man's craft. One Nicostratus Popidius, a surveyor, blazoned his instruments – measuring rods, stakes and the distinctive *groma*, or cross, used for laying out straight

61. In the nineteenth century, the paintings of the *macellum* were among the most admired in the whole town. This part of the decoration particularly captured the visitors' imagination, as the woman was identified as a female painter holding a palette. In fact she was carrying an offering dish, as used in sacrifices.

lines – on the memorial he commissioned for himself, his partner and their children. He had made his livelihood in one of the most characteristic of Roman professions, laying out plots of land, establishing boundaries between properties, advising on land disputes. This is just the kind of man who would have been in demand when Vespasian's agent Titus Suedius Clemens turned up in the town to investigate the problem of the state-owned land that had been illegally occupied by private owners.

Paintings and sculptures can bring these mute instruments of craft to life, or at least show them in use. We have already seen plenty of buying and selling going on (from bread to shoes) in the paintings of life in the Forum. Another celebrated series of tiny painted friezes from one of the entertainment rooms in the House of the Vettii shows some charming cupids (or kitsch, for those who would detect nouveau riche taste here) engaged in all kinds manufacturing activities. Some are busy at wine-making, others at fulling and perfumery. Some appear to be employed in the garland-making business (another commercial use for flowers). Others are producing jewellery and large bronze vessels in what seems to be a metal-working shop (Plate 20). This is an activity also vividly depicted on a marble plaque, which may once have been a shop sign, albeit a rather more elegant one than usual. It shows bronze- or coppersmiths at work – or so it would seem from the finished products on display in the background – focusing on three stages of the production process. On the left a man is weighing out the raw material on a large balance (and refusing to be distracted by junior, who is demanding

62. This sculpture nicely evokes the atmosphere of a metal workers' shop. In addition to the men at work, the scene is completed by a young child and a watching dog. Behind the finished products are on display.

attention behind). In the middle, one of the men is about to hammer the metal on an anvil, while another keeps it in place with a pair of tongs. On the right, a fourth craftsman is putting the final details on a large bowl. And you could want for no better illustration than this of the ubiquity of dogs in Pompeii. Although it looks disconcertingly like a platypus as it is rendered here, the creature crouched on a shelf above the head of the last worker can only be a guard-dog.

Plenty of written material, whether in graffiti or more formal notices and memorials, adds to the picture, or reminds us of occupations that have not left behind such distinctive traces. If you count up all those mentioned in this way (not including such well-known trades as potter or metal-worker not explicitly mentioned in writing), you get to more than fifty ways of making a living in Pompeii: from weaver to gem-cutter, from architect to pastry cook, from a barber to an ex-slave woman called Nigella, who is described on her tomb as a 'public pig-keeper' (*porcaria publica*). Apart from her, women are not mentioned in very great numbers, though they are found in sometimes unexpected contexts. One, named Faustilla, was what we would call a small-time pawnbroker. Three graffiti survive where her clients have written down what they borrowed, the interest they paid (running roughly at the rate of 3 per cent per month), and in two cases what they left as surety – a couple of cloaks and a pair of ear-rings.

It is much trickier to match up these trades to the remains on the site. It is only in a very few types of activity, such as baking or fulling, that permanent installations often allow us to locate a business with certainty. For most of the small commercial units lining the streets, without their furniture, fittings and equipment, there is only occasionally enough that is distinctive remaining to help us work out what was once made or sold inside. A graffito ('Tannery of Xulmus') has helped us identify a tannery, and reasonable guesswork has pinpointed the mat-weaver and cobbler. In any case, all kinds of trades would have been plied from what look like ordinary houses. Faustilla would hardly have needed an office. The home base of the painters (p. 125) can be identified only from the cupboard full of paints. And it would have taken only the addition of a couple more looms and slave girls to an atrium to turn weaving for domestic consumption into a commercial enterprise.

That said, there are even more curious gaps in our knowledge. To judge from the profusion of metal implements found all over the town, and the images on the marble plaque and in the paintings at the House of the Vettii, metal-working must have been big business in ancient Pompeii. But all kinds of puzzles remain. We have little idea how they got hold of the raw materials. And so far, apart from a handful of tentatively identified, small-scale workshops and retail outlets (one of which turned up the only known surviving example of a surveyor's *groma* from the ancient world), only one substantial forge has been discovered, outside the Vesuvius Gate. Perhaps, given the fire risks, this was largely an out-of-town trade. The same must be true of the pottery industry. For only two small potters' premises have been found within the walls, and one of those was a specialist lamp-maker.

For the rest of this chapter, we shall turn to explore just three examples of the commercial life of Pompeii where it is possible to match up the trade with the place – and, almost, with the face of the person concerned: a baker, a banker and a *garum* maker.

A baker

Between the House of the Painters at Work and the main thoroughfare of the Via dell'Abbondanza stood a large bakery that has only recently been completely uncovered. Bakers were a common sight on the streets of Pompeii. More than thirty baking establishments are known in the city. Some undertook the whole process of production: they milled the grain, baked the bread and sold it. Others, to judge from the absence of milling equipment, produced loaves from ready-prepared flour. Though there are some curious clusters (in one road just to the north-east of the Forum there were seven bakeries in just over 100 metres), they were found all over the city, so that no Pompeian was ever far from a bread supply. Besides, bread could also be sold in temporary street stalls and, no doubt, by home delivery on a donkey or mule (Ill. 25, 64).

This bakery on the Via dell'Abbondanza combined milling and baking – and, maybe, other entertainment functions (Fig. 15). It was a two-storey property, with a balcony across part of the frontage above the street. Unusually for Pompeii, considerable parts of the flooring of the upper level have been found and preserved just as it had collapsed into the rooms below – a triumph of archaeological conservation it is true, but a feature that makes it harder for any casual observer to work out the layout and appearance of the place as a whole. At the corner of the property was one of the many street or crossroads shrines we find in the city: a rough-and-ready altar perched on the pavement, with a painting of a religious sacrifice plastered on its outside wall above.

One door from the main street led into the bakery itself, the other (next to the altar) into a reasonably sized two-roomed shop. On the ground floor these appear to be entirely separate units, but the placing of the stairways to the upper floor suggests that the whole property interconnected above. It was all presumably under a single proprietor, even if we must imagine something other than bread being on sale in the shop (for, in that case, they would surely have made a direct connection between the retail unit and the place next door where the bread was made). There was also a side entrance leading into a stable from the alleyway that ran up from the Via dell'Abbondanza, between this complex and the large House of Caius Julius Polybius. This was the alleyway where, as we saw in Chapter 2, the cesspits collecting the latrine waste had been dug up and cleaned out just before the eruption, the piles of refuse still on the ground beside them.

Entering the bakery by the main door, you went into a large vestibule, from which one of several wooden staircases climbed to the upstairs rooms. To judge from the graffiti on the left-hand wall, consisting mostly of numerals, it was here

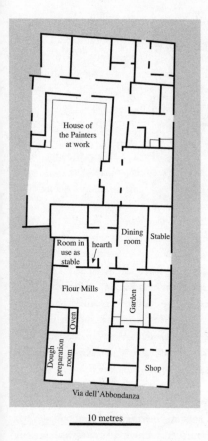

Figure 15. The Bakery of the Chaste Lovers. A commercial bakery doubling as a catering business. At least the dining room (*triclinium*) here is so large that it almost certainly was used by people other than the baker and his family. At the time of the eruption two rooms on the premises were in use as stables.

House of the Painters at work

Dining room

Stable

Room in use as stable

hearth

Flour Mills

Oven

Garden

Dough preparation room

Shop

Via dell'Abbondanza

10 metres

that some of the trade was carried out – checking out consignments of bread, or perhaps even selling it to customers. Any caller would certainly have been able to see and hear the baking at work, for the main oven – rather like a big wood-burning pizza oven in modern Italy – stood just a few metres further in (Ill. 63). On the left was the large room where the dough was prepared. A window had been inserted to bring some light from the outside onto the mixers and kneaders who mixed up the dough in large stone bowls or worked it into shape at a wooden table (the wood does not survive, but the masonry supports which carried it do). It must have been hot work, in a dingy environment. But there had been some attempt to brighten it up: on one wall there was a painting of a naked Venus,

63. The large bread oven from the Bakery of the Chaste Lovers. Somewhat dilapidated, it still shows the cracks caused by the earthquake of 62 and the tremors that no doubt preceded the eruption.

admiring herself in a mirror. It is hard not to think of a pin-up in a modern factory.

When the dough was ready and shaped into loaves, they passed it through a little hatch at the end of the room directly to the area in front of the oven. Occasionally, the individual maker might even have stamped his work. Several carbonised loaves have been found in Herculaneum, for example, imprinted with the words 'Made by Celer, the slave of Quintus Granius Verus' – and very likely some or most of the workers in our bakery would have been slaves too. From the other side of the hatch, the bread would have been loaded onto trays, baked, then removed for storage or sale.

This particular oven had seen better days. One large crack in its structure had been patched up and plastered over some time before the eruption – no doubt after the big earthquake of 62 CE. But further cracks had since appeared, probably thanks to the quakes and tremors in the days and weeks running up to the eruption, and repair work was underway throughout the property. The oven was probably still operating, though on a reduced scale. Sadly, there was no dramatic discovery here like the one made at another bakery in the mid nineteenth century. Eighty-one loaves were discovered still firmly shut in the oven, almost 2000 years overcooked. These are round in shape, and divided into eight sections, just as we sometimes see them in paintings (Ill. 64).

In the back part of this main room stood the flour mills. There were originally four of these, making this one of the larger bread-making establishments in the town. Pompeian mills followed the same standard plan, and were constructed out of stone quarried in northern Italy, near the modern town of Orvieto (a striking

64. A bread stall – or perhaps a free handout financed by some local bigwig. This nineteenth-century copy of the original painting gives a good idea of the kind of wooden furniture and fittings that would originally have been found in shops or outside stalls. Often now it is only the nails, here very visible in the planks of the counter, that survive.

65. A flour mill. It would have been fitted with wooden struts (inserted into the square hole) – to enable the millstone to be turned by slave or mule labour.

example of a specialised import, when presumably the local stone would have done an adequate, if not so good, job). It was a simple system in two parts (Ill. 65). Grain was poured into the upper, hollow stone, which was turned (using wooden struts and handles) against the fixed solid lower block – so as to grind the grain, which fell out as flour into the tray beneath. But at the time of the eruption in this bakery, only one of the mills was in working order with both its elements intact and in place. One of the upper pieces of the other mills had been smashed, and two were being used to hold the lime for the repairs and renovations that were going on.

How were the mills turned? By men or animals? Both are possible, but in this case we can be certain that the process was powered by mules, donkeys or small horses. The remains of two of these animals were actually discovered in the kneading room, where they must finally have been overwhelmed in an attempt to get out. Their stable had been, it seems, one of the rooms that opened into the milling area – a once much grander affair, with decent wall paintings, but later converted into an animal stall, complete with a manger. But these were not the only animals on the property. Five others were more securely penned up in another stable which opened onto the side alley. When first discovered, these were firmly identified – by traditional methods of bone classification – as four donkeys and a mule, of different ages ranging from four years to nine. More up-to-date analysis of the animals' DNA has shown, however, that two were either horses or mules (bred from a female horse and male donkey) and three either donkeys or hinnies (the offspring of a male horse and female donkey). Animal recognition across the centuries is obviously harder than an amateur might imagine.

The skeletons of these animals in the second stable still remain exactly where they were found (Ill. 66), and one day when this property is finally opened to the public they will make a ghoulish display. But they have offered all kinds of glimpses into the life of the bakery and the world of Pompeii more generally. For a start, this number of animals makes it fairly certain that the reduced scale of the operations in the bakery was intended to be only temporary. You would not, after all, have hung on to seven of them, with all the expense of their upkeep, if you were permanently downsizing to a single mill. It also suggests that they were being used both for grinding the grain and for delivering the finished bread. And, unless the absence of any sign of a cart is to be explained by the fact that it had been used by the human occupants in their own escape bid, then they carried out these deliveries laden with baskets or panniers.

But more than this, the careful excavation of the stable has produced the first good evidence we have about the living conditions of the four- rather than two-legged residents of the town. The floor was hard, made out of a mixture of rubble and cement. Some light and air came in from a window looking onto the alley. A wooden manger ran down the long side, and there had been a drinking trough, though this seems to have collapsed before the eruption. The position of two of them suggests that they were tethered to the manger, though one was certainly untethered, or had broken free, for it seems to have been trying to escape through the alleyway door. They were living on a diet of oats and broad beans, which were stored in a loft above the stable. In other words, nothing was much different from how it would be today.

This bakery has sprung one further surprise. For the most part its other rooms are of modest size and decoration, and they presumably housed the baker, his family and slaves, upstairs and down. There was a small internal garden, which also functioned as a light well in what must otherwise have been a fairly dingy atmosphere – and where the slightly mangled remains of an ancient Roman fly were discovered (its exact species is still a matter of debate). And on the kitchen hearth the remains of a last meal were found: a bird of some sort and part of a wild boar had been left cooking. But the real surprise is the oversized and richly decorated dining room, with a large window looking onto the garden. Though out of commission at the time of the eruption (to judge from the pile of lime

66. This victim of the eruption reminds us how important animals were in the various trades of the town – driving machinery and delivering goods. They must also have contributed considerably to the dirt in the streets.

found there), it was painted with a series of alternating red and black panels, featuring at the centre of each of the three main walls a scene of drinking and banqueting, and couples reclining in each other's arms (Plate 10). Compared with some Pompeian scenes of riotous sex, these seem rather decorous expressions of passion, and they have given the place its modern name: House of the Chaste Lovers.

Why such a large *triclinium* in this modest bakery? Possibly, it was the baker's one extravagance. But more likely it was another way in which he made money. Though not a restaurant in the modern sense of the word, this was probably a place where people paid to eat – with food either cooked in the kitchen adjacent or brought in from outside. It was not exactly glamorous surroundings. You would have reached the dining room either via the stable or by going past the bread oven and flour mills. But the room's decor was elegant enough, and it could certainly have accommodated more people than could easily be squeezed into the average living quarters of the poor. It was probably not the only such arrangement in the town. In another house, a similarly oversized dining room is found together with a suspiciously large number of graffiti celebrating the fullers. Could this be, as some archaeologists have guessed, the place that the fullers hired for their communal evenings out?

When not in the midst of repairs, our baker was producing bread on a relatively large scale, and supplementing his income with a catering trade. Who he was, we do not know. We can, however, put a name to the next Pompeian tradesman we shall investigate: the 'banker' Lucius Caecilius Jucundus.

A banker

One of the most extraordinary discoveries in the history of the excavations of Pompeii was made in July 1875: 153 documents which had been stored away in a wooden box in the upper storey of the house now known as the House of Caecilius Jucundus. The main text in each case had originally been scratched into a wax coating over a wooden tablet, about 10 by 12 centimetres (often joined together to form a three-page document, with a summary in ink occasionally written directly onto the wood on the outer faces). The wax, needless to say, has disappeared, but the text remains legible, or partly so, because the metal writing tool or stylus had actually gone through the coating to mark the wood underneath.

All but one of the documents record financial transactions involving Lucius Caecilius Jucundus, between 27 CE and January 62 CE, just before the earthquake. The exception, the earliest text dated to 15 CE, involves a man called Lucius Caecilius Felix, who is probably Jucundus' father or uncle. Most of the documents are to do with auctions that Jucundus has conducted: receipts in which the sellers of the goods concerned formally declare that Jucundus has paid what was due (i.e. the money raised by the sale, minus his own commission and other costs). Sixteen documents, however, deal with various contracts that Jucundus has with the local town council. We now tend to call Jucundus a 'banker', but the modern sense of that term hardly captures Jucundus' role. He was a characteristically Roman combination of auctioneer, middleman and moneylender. He was, in fact, as the tablets make clear, profiting from both sides of the auction process – not only charging commission to the sellers, but also lending money at interest to the buyers to enable them to finance their purchases.

For the history of the Pompeian economy, these documents are a goldmine. They allow us to take a first-hand look at one Pompeian's financial dealings – at what was being bought and sold, when and for how much. Besides, as the documents were witnessed by up to ten witnesses, they offer the most comprehensive

67. The tablets of Jucundus were originally fixed together in several leaves, the writing on the wax inside protected by the outer faces. This made them relatively easy to keep safe as a record of the transactions.

register of Pompeian people that we have. Yet some words of warning are in order too. We do not know why the documents had been kept, what proportion of Jucundus' business dealings between 27 and 62 they represented, or why these had been selected for keeping. Why for example the single document relating to Felix? Had it simply been kept for sentimental reasons as a memento of Jucundus' predecessor? Why do the auction records cluster in the years 54–8, when the man had been in business since 27? And why do they stop in 62? Did he die in the earthquake as some modern scholars have wondered? Or were the more recent documents stored somewhere more convenient, not stashed away in the attic? One thing is certain. We do not have a complete picture of Jucundus' activities for any period. What we have is only a selection of his filing cabinet, perhaps at random, or at least made on principles we cannot now reconstruct.

That said, it is wonderfully vivid material. The one document relating to Caecilius Felix concerns final payment for a mule auctioned by Felix for 520 *sesterces* – and it is the key piece of evidence for the price of such animals in Pompeii. Here both seller and buyer were ex-slaves, and the buyer's proceeds were not handed over to him by Felix himself, but by one of his slaves. Everything was sealed and dated, following the standard Roman system of calling the year after the two consuls in office at Rome itself:

The sum of 520 *sesterces* for a mule sold to Marcus Pomponius Nico, previously slave of Marcus: money which Marcus Cerrinius Euphrates is said to have received according to the terms of the contract with Lucius Caecilius Felix. The aforementioned sum Marcus Cerrinius Euphrates, previously slave of Marcus, declared that he had received, paid down, from Philadelphus, slave of Caecilius Felix. (Sealed).

Transacted at Pompeii, on the fifth day before the kalends of June [28 May], in the consulship of Drusus Caesar and Gaius Norbanus Flaccus [15 CE]

The auction records of Jucundus himself do not always specify exactly what had been bought and sold. In most cases they refer simply to 'the auction of', with the name of the seller. But we do find him on a couple of occasions referring to the sale of slaves. In December 56 CE, a woman called Umbricia Antiochis received 6252 *sesterces* after the sale of her slave Trophimus. This particular slave was obviously a valuable commodity, raising more than four times as much as another slave who was sold for just over 1500 *sesterces* a couple of years earlier. To see this as roughly three times the cost of that mule is an unsettling reminder of the 'commodification' of human beings that lay at the heart of Roman slavery, for all the expectations of eventual freedom that a Roman slave might have. Jucundus is also known to have sold some 'boxwood' (a wood commonly used for writing tablets – but not these, which are of pine) for almost 2000 *sesterces*, and a quantity of linen, the property of one 'Ptolemy, son of Masyllus, of Alexandria'; this is another nice example of an import from overseas and of a foreign trader, though sadly the price raised does not survive.

In general, Jucundus is neither dealing in very large amounts of money nor operating at the very bottom of the range. The largest sum raised at any of his recorded auctions is 38,079 *sesterces*. Whatever the objects of this sale were (it appears simply as 'the auction of Marcus Lucretius Lerus'), they went for more than five times the likely annual turnover of the smallholding we looked at earlier in this chapter. Yet across the archive as a whole there were only three payments over 20,000 *sesterces*, just as there were only three under 1000. The median amount is around 4500 *sesterces*. Jucundus' commission seems to have varied. In two of the tablets it is stated to be 2 per cent. In most cases we can only guess from the final figure paid over to the seller what the likely commission had been – and that is sometimes as much as 7 per cent. Whether Jucundus would have become well off on this depends entirely on how many auctions he conducted, and for what value of goods.

But the auctions were not his sole source of income. The other set of sixteen documents concerns his business contracts with the town administration itself. As was usual in the Roman world, the local taxes of the city of Pompeii were farmed out for private contractors to collect (taking a profit themselves, of course). For part of his career, at least, Jucundus was involved in collecting at least two taxes: a market tax, probably levied on stallholders; and a grazing tax, probably levied on those who made use of publicly owned pasture land. Among his documents we find several receipts for these: 2520 *sesterces* per year for the market tax, 2765 for the grazing tax (sometimes paid in two instalments). He also rented, and presumably worked or sublet, properties that were in public ownership. One was a farm, at an annual rental of 6000 *sesterces*. This rent seems to have been at the limit of what Jucundus could afford – at least if cashflow, rather than inefficiency, was the cause of him being in arrears from time to time. The other was a fullery (*fullonica*), for which he had to find 1652 *sesterces* per year.

It is striking to see here again the economic role of the local government, not merely raising taxes but also owning property in the town and surrounding countryside, which was then rented out for profit. An 'ancestral farm', as the documents describe it, is perhaps not surprising. But quite how the city came to own a fullery is a mystery. So much of a mystery, in fact, that some historians have suspected that *fullonica* here does not mean 'fullery', but a 'tax on fulling'. This was, in other words, another of Jucundus' tax-collecting businesses, not evidence of his further diversification into the textile and laundry trade. Who knows? But whatever the details of these and other properties (Jucundus can hardly have been the city's only tenant), the tablets do give us a clue about the organisation of these affairs from the city's side. The documents show that this day-to-day management of the public assets of the town was not in the hands of an elected official from the city's elite, but of a public slave – or as the documents sometimes officially entitle him, a 'slave of the colonists of the *colonia Veneria Cornelia*'. Two of these are mentioned in Jucundus' tablets: the first was called Secundus, who received the farm rental in 53 CE; he was presumably replaced by Privatus, who received all the later payments.

Together, the buyers and sellers, the servants and officials, and (most numerous of all) the witnesses listed give us the names of some 400 residents of Pompeii around the middle of the first century CE. These range from the public slaves to Cnaius Alleius Nigidius Maius, one of the leading members of the local political elite and owner of the large property for rent we explored in Chapter 3, who turns up as a witness to one of Jucundus' auction documents. Even a quick glance at the archive shows the concern with status that underpinned social and business relations all over the Roman world. When they appear in the documents, the slaves are clearly referred to as slaves, with the name of their owners specified; likewise the ex-slaves. Not so obvious at first sight is the ordering of the lists of witnesses. But careful recent analysis has shown without much doubt that on each occasion the witnesses' names were recorded in order of their social prestige. In the one list in which Nigidius Maius occurs, for example, he takes first place. On two occasions, those nice calibrations of order were disputed, or at least had to be revised. In two lists, the writer had taken the trouble to rub out (or more correctly scrape out) a name and change the hierarchy.

Nonetheless, for all their emphasis on rank, the tablets suggest a mixed society of buying and selling, borrowing and lending, at Pompeii. Bottom of the list though they may have been, ex-slaves were acting as witnesses to the same transactions as members of the oldest, and most elite, families in the town. Women were in evidence too. They did not act as witnesses. But out of the 115 other names preserved on the tablets, fourteen are women's. They are all sellers at auction (one the seller of the slave, Trophimus). This is not a large proportion of course, but it still suggests that women were more 'visible' in the commercial life of the early Roman empire than some of the gloomier modern accounts of their role and standing would have us believe.

Of Caecilius Jucundus himself we know relatively little apart from what is in the documents. The usual assumption (and it is not much more than that) is that he was the descendant of a slave family, though freeborn himself. We do not know where his auctions took place, or whether he operated from an 'office' separate from his house. That house, however, can tell us a little more. It was large and richly painted, which are the clearest signs that his business was profitable. The decoration included a large wild-animal hunt on the garden wall, long faded beyond recognition; a painting of a couple making love, now in the Secret Cabinet of the Naples Museum, but once in the colonnade of the peristyle (a touching or slightly vulgar display, depending on your point of view); an implausibly benign guard dog rendered in mosaic by the front door; and those famous marble relief panels which appear to depict the earthquake of 62 (Ill. 5).

It is just possible too that we have a portrait of him. In the atrium of the house, two squared pillars (or herms) were found, of a type commonly used in the Roman world to support marble or bronze portrait heads. In the case of male portraits, genitals would be attached half way down the herm, making what is, to be honest, a rather odd ensemble. On one of these pillars genitals and bronze head survived – a highly individualised portrait of a man, with thinning hair and a prominent wart on his left cheek (Ill. 68). Both pillars carry exactly the same inscription: 'Felix, ex-slave, set this up to the our Lucius'. What the exact relationship was between this Felix and Lucius and the Lucius Caecilius Felix and Lucius Caecilius Jucundus of the tablets we do not know. The Felix on the herm might be the banker, or he might be an ex-slave of the family with the same name. The Lucius Caecilius Jucundus of the tablets might have nothing to do with this statue at all. But, although archaeologists sometimes insist on grounds of style that the portrait must be earlier than the middle of the first century CE, it is not completely inconceivable that this down-to-earth-looking character is none other than our auctioneer, middle-man and moneylender.

The tablets of Caecilius Jucundus are not the only such written records to be found in the town. In 1959 just outside Pompeii, another large cache of documents from the first century CE were discovered. They detailed all kinds of legal and business transactions at the port of Puteoli – contracts, loans, IOUs and guarantees – involving a Puteolan family of 'bankers', the Sulpicii. How the tablets ended up near Pompeii, some 40 kilometres away from Puteoli across the Bay of Naples, we can only guess.

One particularly intriguing find from Pompeii itself is a couple of wax tablets discovered stashed away with some silverware in the furnace of a set of baths. These record a loan from one woman, Dicidia Margaris, to another, Poppaea Note, an ex-slave. As guarantee of her loan Poppaea Note handed over two of her own slaves, 'Simplex and Petrinus or whatever names they go under'. If she did not repay the loan by 1 November following, then Dicidia Margaris was allowed to sell the slaves to recover the money 'on the ides [13th] of December ... in the Forum at Pompeii in broad daylight'. Careful arrangements were stipulated in case the slaves were to raise more or less than the sum owed. Again, it is striking to see a business arrangement between two women (though in this case Dicidia Margaris is represented by her male guardian). It is striking also to see slaves parcelled up, as it were, and handed over as living surety. But more curious is the date of the document. These arrangements were dated 61 CE, but the tablets were obviously still thought important enough to be hidden away for safe-keeping along with the family silver, eighteen years later. Why? Was there perhaps still some on-going dispute about the repayment of the loan, or the sale of the slaves – and one of the women thought they might still need the written agreement?

Inevitably, this raises the question of the levels and uses of literacy in Pompeii. It is very easy to get the impression that the city was a highly literate, even cultured place. More than 10,000 pieces of writing, most in Latin, but some in Greek

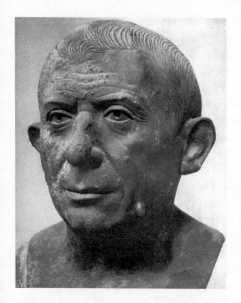

68. Found in the House of
Caecilius Jucundus, this bronze
portrait may be the banker himself
or perhaps, more likely, one of his
extended family or ancestors.
Either way, it is a vivid image of a
middle-aged Pompeian, warts and
all.

or Oscan, and at least one in Hebrew, have been recorded there. Election posters,
graffiti and all kinds of notices – price lists, advertisements for gladiatorial games,
shop signs – cover the walls. Much of the graffiti is of a familiar kind, from pleas
for help ('A bronze jar has gone from this shop. Reward of 65 *sesterces* for anyone
returning it') to laddish boasts ('Here I fucked loads of girls'). But some of it
conveys a more highbrow impression. We find, for example, over fifty quotations
or adaptations from well-known classics of Latin literature, including lines of
Virgil, Propertius, Ovid, Lucretius and Seneca, not to mention a snatch of
Homer's *Iliad* (in Greek). There are also many other snatches of poetry, either
original compositions from some Pompeian versifier or part of a more popular
repertoire.

Modern students of Latin who have been puzzled by that strange genre of
Roman love poetry, which imagines the lover locked outside his girlfriend's house,
addressing his words of anguish to the closed door, will be amused to find just
such a poem in Pompeii, actually written up in a doorway:

Would I might hold around your neck my arms entwined
And place kisses on your lovely lips … etc.

Critics have judged it a rather feeble poetic effort, probably a compilation of various misremembered lines of verse into a not entirely satisfactory whole. They have, moreover, found it hard to decide whether to take literally (or as further evidence of a botched job) the fact that the poem appears to be written *by* a woman *to* a woman.

The recent fashion among historians and archaeologists has been to pour a good measure of cold water on the idea that, appealing and evocative though this material is, it demonstrates widespread literacy and high cultural aspirations among the populace in Pompeii. The snippets from the great works of literature make a strong impression at first sight. But if you look at them more closely you find that they tend to cluster suspiciously around the beginnings of works, or their most famous one-liners. So, for example, twenty-six of the thirty-six quotations from Virgil's *Aeneid* are the first words of either the first or second book of the poem (and four more are the first words of the seventh or eighth books). This looks more like a familiarity with famous sayings than evidence of serious literary knowledge. The ability to scrawl on the walls '*Arma virumque cano ...*' ('Arms and the man, I sing ...', *Aeneid*, 1, 1) no more indicates close acquaintance with the text of Virgil than 'To be or not to be' indicates close acquaintance with Shakespeare.

There have also been doubts raised about quite how far below the elite the ability to read and write extended. It may be convenient to imagine that crude graffiti about sexual exploits were the work of the poorer and less cultured members of Pompeian society. But, in fact, there is no reason whatsoever to suppose that the upper echelons of the town were beyond boasting about their conquests (and, for what it's worth, one of the quotations from the *Aeneid* was actually found in the brothel). It has also been pointed out that many of the graffiti were not street writing at all, but were found on the inside walls of houses – rich houses at that, and not always very high up the wall. They were not written then by the average streetwalker, but by the members of wealthy families, and sometimes (to judge from the height) by the children.

These are all important warnings against taking the literate veneer of Pompeii too much at face value. Yet to argue, as is now often done, that the ability to read and write did not extend much beyond the members of the town council, the rest of the male elite and a few trades- or craftsmen is not necessarily correct. The key here is not the graffiti, even though they are so appealing. Many of those may indeed have been scratched by wealthy kids. Nor is it in the election notices, which few people may have read or taken notice of. The key rather is the kind of documents we find in the dossier of Jucundus, or the carefully pre-served loan agreement between Poppaea Note and Dicidia Margaris or the labels on the wine *amphorae*, recording where the stuff had come from and where it was to be delivered. From these it is clear that for many people well below the level of the wealthy inhabitants reading and writing must have been integral to the way they organised their lives, and to their ability to do their jobs and earn their living.

The garum *maker*

It is from the labels painted on various shapes and sizes of pottery containers, as well as from the mosaics in his atrium, that we can trace the *garum* business of Aulus Umbricius Scaurus and his family. Fish sauce was a staple of Roman cuisine and could be used as a condiment with almost everything. On the best, most optimistic interpretation, it may have been something similar to modern Far-Eastern sauces made from fermented fish (*nuoc-mam* from Vietnam, or *nam-pla* from Thailand). Alternatively it might have been a truly stinking concoction of rotten, salted seafood. The Romans seem to have shared our ambivalence about the product. In one squib, the first-century satirist Martial enjoys a laugh at a man called (ironically enough) Flaccus, who managed to get an erection even after his girlfriend had eaten six portions of *garum*. Elsewhere the same poet refers, appar-ently seriously, to the same substance as 'noble' or 'lordly'. In general, there are plenty of ancient references to its pungent smell, like it or not.

The process of manufacture mixed together pieces of seafood with salt and left it in a vat for a couple of months to ferment in the sun (in the kosher version (pp. 23–4), the maker presumably took particular care about exactly which pieces of seafood went into the mixture). Various different varieties of sauce were the result. The clear liquid that came to the top after the fermentation was the *garum* – though we do not know how that differed from the other term, *liquamen*, which is used. What was left in the bottom of the vats was *allec*, or sediment or lees, which could also be used in cooking. A brine known as *muria* was another side product. This main part of the manufacturing must have been carried out at Pompeii, for Pliny claims that the town was well known for its *garum*. But there is no sign of the equipment needed in the town itself. It was presumably done in large salt pans outside the city, near the coast. The *garum* shop within the city was concerned with distribution rather than production. The sauce was stored in bulk in six large *dolia*, then decanted – for sale at the front of the shop – into *amphorae* and other smaller vessels. Traces of *allec*, in the form of anchovy bones, have survived in the *dolia*.

Umbricius Scaurus and his family certainly marketed, and probably made, all the various forms of fish sauce, carefully distinguished by the labels of the jars. These boasted of their top quality products with the usual hyperbole of a sales pitch: not just 'best fish sauce' (*liquaminis flos*), but 'premium best fish sauce' (*liquaminis flos optimus*) or 'absolutely the best fish sauce' (*liquaminis floris flos*); they also made a point of their pure-mackerel versions of *garum*, which were the most highly regarded by connoisseurs of this stuff. But the labels also give us a hint of the structure of trade and business connections that this family had. For some state clearly that the product was 'from the manufactory of Scaurus'. Others refer, for example, to 'the manufactory of Aulus Umbricius Abascantus' or 'the manufactory of Aulus Umbricius Agathopus'. These names suggest that the men in question had been slaves of Umbricius Scaurus and were now running workshops or other *garum* outlets that were still partly dependent on their old master. Other labels show that the Umbricii Scauri had other strings to their bow. One implies that they were also importing *garum* from Spain (the Roman world's biggest mass producer of fish sauce) for resale in Pompeii.

What is extraordinary about this *garum* business is the scale of the profit involved. The vast majority of the many trades and shops in Pompeii were small-scale and for most of those involved the profits would have been similarly modest, enough to survive and a little bit more. The amount of cash found with the corpses, or left (as it were) in the till, confirms this. It rarely goes above 1000 *sesterces*. But the size of the house and the quantity of his products surviving suggest that a small fortune was at stake. So far as we can tell, this family was not active or prominent in Pompeii before the first century CE. By the middle of the first century, Aulus Umbricius Scaurus had become rich on *garum* and his son of the same name had reached one of the highest offices in the local government of the town, as one of the two annual *duoviri*. He died early, before his father, and is commemorated in a memorial outside the Herculaneum Gate:

In memory of Aulus Umbricius Scaurus, son of Aulus, of the Menenian tribe, *duumvir* with judicial power. The town council voted the land for this monument and 2000 *sesterces* for his funeral and a statue on horseback to be put up in the Forum. His father Scaurus erected this to his son.

This is not quite the lavish funding that they made available for the funeral of

Marcus Obellius Firmus (pp. 3–4) at about the same time. But these are still grand honours being given to one of the most prominent men in the town. We should note, though, that if we did not have other evidence about the commercial activities of this family, we would never have guessed from the tombstone that the Umbricii Scauri were nouveaux riches, who had made their fortune out of rotten fish.

This is one of the reasons why it is so hard to get to the bottom of the Roman economy and who, or what, made it tick.

CHAPTER SIX

WHO RAN THE CITY?

Vote, vote, vote

The younger Aulus Umbricius Scaurus had done as well in the local politics of Pompeii as anyone might reasonably hope. He had been elected by his fellow citizens to serve for a year as one of the pair of *duoviri*, the 'two men' who were the most senior officials in the town. Although his tombstone does not mention it, he must earlier have been elected to the other annual office of 'aedile' (*aedilis*). For that junior position not only gave a man almost automatic entry to the local town council (the *ordo* of decurions) for life, but also allowed him to stand for the higher office. No one, in other words, could be *duumvir* (the correct singular form of *duoviri*) without having been an aedile first. Only one position in the town was more prestigious than that of the regular *duoviri*. Every five years the *duoviri* had the extra task of enrolling the new members of the council and updating the list of local citizens, a responsibility reflected in the special title *duoviri quinquennales*. These men were the really big figures in the town. One, whom we shall meet later in this chapter, had been *duumvir* five times, including two stints as *quinquennalis*. Successful as he was, Umbricius Scaurus had not reached those heights.

The flavour of these annual Pompeian elections is vividly captured in the election posters, more than 2500 of them, painted in clear letters, red or black. These cover the outer walls of some houses, one overlapping the other, as the notices for each new year's campaign were painted over those of the last. They cluster, unsurprisingly, on the main thoroughfares of the town, where they were likely to be spotted by the most people. But they are also to be found on tomb façades, even occasionally on the inside of large properties – such as the House of Julius Polybius, where there is a notice inside (as well as on the façade) urging support for Caius Julius Polybius to become *duumvir*.

The notices conform to a fairly standard pattern. They give the name of the candidate and the position he seeks, aedile or *duumvir* (or they may even give the names of two candidates, who presumably had done a deal to run together as a team). They often, but not always, identify his supporters, and perhaps some reason for supporting him. 'Please elect Popidius Secundus as aedile, an excellent young man' or 'Africanus and Victor are canvassing for Marcus Cerrenius to be aedile' is the typical format. Occasionally, they even make a direct appeal to some potential voter: 'Please elect Lucius Popidius Ampliatus, the son of Lucius, as aedile – that means you Trebius and Soterichus'.

From time to time they give the names of the signwriters too, for it seems that the painting of these notices was an expert job. Altogether we have the names of almost thirty of these skilled propagandists, who no doubt sold their services for a fee. They were not full-time workers, of course. One member of a signwriting team identifies himself by his dayjob, as a fuller ('Mustius, the fuller, did the whitewashing'). These men sometimes seem to have had a local 'patch'. Aemilius Celer, for example, whom we spotted (p. 79) painting up an advertisement for a gladiatorial display 'on his own by the light of the moon', is found signing election notices, clustered in an area in the north of the city close to where he himself lived (to judge from another sign reading 'Aemilius Celer lives here'). On one notice, urging support for Lucius Statius Receptus as *duumvir*, he signed off as 'Aemilius Celer, his neighbour, wrote this' and – obviously fearing that a rival group might turn up with a pot of paint or a handful of lime – he added this warning: 'If you meanly blot this out, I hope you catch something nasty'. How any of these men chose the bit of wall on which to display their slogans we can only guess. But it must usually have been with the tacit agreement, at least, of the owner of the property concerned. If not, the risk was that those carefully painted words would have been painted over by the next day.

Formulaic though the notices are, however, they do give all kinds of insights into the political life of Pompeii. The names of the supporters can tell their own occasionally curious story. Some appear to be simple personal recommendations, even if they were, likely as not, done at the gentle prompting of the candidate himself. A few appeal to Titus Suedius Clemens, the agent of the emperor Vespasian (pp. 48–9), who at one stage used his imperial position to influence (or meddle in) the town's local government. They pointedly declare their candidate 'backed by Suedius Clemens'. Others claim to speak for groups of the town's citizens. The fullers, for example, the millers, the chicken-keepers, the grape-pickers, the mat-makers, the ointment-sellers, the fishermen, and the Isis-wor-shippers are all found parading their support for a particular candidate. A few of these groups are more enigmatic. Who are the 'Campanienses' who canvas for Marcus Epidius Sabinus to be aedile? Or the 'Salinienses' supporting Marcus Cerrinius?

Here we are almost certainly getting a glimpse into the infrastructure of Pom-peian voting organisation. The usual Roman method of conducting elections was to divide the total electorate into sub-groups. Each of these groups would vote amongst themselves to record a single group choice, and the winning candidate was the one who won the support of the majority of the groups. This is a system often compared unfavourably, for its complexity, to the simple mass-meeting show-of-hands adopted by the ancient Athenian democracy, but it is in fact much like the electoral system used by most modern states. In all likelihood the Cam-panienses and Salinienses, together with the Forenses and Urbulanenses found in other notices, refer to four voting groups, based on particular districts of the town, named perhaps after different city gates (we have already seen (p. 20) that what we call the Herculaneum Gate was for the ancient inhabitants the Porta Salis or Saliniensis). There would have been voting districts in the surrounding coun-tryside too.

On the day of the election, we must imagine that the local citizens would have turned up in the Forum, divided into their different districts, returned their dis-trict vote and then acclaimed as winning candidates those who had secured the votes of the majority of the districts. Exactly how they voted is not so clear, but almost certainly by some form of secret ballot. One ingenious recent suggestion is that the main purpose of the closing devices, still visible at the entranceways to the Forum, was to keep out those not qualified to vote on election days.

All these voters were men. Leaving aside the occasional monarchy which pro-duced a queen or two, there was no city or state in the Greek or Roman world that gave women any formal political power. Nowhere did women have the vote. But one of the surprising facts about the electoral notices known in Pompeii is that more than fifty of them name a woman, or a group of women, as the candidate's backers. Does this demonstrate an active interest from women in a political process from which they were excluded? In some cases, yes – even if it was not always a narrowly political engagement that was at stake. Taedia Secunda, for example, who put her name to Lucius Popidius Secundus' attempt to win the office of aedile, was, as the electoral notice explicitly states, the man's grand-mother. On many other occasions family or personal loyalty must have been the reason for the women's support. Nonetheless, the simple fact that it was felt worthwhile to parade their backing is another indication of the *visibility* of women in public life at Pompeii.

But sometimes there might have been more to these slogans than at first meets the eye. Several women's names are found on the outside wall of a bar on the Via dell'Abbondanza lending their support to different candidates: they were Asel-lina, Aegle, Zmyrina and Maria. It is a fair guess that these were the women who worked as the barmaids inside (the single names, two of them, Aegle and Zmyrina, decidedly Greek in origin, suggest that they were slaves). Maybe they had their favourite candidates and commissioned the local signwriters to display these preferences. Or maybe there is a joke, or a bit of negative propaganda, going on here. Some street-corner satirist, or political opponent, has arranged the usual kind of election notices – but inserted the local barmaids' names as the supporters.

Whoever the sponsors behind these posters actually were, Caius Julius Poly-bius and his friends were certainly not pleased. For in the notice in which Zmyrina declares her support for 'C. I. P.' (Julius Polybius was a man so familiar that he could be abbreviated down to his initials) someone has come along later and carried out exactly the kind of defacement that Aemilius Celer had in mind when he threatened anyone who blotted out his handiwork with 'catching something nasty'. Or at least they have partly done so. For here just Zmyrina's name has been obliterated under a layer of lime, the rest left legible, as if the eager candi-date was concerned only to remove that dangerous hint of unsuitable support.

The parade of unsuitable support seems, in fact, to have been the way negative propaganda was delivered on more than one occasion in Pompeian elections. None of the posters we have found so far list the failings of a particular candi-date, or try to dissuade the electorate from casting their votes that way. But we do find some very odd supporters indeed. It may be that the poster which has 'the late drinkers' endorsing Marcus Cerrinius Vatia's campaign to become aedile was a friendly joke – a notice commissioned perhaps after one of their late-night drinking sessions. But it is hard to imagine that the support of 'the pickpockets', or 'the runaway slaves' or 'the idlers' was meant to be anything other than encour-agement to vote against.

What reasons do the supporters give for voting for their chosen candidates? If they are specified at all, these are mostly as formulaic as the notices themselves.

The favourite word, occurring time and time again, is *dignus* – meaning 'worthy' or 'suitable for office'. A more loaded term in Latin than in English, this has important connotations of public esteem and honour (it was, for example, to protect his *dignitas* that Julius Caesar crossed the Rubicon in 49 BCE and embarked on civil war against his rival, Pompey). But there is still very little in any of these posters that even hints at what action might win or justify such esteem, or make a successful aedile or *duumvir*. One graffito – not apparently an election notice, though it has long since disappeared – praised Marcus Casellius Marcellus as 'a good aedile and a great games-giver'. The few attempts to give some concrete reason for electoral support add up to little more than 'he brings good bread' (which may refer either to Caius Julius Polybius' qualities as a bakery owner or to some plans for a distribution of free bread) and 'he won't squander the city's money' (which may hint at Bruttius Balbus' economic prudence in local finances – or, more likely, at his willingness to be generous with his own cash in the public interest).

It is possible, of course, that all kinds of debates about city policy and politics went on amongst the electorate – over dinner, in the Forum or in the bars – that never made a mark on the standardised wording of these posters. Pompeii may have been an intensely political culture. But it is equally likely that for the men in the city, just as for the women, it was family connections, personal loyalty and friendship that were most at issue in choosing a candidate. Taedia Secunda is the only one to make a particular family relationship clear, but a number of the supporters identify themselves as the 'client' or 'neighbour' of the candidate concerned. This is still 'politics', of course, but with a very different flavour. Certainly, the role of the posters was more declaratory than persuasive. That is to say, they were intended to demonstrate support, rather than attempting to change the voters' minds with argument – a process which (on the reasonable assumption that Caius Julius Polybius did live in the house named after him) reaches its logical conclusion in the endorsement of a candidate inside his own house.

No poster has yet been found endorsing the election of young Aulus Umbricius Scaurus, either as aedile as *duumvir*. This is not too surprising because he probably held office a couple of decades before the eruption, even before the earthquake of 62. True, there are some election notices that survive from earlier periods in the town's history. A few even go back slightly before the formal establishment of the colony in 80 BCE and almost a dozen are written in Oscan. But the vast majority are, as you would expect, from the last years of the city's life, and later than the damage caused by the earthquake and the redecoration that it prompted. For this period, there are several candidates who appear in well over a hundred different notices. And this density of evidence has encouraged historians to try to draw even more detailed conclusions about Pompeian politics than what can be extracted from the wording itself.

Some of the most intricate pieces of research have tried to establish, first, a relative order to the electoral campaigns represented – and then, if possible, to work out a complete chronology of the Pompeian elections in its last decade or so. Who stood for what office in what year? The method that lies behind this is effectively an 'archaeology' of the painted surface of the walls, and it is helped by the fact that electoral notices were not washed off or otherwise removed once the particular campaign was finished, but simply covered over the next year with new versions for the new candidates. If you start with the topmost layer of painting, you find that the election notices for some candidates both survive in very large numbers and never appear to be painted over by others. It is logical to suppose that these were the candidates for office in the last elections that took place in 79 CE (probably in the spring, to take up office in July). If so, then the candidates for the post of aedile in the last year of the city's life were Marcus Sabellius Modestus, who seems to have been running with Cnaeus Helvius Sabinus, against Lucius Popidius Secundus and Caius Cuspius Pansa. The candidates for the office of *duumvir* were, on the same line of reasoning, Caius Gavius Rufus and Marcus Holconius Priscus.

Peeling back through the layers of posters, the next task is to determine which overlie which – and so which are later than others. From this it should be possible in theory to build up a chronology of candidates. This operation is much trickier than merely identifying the very latest candidates. As the walls decay and the paintings fade, it is not always easy to establish the precise relationship between different notices, not to mention the fact that co-ordinating the evidence from different parts of the city is very complicated indeed. There is no single list of candidates even for the 70s CE that has convinced everyone. That said, one thing is universally agreed: that there were many more candidates for election to aedile than to *duumvir*. In fact, on one reconstruction, between 71 and 79, there were only ever two men each year standing for the duovirate: only as many candidates as there were places, in other words.

If that were the case (and it certainly was in some years), then the purpose of the posters could not have been to persuade the voters to choose one candidate over another. At first sight, it also gives a gloomy impression of Pompeian democracy. That is to say, despite the appearance of a lively democratic culture, no choice was offered to the electorate in filling their major elected office. On reflection, things seem rather different. For since it was the rule in Pompeii (as in Roman towns in general) that no one could become *duumvir* without first having been aedile, and since only two aediles were elected each year, competition for the higher office would by definition be almost non-existent.

There was sometimes strong competition to become aedile: Cnaeus Helvius Sabinus, a candidate of 79, had made at least one previous and unsuccessful attempt to be elected, as we can tell from what must be earlier notices. There need only have been competition to become *duumvir* if more than two of those eligible were keen to hold the office in the same year – perhaps because they were particularly keen to be elected to the more prestigious post of *duumvir quinquennalis*, or because they wanted to hold the office more than once. In fact, unless every ex-aedile was available to be elected *duumvir* (and a few at least would have died in the intervening years, or moved away, or changed their minds about public office), then some men would have had to become *duumvir* more than once, simply in order to fill the slots. In other words, the competitive gateway to public office and prominence in Pompeii was the office of aedile.

The crucial fact to remember, however, in thinking about political life in Pompeii is that the number of electors was small. Suppose we return to the rough estimates of total population that I suggested in the last chapter: 12,000 in the town, 24,000 in the surrounding countryside. If we follow one very rough-and-ready rule of thumb commonly used in calculations like this, we can reckon that approximately half of those people would have been slaves. And of the remainder more than half must have been women and children, not entitled to vote. This means that in the town itself the electorate would have been something in the region of 2500, in the countryside round about, perhaps 5000. In other words, the voters resident in Pompeii itself were roughly the same in number as the pupils in a large British comprehensive school or US high school. The grand total, including those resident in the surrounding area, was less than half the student population of an average British university.

These comparisons give a useful sense of proportion. There has been much talk in recent discussions of Pompeian elections of the role of 'electoral agents' or of various means of 'marshalling support', and I myself have referred to 'propagandists' and more than once to an electoral 'campaign'. But all these expressions suggest a process on much too grand a scale and much too formally organised. Of course, all kinds of ideological controversies might have divided the Pompeian population, especially in that period when the colonists were imposed on the town after the Social War and we have hints of various kinds of internal tension (pp. 42–3). But it is hard to resist the likely conclusion (as the election posters themselves suggest) that in the final years of the city's life most elections were conducted as an extension of family, friendship and other personal relationships. It is often asked how in a community like Pompeii, with no sign of any official way of proving one's identity or right to vote, participation in the elections was policed. How, for example, did they stop slaves or foreigners turning up and usurping political rights? The answer is very simple. By the time the few thousand voters had arrived at the Forum, been let through the barrier and divided into their various voting districts, any interloper would have been easily spotted. These were people who knew each other.

The burdens of office?

Size is not the only factor in understanding the political culture of Pompeii. There is also the question of the degree of autonomy the town enjoyed and the type of decisions that fell to the local community. In Pompeii, the male citizens came together to elect their aediles and *duoviri*. The assembly of citizens had no other functions than that (any wider powers they once held in the pre-Roman period had been lost when the town became a Roman colony). Indirectly, though, since the aediles were drafted into the local council or *ordo*, the assembly also elected the council – or, as we shall soon see, the majority of it. But what did these elected officials do? What powers did they or the *ordo* have? Why might the electorate's choice matter? As a Roman town from the early first century BCE, Pompeii had no big decisions of peace and war or national policy to make. Those were made in the capital. But it was Roman practice to leave local communities to govern their own local affairs. So what exactly was at stake?

We have some evidence for this from the town itself. Surviving texts inscribed on tombstones, public buildings, or the bases of statues, but also Lucius Caecilius Jucundus' wax tablets and other less formal documents, record or refer to the actions and decisions of the local officials and the council. We have already seen the *ordo* deciding to bring the Pompeian system of weights and measures into line with Roman standards, and aediles assigning or confirming traders' sales pitches. We have also seen in the tablets of Jucundus that local taxes were raised, and that the town itself owned property which was rented out by the council and the elected officials, even if the day-to-day management was in the hands of a 'public

69. What went on in the Covered Theatre? This nineteenth-century fantasy of music and dance is a very bad guide to the kind of performances that were presented. But it does give some idea of how the now open-air theatre would have appeared when its roof was in place.

slave'. The titles of the two main Pompeian offices also give a clear indication of the nature of some of the duties involved. The '*duoviri* with judicial power' presumably handled matters of law. The aediles, to judge at least from the duties of the aediles in the city of Rome itself, would have been particularly concerned with the fabric of the city, buildings and roads. In fact, they are occasionally referred to not as aediles, but as '*duoviri* in charge of streets and of sacred and public buildings'.

Other activities are revealed in other texts. It is clear that the town council had the authority to decree that statues be erected to local notables or members of the imperial family. In other cases it might grant the land for such marks of honour: a private citizen could take the initiative and pay for a statue himself, but he would still need the *ordo*'s permission to set it up in public. The council likewise could assign money to pay for a public funeral for prominent members of the community, as well as a prestigious burial place. In the case of public buildings, the council would set the budget, then the *duoviri* would find the contractors and be responsible for approving the job at the end. This is the procedure referred to in an inscription set up at the entrance to the Covered Theatre (or 'Odeon'), which was built in the early years of the colony (Ill. 69): 'Caius Quinctius Valgus, son of Caius, and Marcus Porcius, son of Marcus, *duoviri*, by decision of the councillors, awarded the contract for building the Covered Theatre and likewise approved the work'. This was a tradition which went back before the Roman takeover of the city. As we have seen, the Oscan inscription on the sundial in one of the main town baths records that one of the town officials in the second century BCE, Maras Atinius, son of Maras (a good Oscan name), had set it up 'with the money raised from fines'.

The particular emphasis here on honorific statues, funerals and building work is perhaps misleading. It has a lot to do with the fact that much of the evidence we have comes from statue bases, tombstones and inscriptions on public buildings. But the underlying theme of donation, benefaction, and both public and private generosity is an important one. For it is clear that, whatever else they did, the elected officials were expected, even required, to give generously to the local community out of their own funds. The same pair of *duoviri* who saw to the construction of the Covered Theatre also built the Amphitheatre at their own expense 'and gave it to the colonists in perpetuity'.

On a more modest scale, though still a very substantial series of benefactions, the gifts made to the city by Aulus Clodius Flaccus in the early first century CE on each of the three occasions he was *duumvir* were recorded in detail on his tomb. The first time, he presented the games in honour of Apollo in the Forum – with a procession, bulls and bullfighters, boxers, musical shows and cabaret, including a well-known performer, Pylades, who is singled out by name. (This is another striking use for the Forum and – given those bulls – another reason for making sure that its entrances and exits could be secured.) The second time he held the office, as quinquennial *duumvir*, he presented more games in the Forum with much the same line-up, minus the music; and on the next day he showed 'athletes', gladiators and wild beasts (boars and bears) in the Amphitheatre, some paid for by himself alone, some with his colleague. The third time was either a less lavish display, or it was described more reticently on the tomb: 'with his colleague he gave games with a first-rate troupe and extra music'.

Games and spectacles, it seems, were the norm for this type of benefaction. Cnaeus Alleius Nigidius Maius put on a large gladiatorial display when he was quinquennial *duumvir* in the 50s, 'at no expense to the public purse', as one of the painted advertisements underlines. But building work might be substituted. A series of inscriptions in the Amphitheatre record the fact that various magistrates built sections of stone seating (probably to replace the original wooden versions), 'instead of games and lights, by decision of the councillors'. This implies that the *ordo* allowed them to spend the required money on upgrading the facilities, rather than on a show itself and on whatever 'lights' meant. Were some displays perhaps held at night, with the special lighting?

There was also a direct transfer of cash from *duumvir* or aedile to the public funds. Aulus Clodius Flaccus notes that 'for his [first] duumvirate, he gave 10,000 *sesterces* to the public account'. This was probably the fee that we know of elsewhere in the Roman empire usually paid by local officeholders and new members of the *ordo*. Taken altogether, these fees represented a significant part of any town's budget. Flaccus' heirs emphasised this particular payment no doubt, because they wanted to make clear that he had paid more than the going rate.

The underlying philosophy of local officeholding in the Roman world was quite different from our own. We expect local councillors to be compensated for the expenses they incur in the course of representing their community. The Romans expected men to pay for the privilege of being a member of the *ordo* or one of the elected officials: status came at a price. To put it another way, when the Pompeian voters were choosing between the different candidates for office, they were choosing between competing benefactors.

There is one document never found in the excavations that would have allowed us to fill in the details of the town's government, the duties of its officials and the regulations for its council. As a Roman colony, Pompeii would have had a formal constitution or charter (in Latin, *lex*), most likely inscribed on bronze and publicly displayed in a temple or other civic building. This has never come to light – perhaps it was rescued (or stolen) by salvage parties just after the eruption. In its absence, scholars have tried to fill in the picture of Pompeii's constitution from other such documents which have survived. The basic justification for doing this is that Roman legal provisions were for the most part applied even-handedly across the Roman world. What was laid down for a colony in, for example, Spain probably went for Pompeii too.

There is a good deal of truth in this argument (even though we tend to attribute far too much uniform consistency to the Romans in law as in much else). The surviving constitutions in some respects certainly match the practices we have seen in other sorts of evidence at Pompeii. One formal requirement in a Spanish charter is that the *duoviri* and aediles should present games, partly from their own money. In the legalese of the *lex*, it runs:

> Whoever shall be *duoviri*, except for those who shall be first appointed after this statute, they during their term of office are to organise a show or dramatic spectacle for Jupiter, Juno, Minerva and the gods and goddesses, during four days, for the greater part of the day, as far as shall be possible according to the decision of the council, and each one of them is to spend on that spectacle and on that show not less than 2000 *sesterces* from his own money, and it is to be lawful to take and spend out of public money up to 2000 *sesterces* for each *duumvir*, and it is to be lawful for them to do so without personal liability …

This is a typical piece of careful Roman drafting: note how they lay down explicitly that the shows should last 'for the greater part of the day' (there was to be no getting away with just a morning's worth). It is almost certain, to judge from the tombstone of Aulus Clodius Flaccus, that some very similar clause was included in the Pompeian constitution too.

The surviving constitutions remind us also of the kinds of issues that the Pompeian version must have covered. These range from particular questions of legal practice and procedures (what cases could be heard locally, or under what circumstances might they be referred to courts in Rome itself?) to arrangements for the timetabling of meetings of the *ordo* or rules on where councillors should live (the same Spanish constitution specifies a five-year residence requirement in the town or within a mile of it). But it is much harder to know exactly how closely any of the details would be reflected in the lost Pompeian document.

Another clause from the Spanish version lays out precisely what attendants each of the officials should have, and how much they should be paid. It is in the same formal legal style:

> Whoever shall be *duoviri*, there is to be the right and power for those *duoviri*, for each one of them, to have two lictors, one servant, two scribes, two messengers, a clerk, a crier, a *haruspex*, a flute-player ... And the fee for them, for each one of them, who shall serve the *duoviri*, is to be so much: for each scribe 1200 *sesterces*, for each servant 700 *sesterces*, for each lictor 600 *sesterces*, for each messenger 400 *sesterces*, for each clerk 300 *sesterces*, for each *haruspex* 500 *sesterces*, for a crier 300 *sesterces*.

This is not only carefully drafted. Note how the wording makes it absolutely clear that this is the staff which *each duumvir* will have (though, less carefully, the pay for the flute-player seems to have been omitted). It also offers a vivid glimpse into the role of a local official and how he might carry it out. The *haruspex* and flute-player hint at the religious duties of the *duumvir* (a *haruspex* would examine the entrails of sacrificed animals for signs from the gods (Chapter 9)). The scribes – by far the best paid – and the clerk imply that a good deal of writing was involved in the job, though the crier makes it clear that there were oral as well as written ways of transmitting information. The mention of lictors, attendants who in Rome itself carried the bundles of rods and an axe, the *fasces*, that were the symbol of official Roman authority, suggests that the *duoviri* were surrounded by a certain degree of pomp and ceremonial.

The question is, can we assume that the Pompeian *duoviri* enjoyed the services of the same or similar staff. They are certainly not prominent in the written evidence from the town – hardly extending beyond the single 'public slave' doing the city's business in the Jucundus tablets, and a group of four 'clerks' who sign their names on an inn wall. This does not prove that they did not exist. As the old archaeological cliché goes, 'absence of evidence is not evidence of absence'. All the same, it is hard not to suspect on the basis of what survives that the Pompeian *duoviri* worked with a more skeleton staff than some of their equivalents elsewhere. Certainly, if this was his entourage, the salary bill alone would have eaten up almost 75 per cent of what Aulus Clodius Flaccus paid when he entered office as *duumvir*.

70. A sketch reconstructing the interior of the Basilica in the Forum, an imposing building for a small town. The columns provided a convenient place for local graffiti artists to leave their messages.

But there is a more significant point here. For we must always remember that many of the confident claims of modern scholars about how local government worked in Pompeii are drawn not from the evidence found in, or about, the town itself, but from documents that refer to other – albeit similar – communities. Of course it may well be true, as it is so often stated, that the *ordo* at Pompeii was made up of a hundred members; or that the *duoviri* and aediles wore the *toga praetexta* (the toga with a purple border worn by senators in Rome itself). It is, however, a conjecture, based on what is known in other similar towns.

Perhaps the most intriguing gap in our knowledge of the way the city was run lies in the simple, day-to-day practicalities of Pompeian political life. What, for example, went on in a meeting of the *ordo* of decurions? How did a *duumvir* or aedile spend his day? Even simpler, where did formal political business take place? It is a reasonable assumption that most of it was conducted in the Forum, but exactly where we do not know. The three buildings at the southern end of the piazza are usually thought to be connected with the local government and are marked on many modern maps of the town as 'council chamber', 'government office' and 'archive' (Fig. 14). But the only evidence for this is their location, the fact that they have no other obvious purpose, and that the council and other officials surely need a meeting place somewhere. Hardly an overwhelming argument: in Rome itself, the senate often met in a temple – why not here too?

Legal cases may well have been conducted in the large and grandly decorated building in the Forum known as the Basilica (Ill. 70). The *duumvir* would perhaps have directed proceedings, and made his judgement from the raised platform at the far end – though the fact that there is a base for a statue right in front of the platform, blocking the view, makes that reconstruction rather less likely than it might seem at first sight. In any case, to think of this as a permanently designated courtroom, and only as a courtroom, would be to exaggerate the time spent on legal business in the town. Legal geniuses the Romans may have been, but the chances are that in Pompeii, as elsewhere in the ancient world, most disputes were settled, and most crimes punished, outside the full mechanisms of the law. Even the *duoviri* might have operated relatively informally, as we saw in the paintings of the Forum, where some kind of dispute was apparently being settled under the colonnade (Ill. 28).

The one thing we know for certain about the Basilica is that lots of people stood around there with plenty of time on their hands: for it has provided one of the richest stocks of graffiti anywhere in the city, hundreds and hundreds of them. Almost none of these have any obvious legal flavour (although the scrawled maxim 'A tiny problem becomes a vast one if you ignore it' might appeal to a tidy legal brain). Most are the kind of street-talk we have seen before, including a memorable couplet wishing on some unfortunate person called Chius even worse piles than he already has ('so that they burn more than they've burned before'). There is one graffito, however, which may refer to the *duoviri* and their staff, albeit under the cover of a crude pun. It reads: 'If you bugger the *accensus*, you burn your prick'. *Accensus* in Latin can mean 'fire'. So at first sight, this is more of the usual earthy style of humour ('If you bugger the fire, etc. …'). But there is another sense of the word *accensus*, found in the Roman city constitutions: it means the 'servant' of the *duumvir* or aedile. Is this a different sort of joke then – about meddling with the *duumvir*'s assistants?

Maybe there is a hint here about how we should picture Pompeian public life: less formal and, at the same time, less familiar than the image we so often draw from a combination of upmarket Latin literature, nineteenth-century paintings and novels, and sword-and-sandals movies. We cannot hope to be able to reconstruct with any accuracy a meeting of the Pompeian *ordo*. We do not know where, or how often, it met, or how many members it had, or what particular topics it would have discussed. (Did it normally 'fix' the elections to the duovirate, by prearranging which ex-aediles would stand? Did it discuss the management problems of the city's farm, or Lucius Caecilius Jucundus' arrears of his rent?) But it is very unlikely that it was ever full of starchy figures in togas, standing to orate in grave and earnest style, as if rulers of the world (that is probably a misleading image even for the senate at Rome itself). It was probably much more down to earth, much less pompous – even in our terms, I suspect, a little seedy.

The same goes for the business of the *duoviri* and aediles. True, there must have been some elements of pomp and grandeur in holding these offices. That is certainly the image implied by the tombstone of Aulus Clodius Flaccus, and by the references in other city charters to lictors and fancy togas. But it is hard not to suspect that the day-to-day reality was altogether less grand, more improvised and more rough and ready. It is easy enough to invent, as scholars often have, an impressive-sounding schedule for these local bigwigs: rise and receive clients at the morning *salutatio*, leave home for the Forum, handle financial affairs, sign contracts, deal with law cases, network at the baths, entertain over dinner ... There is some evidence for almost all of these activities (and, interestingly, the times of day noted on the signed documents from Puteoli (p. 182) do show a clear preference for financial business in the early to mid-morning). But how regular and systematic such a schedule was, and how far we can work out what most of these activities actually entailed, is another matter. How busy these officials were, how many hours a day they spent on their official duties, what expertise they could draw on in managing the city's affairs, how they conducted legal business when many of them could have had little or no legal training are just some of the curious puzzles, for us, of life in Pompeii.

The face of success

We know a good deal more about the men who held office in Pompeii than we do about the day-to-day practicalities of local government. Even in those earlier periods where the electoral posters are lost (and with them the names of the candidates standing for office), we can still work out in many cases who the elected *duoviri* and aediles were, and even in which year they held office. It is a delicate business of piecing together a list from the names and dates found, for example, in Jucundus' tablets, from inscriptions commemorating those who sponsored building works or gladiatorial shows, and the names and offices blazoned on tombstones.

The end result is that for some decades we know the names of over half the local officeholders; during the reigns of Augustus and Tiberius (partly because there was so much building work going on in Pompeii), that figure rises to at least three quarters. Some of these remain just names. Others we can get to know much more intimately: we can see something of their individual achievements and aspirations, and of how they chose to be remembered. Just occasionally we can put a face to a name.

These officeholders conformed to a certain type. Not everyone in Pompeii would have been eligible to stand for election, not even all the free citizens. Assuming that it was organised like other towns in the Roman world, those who put themselves forward to become an aedile or a *duumvir* were formally required to be male, adult, of free-citizen birth, respectable and rich. This means, for example, that no ex-slave could hold public office at this level. A slave granted his freedom by a Roman citizen became a citizen himself and could vote in elections, a strategy of incorporation almost without parallel among other slave-owning societies. But it was only in the next generation – for their sons were under no such restriction – that the family of an ex-slave could begin to play a completely free part in local government. It also means that the poor were not merely discouraged from standing for office by its various obligations (for how could they have afforded the entrance fee and the required benefactions?). They were also formally prevented from doing so by a minimum property qualification: in other towns, 100,000 *sesterces*' worth was a common minimum. There were also rules which excluded a variety of unsuitable professions, such as actors, and laid down the minimum age for office. At Pompeii, no one under twenty-five, or perhaps thirty, was allowed to be an aedile.

There was still room, however, for plenty of variety among the officeholders at Pompeii: from those who must only just have reached the property qualification to men of very considerable means; from the local landed aristocracy to the newly rich. Aulus Umbricius Scaurus' family, as we have seen, had recently made their money out of *garum*. Caius Julius Polybius has a name which hints that his family was descended from a slave in the emperor's household. Others, like Marcus Holconius Rufus, whom we shall shortly meet face to face, belonged to a family prominent in Pompeii for generations and whose wealth derived mostly from its land.

Generations of scholars have looked for a pattern in these variations. Can we, for example, spot periods when the nouveaux riches become more prominent? After the earthquake, perhaps? Despite an enormous amount of work (and ingenuity) the only safe conclusion is an unsurprising one. Some old families were prominent in the town's hierarchy from the early first century BCE until the eruption. Throughout this period members of newer families often gained public office, making up around 50 per cent of aediles and *duoviri*, but they seem rarely to have gained a permanent foothold in the elite. A mixed society, in other words, but one where old money always counted.

Just occasionally we find an interloper, when one of the *duoviri* came from outside the local community. This may have broken the rules for local residence, but in these cases that would hardly have been a worry – for the officeholder concerned was the emperor himself or an imperial prince. Caligula was twice *duumvir* of Pompeii, once in 34 CE in the reign of Tiberius (when, for what it's worth, he must also have been considerably below the minimum age required for the office), and once as emperor six years later. In fact, when Caligula was assassinated in January 41 CE, he was halfway through his term of office as *duumvir quinquennalis* at Pompeii. There seems to have been no illusion that he would have undertaken any practical duties of the duumvirate, for on each occasion we find an additional 'prefect with judicial power' in office – acting, as is explicitly stated in one inscription, on the emperor's behalf. This office of 'prefect' proved a useful stand-by on other occasions too. Experienced men obviously deemed 'a safe pair of hands' were appointed as *praefecti* following the riot in the Amphitheatre and after the earthquake of 62 to take the lead in the emergency.

How exactly would Caligula's duumvirate have been arranged? And where would the initiative have come from: the imperial palace or Pompeii itself? One theory is that by inserting an emperor or prince into the local government, even in an honorary capacity, the central authorities in Rome were attempting to gain some control of affairs in the town. It was, in other words, a punishment or a rescue bid after some crisis in the town's management. Hard as it is to imagine the mad Caligula ever being more of a help than a hindrance, maybe even a nominal imperial presence would make scrutiny and central government intervention easier. But more likely an imperial name among the *duoviri* would be considered an honour for the town, and the initiative would have come from the Pompeian side. Caligula's agreement to accept the office would have been the result of careful negotiation between Pompeii and palace officials – not unlike, I imagine, the delicate protocols that lie behind securing the visit of a British 'minor royal' to a school fete.

Honour was also at stake in some extraordinary appointments to the town council. One young lad, Numerius Popidius Celsinus, was given membership of the *ordo* 'without payment' at the age of only six, because he had rebuilt the temple of Isis at his own expense. Or so the inscription says – presumably his father, an ex-slave, rebuilt it in his son's name and so eased the boy's path into the local elite. Another precocious councillor was a young member of that long-established elite family whose burial ground has been discovered at Scafati (p. 155). Decimus Lucretius Justus was nominated to the council without charge when he was only eight years old; he died at thirteen. Almost certainly these 'honorary members' did not have full rights within the *ordo*. Documents from elsewhere in the Roman world suggest that there may well have been different ranks of councillors, some who would not have had the right to speak in discussion. All the same, a handful of pre-teens makes a startling addition to our picture of the *ordo*.

Aediles, *duoviri* and councillors were the very top notch of Pompeian society, in wealth, influence and power. They formed the local ruling class – or the 'decurial class' as they are often now called (from 'decurion', meaning councillor). Even so, these local bigwigs fell far behind the rich powerbrokers of the capital itself. A property qualification of 100,000 *sesterces* (if that is what it was at Pompeii) is substantial enough. From the reign of Augustus on, it took ten times that amount, 1,000,000 *sesterces*, to qualify to be a senator at Rome, the very top rank of the Roman social hierarchy. In fact, many Roman senators did have their origins in the country towns of Italy. But there is not a single senator whom we know for certain came from Pompeii or a Pompeian family; they might have owned attractive seaside villas in the neighbourhood, but it was not their ancestral home.

This is not to say that the citizens of Pompeii were without influence and connections with the world of the capital itself. After they had gained Roman citizenship in the Social War and before the one-man rule established under the first emperor Augustus (31 BCE–14 CE) effectively stamped out democratic voting in the capital, Pompeians were eligible to vote at Rome, both at elections and in making laws – if they could be bothered to travel there, that is. They were mostly enrolled in the same voting group (the 'Menenian tribe'), whose name they still included in their formal titles ('Aulus Umbricius Scaurus, son of Aulus, of the Menenian tribe' (p. 186), long after voting had died out. But some of them had closer links to the centre of Roman power, as we can see if we look at the career of just one leading Pompeian. He is Marcus Holconius Rufus: five times *duumvir*, and twice quinquennial, who lived in the reign of the emperor Augustus. Hardly a typical councillor, he was a member of an old family known for their wine production (the 'Horconian' or 'Holconian' vine is mentioned by Pliny as a local speciality). He probably counts as the most powerful Pompeian we know, and one who made a major impact on his city.

Now in the museum at Naples, the life-size marble statue of Marcus Holconius Rufus once stood at the crossroads of the Via dell'Abbondanza, in its widest part (almost a little piazza) outside the Stabian Baths, next to a large arch which spanned the road and may have carried statues of other members of his family

71. Marcus Holconius Rufus, one of Pompeii's most successful citizens – shown here in his statue from outside the Stabian Baths. He looks grand enough to be an emperor. In fact this head probably *was* recut from a portrait head of the emperor Caligula.

(Ill. 71). This is not far from the Forum, where most of the other images of local worthies and imperial grandees stood, erected by a grateful (or carefully calculating) city council – the emperor and his relations occupying the most prominent positions in the piazza, the locals arranged round about so as not to upstage the imperial family. But Holconius Rufus would have stood out by being slightly separate from all the rest, and it is probably this location that accounts for the statue's survival. The Roman salvage operations after the eruption seem to have made a bee-line for the statues in the Forum, leaving very few to be found by modern archaeologists. The salvagers missed Holconius Rufus, who was standing away from the main group, a little way down the street.

The statue is a proudly military figure, dressed in an elaborate cuirass and a cloak, his right hand originally holding a spear. When he was rediscovered in the 1850s, clear signs of paint were still visible: the cloak had once been red, the tunic under the breastplate white with a yellow border, the shoes black. It is a splendid piece. The only jarring element is the head, which looks somewhat too small to fit. Indeed, it does not fit. The head, as we have it, is a replacement, perhaps for the original damaged in the earthquake of 62 (or that is one guess). Careful examination shows that it was not originally made for our statue at all. Another portrait head has been recut with the features of Holconius Rufus and inserted into the neck.

So whose portrait suffered the indignity of removal and reworking, in this ancient version of identity theft? One ingenious idea is that the replacement head had belonged to a statue of the emperor Caligula, and had been surplus to requirements after his assassination in 41. Not only was the city very likely to have commissioned a statue of Caligula, given his two periods as *duumvir*, but archaeologists who have closely examined the reworked head think they can detect some telltale traces of Caligula's distinctive hairstyle surviving the otherwise complete makeover. To us, the idea of recycling the head of a disgraced emperor to play the part of Holconius Rufus seems faintly ridiculous, but this practice of 'changing heads' is in fact surprisingly common among the portrait statues of the Roman world.

Underneath the statue, still visible on the pedestal outside the Stabian Baths, is an inscription detailing the main offices he held. There we can see his repeated holdings of the Pompeian duovirate. But headlined is one called 'military tribune by popular demand'. 'Military tribune' was a well-established post in the Roman army for young men of officer class. But 'by popular demand'? This seems to refer not to any truly military office, but to an honorary position awarded by the emperor Augustus on the recommendation of local communities, hence the 'popular demand'. It brought with it the formal Roman rank of a 'knight' (the next rank down from senator) – gratifying to the recipient no doubt, and useful in other respects for the emperor himself. As the Roman biographer Suetonius writes of this general initiative in his *Life of Augustus*, 'his aim was to maintain a proper supply of men of respectable standing', and loyalty too, he might have added.

The honour almost certainly involved some contact with the emperor himself, or with those close to him. For the inscription records that Holconius Rufus was also 'patron of the colony', a semi-official role which might involve intervening on the town's behalf with the powers that be at Rome (the patron might be expected, for example, to help arrange for a prince or emperor to hold a local duumvirate). Finally, he was 'Priest of Augustus' in the town. Even before the first emperor had died, he held a panoply of religious honours almost as if he were a god (p. 299) – coordinated here in Pompeii by the loyal Holconius Rufus.

Looking back to the statue, we can now see the point of the military garb. There is no reason to suppose that Holconius Rufus had ever been in the army. The elaborate cuirass is a visual reminder of his prestigious, but entirely noncombatant, military tribunate. For those viewers who knew the monuments of the city of Rome itself, however, there was also a nice – even if slightly over-the-

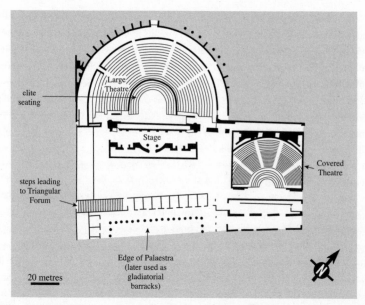

Figure 16. Plan of the Large Theatre and its surroundings. The Large Theatre was restored and enlarged by Marcus Holconius Rufus according to the policies of Augustan regime. The male elite sat in the front, carefully cut off from the ordinary people behind. Adjacent to this building are both the Covered Theatre, and the *palaestra* used by gladiators in the last years of the city (Ill. 94), and above the Triangular Forum with the old Temple of Minerva and Hercules.

top – reference to one of Augustus' most lavish new buildings, the so-called Forum of Augustus. This vast development in the middle of Rome, packed with statues, artworks and gleaming coloured marbles, was focused on a temple of 'Mars the Avenger' – a reminder, if such was needed, that Mars the god of war had brought vengeance on those who had assassinated Augustus' uncle, and adoptive father, Julius Caesar. The original statue of the god in the Forum of Augustus has not survived. But, from various versions and replicas of it, we can be certain that the designs on Holconius Rufus' cuirass were copies of those on the cuirass of Mars himself. Our Pompeian bigwig, in other words, was here dressed in the image of one of Augustus' divine protectors.

Unsurprisingly perhaps, Augustus is reflected in some of the building work sponsored by Holconius Rufus, as *duumvir*. During his third period of office, we know that he did some renovation in the temple of Apollo – building upwards. For a surviving inscription states that he and his colleague paid 3000 *sesterces* to the owner of the adjoining property (who had presumably objected) in recompense for blocking of his light with the new wall. But later, along with Marcus Holconius Celer (either brother or son), he funded a much bigger and more costly improvement scheme in the old Large Theatre, originally built in the second century BCE (Fig. 16). Inscriptions again, probably originally placed over the building's main entrances, record that the Holconii built 'at their own expense, the covered gallery, the boxes and auditorium'.

This list does not quite capture, for us, the impact of the changes. Not only was the number of seats increased, but the refurbished covered gallery effectively became the divider between the new seats on the upper levels (explicitly earmarked for the poor, slaves, maybe women), with their own frankly shabby entrance staircase leading up from outside the building, and the upmarket seats below, which were occupied by the elite male citizens. This was a renovation, in other words, which accorded exactly to the policy of the emperor Augustus, to make sure that spectators in the theatre were carefully segregrated by rank – a segregation not achieved, as in the world of the modern theatre, by the price of the seats, but by law. It is no coincidence that as well as further inscriptions honouring Holconius Rufus in the theatre, there is also one honouring the emperor Augustus.

This is a good example of how the wishes of the emperor, and changes in policy at the centre of the Roman world, were transmitted to places like Pompeii through intermediaries such as Holconius Rufus – with a foot, as it were, in both camps. It also offers a nice hint about how family success might be achieved down the generations. At least, if Holconius Rufus hoped that his own and Celer's costly benefactions in the theatre might help to guarantee the prestige of the Holconii into the future, he would not have been disappointed. One of those men aiming to become *duumvir* in the last elections the town would ever see was Marcus Holconius Priscus, very likely his grandson or great-grandson.

Beyond the male elite?

It is easy to get the impression from the election posters, the records of benefactions and the lists of *duoviri* and aediles, that it was only the male elite that counted in Pompeii. In some senses that is formally true: no one without the required wealth could hold one of those main offices, nor could any ex-slave however rich, nor any woman no matter how capable or ambitious she was, or how aristocratic her birth. Yet there are plenty of hints that other more or less official groups of citizens, from lower down the formal social pecking order, could and did make an impact in the public world of Pompeii. And there is clear evidence of the impact of leading women at the very heart of the town.

To return for a moment to the family burial ground recently found outside Pompeii at Scafati. The most distinguished of the family members commemorated (probably called Decimus Lucretius Valens, though the name does not actually survive) was, like Marcus Holconius Rufus, a Roman knight; he had been granted that status by the emperor Tiberius. He had been the local sponsor of very generous gladiatorial games, and – as we would by now expect – 'in return for this generosity', as the text of the inscription puts it, the local council had decreed him a statue on horseback at public expense, as well as a funeral (though the word itself has been lost), a burial place and a eulogy.

So far, no surprises. But the inscription goes on to record other votes of honour. The *Augustales* (and possibly some other group – for frustratingly the next word hardly survives) voted him *statuae pedestres*, full-length standing statues, as did the attendants of the *Augustales*, along with the *nates* and *scabiliari*. The *forenses*, whom we have met before, voted him 'shields' (that is, his portrait on shields). The *nates* and *scabiliari* are more of a puzzle. The best guess is that the *scabiliari* were the 'clapper beaters' in the theatre, assuming that the word is connected with the Latin *scabellum*, meaning a large foot-operated castanet, often used in pantomime (p. 256). If so, the *nates* might have been the cushion sellers, cushions being a desirable commodity if you were to sit for hours on the hard stone seats. But that is largely a deduction from the one attested meaning of the Latin word *natis/nates* that we have: namely, 'buttocks'.

But whoever exactly these different groups were, it is clear that there were numerous organisations in the town, in addition to the local council, who might not only have an interest in honouring a leading citizen, but also the institutional structure to make (and to follow through) a decision to do so, not to mention the cash to pay for it. As well as those mentioned on Lucretius Valens' memorial, a couple of very fragmentary painted lists, one firmly dated to the 40s BCE, record 'presidents' and 'attendants' – a mixture of slaves, ex-slaves and freeborn men – in charge of some sort of local association in the city, probably based around the crossroads and the shrines often found there. We also find reference elsewhere to the 'Fortunate Augustan Suburban Country District', which not only had its own officials but also acted as a benefactor, paying for some of the seating in the theatre. Some scholars have assumed that this was mainly a rural voting district, which had developed extra social and institutional functions. But the fact that it seems to have been reorganised in 7 BCE has suggested to others a slightly different role. For this was exactly the same year as the emperor Augustus reorganised the local neighbourhood associations in Rome, turning them partly into loyalty organisations focused on the emperor himself. Was there influence or initiative from Rome lying behind this 'Fortunate Augustan Suburban Country District'? Certainly, as we shall see in Chapter 9, the religious worship of the Roman emperor in Pompeii involved organised groups of relatively humble city residents.

Predictably enough, once we get below the level of the *ordo* the evidence is much thinner and it is even harder to pin down exactly what these groups did or how they were constituted, or just how 'official' they were. We can guess, for example, that there was some difference in status between the 'cushion-sellers' (if that is what they were) and the *forenses*. But what exactly? Some were even on the margins of legality. Tacitus explains that one of the Roman government's responses to the riot in the Amphitheatre was to disband 'the illegal clubs'. Which were these?

Murky as these groups are, however, the important point is not just that there were organisations in the town which involved those who would have been excluded from the *ordo* itself. It is also that they seem to have operated on similar principles to those of the local elite, and with sometimes similar rewards. Benefaction, for example, played an important role at this level too – whether statues or theatre renovation. Pompeii was a culture of *giving*, at all levels. Public office of any sort entailed public generosity.

Probably the most important of these groups were the *Augustales*, one of those associations that voted to honour Decimus Lucretius Valens, and which may almost have amounted to an *ordo* for ex-slaves. The evidence for this group in Pompeii itself is very fragmentary: we have plenty of evidence for its individual members, but little for what the *Augustales* as a whole did. Again our picture must depend on piecing together what we know from other towns in Italy. Their name makes it fairly clear they were involved with the religious worship of Augustus and later emperors, but they were not a specialised 'priesthood' in any narrow sense. For the most part, we find them engaged in sponsoring banquets and buildings, and even – like the *ordo* itself – paying an entrance fee to get into the group.

The large tomb monuments of some of those commemorated as *Augustales* in the cemeteries outside Pompeii suggest that they were individuals of wealth and power in the town. One in particular, the memorial to Caius Calventius Quietus

72. This tomb of an ex-slave, erected as was usual alongside one of the roads leading out of the city, boasts of the civic honours won by Caius Calventius Quietus. In death it can be hard to distinguish the monuments of the old Pompeian aristocrats from those of the new rich.

(almost certainly an ex-slave), boasts that 'on account of his generosity' he had been awarded, 'by the decision of the council and the agreement of the people', a *bisellium* – a special, and specially honorific, seat in the theatre that was awarded to the city's leading men (Ill. 72). What the Marcus Holconius Rufuses of the Pompeian world said about the likes of Caius Calventius Quietus we cannot now know. But in death at least there is nothing to distinguish him from the members of the oldest landed families. Fiercely hierarchical society though it was, the routes to prestige at Pompeii, even for those outside the decurial class, were more varied than they might seem at first glance.

But the biggest surprise in this male hierarchical world is to be found in the Forum itself. The largest building in the area, standing at the south-east corner, was erected in the reign of Augustus (Fig. 14, Ill. 73). Its function has long been a cause of controversy, like so many of the Forum buildings: market, slave market, multi-purpose hall? But its inspiration is clear. We have already seen that two of the statues on its façade were copied from the Forum of Augustus. The carved marble door frames, decorated with scrolls of acanthus, reflect the contemporary style of the capital, and are very close to those on another celebrated Augustan monument, the Altar of Peace. Some art historians have compared its conception to a huge portico erected in Rome by Augustus' wife, the empress Livia.

73. The Building of Eumachia as it is shown on this detailed nineteenth-century model of the excavations, displayed in the Archaeological Museum in Naples. The Via dell' Abbondanza runs along the right, the large open courtyard of Eumachia's foundation is in the centre, the Forum colonnade is at the bottom.

That is a good comparison in more ways than one. For this building, known as the Building of Eumachia, was also sponsored by a woman. Inscriptions over the two entrances declared that Eumachia, who was a priestess in the town, daughter of one leading family and married into another, built it 'in her own name and that of her son ... at her own expense'. Her statue stood at one end of the building (Ill. 74), paid for by the fullers (hence the fantasy that the whole building might be a cloth-workers' hall). We know almost nothing about Eumachia, and can only guess at all the different circumstances that might lie behind her building of this monument, and the different degrees of active involvement she might have had in the planning and design. Most likely she was attempting to advance the career of her son. But one thing is certain: the finished product is stamped with her own name almost as firmly as the theatre is stamped

74. The statue of Eumachia from the building which she founded in the Forum. It is instructive for us to remember that this modestly clad figure could finance one of the largest buildings in the town.

with that of Holconius. Eumachia here represents a similar conduit for the culture of the capital to make its way to Pompeii. And Eumachia was not the only such female benefactor. An inscription found in the Forum makes it clear that another of the major buildings there was the work of another priestess, one Mamia.

We should not, for this reason, overestimate the degree of power held by women in this town. To be a priestess, public office though that was, was not the same as being *duumvir*. Even large-scale benefaction was a long way from formal power. That said, Eumachia is another example of the varied routes to public prominence the town offered. She is another 'face of success'.

CHAPTER SEVEN

THE PLEASURES OF THE BODY: FOOD, WINE, SEX AND BATHS

Dormice for starters?

A curious pottery object, unearthed in the mid-1950s in a small house not far from the Amphitheatre in Pompeii, was almost instantly identified as a 'dormouse-jar' (Ill. 75). The idea is that the dormice lived inside, running up and down the spiralling tracks moulded into the sides of the jar (the Roman equivalent of a hamster's wheel). A couple of feeding trays could be filled up from the outside, and a series of small holes let in air and a little light. For a lid was fitted on the top, to keep the creatures inside and, perhaps, to confuse their body-clocks with the constant gloom, so that they did not hibernate – although you might equally well predict that the dark would have sent them to sleep.

Unlikely as this reconstruction may seem, the strange pot does in fact match up almost exactly with a description offered by one first-century BCE writer on agriculture: 'Dormice are fattened up in jars,' he writes, 'which a lot of people keep even inside their houses. The potters make them in a special shape. They make runs in their sides, and a basin for holding food. Into these jars, you put acorns or walnuts or chestnuts. When the lid is fitted, the animals grow fat in the dark.' Several others have been found in Pompeii or round about. This leaves no doubt that a nice plump dormouse could be a delicacy of Roman cuisine. The one surviving Roman cookery book – a compilation of the fourth or fifth century CE, attributed to a well-known gourmet called Apicius, who lived centuries earlier and almost certainly had nothing whatsoever to do with the book – includes a recipe for stuffed dormice ('Stuff dormice with pork stuffing and with the meat

75. A Pompeian dormouse holder.
Occasionally the Romans really did eat
dormice, just as they do in the movies.
They would have been placed in this
small pottery jar (some 20 centimetres
tall), with a lid – to be kept and fattened
before consumption. The ridges in the
side of the jar acted as exercise runs for
the doomed creatures.

of whole dormice crushed with pepper, nuts, *silphium* [perhaps a kind of fennel]
and fish sauce'). And at Trimalchio's extravagant banquet that is the centrepiece
of Petronius' novel, the *Satyrica*, the starters included 'dormice dipped in honey
and sprinkled with poppy seeds'.

But these poor little creatures played a smaller role in Roman cookery than they
do in modern fantasies about the luxury and excess of Roman eating habits, which
are one of the most celebrated and mythologised of all aspects of Roman life. The
lavish banquet at which men and women recline together in various states of
undress, being fed grapes by battalions of slaves or tucking into silver platefuls of
stuffed dormouse in *garum*, is a familiar image from sword-and-sandals movies
and even TV documentaries. And the weirder aspects of Roman cuisine are regularly imitated at student toga parties and the occasional brave, if short-lived,
modern restaurant (some concoction of anchovy usually standing in as a pale imitation of proper Roman fish sauce, and sugar mice doing duty for the real thing).

This chapter will explore a series of Pompeian pleasures, from eating and
drinking to sex and bathing. We shall find (as the dormouse-holder has already
shown) that the modern popular image of the Romans at play is not entirely
wrong. But in each case the picture turns out to be more complicated and interesting than the hedonistic, excessive and raunchy stereotype implies.

You are what you eat

The Romans themselves had a hand in mythologising their eating and dining.
The biographers of emperors made much of the ruler's habits at table. Banquets
were imagined as an occasion to enjoy his hospitality, but also to see the

hierarchies of Roman culture sharply reinforced. True or not (and probably not), it was said of Elagabalus, a particularly strange third-century CE emperor, that he hosted colour-coded dinner parties (on one day all the food being green, on another blue) and that to make sure that the inferior guests knew their place he served them food of wood or wax, while he himself consumed the edible version. Other Roman writers discussed in minute detail the rules and conventions of elite dining. Should women recline with the men, or should they sit upright? Which position on the shared couch was most honorific? At what time was it polite to arrive at a dinner party? (Answer: neither first nor last, so it might be necessary to hang around outside to make a well-timed entrance.) In what order should the different dishes be eaten?

Meanwhile fantastic culinary creations caught the Roman imagination as much as they do the modern. At Trimalchio's fictional banquet, a running joke is that none of the food is quite as it appears (rather like Trimalchio himself – an ex-slave pretending to be an aristocrat). One of the courses consisted of a boar, surrounded by piglets who turned out to be made of cake. When the boar was carved, a flock of thrushes flew out of its innards. A rather more mundane artifice, but with similar 'deception' in view, is recommended in Apicius' cookery book. One memorable recipe is for 'Casserole of anchovy without anchovy'. A mixture of any kind of fish, 'sea nettles' and eggs, it promises to pull the wool over the eyes of every diner: 'at table no one will recognise what he's eating.'

At Pompeii itself we find wall paintings depicting extravagant parties that fit nicely with our own modern stereotype of Roman dining. One scene (Plate 10) in the dining room in the Chaste Lovers bakery shows two couples reclining on couches covered with rugs and cushions. Though hardly a picture of sexual debauchery, other types of excess are on display. The drink is set out on a pair of tables nearby. A considerable quantity has already been consumed, for a third man has passed out on one of the couches, while a woman in the background has to be supported by her partner or slave. Another painting from the same room shows a similar scene, but this time in the open air, with the couches covered by awnings, and a slave mixing up the wine in a large bowl (wine was usually mixed with water in the ancient world).

In the House of the Triclinium, named for the paintings in its dining room, we find other variations on this theme. In one scene, a man who must just have arrived at the party is sitting on a couch, as a slave removes his shoes, while one of the other guests is already vomiting (Ill. 76). In another scene, in which entertainers perform for the guests on their couches, we glimpse a striking piece of

76. A nineteenth-century copy of a painting of a Roman party, from the House of the Triclinium. Notice how the servers, whether slaves or free, are shown as smaller than the guests. But they are very useful adjuncts to the occasion: one (on the left) removes a guest's shoes; another (on the right), takes care of someone who is already being sick.

furniture. What looks at first sight like a living waiter, is in fact a bronze statue of a young man, holding a tray for food and drink.

So do the dining rooms and dining customs of Pompeii match up to these images on its walls? In part, yes. We saw in Chapter 3 that, even for the city's elite, formal dining of this type was probably restricted to special occasions, most food being taken on the run, sitting at tables, or perched in the peristyle. That said, some *triclinia* have been excavated which show an exquisite attention to detail and to luxury – as, for example, the dining installation overlooking the garden in the House of the Golden Bracelet, with its shining marble and babbling water (Ill. 35). The silver tableware and other elegant pieces of dining equipment occasionally discovered in and around Pompeii also conjure up an image of rich Roman dining, with all its stereotypes, jokes and cultural clichés.

In the House of the Menander, 118 pieces of silver plate, most of it dining ware, were found, carefully wrapped in cloth, stashed away in a wooden box in a cellar under the house's private bath suite. Whether put here as the occupants fled, or more likely – as there was no sign of hurried packing – in storage during renovations to the house, this collection includes matching sets of drinking cups, plates, bowls and spoons (knives would have been made from tougher metal). There are even a pair of silver pepper or spice pots, in 'Trimalchian' disguise, one in the shape of a tiny *amphora*, the other in the shape of a perfume bottle.

A few miles outside the city, in a country house at Boscoreale, over a hundred silver pieces were unearthed at the end of the nineteenth century. These had almost certainly been hidden away for safe-keeping as the volcano erupted, in a deep wine vat where the body of a man – owner or maybe would-be robber – was also found. Among the precious service were a pair of cups which again strike a chord with Trimalchio's banquet. In the middle of his feast a silver skeleton was brought onto the table, prompting Trimalchio to sing a dreadful ditty on the theme of 'eat, drink and be merry, for tomorrow you die' (a favourite topic of Roman popular moralising). Two of the silver drinking cups from Boscoreale are decorated with a jolly party – of skeletons (Ill. 77). Several are given the names of learned Greek philosophers, and are accompanied by suitable philosophical slogans: 'Pleasure is the goal of life' etc.

In some cases, we can point to an almost exact match between objects depicted in the paintings of drinking and dining on Pompeian walls and those found in the excavations of the city. The collection of silver plate shown on the walls of one rich tomb could almost be part of the dinner service from the House of the Menander. Even more striking is the free-standing bronze statue discovered in a large room in the House of Polybius (once a dining room, it was being used for storage or safe-keeping at the moment of the eruption). Imitating the distinctive 'archaic' style of Greek sculpture in the sixth century BCE, this figure holds its arms out, presumably to carry a tray. Though it is often assumed that this tray would have held lamps, making the statue an elaborate and expensive lamp-stand, it could equally well have been a 'dumb-waiter', holding food just as in the painting from the House of the Triclinium. That idea is certainly seen on a smaller scale in a group of table settings from another house in the city: four elderly men, naked, with long dangling penises, each supporting a small tray, for holding appetisers, titbits or any dainty food (Plate 12). Part of this design has had a surprising afterlife: overlooking the dangling penises, a well-known Italian kitchenware company is now marketing an expensive mock-up of this very tray.

77. A clever message for a rich dinner party. This silver cup from Boscoreale features some jolly skeletons, with moral slogans inscribed next to them.

But there are reasons for thinking that even on the grandest occasions, the reality of Pompeian dining would have been rather different from the images that surrounded it, and a good deal less sumptuous or elegant. The paintings on the walls, in other words, might have reflected an ideal of dining (vomiting and all) rather than the reality. Of course, the hard stone of the fixed couches would have been made much more comfortable and attractive by the addition of rugs and cushions. And no doubt, with practice, the idea of eating with your right hand, while leaning – semi-recumbent – on your left elbow would have come to seem entirely natural. All the same, many of the Pompeian dining rooms, where the couches still survive, seem with a practical eye to be awkward and cramped for the diners. Even in the top-of-the-range installation in the House of the Golden Bracelet, simply mounting the couches looks as if it could have been a difficult operation, at least for the less nimble. Some wooden steps, or their human equivalent in the shape of slaves, would have helped, but not entirely solved the problem. Besides, three people on these couches would feel to us rather crowded. Maybe in fact it did to the Pompeians too. The fact that the different utensils in the silver dinner services are arranged in pairs rather than threes may hint that the canonical 'three on a couch' was not always the practice in real life.

The details of the serving arrangements are also puzzling. Movable couches in a large display room would allow for flexibility and plenty of space. Not so the 'built-in' *triclinia*. Where there are fixed couches, there is also often a fixed table in the centre, on which the food and drink must have been placed. But it was not

78. Pompeian cooking equipment, fit for a banquet. On the lower level, large buckets and vessels. Above, more sophisticated utensils – ladles, pans, moulds and what look like egg poachers.

large and there would have been little room to spare after nine (or even six) plates and drinking cups were put there. That suggests that portable tables and slaves would have had an important role, but there is little room for these either – particularly since servers could not move *behind* the diners to replenish food and drink as in a modern restaurant. And what of those cases where, as in the House of the Golden Bracelet, the central table is a pool of water. Here the younger Pliny, who kept well clear of the eruption of Vesuvius when his uncle went to investigate, and lived to tell the tale, can perhaps point us in the right direction. In one of his letters, he describes a villa he owned in Tuscany. This included an elaborate garden, with a dining area at one end with a pool of water in front of it, filled by water spouts that gushed from the couches themselves. He explains that larger dishes were placed for the diners on the edge of the pool, but that smaller dishes and garnishes were set floating on the water. That may well have been the principle in the House of the Golden Bracelet. If so, it's hard not to suspect that, however elegant the arrangement was in theory, some of the food, not to mention the guests, became rather damp.

This raises questions about the kind of food that would have been served in these fitted dining rooms. Influenced by Petronius, we tend to think of large elaborate dishes: whole boars with a stuffing of live birds being only one of many extravagant options. And it is true that some of the cooking equipment found at

Pompeii suggests that some complicated confections were possible, even if not quite so showy as those offered by Trimalchio. Discoveries include plenty of large saucepans, frying pans, colanders, strainers and elaborate moulds for mousses (strikingly reminiscent of the shapes still used for modern jelly moulds: long-eared rabbits and fat pigs) (Ill. 78). Probably all that was feasible in a large room with movable couches. Not so in the smaller versions, however elegant. There the practicalities of space, and of eating with just one hand, prompts the suspicion that what was served was often simple and small, or at least already cut up into bite-size chunks. Against the lavish image of movie-style Roman banquets, we have to set an often more cramped and uncomfortable reality, with anything more substantial than the equivalent of a modern finger buffet making for awkward, messy eating.

Not that these considerations would have worried the poor, for whom stuffed boar and honeyed dormice were probably not even a part of their wildest fantasies. *Triclinium* dining was for the wealthy, or for those in the ranks below who might occasionally take a special meal in a place such as the dining room in the Chaste Lovers bakery, where you could pay to eat in that style (even if it was located unglamorously between the pack animals and the flour mills). Everyday food for most Pompeians was far from showy. In fact it must have been a repetitive, if healthy, diet of bread, olives, wine, cheese (more like ricotta than cheddar), fruit, pulses and a few cottage garden vegetables. Fish would have been available too (caught in the Bay nearby, less polluted then than now), and more rarely meat. By far the commonest form of meat was pork, and that probably more often in the form of sausage or black pudding than a large roast joint. Chicken and eggs, as well as sheep or goat's meat, provided some variety.

That is the picture of meat distribution discovered in the excavation of even the larger houses. In just one year's explorations of the House of the Vestals, for example, some 250 identifiable animal bones were found (more than 1500 could not be identified). Almost a third of them were from pigs, just over 10 per cent from sheep or goats, a mere 2 per cent from cows. This is a rough-and-ready figure, probably under-representing some classes of evidence (a total of twelve identifiable chicken bones seems implausibly small); and the large number of 'unidentifieds' necessarily puts a question mark over any firm conclusions. Nonetheless, it fits nicely with the pattern of evidence we have from throughout the Roman world that pork was the standard meat; the pig discovered at the Villa Regina (p. 158) would have been destined for the dinner table.

The basic diet of ordinary Pompeians is vividly illustrated by a neatly written list, scratched into the atrium wall of a house, with connecting bar, in the centre of the city. As usual with such graffiti there is no explanation of its purpose, but it appears to be a list, with prices, of food (and a few other essentials) bought on a series of eight days in an unknown month of an unknown year, which can hardly be very long before the eruption. Presumably it represents an attempt by someone – whether resident in the house or a visitor – to keep track of his, or conceivably her, recent expenditure. We cannot now decode all the Latin terms for the purchases: the *sittule* which cost '8 *asses*' (there were 4 *asses* to one *sesterce*) may have been a bucket; the *inltynium* at the cost of 1 *as* may possibly have been a lamp; the *hxeres* at 1 *denarius* (or 16 *asses*) may have been dried fruit or nuts – and, if so, rather expensive.

If it is a full record of a week's shopping (and that is a big if), it suggests a dreary diet, unless whoever it was had other foodstuffs in store, or was growing his own. Everyday he bought bread, one or more of three different types: 'bread', 'coarse bread' and 'bread for the slave'. On the first day of the list, 8 *asses* were spent on 'bread'; on the second day, 8 on 'bread' and 2 on 'bread for the slave'; on the final day, 2 *asses* went on both 'bread' and 'coarse bread'. The 'bread for the slave' may have been either an accounting category, or it may refer to a particular kind of loaf; but it was not the same as 'coarse bread', since on one of the days in question both were purchased. Either way, the list not only gives us a glimpse into the range of different products made by a Pompeian bakery, but also underlines the importance of bread as a staple of the average Pompeian diet. At 54 *asses* (or 13½ *sesterces*) in total, it was the biggest item in the week's expenditure.

After that came oil, bought on three days, at a total of 40 *asses*, and wine, also bought on three days, for 23 *asses* in all. The more occasional, or less expensive, purchases ranged from 'sausage' (for 1 *as*) and cheese (bought on four days, in two varieties, but for just 13 *asses* in all) to onions (5 *asses*), leeks (1 *as*), whitebait (2 *asses*) and possibly – or so the word hints – something bovine (*bubella*, for 1 *as*). It is basically a diet of bread, oil, wine and cheese, with a few extras thrown in, but hardly any meat. A couple of other, shorter, lists which also appear to record food purchases confirm that general picture. Both list bread. One includes wine (1 *as*), cheese (1 *as*), oil (1 *as*), lard (3 *asses*) and pork (4 *asses*). The other, which may reflect a recent trip to the vegetable market, has cabbage, beetroot, mustard, mint and salt (all at 1 *as*, except the pricey cabbage at 2).

It is easy to feel romantic about the simple and healthy diet that these lists seem to represent. Indeed Roman poets, a comfortably off crowd whatever their protestations of poverty, often waxed lyrical about the wholesome fare of the peasant. Cheap local plonk, they crowed, and some simple bread and cheese, was better than a banquet if the company was right. So indeed it might have been. But the eating habits of the ordinary Pompeian were a very far cry from the image of Roman dining in modern movies, or even from the image of dining displayed on the walls of Pompeii itself. I suspect that, if we are honest, most of us, given the choice, would prefer to dine with Trimalchio.

Café society

The best way to escape a diet of bread, cheese and fruit, eaten in small lodgings over a shop or workshop, where there were limited or no facilities for cooking anything more interesting, was to eat out. Pompeii has long been thought of as a cheap café culture, with bars, taverns and *thermopolia* (as they are often called in modern guidebooks, though this was certainly not the standard ancient term) lining the streets, catching the passing trade – from visitors with time on their hands to local residents with nowhere nice of their own to be. In fact the masonry counters facing the pavements, with large jars (*dolia*) set into them and display stands behind, are one of the most familiar elements in the Pompeian street scene (Plate 4).

Often brightly decorated, these counters run the gamut of Pompeian decorative taste: sometimes faced with a nice patchwork of coloured marble, sometimes elegantly painted in flower patterns, sometimes featuring lusty phallic images. The façades of the buildings might carry signs or enticing advertisements for what lay inside. One bar near the Amphitheatre, with a small vineyard attached, sported a wonderful phoenix on its exterior wall, next to the slogan: 'The phoenix is happy and so can you be'. This is the bar owned by Euxinus, 'Mr Hospitality' (p. 20). It is nice to think of him advertising the warm welcome at his bar with a painting of the mythical bird that rose from the ashes. What better way to parade the kind of 'pick me up' you would find inside at Bar Phoenix.

There are over 150 such establishments so far discovered in the excavations at Pompeii (with estimates for the whole city rising well above 200). It is easy to get the impression of a town crammed full of fast-food joints serving, from the *dolia* set in the counters, wine and filling stews to a hungry populace – albeit in an atmosphere less 'family-friendly' than the modern McDonald's. For Roman writers certainly tend to portray such bars and taverns as shady premises, associated with a range of vices that went beyond drunkenness and the over-consumption of cheap food. They were said to be places of sex, prostitution, gambling and crime, run by unscrupulous landlords, who were crooks and cheats.

The poet Horace, for example, writes of the bailiff of his country estate longing for the disreputable pleasures of the town: 'the brothel and the greasy tavern', a no doubt significant pairing and a hint at the type of fare on offer. Juvenal, in what is admittedly an extravagant satire, conjures up the image of a bar at the Roman port of Ostia filled with all kinds of unsavoury types, from thieves, murderers and hangmen to coffin makers and the eunuch priests of the goddess Cybele taking time off to get drunk. Emperors too seem to have thought that bars were in need of legislative control. Nero is said to have forbidden the sale of anything cooked apart from vegetables and beans; Vespasian limited it to just beans. Though how effective these bans were – and how exactly they were supposed to improve the moral climate – is unclear.

Sex, prostitution, gambling and crime: all these were certainly present in Pompeii, whether in bars or elsewhere. But the reality of much tavern life was less lurid and more varied than those upper-class Roman authors and lawmakers – always ready to brand places of harmless popular pleasures as morally disreputable – would suggest. What has been uncovered in Pompeii presents a rather more complicated and diverse picture of these establishments than is often allowed.

For a start, were there really 200 bars in the town? Reckoning the population of the city at around 12,000, that would mean one for every 60 inhabitants, whether men, women, slaves or babies. Of course, the resident population may not be a particularly meaningful figure here. For food and drink outlets would cater for many visitors: for sailors from the port, for those who had come in from the countryside for a day, or for those stopping off on some longer journey by road. A town is always likely to have facilities for more than those who live there permanently. All the same, 200 seems a considerable over-provision (and hardly a money-spinner for the landlords), especially when you take into account all those people who were unlikely to have made heavy use of the bars – many of the slaves, for example, or the upper-class ladies.

The fact is that a good number of what we now label as 'bars' (or whatever sub-category of 'tavern' or 'inn' we prefer to call them) can have been nothing of the sort. Their counters, inset *dolia* and display racks would certainly have been for selling something, but it could have been a whole variety of products, not necessarily food and drink for instant, on-the-spot consumption. The chances are, in other words, that some of these bars were really grocery shops or the like, selling nuts, lentils and beans from their counters.

Indeed, even when the establishment is certainly a bar, the conventional picture of mine host ladling wine and stew out of the large jars set in the counter cannot be correct. These jars were made of porous pottery. There is no sign that they were sealed with pitch. And it would have been extremely difficult to clean them or even to get the last scraps of any liquid content out of them. In nearby Herculaneum, where traces of their contents more often survive, it seems they were filled with dry goods – dried fruit, beans or chick-peas – some of which at least might have been sold as snacks. The wine was stored in jars on the floor or in racks on the wall, as the occasional remains of fixings and supports suggest, and presumably decanted directly into jugs for serving. Hot food would have been cooked up on a separate stove and served from the pan.

Quite how disreputable these places were is a moot point. The attempts to detect some rudimentary zoning in the urban layout of the city, and to link the bars and the brothels to areas of 'deviant behaviour' away from the formal, public and ceremonial areas of the city, are only partly convincing. It is true, as we saw in Chapter 2, that there are fewer in the immediate vicinity of the Forum than in other busy areas of the town (canny landlords would obviously try to choose a location with maximum access to potential trade). But not only is their relative absence partly illusory (three, as we noted, once stood where the modern restaurant is), but all kinds of factors, such as property prices or rent, may be at work here too. That said, there is no doubt – as we shall see by taking a look at one or two – that bars were associated with the combined pleasures of food, alcohol and sex.

The women whose names appeared (and were in some cases erased) in the election slogans on the wall of the bar on the Via dell'Abbondanza (p. 191) probably worked as barmaids or waitresses inside: Asellina, Zmyrina, Aegle and Maria. This was only partly excavated in the early twentieth century, and we do know how far its facilities extended beyond the single room we now see – if there were four barmaids, presumably it extended some way. But nonetheless the surviving decoration and the collection of objects so far unearthed on its premises give us a good impression of the ambience and equipment of a Pompeian bar.

Outside the lower part of the walls were painted red, with the electoral slogans above that. There is no obvious shop sign or advertisement on the façade, but on the street corner, a couple of doors away, a painting of some smart bronze drinking vessels must have been meant to alert potential customers to a bar in sight. The bar has a wide opening onto the street, though it is partly blocked by the

79. With bells on ...? This extraordinary phallic lamp hung over the entrance to a bar. It provided some light at night, and must have jangled, like wind-chimes, in the breezes. The little statue in the centre is just over 15 centimetres tall.

L-shaped counter: a solid masonry structure, painted red on its sides and covered on top with a patchwork of marble fragments. Four *dolia* are set into it, and at the end is a small oven, with a bronze container built in, presumably for heating water – the ancient equivalent of having a kettle on the boil. The wine jars were stacked against the wall behind the counter, where (to judge from the find-spots of the various objects) there was a wooden shelf carrying more of the bar equipment. At the back of the room, stairs led to an upper level.

Customers were greeted by a bronze lamp that hung over the counter on the street side (Ill. 79). This ingenious creation was so shocking to the original excavators that they chose not to illustrate it when they first published the finds. For the lamp itself is attached to a small bronze figure of a pygmy, largely naked, with an enormous phallus almost as big as himself. Although his right arm is damaged, he would probably have been holding a knife, as if making to cut off his vast penis, which is itself already growing another mini-member from its tip. To cap it all, six bells dangle from different parts of the whole ensemble. One of several such objects found in Pompeii or nearby (which is how we can be fairly certain about the knife), hanging over the counter it acted as a combination of lamp, wind-chimes and service bell. Welcome to the world of the bar?

This was a night-time, as well as a day-time world, to judge from the seven other pottery lamps found in the single room (one an elegant specimen in the shape of a foot). The rest of the objects discovered were a mixture of the practical and homely, with some little touches of luxury and whimsy. There was a good collection of bronze jars, for water or wine, as well as a bronze funnel which must have been an essential piece of equipment for decanting the wine from the storage vessels to the servers. So characteristic an accessory of the bar was it that a funnel had its place among the other drinking paraphernalia in the painted advertisement on the corner. Glass seems to have been the material of choice for drinking vessels – in general a much more common presence on Pompeian tables than we tend to imagine, misled by its relatively low rate of survival. Not only did it often smash in the eruption itself, but it has had bad luck in modern times too. Several of the glass vessels from this bar, in fact, were destroyed in the Second World War, but the finds originally included a nice set of delicate glass bowls and beakers (as well as a mysterious mini-*amphora* in glass, with a hole in the bottom, perhaps for dropping tiny quantities of special flavouring into water or wine). The utensils were completed with some cheaper pottery cups and plates and an engaging pair of jugs (one in the shape of a cockerel, the other of a fox) and a knife or two.

For the rest, there are enough surviving traces to show that the whole place was originally less bare than it appears now. Bone fittings and hinges hint at the presence of some wooden furniture, cupboards perhaps, or storage boxes. The recent takings were also discovered: 67 coins in all, a few (totalling just over 30 *sesterces*) in higher denominations, the rest in *asses*, two-*as* pieces or tiny quarter-*asses*. From their exact find-spots, it seems that the counter service was mostly dealing in *asses*; a couple were even found in the *dolia* – which might hint at another use for these jars in the counter. Most of the higher denominations had been put away on the shelf behind. This amount of cash fits well with other evidence we have for the prices at a Pompeian bar. A graffito at another establishment suggests that you could get plonk (a glass? a pitcher?) for 1 *as*, something better for 2 *asses* and top-notch Falernian wine for 4 *asses*, or 1 *sesterce* (though, if Pliny is to be trusted when he says that you could set Falernian alight with a flame, then it must have been more like brandy than wine, until it was mixed with water). Apart from the welcoming pygmy, the nearest we get to any signs of depravity are the fragments of a couple of mirrors.

But it is the behaviour of the staff and customers that counts; and you cannot necessarily reconstruct the conduct within from the physical surroundings. We get a precious glimpse of the atmosphere of a bar, people and all, from two series of paintings in two other drinking establishments in the town – where the images on the walls were obviously meant to entertain the customers with scenes of the 'bar life' they were enjoying. Humorous, parodic, idealising, though these may be, they are our best guide to Pompeian café culture.

The first series is from the so-called Inn (or Bar) of Salvius ('Mr Safe Haven'), a small establishment on a desirable corner site in the city centre: four images, originally running along one wall of the main front room, opposite the counter, now in the safety of the Naples Museum (Plate 13). On the left, a man and a woman – both brightly clad, she in a yellow cloak, he in a red tunic – enjoy a rather awkwardly posed kiss. Above the figures is the caption 'I don't want to ... [the key word is sadly lost] with Myrtalis'. Whatever the man did not want to do with Myrtalis, or who she was, we shall never know. Perhaps this is a vignette of the fickleness of passion, much the same then as now: 'I don't want to hang around with Myrtalis any more, I'm getting off with this girl.' Or perhaps, given the stiffness of the pose, this girl *is* Myrtalis and the point is that the man is none too keen on the encounter.

In the next scene, a couple of drinkers are getting served by a waitress, but there's competition for the wine. One of them is saying, 'Here', the other, 'No it's mine.' The serving woman isn't going to get involved: 'Whoever wants it, take,' she says to them. Then, as if to taunt them by offering it to another customer, says, 'Oceanus, come and have a drink.' This is not deferential service; and the waitress is more than ready to answer back. Drinking is followed by a game of dice in the next scene, and another argument is brewing. A couple of men are sitting at a table. One shouts, 'I've won', while the other objects, 'It's not a three, it's a two.' By the final scene in the series, they have come to blows and abuse: 'You scum, I had the three, I won', 'No, come on, cocksucker, I did.' It is too much for the landlord, who throws them out. 'If you want to fight, go outside,' he says in the usual landlord's way. The customers, as they looked at the paintings, were presumably supposed to get the message.

The paintings suggest a familiar and slightly edgy mixture of sex, drink and play, but no terrible moral turpitude: some kissing, plenty of tipsy banter (but hardly the vomiting we saw in the dining-room images), a row over a game getting a bit out of hand, and a landlord who doesn't want his bar trashed. We find much the same kind of pictures in the other decorated bar a few blocks away, also on a good corner site and usually now called after its location, the Bar on the Via di Mercurio. This had a back room with a direct entrance onto the street, and presumably waitress service from the counter next door to four or five tables,

80. Life in the bar. This nineteenth-century drawing shows four men around a table, enjoying a drink, served by a diminutive waiter. Above them hang some of the bar's food supplies.

maximum. It was on the walls of this room that the paintings were set, at just the right height to be enjoyed by someone sitting at a table. There are captions to some of them, not here painted as part of the original design, but graffiti scratched on by the customers.

Once again we find men (this does seem to be a world of *male* drinking) having their glasses replenished by willing, or not so willing, servers. In one painting a waiter (or waitress, it's hard to tell) is topping up a glass that a customer holds out. Someone has scratched above his head 'Give me a little cold water' – to mix, that is, with the wine in the glass. In another similar scene, the scrawled caption reads: 'Another cup of Setian', referring to the wine that had been the favourite of the emperor Augustus, and was reputed to be especially nice when chilled with snow. There are scenes of gambling here too (Plate 6), and one particularly evocative view of the inside of a bar (Ill. 80). A group of what seem to be travellers (a couple are wearing distinctive hooded cloaks) are sitting round a table having a meal. Above them is one solution to the storage problem in these small places: a selection of food, including sausages and herbs, hangs from nails attached to a shelf, or even to some kind of framework suspended from the ceiling.

But there is a strikingly different theme in a painting that once decorated the end wall of this room, long since lost or destroyed (all except a couple of remaining human feet and shins), and known only from nineteenth-century engravings (Plate 11). It apparently shows an extraordinary balancing act. A man and an almost naked woman perch on a pair of tightropes, each holding or drinking from a large glass of wine. And as if that wasn't difficult enough, the man simultaneously inserts his large penis into the woman from behind. In fact, it is something of a relief to discover that the original picture was not quite as weird as this engraving makes it seem. For more than likely the whole tightrope element was introduced by the modern artist, who mistook the faint traces of the painter's guidelines, or possibly painted shadows, for this ingenious contraption. But even minus that particular bit of the balancing act, it is a provocative contrast to the decorous kiss from the other bar. What does it represent? Some archaeologists have thought it a scene drawn from a raunchy act in the local theatre (and so the large penis might be a pantomime-style appendage). Others, bearing in mind that the companion pictures are all of tavern life, conclude that this must be one of the activities you would find in the bar itself – whether it's a do-it-yourself cabaret, or something the drinkers might end up doing (or hope to end up doing) with the barmaids by the end of the evening.

Does this painting suggest that we should take the accusations of Roman writers more seriously? Certainly, in addition to the eating and drinking, gaming and flirtatious banter, there are many hints that the sexual encounters in at least some of these bars went beyond kissing. On the outside wall of one bar, for example, a small graffito (written entirely within a large letter O of an electoral slogan) reads: 'I fucked the landlady'. In others, we find women's names written on the wall in a clearly erotic context and sometimes with a price: 'Felicla the slave 2 *asses*', 'Successa the slave girl's a good lay', and even what has been taken to be a price list, 'Acria 4 *asses*, Epafra 10 *asses*, Firma 3 *asses*'.

We have to be careful in interpreting this kind of material. If today we were to see 'Tracy is a whore' or 'Donna sucks you off for a fiver' daubed up at a bar or bus shelter, we would not automatically assume that either of them was actually a prostitute. Nor would we assume that 'a fiver' was an accurate reflection of the prices charged for these sexual services in the area. They are just as likely to be insults as facts. So too in Pompeii – despite the attempts by some over-optimistic modern scholars to use evidence like this to construct lists of Pompeian prostitutes or even to work out an average price for the job. In fact that 'price list' may be nothing of the sort. The inclusion of *asses* is a modern addition; the original has simply three names with a number.

Yet the clustering of explicitly erotic scribble around some bars cannot be explained away, especially when it is combined with matching decorations. It has led to the conclusion that, while some drinking establishments in the town were just that, with a bit of sex on the side, some were not so much bars as fully fledged brothels. Both the bar on the Via dell'Abbondanza that we looked at and the Bar on the Via di Mercurio have often been identified as such: the first largely on the basis of the pygmy lamp, the second on the basis of the tightrope walkers (and perhaps another painting of which only a head survives, but which might originally have shown a couple making love). On some recent calculations, these are just two of a grand total of thirty-five brothels in the town. Pompeii, in other words, was a town in which there was roughly one brothel for every seventy-five free adult males. Even adding in the visitors, the country dwellers and the slaves who might have chosen to spend their pocket money in that way, it seems at first sight an over-generous ratio – or a level of sexual supply that would justify the worst fears of Christian moralists about pagan excess.

That, in a nutshell, is the 'Pompeian Brothel Problem'. Can we really believe that there were as many as thirty-five brothels in this small town? Or was there, as the most sober estimates have it, just one? How do we recognise a brothel when we find one? How do you tell the difference between a brothel and a bar?

Visiting the brothel

Roman sexual culture was different from our own. Women, as we have seen at Pompeii, were much more visible in the Roman world than in many other parts of the ancient Mediterranean. They shopped, they could dine with the men, they disposed of wealth and made lavish benefactions. Yet it was still a man's world in sex as it was in politics. Power, status and good fortune were expressed in terms of the phallus. Hence the presence of phallic imagery in almost unimaginable varieties all round the town.

This is one of the most puzzling, if not disconcerting, aspects of Pompeii for modern visitors. In earlier generations scholars reacted by removing many of these objects from public view, putting them in the 'Secret Cabinet' of the museum at Naples or otherwise under wraps. (When I first visited the site in the 1970s, the phallic figure at the entrance to the House of the Vettii was covered up, only to be revealed on request.) More recently the fashion has been to deflect attention from their sexuality by referring to them as 'magical', 'apotropaic' or 'averters of the evil eye'. But sexual they cannot avoid being. There are phalluses greeting you in doorways, phalluses above bread ovens, phalluses carved into the surface of the street and plenty more phalluses with bells on – and wings (Ill. 81). One of the most imaginative creations, which once jingled in the Pompeian breeze, is the lusty phallus-bird, a combination (I guess) of a joke and an unashamed celebration of the essential ingredient of manhood.

In this world, the main functions of respectable, well-off married women

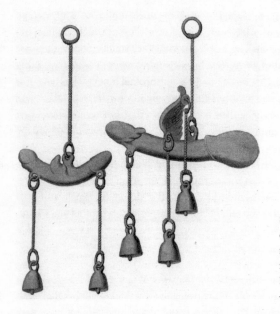

81. The 'phallus bird' was one of the Roman world's most extraordinary mythical creatures. Impressive, powerful – or just silly?

– that is, the occupants of the larger houses at Pompeii – were twofold: first the dangerous job of bearing children (childbirth was a big killer in ancient Rome, as it was in every period up to the modern era); and second the management of house and household. One tombstone from Rome famously hits the nail on the head. It is a epitaph put up by a husband to his wife Claudia. It praises her beauty, her conversation, her elegance; but the bottom line is that 'She bore two sons … she kept the house, she made wool.' The lives of poorer women might in practice have been more varied – whether as shopkeeper, landlady or moneylender – but I doubt that the underlying assumptions about their role were very much different. This was not a society where women were in control of their lives, their destinies or their sexualities. The stories told by Roman poets and historians of racy, licentious and apparently 'liberated' women of the capital are part fantasy, part applicable only to such truly exceptional characters as those in the imperial house itself. The empress Livia was not a typical Roman woman.

For elite men, the basic message was that sexual penetration correlated with pleasure and power. Sexual partners might be of either sex. There was plenty of male-with-male sexual activity in the Roman world, but only the very faintest hints that 'homosexuality' was seen as an exclusive sexual preference, let alone lifestyle choice. Unless they died too young, all Roman men married. Sexual fidelity to a wife was not prized or even particularly admired. In the search for pleasure, the wives, daughters and sons of other elite men were off-limits (and crossing that boundary might be heavily punished by law). The bodies of slaves and, up to a point, of social inferiors, both men and women, were there for the taking. It was not simply that no one minded if a man slept with his slave. That was, in part at least, what slaves were *for*. Poorer citizens, with a less-ready supply of servile sexual labour, would no doubt use prostitutes instead. As with dining, the rich provided for themselves 'in-house', while the poor looked outside.

Not that this made for a carefree sexual paradise, even for the men. As in most aggressively phallic cultures, the power of the phallus goes hand in hand with anxieties – whether about the sexual fidelity of one's wife (and so the paternity of one's children) or about one's own capacity to live up to the masculine ideal. In Rome itself, insinuations that a man had played the part of a woman, that he had been penetrated by another man, could be enough to blight a political career. In fact, many of the insults that scholars have sometimes taken as signs of Roman disapproval of homosexuality as such are directed only at those whose played the passive part. And, to return to Pompeii, whatever other associations that tiny bronze pygmy might have had, caught for ever in the act of attacking his own giant penis, it surely exposes some kind of sexual unease. Funny, fantastic, carni-valesque, it may have been. But it is hard to escape a more uncomfortable message too.

Nor is it the case that individual relations between Roman men and women were as unnuanced and mechanical as my stark summary might suggest. All kinds of relationships of care and tenderness flourished, whether between husband and wife, master and slave, lover and beloved. A expensive gold bracelet, for example, found on the body of a woman at a settlement just outside Pompeii is inscribed with the words 'From the master to his slave girl'. It reminds us that affection can exist even within these structures of exploitation (though how far that affection was reciprocated by the 'slave girl' concerned, we of course do not know). And the walls of Pompeii, both inside and out, carry plenty of vivid testimony to passion, jealousy and heartbreak with which it is hard for us not to identify, even if anachronistically: 'Marcellus loves Praestina and she doesn't give a damn', 'Restitutus has cheated on lots of girls'. All the same, the basic structure of Roman sexual relations was a fairly brutal one, and not one that was female-friendly.

Within this context prostitution had a place both on the streets (or in the brothel) and in the Roman imagination. For the Roman government, prostitution could be a source of revenue. The emperor Caligula, for example, is said to have imposed a tax on prostitutes – though how exactly it was levied, where it was applied and how long it remained in force is anyone's guess. Revenue apart, the main concern of the authorities was not to police the day-to-day activities of prostitutes but to draw a firm line between them and 'respectable' citizens, especially the wives of the Roman elite. Prostitution belonged to a motley group of occupations (including gladiators and actors) that were officially judged *infamis* or 'disgraceful', a stigma which carried with it certain legal disadvantages. Some prostitutes would anyway be slaves, but even those who were free citizens did not, for example, enjoy the protection against corporal punishment that usually went with Roman citizenship. Pimps and male prostitutes (who were, by the logic of Roman sexuality, effectively female) could not stand for public office. Tradition even had it that women prostitutes were not allowed to wear standard women's clothes, but dressed in a man's toga. This was a crossing of gender boundaries that firmly distinguished them from their respectable counterparts.

Prostitutes loomed perhaps even larger in the Roman imagination than in reality, from images of 'happy hookers' to the tragic victims of abduction sold off for sexual labour or the objects of public abomination or derision. In Roman stage comedies of the third and second centuries BCE, prostitution is a major theme. One of the characteristic romantic plots of these plays concerns the young man of good family who has fallen in love with a slave prostitute, controlled by a malevolent pimp. Despite their love, marriage is impossible, even if the young man could raise the money to buy her, because his father would not countenance such a wife for his son. But there is a happy ending. For it turns out that the object of his desire was actually a respectable girl all along: she had been the victim of a kidnapping and sold to the pimp; so she was not a 'real' prostitute after all. In comedy, at least, we are allowed to glimpse the awkward truth that the boundary between respectability and prostitution might not be quite so clear as we thought.

It is against this background that archaeologists have tried to pinpoint the prostitutes of Pompeii, and to identify the physical remains of the brothels. The total number they come up with depends entirely on the criteria they choose to adopt. For some the presence of erotic paintings can be enough to indicate a place for commercial sex. So, on this interpretation, a small room near the kitchen of the House of the Vettii, decorated with three paintings of a couple, man and woman, making love on a bed, is a dedicated place of prostitution – a money-spinning sideline for the owners (or for their cook). It can be linked for good measure to a tiny scratched graffito in the front porch of the house which may offer the services of 'Eutychis' for 2 *asses*. Alternatively, of course, the room has just been decorated in this way to please a favourite cook (whose lodgings, next to the kitchen, it may well have been), and the scrawled information (or insult) about Eutychis is nothing to do with it at all.

Others place the qualifying standard for a brothel rather higher. One scholar lists three conditions that more reliably indicate that we are dealing with a place primarily used for sex for profit: a masonry bed in a small room easily accessible to the public; paintings with explicitly sexual scenes; and a cluster of graffiti of the 'I fucked here' type. Needless to say, if you require all of these conditions to be met, the number of brothels in the town goes down – to one. On this argument, the upstairs or backrooms of bars might well have provided a place where some people sometimes paid for sex, but that is different from a brothel, in the strict sense of the word.

There are all kinds of traps for the archaeologist here. We have already noted the difficulties in interpreting the erotic graffiti and in deciding if the plain single rooms with masonry beds and doors directly from the streets were places of prostitution or just very small lodgings for the poor (why, after all, must we imagine that stone beds were particularly suited to prostitution?). But the key question concerns the difference between the dedicated brothel and any of the many other places in the town where sex and money were not kept entirely separate.

We have probably been rather too easily taken in by the Romans' own attempts to insist that prostitutes were a clearly separate class of women (or men) and by the institutional image of the brothel and pimp given by Roman comedy. Most of the 'prostitutes' in Pompeii were probably the barmaids or the landladies (or the flower-sellers, or the pig-keepers, or the weavers for that matter) who sometimes slept with customers after closing-time, sometimes for money, sometimes on the premises, sometimes not. I very much doubt that many of them really wore togas (a classic piece of Roman elite male myth-making), thought of themselves as prostitutes or defined their place of work as a brothel – any more than the modern massage parlour is a brothel, or a hotel where, if you ask, you can rent a room by the hour. The search for the Pompeian brothel is, in other words, a category mistake. Sex for money was almost as diffused through the town as eating, drinking or sleeping.

Except in one case: a building five minutes' walk east of the Forum, just behind

82. This image of love-making from the brothel is set in more luxurious surroundings than the brothel itself seems to have offered. The bed is comfortably appointed, with a thick pillow. Next to it, on the left, stands a lamp, a hint that we are to imagine that the scene is set at night time.

the Stabian Baths, which meets all of the toughest criteria there have been for such an identification. It has five small cells, each with its own built-in bed and a series of explicitly erotic paintings, showing couples making love in a variety of different positions (Ill. 82). It still contains almost 150 graffiti, including a good number of the 'I fucked here' type (though not all are of that kind: one person at least was moved to scratch a quotation from Virgil). It is a rather dark and dingy place. Set on a corner, it has a door onto both streets (Fig. 17). What is now the main entrance in the one-way system used to cope with the crowds of tourists was probably the main entrance in antiquity too. If you enter this way you find yourself in a wide corridor, with three cubicles on the right and two on the left. At the end of the corridor, a masonry screen blocks the view of what lies beyond. That turns out to be the latrine – so clearly some care had been taken to ensure privacy for toilet-users, or alternatively to ensure that incoming clients were not greeted by the sight of another customer on the toilet.

The walls are mostly painted white, in what had been a relatively recent redecoration before the eruption (the imprint of a coin of 72 CE has been found in the plaster). High up above the level of the entrance to the cubicles are the erotic paintings, which show men making love to women from behind, underneath, on

Figure 17. The brothel. Nothing fancy here. The brothel was small and cramped. Apart from the lavatory, there was nothing but five tiny cubicles off a hallway. Where the money changed hands is far from clear – as is the use of the upper floor. Was it a separately rented apartment, or did it house the pimp and the girls?

top, and so on. There are just two significant variants. One painting shows a single male figure with not just one, but two large erect phalluses (on the 'two is better than one' principle, presumably); another shows a man on a bed and a woman standing by his side, not engaging in lovemaking, but looking at some kind of tablet – perhaps meant to be, in a nice self-referential joke, an erotic painting.

The cubicles themselves are small, with short masonry beds, which would (one hopes) have been covered with cushions and covers, or at least something a bit softer than the hard stone. There is now no sign of any way of screening off the cubicles; but that may well be a consequence of the rough techniques of the 1860s excavators. If the view to the latrine was blocked by a substantial barrier, it is hard not to imagine at least a curtain which could be pulled across these door-ways. Most, though not all, of the graffiti comes from inside the cubicles, and it is from these scraps of writing that we get some hints of who used the brothel and how.

The men who came here were not afraid to leave their names on the wall. So far as we can tell, these names include none of the well-known figures of the Pompeian elite. Prostitutes, as we already noted, were probably for those without ready access to the sexual services of their own slaves. The one man who clearly notes his job was an 'ointment seller'. In fact, this collection of graffiti is one of the best indications we have that some command of reading and writing was found widely among the relatively humble people at Pompeii. Most of them sign up as individuals: 'Florus', 'Felix went with Fortunata', 'Posphorus fucked here'. But occasionally, it seems, the customers came on a joint outing: 'Hermeros with Phileteros and Caphisus fucked here'. This was possibly group sex, but more likely a boys' night out.

The prostitutes themselves are harder to place. The names on the walls include a number of Greek or eastern women's names (including, interestingly, a 'Myrtale' (p. 230), which can often indicate slave status. But these may be 'profes-sional' names, assumed for the job, and so tell us nothing about the real background of the girls concerned. There is no clear evidence of any male prostitutes, though there are some references in the graffiti to sexual practices (such as buggery: in Latin *pedicare*, usually referring to men) which would not absolutely exclude the possibility that men as well as women worked here. Where there is a sign of prices, they are rather above the '2 *asses*' we often find on the walls of bars. One man, for example, claims that he 'had a good fuck for a *denarius* [that is 16 *asses*]'. This may mean that sex on the side with a serving girl came cheaper than in the brothel itself. It could be a further hint that the '2 *asses*' line was more of a conventional insult than a real price.

The layout of the graffiti within the building may tell us even more. One recent study has pointed out that the first two cubicles nearest the main entrance contain between them almost three quarters of the graffiti. Why? Possibly because they were used not just for sex itself, but as waiting rooms, so men had time here to scratch their thoughts and their boasts into the plaster. More likely, and more simply, these were the cubicles next to the street which were used more. You came in and took the first available 'slot'.

How the brothel was organised, we can only guess. Were the girls who worked here slaves with a pimp owner who ran an organised business? Or was it all rather more casual? More freelance? One relevant factor is an upper floor, accessed by a separate entrance on the side street. This had five rooms, one considerably larger than the others, linked by a balcony serving as a corridor between them. There are no fixed beds here, nor erotic paintings nor surviving graffiti of any sort (though there is much less surviving decoration at all). There is nothing to prove what happened on this level. It could have been more prostitution. Or it could have been where the girls lived (and on this model the pimp perhaps occupied the larger room). Alternatively it was not directly linked to the brothel at all, but was a separate rented apartment (address: 'above the brothel'). In which case, the working girls might simply have worked, lived and slept in those small cubicles.

It is, frankly, a rather grim place. And it is hardly improved by the stream of visitors who – since its restoration a few years ago – now make a bee-line for it. It usually proves to offer the tourist only a brief pleasure. It has been calculated that the average visit lasts roughly three minutes. The local guides meanwhile do their best to make it appealing, with not entirely accurate stories about the peculiar encounters that once took place in it. As some have been heard to explain: 'The paintings have a practical purpose. The prostitutes couldn't speak Latin, you see. So the clients had to point to a picture before they went in to let the girls know what they wanted.'

A good bath

A tombstone from Rome, put up some time in the first century CE to an ex-slave, Tiberius Claudius Secundus, by his partner Merope, includes the following piquant observation: 'wine, sex and baths ruin our bodies, but they are the stuff of life — wine, sex and baths'. Tiberius Claudius Secundus had not, in fact, done too badly, for he had lived to be fifty-two years old. But the wry sentiment blazoned here was almost certainly a popular Roman maxim. A version of it turns up, for example, as far away as Turkey: 'Baths, wine and sex make fate come faster'.

So far in this chapter we have looked at the wine and the sex of ancient Pompeii. What about the baths: those three large sets of public bathing complexes in the town (now called, from their locations, the Stabian, Forum and Central Baths) and a number of smaller privately owned commercial establishments, catering to a public or semi-public trade?

Roman bathing was synonymous with Roman culture: wherever the Romans went, so too did Roman baths. Bathing in this sense was not simply a method of washing the body, though cleanliness was one part of its purpose. It was a mixture of a whole range of (for us) different activities: sweating, exercising, steaming, swimming, ball-gaming, sunbathing, being 'scraped' and rubbed down. It was Turkish bathing plus, with all kinds of further optional extras that might be added on, from barber's services to – in the very grandest metropolitan versions – libraries. The bathing complexes that were designed to house all these activities were some of the largest and most elaborate and sophisticated pieces of architecture in the Roman world. In Pompeii, the three main public baths together occupy a space larger than the Forum itself, even though they are tiny by comparison with the vast schemes of the capital. The whole of the Forum Baths at Pompeii would fit easily into the swimming pool of the third-century CE Baths of Caracalla at Rome.

The baths were both a social leveller and one of those places where the inequalities of Roman society were most glaringly on display. Everybody except the very poorest went to the baths, including some slaves – even if they were only acting as retinue for their master. The very richest did have their own private baths at their home, as in the grand House of the Menander at Pompeii. But, as a general rule, the well-off would have shared their bathing with those less fortunate than themselves. In other words, unlike for dining, they went *out* to bathe.

On the one hand, the conventions of bathing brought everyone down to size. Bathing naked, or nearly naked (there is evidence for both practices), the poor were in principle no different from the wealthy – possibly healthier and of finer physique. This was Roman society on display to itself, without all those usual markers of social, political or economic rank: striped togas, special 'senatorial' sandals or whatever. It was, as one modern historian has put it, 'a hole in the ozone layer of the social hierarchy'.

On the other hand, the stories which Roman writers tell about baths and bathers return time and again to competition, jealousy, anxiety, social differentials and ostentation. This was partly a question of the body beautiful, for both men and women. According to one ancient biographer, the emperor Augustus' mother could not bear to go to the baths ever again, after an unsightly mark appeared on her body when she was pregnant (it was in fact a sign of the divine descent of her son). And the poet Martial wrote a pointed epigram about a man who laughed at those with hernias, presumably in the baths, until he was bathing one day and noticed he had one himself.

But it was also a question again of displaying (and pulling) rank. A notorious incident in the second century BCE involved a consul's wife, who was travelling in Italy and decided that she wanted to use the men's baths in a town not far from Pompeii (the men's suite must have been better appointed than the women's). So not only did she have the men thrown out, but her husband had the local elected *quaestor* flogged for not clearing them out quickly enough, and not keeping the baths themselves clean.

One nice variant on this theme, with a happier ending, concerns the emperor Hadrian. The story is told that when he was visiting the baths one day (for even emperors might bathe in public – or make a point of so doing once in a while) he noticed a retired soldier rubbing his back against the wall. When questioned, the man explained that he could not afford a slave to rub him down. So Hadrian gave him some slaves and the cost of their maintenance. Returning on a later occasion, he found a whole group of men rubbing their backs on the wall. The cue for another act of imperial generosity? No. He suggested that they should rub each other.

There was also some edgy ambivalence about the moral character of the baths. True, many Romans assumed that bathing was good for you, and indeed it might be recommended by doctors. But there was at the same time a strong suspicion that it was a morally corrupting habit. Nakedness, luxury and the pleasures of hot, steamy recreation were in the eyes of many a dangerous combination. It was not only the noise that worried the philosopher Seneca, when he complained about living above a set of baths (p. 108).

Archaeologists have tended to stereotype and normalise Roman baths much as they have Roman houses. An array of Latin names are applied to the various parts of the cycle of cold and hot rooms: *frigidarium* (cold room), *tepidarium* (warm room), *caldarium* (hot room), *laconicum* (hot sweat room), *apodyterium* (changing room) and so on. These terms were sometimes used by Romans themselves. In fact, an inscription in the Stabian Baths at Pompeii records the installation of a *laconicum* and a *destrictorium* (a scraping room). But they were not the standard everyday words that modern plans and guidebooks suggest. I very much doubt that many Romans would, in practice, have said, 'Meet you in the *tepidarium*.'

Nor was there the kind of fixed procedure in the baths that these impressive Latin terms encourage us to think. Archaeologists are almost always too keen to systematise Roman customs. Although we are often told by experts on the baths that the principle of Roman bathing was to move through progressively hotter rooms, before going back to the beginning and finishing with a cold plunge, there is no firm evidence for that. All kinds of different pathways would have been possible (and, in fact, some experts hold the opposite view that they worked through from hot to cold). Nor is there any reason to suppose that a visit would always have required a couple of hours, minimum, or that visits for men were always in the afternoon. Practice was almost certainly much more varied, procedures much more 'pick and mix', than the modern desire to impose rules and norms would have us believe.

The variety of opportunities and entertainments offered by a relatively large bath complex will become clearer if we take a look at the Stabian Baths at Pompeii (Fig. 18). One of the three main sets of public baths in the centre of the town, these were – like so much else – under repair at the time of the eruption, with only the women's area in full working order. In fact there must have been a certain pressure on bathing space in Pompeii in 79. Of the public baths, only the Forum Baths were operating to capacity. A brand-new set (the Central Baths) were being built to the most up-to-the-minute designs but had not yet been completed. Even the private commercial establishments, which tended to be smaller than those operated by the city, and which might have been more picky about their clientele, were not all up and running. One, for example, had been in ruins for many years (perhaps a commercial failure), and the so-called Sarno Baths on the lower floors of an apartment block (pp. 107–8) were being restored. Those on the Estate of Julia Felix, 'an elegant bath suite for prestige clients' as the rental notice puts it (p. 110), were one of the few in operation – and were presumably, given the likely demand, a nice money spinner.

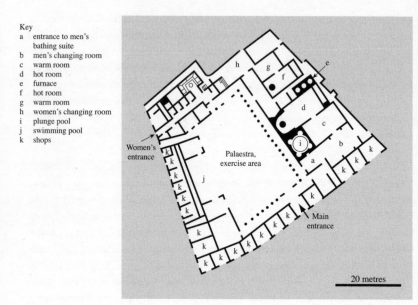

Key
a   entrance to men's
    bathing suite
b   men's changing room
c   warm room
d   hot room
e   furnace
f   hot room
g   warm room
h   women's changing room
i   plunge pool
j   swimming pool
k   shops

Women's entrance

Palaestra, exercise area

Main entrance

20 metres

Figure 18. The Stabian Baths

The Stabian Baths were the oldest in the city, going back long before the Roman colony. The different phases of their construction are very complicated to disentangle (and not helped by the fact that the notes of one major study of the fabric were destroyed in the bombing of Dresden in the Second World War). The very first building on the site, which some archaeologists have dated as early as the fifth century BCE, took the form of an exercise court (*palaestra*) and a row of 'hip baths' in the Greek style. But the baths as we see them now were the result of a major redevelopment in the middle of the second century, with a series of improvements and refurbishments going on right up to the end of the city's life, including the provision of water direct from the aqueduct, rather than from the earlier well (Ill. 83). We assume that they were publicly owned and administered, not only because of their size (it is hard to imagine a complex this large being private enterprise), but also thanks to inscriptions which record the investment of public money: the sundial, with its Oscan text noting that it was set up with the proceeds of the fines; and building of the *laconicum* and *destrictarium* by *duoviri* in the first century BCE, 'out of the money', as the inscription states, 'which they were legally obliged to spend either on games or on a monument'.

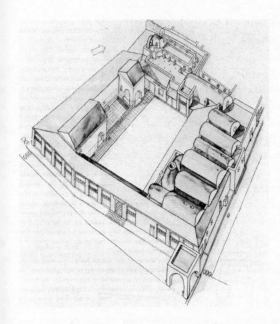

83. The Stabian Baths. In the centre of this reconstruction drawing is the open exercise area. On the right are the vaulted rooms which form the men's and women's bathing suites. The Via dell' Abbondanza runs along the front face of the complex (bottom left) – with the large arch, associated with the family of Marcus Holconius Rufus.

The main entrance was from the Via dell'Abbondanza, just near the statue of Marcus Holconius Rufus, where the street widens to form a little piazza. A row of shops fronted the street itself, but going through the vestibule you came into a colonnaded courtyard, which was the exercise (and sitting) area. At some point money may have changed hands. For while some public baths made no charge, others levied a small fee. We do not know which was the case here, but the easiest place to have taken any cash would have been at the entrance to the main bath suite at (*a*).

The layout of the bathing rooms themselves is extremely practical. In the Stabian Baths the heating is provided by a single wood-burning furnace, which was connected to the underfloor heating system or 'hypocaust'. The earliest example of this system to survive in the Roman world (it was probably invented in Campania), this provided a much more powerful way of heating the rooms than the earlier system of braziers, which was still in use at the Forum Baths (Ill. 84). The basic principle was that the floors of the rooms to be heated were raised on small pillars of tile, so providing an air space underneath. This was warmed by the heat of the fire – the nearer to the furnace each room was, the hotter it would become. The arrangement in the Stabian Baths allows two sets of room to be heated on either side of the fire: two very hot rooms, (*d*) and the smaller (*f*), and two warm rooms, (*c*) and the smaller (*g*).

Why two sets? The smaller set was for women, whose bathing was here segregated from the men's. They did not use the impressive main entrance to the baths on the Via dell'Abbondanza, but entered up a side street through a door, which is said to have carried the painted sign 'Women' (visible soon after the original excavations, it is now completely illegible). Instead of emerging into an airy courtyard, they had to make their way down a long, poky corridor before they reached a place they could perhaps pay to leave their clothes (*h*) and enter their own smaller suite of rooms. This was the arrangement at the Forum Baths too, where there was a second less elaborate series of female bathing rooms. In the Central Baths, no such separate provision was planned: either women would have been excluded, or they would have bathed at separate times, or it would have been that red rag to ancient moralists – mixed bathing.

For the men visiting the Stabian Baths, the choices would have been many. They left their clothes in the changing room, (*b*), a beautifully stuccoed room, where the individual niches for the bathers' belongings still survive (Ill. 85). We may guess that the establishment's staff included a guard for this facility, but Roman writers tell many tales of petty thieving at the baths. Maybe it was better to leave your valuables at home. They could then move outside for all kinds of games and exercise. There was a swimming pool, (*j*), and, if the discovery of a couple of stone balls is significant, perhaps a place where you could play some form of bowls. The oiling and scraping that traditionally went with Roman exercise may have been provided by the visitor's own slaves (brought with him for the purpose), or on a Hadrianic self-help basis. But there may have been staff at the baths for this too – though where the 'scraping down room' built by the *duoviri* was, we do not know. Inside the bath-suite itself, there was the possibility to sweat in the heat, to sit around in the small pools (rather like a modern hot tub), or to plunge into the cold bath, (*i*) – which is reckoned to be a later conversion of the earlier *laconicum*.

For those who lived in small dingy houses, or perched over their workshop, these baths must have been a real People's Palace (Plate 16). Not only were they marvellously spacious, with all the pleasures of swimming and splashing and whatever kind of exercising took your fancy, but they were decorated in lavish style. The barrel vaults of the bathing suite were painted in rich colours, while the sun streamed in dramatically through roundels in the ceilings. Where the sun did not stream, the rooms were kept brightly twinkling with a battery of lamps. In one corridor of the Forum Baths a store of 500 lamps was discovered.

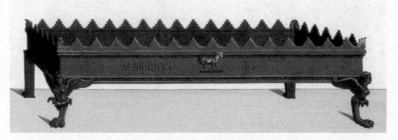

84. Bronze brazier from the Forum Baths, carrying a characteristic Pompeian visual pun. It was a gift to the Baths from a man called Marcus Nigidius Vaccula. 'Vaccula' means 'cow' – and so he emblazoned a cow as an emblem on this piece of metalwork.

It is not only the modern visitor who is drawn to reflect on quite how hygienic it all was. There was no chlorination in the pools to mitigate the effects of the urine and other less sterile bodily detritus. Nor was the water in the various pools constantly and quickly replaced, even if there was sometimes an attempt to introduce a steady flow of new water into them, which would at least have diluted the filth. The hot tubs in the bathing suite itself must have been a seething mass of bacteria (just as many eighteenth-century European spas). Martial jokes about the faeces that ended up in them, and the Roman medical writer Celsus offers the sensible advice not to go to the baths with a fresh wound ('it normally leads to gangrene') . The baths, in other words, may have been a place of wonder, pleasure and beauty for the humble Pompeian bather. They might also have killed him.

Unsurprisingly, given the nakedness and the possible mingling of women and men (at least in Roman fantasy), baths were also associated with sex. Just like bars, some of them have been thought to be brothels masquerading under another name, with prostitutes lingering to pick up clients. The problem exercised Roman legal writers and jurists too. In trying to work out who exactly should suffer the legal penalty of being *infamis* for their involvement in prostitution, one writer cites a practice known 'in certain provinces' (not in Italy, in other words), where the bath manager has slaves to guard the bathers' clothes, who offer a much wider range of services. Should he count as a pimp, Roman legal brains pondered – in theory.

In Pompeii we come face to face with this issue, in practice, in a set of baths situated just outside the city walls, next to the Marine Gate, and known now as

85. The men's changing room from the Stabian Baths, before its restoration. Clearly visible are the stuccoed ceiling and, on the right, the 'lockers' for leaving clothes.

the Suburban Baths. Excavated in the 1980s, these baths were a private commercial operation, located on the ground floor of a building which had domestic and other accommodation above. Much smaller than the public bathing complexes in the town centre, and with no sign of a women's section, their attraction must have been the wonderful views they commanded over the sea, which bathers could enjoy from a spacious sun terrace (this was not the place to come to exercise). First built in the early first century CE, these too were undergoing repairs at the time of the eruption.

Their modern claim to fame is the changing room. High up on one wall you can still see eight scenes of athletic sexual intercourse, mostly couples (one of which *may* be two women), but also a trio and a foursome enjoying group sex (Ill. 86). These now survive on one wall only, but originally they would have appeared on two other walls, adding up to perhaps twenty-four different varieties of sexual position in all. Under the erotic scenes themselves, we find paintings of a series of wooden boxes or baskets, each one numbered (I–XVI still survive). Why the pictures of sex, and why combine them with pictures of numbered boxes?

The most likely answer lies in the simple fact that this was the changing room.

Plate 13. Almost a 'comic strip' series of paintings on the wall of the Inn of Salvius (p. 230). The couple in the first scene used to be taken for two men until cleaning revealed that the left hand figure was female. Although the final scene is damaged, it is clear enough that that landlord is laying down the law: 'If you want to fight, go outside.'

Plate 14. Among the gathering of humans and gods that makes up the Villa of the Mysteries frieze (p. 132), a boy reads out from a scroll, watched over by a woman, perhaps his mother. Part of the visual 'joke' lies in that fact that we the viewers can neither see nor hear what he is reading out.

Plate 15. The face of the defeated king Darius from the 'Alexander Mosaic' in the House of the Faun (p. 28).

Plate 16. The baths offered a glimpse of luxury to the ordinary Pompeian bather. This nineteenth-century painting recreates the ambience of the Stabian Baths (p. 246).

Plate 17. In the centre (*tablinum*) of the House of the Tragic Poet (Fig 6), this mosaic depicted a group of actors preparing to go on stage. The performance is to be a satyr play, hence the thespians are squeezing into goat costumes (pp. 254–5).

Plate 18. A painting from the sacred precinct of Isis in a nineteenth-century copy. The Greek priestess Io, one of Zeus' lovers, is received in Egypt by the goddess Isis. According to the myth, Io had been hounded by the jealous Hera, Zeus' wife – who at one stage had turned her into a heifer, hence the horns. She is supported by a river god (p. 306).

Plate 19. The garden wall of the House of the Ancient Hunt, named after this painting.

Plate 20. A nineteenth-century version of a miniature frieze in the House of the Vettii, showing cupids as metal workers.

Plate 21. Here, in the original paintwork from the House of the Vettii, the cupids have a chariot crash. (p. 126).

Plate 22. A vista onto a foreign world. In this painting, pygmies get into all kinds of adventures. One is riding a crocodile, another is apparently being eaten by a hippo, though help is at hand.

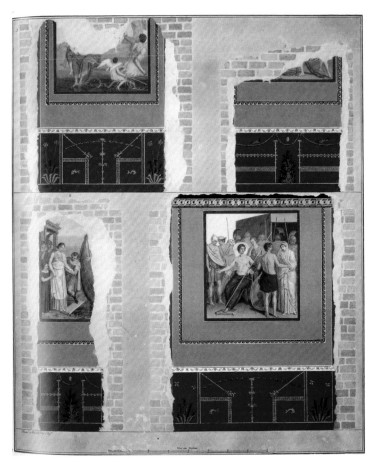

Plate 23. A composite image of the walls of the House of the Tragic Poet. On the lower left Helen departs on her journey to Troy. On the right, in another moment from the Trojan War, the prisoner Briseis is taken from Achilles to be given to Agamemnon (pp. 147–8).

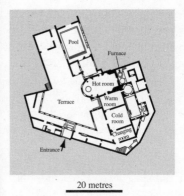

Figure 19. The Suburban Baths. This small set of privately owned, commercial baths, was arranged around a large central terrace overlooking the sea. The notorious erotic paintings come from the changing room.

20 metres

Unlike the equivalent in the Stabian Baths, there were no built-in niches to leave your clothes, but still visible are the traces of a shelf running round the room under the paintings – on which individual boxes or baskets would have been placed. The paintings above serve to number the various baskets and to give the

86. The changing room of the Suburban Baths. The details of the design may now be hard to make out, but on the lower register a series of numbered boxes is shown, in perspective (here III to VI). Above each one is a scene of love making.

bather an amusing *aide mémoire* for remembering where he had left his kit: 'number VI – that's the threesome'. Others have wanted to push the interpretation further and suggest that these paintings acted as an advertisement for a brothel on the upper floor, or even as a menu of options for sale ('Half an hour of number VII, please'). Perhaps this is also a case (as 'in certain provinces') where the slave girls in the changing room were doubling as prostitutes. Perhaps the graffito near one of the entrances to the upper floor, apparently advertising the services of Attice for the (high) price of 16 *asses*, is to be connected to these paintings.

We do not know. But there is a curious sting in the tail to the story of these paintings. Although we can now see eight of them in quite good condition, they all seem to have been painted over sometime before the eruption. The decoration of the rest of the room was left untouched: someone wanted to cover up just these. Why? One argument suggests that there had been a change in baths manager (and no longer one with an investment in the supposed brothel upstairs). But maybe it was an even simpler explanation.

Maybe even some Pompeians had occasionally had enough of pictures of sex.

CHAPTER EIGHT

FUN AND GAMES

The throw of the dice

A fourth-century CE Roman historian, with little time for the poor, referred disdainfully to the strange snorting noise that you might hear, late at night, in the taverns of the city of Rome. It was nothing to do with any sexual fun and games; it came instead from the gaming tables. The players were so intent on their dice that they produced this disgusting sound, as they drew breath into their rattling nostrils. This is one of the rare occasions where we can instantly reconstruct the sound of Roman life – a sound that would no doubt have been heard loud in the bars of Pompeii where, to judge from the paintings we looked at in the last chapter, gaming and dicing were a major accompaniment to the food and drink.

We do not know exactly what game the men in the paintings were playing. Roman board games, like our own, came in many different varieties, with different titles. 'Little Robbers' or, perhaps, 'Little Soldiers' (*latrunculi*) was one of the favourites, and was certainly played at Pompeii; for one election poster offers a candidate the support – unwanted maybe – of the '*latrunculi* players'. Another which is often mentioned in Roman literature was called 'Twelve Writings' (*duodecim scripta*). No rulebook survives for any of these games, and there have been all kinds of scholarly attempts to reconstruct the play from casual references. *Latrunculi*, for example, may have involved trying to blockade or hem in your opponent's pieces in a way somewhat reminiscent of modern draughts. But most of them, then as now, followed the same basic principle: a dice throw allowed the player to move his counter or counters on the board, or towards the winning goal; the sheer chance of the fall of the dice was the crucial element in success, but varying amounts of skill could no doubt be deployed in the movement of the pieces. There was certainly enough skill involved for the emperor Claudius to write a book (sadly lost) on the art of *alea*, a generic term for such dice games.

Gambling on the outcome was also a crucial element. Tavern games could win the contestants a lot of money, or lose it. One graffito from Pompeii boasts of a particularly spectacular win: 'I won at Nuceria playing *alea*, 855 ½ *denarii* – honestly, it's true'. This was a grand sum, amounting to 3422 *sesterces*, which was almost four times the annual pay of a legionary soldier. Most prizes must have been much lower, as the lucky winner at Nuceria hints with his insistence on the truth of his claim. All the same, it helps us get a little closer to understanding the social level of Pompeian café culture. These men may have been humble, and very poor by the standards of the local elite, but they still had a bit of time and cash to spare. Gambling is not, and was not, an occupation of the destitute.

The Roman authorities legislated against games and gambling of this sort with an enthusiasm that they never showed for regulating prostitution. Ineffectually no doubt, and with glaring double standards. For it is clear that all these games (as the emperor Claudius' passion for them shows) were played right across the social spectrum. Gambling was such a distinctively Roman habit that one eccentric theorist in the first century BCE could argue that Homer must have been a Roman, because he depicts the suitors of Penelope in the *Odyssey* playing dice. No gaming boards actually survive from Pompeii, though they have been found elsewhere in the Roman world. The Pompeians presumably played on wood. And there is a good deal of debate about whether the objects sometimes identified as dice throwers are not in fact small cups. But gaming counters and dice have been found right across the town, including in the very richest houses: a couple of lovely dice, and a handful of counters, were discovered in the House of the Menander for example.

It was tavern, rather than domestic, gaming that the Romans wanted to restrict. Why? Partly, no doubt, because it risked destabilising the social and economic hierarchies. A culture which ranked its members so strictly by the amount of wealth they owned would almost inevitably resist the idea that the mere throw of the dice could change a person's status. Seen in those terms, the man who had his windfall at Nuceria was not simply lucky but a dangerous disruption of the social order. But an interesting recent suggestion is that the problems of the Roman elite with tavern gaming also related to more general questions in Roman culture about the use of leisure (*otium*). How was leisure properly to be spent? What was the right time for leisure? Were particular leisure activities suited to particular contexts only? Was gaming acceptable within the confines of a rich private house but not in a bar?

But proper or decidedly improper, dice and gaming were a favourite leisure activity in Pompeii. As we move on now to consider other ways of using *otium* – the shows and spectacles which, with their theatres and Amphitheatres, have left a much bigger imprint in the archaeological record than a humble game of dice – it is worth reflecting that more man-hours were spent (or wasted) at Pompeii at the gaming board than were ever spent in front of actors or gladiators.

Starstruck?

Pompeii was a theatrical town. In 79 CE it had two permanent stone theatres, though in varying states of disrepair. One went back to the second century BCE but was refurbished and enlarged by Marcus Holconius Rufus so that it would seat some 5000 people (Ill. 87). Parts of the permanent brick stage set are still visible, as well as the fittings for the curtain (in Rome the curtain did not fall, as in the modern theatre; it was pulled up from the ground). The other, directly next to it, was a smaller Covered Theatre seating up to 2000 people, erected in the early years of the Roman colony by the same men who built the Amphitheatre (Ill. 69). By the time the first permanent stone theatre was put up in the city of Rome in the 50s BCE, financed from the spoils of Pompey the Great's Eastern wars, little Pompeii had had two theatres for almost two decades.

More than this, if you walk through the richer houses of the town, or through the galleries of paintings and mosaics now in the museum at Naples, you are repeatedly confronted with images of the stage, drama and theatrical perform- ance. The name of the House of the Menander, as we have seen, is taken from the painting of the fourth-century BCE Greek comic dramatist in the central niche of the peristyle, directly aligned with the main entrance to the house (Ill. 44). Menander is shown seated holding a papyrus roll; he is clearly named both under the chair and on the roll. Opposite him was another similar figure, now barely visible, but almost certainly representing another dramatist: Euripides is one guess.

A nice complement to the Menander are two mosaics from the Villa of Cicero just outside the city walls. Made out of exquisitely small *tesserae*, they are 'signed' by their artist: Dioskourides of Samos. One shows three women seated drinking round a table, the other a group of musicians playing tambourine, cymbals and

87. The view towards the stage of the Large Theatre – and towards the more spacious seats for the elite on the front rows. The wooden stage in this photograph has been inserted for a modern performance.

flute (Plate 1). All the figures wear theatrical masks (one of the women is an impressive 'old hag'), showing that these are scenes from plays, not real life. But which? A lucky find of similar mosaics on the Greek island of Lesbos, but this time with titles, makes it almost certain that they are intended to be scenes from comedies of Menander: the women are taken from his *Women at Breakfast*; the musicians probably from his *Girl Possessed by the Gods* (in which music is used to test out whether a girl who *says* she is possessed really is). Meanwhile a scene from a tragedy of Euripides, *The Children Heracles*, has been identified in a painting in the House of Casca Longus. Again the characters are shown fully masked, and the painting makes a companion piece to a scene taken from some unidentified comedy, featuring a wonderfully pot-bellied old slave holding forth in front of a young couple.

There is an interest in the backstage world too. The mosaic that held pride of place in the centre of the *tablinum* in the House of the Tragic Poet showed actors getting ready to go on stage (Plate 17). The performance for which they were preparing was neither a traditional tragedy or comedy, but a 'satyr play' – a kind of lusty burlesque that in the fifth-century BCE Athenian theatre had followed a series of three tragedies, offering the audience some much-needed light relief. In this scene the couple on the far left are already wearing the distinctive goat costumes of the chorus in this style of show (a chorus made up of satyrs – half-goats, half-men). The rest of the company is not entirely ready yet. The actor at the back is still squeezing into his costume (another goaty-outfit), the flautist is practising his tunes, while the director in the centre is giving his final instructions. At his feet and on the table behind are masks waiting to be put on – though these also serve as a signal to us of the theatrical nature of the scene. In fact, throughout the repertoire of Pompeian domestic decoration, masks such as these are one of the commonest elements, perched on those fantastic painted architectural extravaganzas or floating in the middle of walls. It as almost as if the theatre provided a model for the whole spectacle of Pompeian wall-painting itself: painting made a theatre out of a house.

The big question is how we put these paintings and mosaics together with the surviving remains of the theatres themselves. We have seen on other occasions that the decoration of house or bar may reflect, in idealised or humorous form, the activities of the residents and the painting's viewers – whether drinking, dining, or gambling. Do these scenes of the classics of Greek drama on the floors and walls of Pompeian houses suggest that the local theatres were the venues for revival performances of this kind of play. When the *duoviri* sponsored dramatic performances as part of their required munificence to the town, did they choose reruns of old and rather upmarket favourites, such as Menander and Euripides, in Greek or in Latin translation?

A few modern scholars have thought so. But the short answer is that we have little hard, direct information on what was performed in either of these theatres, nor how often performances in them would have taken place. Unlike the gladiatorial fights, for which we have almost the ancient equivalent of programmes, no playbills or painted advertisements for shows in the theatres survive. Most historians have been unconvinced by the idea that classic Greek drama was much in evidence on the Pompeian stage. There are, after all, no examples of it in the literary quotations scrawled on Pompeian walls (in fact, these include no recognisable quote from any play at all, except for a single line from a tragedy of Seneca). And many of the paintings and mosaics which depicted classical drama were no doubt based on famous works of Greek art and were intended as a more general symbolic reflection of the cultural world of ancient Greece and its symbols. They were not a direct reference to local performances.

The favourite candidates for the Pompeian stage have usually been various Italian genres. Often cited have been so-called 'Atellan farces', a type of comedy of which only a few fragments survive, but is supposed to have been originally an Oscan invention. Featuring stock characters such as Manducus, the glutton, or Bucco, the braggart, they have been compared to the Morality Plays of the Middle Ages. Also in the frame are other styles of Roman comedy, such as survive in the plays of Plautus and Terence, and even performances that are not theatrical in our sense of the word. One idea is that the Covered Theatre was not designed for drama at all, but was built to be the assembly hall of the early colonists.

All of these suggestions are perfectly possible, but no more than that. Some careful detective work, however, does allow us to get a little closer to the staples of the Pompeian stage. Scholars have only recently turned their attention to two genres of theatrical performance, again very largely lost, that were hugely popular, among emperors as well as paupers, in Italy during Pompeii's last hundred years or so. They are mime and pantomime. Mime came in many forms, performed as street entertainment, in private houses, as short interval entertainment in the theatre and as the main feature. Ribald comedy, going under such titles as 'The Wedding', 'The Fuller' or 'The Weaving Girls' (perhaps, as one scholar has suggested, the ancient equivalent of a play called 'The Swedish Masseuses'), it was played by both male and female actors who, unusually, did not wear masks. Sometimes it was improvised according to the lines of a plot invented by the *Archimimus* ('chief mime'); sometimes it was scripted. Despite the title and our own understanding of 'mime', it was not silent – but a mixture of words, music and dance.

Pantomime was a different genre, usually tragic rather than comic, and certainly not to be confused with the modern performances of the same name. Ancient pantomime is more the ancestor of modern ballet than of our 'pantomime'. Said to have been introduced to Rome in the first century BCE, it featured a star performer who gave a virtuoso display of dance and mime (in our sense of the word 'mime') to a libretto that was sung by the supporting members of the troupe, male and female. These formed a vocal 'backing group', along with others who provided the music. The *scabellum*, or large castanets, was a distinctive, and noisy, part of the show. The star alone took all the different roles in the plot, hence the title: '*panto* – mime', or 'miming *everything*'. In the process, he changed his mask (which had a closed rather than an open mouth, as in conventional ancient theatre) to indicate the different parts he was adopting. All kinds of themes were performed, drawn from the repertoire of classic Greek tragedy, Euripides' *Bacchae*, for example, or the story of Iphigeneia. Historians now reckon that there was more to pantomime than just degenerate theatre. It was probably one of the main ways that the general population in the Roman world picked up their knowledge of Greek myth and literature.

There are clear signs that mime and, especially, pantomime were major attractions at Pompeii, in the theatre and at other venues. A portrait set up in the Temple of Isis commemorates a man called Caius Norbanus Sorex 'a player of second parts'. Another statue of the same man stood in the Building of Eumachia in the Forum (the inscribed base, though not the portrait itself, survives), and another

88. Actor and benefactor? Although he was a member of a 'disgraceful' profession (p. 236), this is one of two bronze portraits in Pompeii to have publicly honoured the mime actor Caius Norbanus Sorex. Another portrait of the same man is known from Nemi, near Rome.

in the sanctuary of Diana at Nemi, just outside Rome, where he is called 'mime actor in second parts'. He was presumably a member of a travelling mime company who worked in various places in central and southern Italy. Though not the lead player in his troupe, he had done enough in Pompeii (maybe he contributed to the restoration of the Temple of Isis after the earthquake) to be honoured by two bronze portraits. The fact that, as an actor, he was legally *infamis* ('disgraceful') did not seem to get in the way of public commemoration, 'on land given by decision of the town council', in the centre of Pompeii.

We have already seen a few hints of pantomime performance in the city. According to the exact words of his tombstone, the shows presented by Aulus Clodius Flaccus at the games of Apollo (p. 198) featured 'pantomimes, including Pylades'. Pylades was the name of the emperor Augustus' favourite pantomime performer, who played at some of his private dinner parties. It may be that this notable performer himself was brought to Pompeii by the generosity of Flaccus, or it may be a later star who had adopted a famous theatrical name – a common,

89. This wallpainting from a private house in Pompeii may well evoke pantomime performances. Various characters are shown against a façade similar to that of the Large Theatre.

but for us confusing, practice among ancient actors. Another tomb inscription, the epitaph of Decimus Lucretius Valens (p. 211), gives us a passing reference to the loud music of the pantomime. For, if my translation is correct, the 'clapper beaters' or 'castanet players' (*scabiliari*) were one of the groups who had honoured the dead man with statues.

The enthusiasm of the Pompeians for pantomime can be detected in a handful of difficult to decipher, poorly preserved, but intriguing graffiti. They seem to refer to different members of a pantomime troupe headed by one Actius Anicetus, who is also found at nearby Puteoli under the name of 'Caius Ummidius Actius Anicetus, the pantomime'. 'Actius, star of the stage' reads one apparent fan message scrawled on a tomb outside the city wall, 'Here's to Actius, come back to your people soon,' reads another. And it may be that those who occasionally call themselves 'Anicetiani' are the self-styled fans of Anicetus, rather than other members of his troupe. Some of those supporting members can, in any case, be tracked down in other graffiti at Pompeii. In the private bath of a large house someone has written the words *histrionica Actica* or 'Actius' showgirl', perhaps an admirer of a female member of the company, who did not know her exact name. Elsewhere a man called Castrensis appears often enough in graffiti alongside Actius Anicetus for us to imagine that he too is another player in the troupe. So also does a 'Horus': 'Here's to Actius Anicetus, here's to Horus' as one graffito runs. We seem to be dealing with a popular group of perhaps seven or eight players altogether.

With the popularity of pantomime in mind, we can return to the paintings on the walls of Pompeii. For tucked away among all those evocations of the distant world of classical Greek theatre there are one or two that may in fact capture the more staple fare of the Pompeian stage. One likely candidate is an overblown painting of a stage set which is now faded almost beyond recognition. But in earlier drawings we see what looks very much like the elaborate architectural backdrop of the stage that is found in the Large Theatre of Pompeii, with its large central doorway (Ill. 89). A clever suggestion is that this particular design reflects a pantomime on the theme of the myth of Marsyas, who picked up the flutes of the goddess Minerva and challenged Apollo to a musical contest. If so, we see in the main openings of the stage, from left to right, Minerva, Apollo and Marsyas, as they would be portrayed in turn by the star dancer. The chorus, meanwhile, peep around the background.

This may be the closest we can now get to the Pompeian theatre.

Bloody games

A day out for the Pompeians could involve a much bloodier spectacle than this harmless if raucous pantomime. When Lord Byron coined the famous phrase 'butchered to make a Roman holiday', he meant exactly that. One of the ways that Romans spent their leisure time was watching men pitted against wild animals, and the combat of gladiators, who sometimes fought to the death. An enormous amount of scholarly effort has been spent in trying to discover where and when gladiators in particular originated. Did they come to Rome via the mysterious Etruscans? Was the institution a south Italian era invention from the region of Pompeii itself? Did it have its prehistoric origins in human sacrifice? And perhaps even more effort has been devoted to working out why the Romans were so keen on such practices anyway. Were they a substitute for 'real' warfare? Did they function as a collective release of tension in a highly ranked and rule-bound society? Or were the Romans even more bloodthirsty than those modern audiences who are happy to watch boxing or bull-fighting?

The material that survives from Pompeii does not help much with those questions. Their answers will always remain speculative at best. What we do get from the buildings, paintings and graffiti in the town is the best insight from anywhere in the Roman world into the practical infrastructure and organisation of wild-beast hunts and gladiatorial games, and into the lives (and deaths) of the gladiators themselves. We have posters advertising the shows and the facilities offered. We can visit the gladiators' barracks and see what they wrote on their own walls. We can even inspect cartoons of real gladiatorial fights, recording the results of the contest, and whether the losing fighter was killed or let off with his life. We

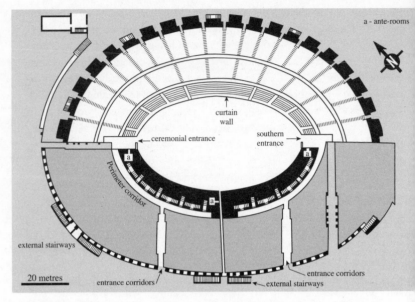

Figure 20. The Pompeian Amphitheatre. The plan shows the pattern of the seating (above), and (below) the system of internal corridors and access ways which ran underneath the seating, largely invisible from above.

come closer here to the day-to-day culture of the Roman Amphitheatre than we do by reading the bombastic accounts in ancient writers of the blockbuster shows occasionally presented by Roman emperors, with – or so the writers claim – their mass human carnage and whole menageries of animals put to death.

The Amphitheatre, where most of the gladiatorial shows and hunts took place, is still one of the most instantly impressive monuments in the whole city of Pompeii. Built at the very edge of the town, thanks to the generosity of Caius Quinctius Valgus and Marcus Porcius in the 70s BCE (pp. 40, 42), it is the earliest permanent stone building of its type to be found anywhere and is of a substantial size even by metropolitan Roman standards. The Colosseum in Rome, which was built 150 years later in a city with a total population of around a million, is only just over twice as big: the Colosseum could accommodate about 50,000 spectators, the Pompeian Amphitheatre some 20,000. Amphitheatres now can be disappointing to visit: high on initial impact, but low on rewarding details. They do not always repay careful inspection. In Pompeii, however, we can piece together

90. The arena of the Amphitheatre. The front rows of seating for the elite are clearly visible, marked off from the main seating behind. The main entrances for gladiators and animals lie at either end of the oval fighting space.

from what has been discovered the Amphitheatre's sometimes surprising history.

The plan of the building as it was buried in 79 gives us a good idea of how the Amphitheatre worked. The seats surrounding the display area were carefully ranked. The front rows were reserved for the local elite, who enjoyed spacious seating and a ringside view – though at the cost of sometimes being uncomfortably close to the action and to the wild animals on the loose. The women were probably relegated to the very back, if the rules that were introduced by the emperor Augustus in Rome applied, and were enforced, here too. Spectators entered the building by different routes, according to where they were sitting. Those in the main seating area made their way up the steep stairways on the outside of the building, which led onto a walkway that ran round the top of the seating. From here they would take the appropriate stairway down again to their place. Those in the posh seats went in through one of the lower entranceways, which led to an internal corridor running around the perimeter of the arena. From here they would take one of the series of stairways that led up to the front rows of seating. On this system the rich would never have had to cross paths, or rub shoulders in the mêlée, with the great unwashed. And just to be on the safe side, there was a hefty barrier in the seating area between the places reserved for the elite, and the rest above.

The main ceremonial way-in was the entrance on the north side, decorated with statues. The gladiators and animals would also have entered and left here, or at the opposite end, to the south. Unlike in the Colosseum at Rome, there were no cellars or underground passageways beneath the floor of the arena which could accommodate the waiting fighters (human or animal) and then release them through trapdoors when their turn came, into the spotlight above. The only place in this design for either men or (small) beasts to wait before their fight were the cramped rooms, (a), by each of the main entrances. Any larger animals must have been caged up outside, forming a mini-zoo, no doubt to the amusement, and terror, of passing spectators.

What has been lost? First the wooden seats. Even in the Amphitheatre's final phases, the seats were not all made of stone. Where the areas of grass now are, the seats were wooden. The stone versions had been added piecemeal, through the benefaction of various local officials. When Quinctius Valgus and Marcus Porcius first built the monument, the structural frame was in masonry, but all the seats were in wood. More disappointingly, the paintwork has also been lost. When the building was first excavated in 1815, brightly coloured decorations were discovered covering the curtain wall that surrounded the arena, just below the seats of the elite. These all disappeared in the cold weather of the following winter – but luckily not before they had been copied by artists working on the site.

The pictures showed a wonderful array of mythological figures (a Victory balancing on a globe and holding a palm branch, to symbolise success, was a recurring element) and images of gladiatorial equipment leaning against paintings of statues. But the main panels evoked the combats of the arena. There were scenes of wild animals charging through a mountain wilderness, reminiscent of the hunts that were staged there (and of the scenes on some garden walls). The artist had indulged his fantasy by including lions which, so far as we know, were never actually part of the display at Pompeii, even if they roamed the audience's imagination.

Of course, there were gladiators too. One of the paintings shows the start of a bout (Ill. 91). The referee stands in the middle between two gladiators who are not yet fully kitted out for their fight. The one on the left is blasting a note on a large curved horn with an ornamental handle to signal the start of proceedings.

91. The start of a bout. The lost paintings on the curtain wall of the arena included this scene of a pair of gladiators during the preliminaries to their fight. Interestingly the referee and support staff easily outnumber the fighters themselves.

Behind him a couple of attendants wait with his shield and helmet. On the right his opponent is already equipped with his shield, though his attendants have still to hand over his helmet and sword. A pair of Victories hover in the background, waiting to award palm branch and wreath to whichever one is the winner. Another image depicts the end of a contest between two rather burlier fighters. The loser has dropped his shield, carries a hopelessly buckled sword and has blood pouring out of his left arm.

This particular decoration was installed in the last years of the city, after the earthquake of 62 – for, unlike both the theatres, the Amphitheatre was in full working order at the time of the eruption. That famous painting of the riot in the Amphitheatre in 59 CE (Ill. 16) would suggest that the new scheme replaced a less complex design. If we can trust the artist's accuracy, at the time of the riot the curtain wall was decorated with a painted pattern to imitate marble, a common Roman conceit. But whether it is a question of imitation marble or gory scenes of combat, we find that the austere monochrome image of the surviving ruins belies, as so often, the vivid, even garish, original appearance of the monument.

The Amphitheatre did not stand alone. Some parts of the festivities connected with gladiatorial shows would have spilled over into the so-called Large Palaestra next door – a generous open space, surrounded by colonnades with a swimming pool in the centre and shady avenues of trees. Its original date and function are uncertain, though the size of the tree roots indicates that they had been planted about a hundred years before the eruption. One theory is that its main purpose was to provide an exercise ground for the city's youth; or at least for the wealthy boys, who may – following the policy of the emperor Augustus – have been organised into a paramilitary 'corps' (a cross between the boy scouts and the territorial army). There is, in fact, precious little evidence for this. The graffiti surviving on the colonnades suggest instead a much more mixed set of leisure and business uses, from shady park to open-air market and school. It must have come into its own when there were 20,000 people in the Amphitheatre, offering a place for a break, for eating and drinking, and for the lavatory. So far as we have been able to tell there was no latrine in the Amphitheatre: 20,000 people and nowhere but the stairs and corridors to take a piss.

Advertisements for forthcoming shows in the Amphitheatre, painted in the same style and by the same signwriters as the electoral slogans, give us all kinds of information about who the sponsors were, what the programme contained, how long it lasted, what facilities or extra attractions might be laid on. This evidence can sometimes be combined with memorials on tombs, where families might boast about the generosity of the deceased in financing shows. For gladiatorial spectacles and wild-beast hunts were a major part of the culture of benefaction we have already noticed in the town. Elected officials would stage these shows during their year of office. So would civic priests, or even in one case we know of an *Augustalis*. So too, for that matter, might men, like Livineius Regulus in 59 CE, looking to curry favour with the locals, for motives good or bad. Occasionally the advertisements make a point of stressing that the shows are to be put on 'at no public expense'. Perhaps it was normal practice for the city council to make some contribution to the cost too. Either way, there is no sign that any charge was made to those attending. This looks like free entertainment.

One especially lengthy series of shows extending over five days was advertised in the poster painted on a street wall by that active Pompeian signwriter Aemilius Celer (Ill. 92). It was on this occasion that he chose to inform his readers that he was working 'alone by the light of the moon' (p. 79). The advertisement ran in typical wording:

> Decimus Lucretius Satrius Valens, permanent priest of Prince Nero, the son of the emperor, is presenting twenty pairs of gladiators. Decimus Lucretius Valens his son is presenting ten pairs of gladiators. They will fight at Pompeii on 8, 9, 10, 11, 12 April. There will be a wild-beast hunt according to the usual rules and awnings.

There is no doubt that this act of generosity was intended to enhance the prestige

D·LVCRETI·
SCR CELER

SCR
AEMILIVS

SATRÍ·VALENT IS ·FLAMINIS· NERÓNIS· CAESARIS· AVG· FÍL I· CELER·SING
PERPETVÍ·CLADIATÓRVM·PARIA·XX·ET·D·LVCRETIO·VALENTIS·FÍLI·AD LVNA
GLAD·PARIÁ· X·PVG· POMPEÍS· VI· V· IV· III·PR· ÍDVS· APR· V É NATIÓ· LEGITIMA·
ET·VELA· ERVN T

92. An elegant advertisement. Careful work by the sign writer Aemilius Celer, advertising gladiatorial games put on by Decimus Lucretius Satrius Valens. (The translation is on p. 264).

and reputation of Satrius Valens, whose first two names appear in letters about ten times as big as everything else. He was giving these games in his capacity as priest, but by including his son in the enterprise (albeit with half as many gladiators to his name) he was no doubt also intending to give the younger man a leg-up in the politics of the local community. The place and date are very simply stated. There was obviously no need to specify that the show was to be held in the Amphitheatre. We know that in many Italian towns, including Rome itself, the forum could be used for shows, and we have already seen one occasion when animal displays were conducted in the Pompeian forum. But the distinctive combination of gladiators and wild-beast hunt must have been enough to tell people where to go. The crucial message to get across was that the occasion was to be held *at Pompeii*. For the walls of the town carried advertisements for shows at other local venues – Nola, Capua, Herculaneum, Cumae – for those who could be bothered to make the trip. People did not need to be told a precise time either. So long as they knew the date, they could rely on a standard kick-off time.

Five days is the longest series of gladiatorial shows we know of at Pompeii. Many are advertised for just a single day, some for two, three or four. Even if we were to assume that most of the elected officials, plus some priests, chose to provide these bloody games as their benefaction to the town, and even allowing for some extra performances perhaps put on commercially, there could hardly have been more than twenty days of shows in the Amphitheatre each year. Most of the time it must have been empty and locked up, or taken over for anything else that could use a large open space. Pantomime perhaps?

How, in the case of the games of Satrius Valens and son, the gladiators and the hunt were spread over the five days is puzzling. We do not know how long each pair would keep going. But on other occasions just a single day's show features thirty pairs of fighters plus a hunt. So do we imagine that Satrius Valens' generosity consisted mostly in spreading his fighters more thinly across the allotted time? Or did the gladiators appear on more than one day? Some advertisements specify that 'substitutes' will be provided, to take the place of a dead or wounded fighter, and sometimes it is clear that individual gladiators went into battle several times in the same games. Maybe Satrius Valens had that in mind. But did he have access to enough spare animals to present hunts on each of five days?

At the end of the advertisement we learn that the hunt is to be conducted 'according to the usual rules' (*legitima*). The point of this is not at all clear, though some historians imagine that it means little more than 'the hunt that normally goes with a gladiatorial show', or just 'a regular hunt'. We also learn that the awnings will be in use over the building, to bring shade to spectators if it turned out to be a hot sunny day, and presumably at extra cost to the sponsor. Even in the balmy Mediterranean climate, the weather seems to have been on the mind of those who planned these events. From the recorded dates, it seems that the hottest months of July and August were not favourite times for the shows. But wet weather could be a problem too. Some advertisements add the cautious warning: 'weather permitting'.

Satrius Valens and his son (assuming that it was they who chose the wording) make no mention of one other extra that many wealthy sponsors of the games include: *sparsiones*. This is a term that can mean anything 'sprinkled' or 'showered' over the audience. Sometimes it was perfumed water sprayed over the audience in their seats, sometimes little presents thrown into the crowd (as at a modern Christmas pantomime before Health and Safety regulations prohibited it). Such a flourish was perhaps beyond even this family's generosity, over five days.

Nor do they mention, as some do, any special occasion or commemoration linked to their shows. One of the most intriguing of these is found in the single day of displays put on by Cnaius Alleius Nigidius Maius 'at the dedication of the painting work'. No one is exactly sure what this 'painting work' was. But one nice suggestion is that these shows were a day of celebration to commemorate the completion of those splendid paintings that once covered the circuit wall of the arena.

We can fill out the picture given by the advertisement thanks to a number of paintings and sculptures from the town which depict the games in the Amphitheatre and occasionally the festivities and rituals that surrounded them. A

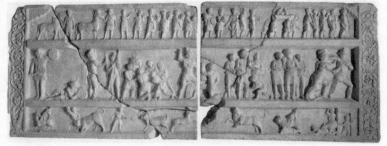

93. Different elements of the gladiatorial games are shown on each register of this sculpture. On the top level: the procession leading to the Amphitheatre. In the middle: the gladiatorial fights themselves. Below: in the animal contests one human fighter on the right is being finished off by a bear, while on the left a bull is being killed.

precious piece of evidence comes from one of the town's cemeteries and must once have adorned an expensive tomb (Ill. 93). It includes three bands of sculpture. The bottom band depicts a wild-beast hunt. Part of the spectacle appears to consist of animals fighting each other. A pair of dogs are busy attacking a goat and a wild boar. The human combatants concentrate on the larger animals. One is skewering a bull, another is about to dispatch a boar. One has lost out in his encounter with a bear, which is already taking a large bite out of him, to the despair of two attendants.

The middle and widest band shows various groups of gladiators, some in the midst of fighting, some claiming victory, some collapsed in defeat. The most striking thing about the scene is that there are as many attendants and officials in the ring as there are gladiators. No fewer than five are supporting a fighter who has almost fallen to the ground. Five more, on the right, are looking after a pair who are taking a break: one is having treatment on his wounded leg; the other is being giving refreshments. There is something disconcertingly like modern sportsmen and their trainers in this image.

Even more interesting is the upper band of sculpture. For this shows the grand preliminaries to the games which – in our fascination with, or disgust at, the gory sides of the occasion – it is all too easy to forget. The whole proceedings started with a procession through the streets of the town. Here we see it when it has already reached the Amphitheatre, as the awnings at the upper corners must indicate. On the right, leading the way are two musicians and three lictors, staff who are mentioned elsewhere as being assigned to local *duoviri*. Behind them comes a curious platform, carried on the shoulders of four men. On top of it two figures, models presumably, crouch around an anvil, one holding a hammer in the air and about to strike. You might expect the gods to be honoured in this procession (and indeed statues of deities were often carried on platforms much like this in religious and civic processions), but what are these little blacksmiths doing here? The best suggestion is that this is intended to celebrate their metal-working, the skill on which the whole occasion depended. Next in line is a man carrying a placard, perhaps naming the sponsor of the show or the reason for its performance, and next someone carrying a palm, the symbol of victory. Then comes a man dressed in a toga. This is almost certainly the sponsor himself, who is followed in turn by a procession of men parading the gladiators' armour, piece by piece, the fruit of the blacksmiths' labours. Bringing up the rear are a trumpeter and two more attendants leading horses decked in obviously ceremonial trappings, for a festival occasion.

This is a rare glimpse of the rituals, the varied spectacles, the community involvement – from sponsor to blacksmiths – which gave a context to these bloody games. Was all this also stopped when shows were banned in Pompeii for ten years in 59? Whatever the reason for the riot (whether a combination of fraying tempers, local rivalry and alcohol-fuelled exuberance, or something more sinister), such a total ban would have hit very hard at the life of the town, its shared pursuits, its structures of patronage and hierarchy.

The answer is probably not. Tacitus' Latin account is vague on this point: he refers only to the prohibition on 'any public gathering *of that kind*'. But a handful of surviving advertisements give notice of forthcoming games which are to include wild-beast hunts, athletes, awnings and *sparsiones*. This was everything the audience might have hoped for – except the gladiators. The nearest thing to them are the 'athletes'. Almost certainly these advertisements refer to shows held between 59 and 69. The ban, in other words, applied to the gladiators alone. The rest continued much as normal, even if many Pompeians no doubt felt that athletes and even wild beasts were a poor substitute for the star attraction. In fact, one of the shows concerned is the celebration presented by Nigidius Maius for the 'dedication of the painting work'. If that 'painting work' really was the decoration of the arena's curtain wall, it must have seemed a sad irony to be dedicating those splendid images of gladiators in combat at a show that could present no gladiators at all.

Heartthrobs of the girls

So far we have seen the shows from the point of view of spectators and sponsors. But what about the gladiators and beast-fighters themselves? Who were they? How were they organised? Can we reconstruct anything of their perspective on the Amphitheatre? Was the life of a gladiator bound to be bloody and short?

Gladiators were almost always men. Although modern scholars have often become very excited at the transgressive prospect of female gladiators, in truth there are only a handful of plausible candidates from anywhere in the Roman world. There are none at all in Pompeii. In terms of formal, legal status, gladiators were at the bottom of the pile of Roman society. Many were slaves, others were condemned criminals: those were the conscripts, willing or unwilling. A few others were volunteers. For signing up as a gladiator might have been one of the very few routes out of total destitution in the Roman world. Survival, in the short term at least, might be bought at a high price that amounted to more than just danger. It would have involved a loss of day-to-day freedom almost akin to slavery itself, under the control of the troupe manager or, in Latin, *lanista*.

The *lanista* was a crucial middleman in the whole business (and for them it *was* a business) of gladiatorial shows and beast hunts. The elite sponsors of the games did not keep their own gladiators for display. When they wanted to put on a show, they would have negotiated a price with one of these troupe managers. Trade was probably not so brisk that there would have been a very large number to choose from, but in Pompeii itself we know the names of three *lanistae* operating in the last forty years of the city's life.

The best attested is a man called Numerius Festus Ampliatus. An advertisement on the wall of the Basilica in the Forum, for example, gives notice that 'the gladiatorial "family" [*familia*] of Numerius Festus Ampliatus will fight again ... on 15 and 16 May'. As is normal, Ampliatus' troupe is called his 'family' or 'household' (more an indication of the wide range of meanings of the Latin *familia* than the barefaced euphemism it might seem). The fact that no sponsor is named may suggest that this show was a purely commercial occasion, capitalising – as the word 'again' hints – on some earlier success. He certainly had more than a local Pompeian trade. Another advertisement publicises the appearance of his *familia* at the town of Formiae, which lies to the north, halfway to Rome.

The job of the *lanista* involved acquiring the gladiators for his troupe, which would presumably have meant scouting for talent at local slave auctions. But once acquired they needed training. Gladiators were expected to perform in various specialist roles, and with different types of equipment. The 'Thracian' (*Thrax*), for example, fought with a short curved sword and a small shield. The 'fish-heads' (*murmillones*, so called after the emblem of a fish on their helmets) had a large, long shield. The 'net-man' (*retiarius*) fought with a trident and a net, in which he tried to ensnare his opponent. The art of the *lanista* must have been in training up his men to these roles, then making clever fighting combinations: a fish-head against a net-man was, for example, a popular combination.

Occasionally, he might hire in extra men from other gladiatorial troupes, to fill gaps or to acquire a star fighter temporarily. One graffito, now detached from its original wall and in the Naples Museum, seems almost to replicate a show's programme originally stretching over four days. It gives the name of the *lanista*, Marcus Mesonius, then it lists the different bouts, giving the names of the gladiators and who won. A number of them are described as 'Julian' or 'Neronian' gladiators, meaning that they had been trained at the emperor's own gladiatorial training school at Capua. They must have been either permanent or temporary hirings by Mesonius. It would be hard to avoid the comparison with the British football transfer market – but for the fact that the job in question was real fighting, not kicking a ball around a pitch.

The *lanista* probably also trained the beast-fighters (employed on much the same terms as the gladiators proper) as well as acquiring the animals for the hunt. The advertisement for Ampliatus' 'repeat show' certainly includes a hunt and, in any case, the animals may not have required any particular expertise to acquire and house. At Rome itself the emperors occasionally put such exotic animals as lions, elephants or rhinoceroses on display (and to death) – acquired and transported, we know not how, from distant parts of the empire. In 1850, to bring a young hippo from Egypt to London, it took a specially built steamer, with a 2000 litre water tank, and a host of keepers and smaller animals for its food. How the Roman imperial agents managed similar transport is a complete mystery. But at Pompeii, there was nothing nearly so exotic. All the evidence we have suggests that the beasts were obtained locally; and even then dogs and goats were commoner than bulls and bears. The truth is that the Pompeian arena was stocked more like a modern 'children's corner' of a zoo than a wild-game park.

Gladiators and beast-fighters mostly lived on the job. Two places in Pompeii have been identified as gladiatorial barracks. How exactly the gladiators lived in these places, how many of them there were, and under what degree of imprisonment is very unclear – and much less certain than the movie image in *Spartacus* or *Gladiator* would suggest. Nor is it certain whether they were the permanent

94. This large open space, with accommodation around it, provided a base for gladiators in the last period of the city's life – to judge at least from the gladiatorial equipment (Ill. 95) found there.

base for a single *familia*, or temporary housing for any troupes passing through. But both buildings have a very close connection with gladiators.

The first is what was originally a sizeable private house in the north of the city, converted in the early first century CE to house gladiators in rooms around a large peristyle, which would (or so we imagine) have been used for training. The gladiatorial connection is absolutely clear, thanks to more than a hundred graffiti by or about gladiators plastered around the peristyle. But this building was not in use in the final years of the city. Maybe after the earthquake of 62, or perhaps when trade picked up after the end of the gladiatorial ban, gladiators took up residence in what had been a large colonnaded open space connected to the Large Theatre.

This seems to have consisted in a large training area with rooms for the fighters around the edge of the complex (Ill. 94). Many of these had an internal wooden gallery, making a two-level apartment, though it would still have been cramped for two or three gladiators sharing. No traces of beds have been found, which suggests that, at best, they slept on mattresses, directly on the floor. This picture can be filled out by suggesting that some of the larger rooms on the east side may have provided communal, social space, with an apartment for the *lanista* or one of his sub-managers above. Maybe. But in truth there is little evidence for

95. One of the bronze helmets found in the gladiators' accommodation. Like the others, it is so richly decorated (here with an image of the goddess 'Rome') and in such good condition, that it is hard to imagine that it has seen active combat. Much more likely it is part of the gladiators' ceremonial or parade dress.

that beyond modern fantasy. There was even one room which may have served as a prison or punishment area, complete with iron shackles – though the skeletons found there during the excavations in the eighteenth century were not apparently chained in this way, and to be honest the shackles did not necessarily have anything to do with the gladiators.

How are we so certain that these were gladiatorial quarters? The simple answer lies in the extraordinary finds of bronze gladiatorial armour and weapons in ten of the rooms around the peristyle. These added up to fifteen richly decorated bronze helmets, fourteen shinguards, six shoulder-guards, as well as a small assortment of daggers and other weapons. Most of these are richly decorated, with scenes from classical myth or emblems of Roman power. One helmet, for example (Ill. 95), displays a personification of Rome itself, surrounded by defeated barbarians, prisoners and trophies of victory. Strikingly they are all in a perfect state. Not one shows any sign of ever having been used in fighting. These may well have been the parade collection, such as we saw carried along in the representation of the opening procession at the games. If so, nothing survives of their day-to-day fighting equipment.

The prospects for these gladiators were grim, but not quite as bad as we might fear. The good news for them was that they were an expensive commodity. Many of them would have been bought at a price; and all of them would have used up many of the *lanista*'s resources in their training and keep. He would not want to waste them. Even if gladiatorial shows in which no one was ever killed would hardly be crowd-pullers, and even if the sponsor wanted his money's worth, it

96. This vivid record of three gladiatorial bouts at Nola (the place is mentioned next to the topmost pair of fighters) was found scrawled on the outside of a tomb. One of the fighters is a first-timer. The middle register features M(arcus) Attilius who is marked down as a 'novice' ('T' for *tiro*). After his first victory ('V' stands for *vicit*), he goes on to win his second fight against the more experienced L(ucius) Raecius Felix. The musicians shown at the top remind us of what a noisy occasion these games must have been.

would be in the troupe manager's interests to keep the deaths to a minimum. It would surely have been part of the deal between *lanista* and sponsor that when a fighter lost, more often than not the sponsor should give a lead to the crowd in allowing him to be reprieved, not to put him to death there and then. Needless to say, that must have been the instinct of the gladiators too. Training and living together, and no doubt becoming friends, they would hardly have been going all out for the kill.

That is certainly the picture we get from the Pompeian graffiti which record the results of particular bouts of fighting. One of the most evocative examples is a set of drawings with accompanying captions found on a tomb, depicting a four-day series of games at nearby Nola (Ill. 96). The gladiators are a mixture of old hands, with thirteen or fourteen fights to their name, and a novice undertaking his first two fights. None of the losers are killed, for next to each of their pictures there appears the letter 'M' for *missus*, or 'reprieved'. From the record of the gladiators' 'form' that is also recorded ('fought 14, victories 12') we can tell that two of the losers had been spared at least twice before. In the show presented by Mesonius, on one day nine pairs of gladiators fought. Out of these eighteen, we can still identify eight outright victors, five men reprieved and three men killed. Occasionally a Pompeian gladiator is recorded as fighting more than fifty fights.

Nonetheless, even if defeat often did not mean death, the loss of life must have been by our standards considerable. To put exactly the same figures in a less upbeat way, three dead out of a total of eighteen gladiators, suggests a death rate of about 1 in 6 in each show. Small as the sample is, it fits with the overall record of numbers of fights fought by each gladiator for whom that total is recorded. True, there are a few old-stagers, but only a quarter of those we know have more than ten fights to their name. If we reckon, the other way round, that three quarters would have died before their tenth fight, that means a loss rate of some 13 per cent per fight. Even assuming that they did not fight very often (two or three shows a year is one estimate), if they entered the arena at the age of seventeen they could expect to be dead by the time they were twenty-five.

But if longevity did not come with a gladiatorial career, celebrity perhaps did. There were clearly some star gladiators whose names were paraded on the advertisements for shows, including one beast-fighter too, called Felix, whose match against some bears was specially highlighted in one notice. The figures of gladiators, in their distinctive armour, are also found throughout the town, and in every medium you can think of. They turn up as little figurines, as images on pottery lamps, and forming the handles of bronze bowls. One statue of a gladiator, more than a metre high, seems to have done duty as a kind of trade mark, or inn sign, at one tavern near the Amphitheatre. Gladiators would have seen their own images all over the place.

It is also commonly said that they had enormous sex appeal for the women of Pompeii and elsewhere in the Roman world. The satirist Juvenal writes of some imaginary upper-class Roman lady who runs off with the great brutish figure of a gladiator, obviously attracted by the ancient equivalent of 'rough trade', and by the glamour that his dangerous life brought. The Roman imagination certainly saw the gladiator in these terms. But we find a cautionary tale when we try to follow this fantasy through to the real life of Pompeii. We have already seen (p. 5) that the myth of the upmarket Pompeian lady being caught red-handed in the gladiatorial barracks, with her gladiator lover, is just that: a myth. But some of the other evidence for the sex appeal of the gladiators requires a second look too.

Some of the most famous graffiti from Pompeii are about two particular gladiators and their female fan club. 'Celadus, heartthrob of the girls', 'Celadus, the girls' idol', 'Cresces, the net-man, puts right the night-time girls, the morning girls and all the others'. It would be nice to think of some love-struck Pompeian women wandering around the town and immortalising their passion for Celadus and Cresces on the walls they passed. And that indeed is how they are often treated by modern scholars. But it is not so simple. These graffiti were found inside the old gladiatorial barracks. They are not the fantasy of the girls. They are written by the gladiators themselves – simultaneously bloke-ish boasting and the poignant fantasies of a couple of young fighters, who faced a short life and may never have got their girl, or at least not for long.

When it comes to reconstructing the everyday life of an ancient, it matters a very great deal where exactly your evidence is found.

CHAPTER NINE

A CITY FULL OF GODS

Those other inhabitants

Pompeii teemed with gods and goddesses. Whatever they would have made of the rest of my account, it would certainly have surprised the inhabitants of the ancient city that, so far, I have tended to leave in the background the various deities who bulked large in their lives. The city contained literally thousands of images of these gods and goddesses. If you count them all, big and small and in every medium, they were probably more in number than the living human population.

They certainly came in all sorts, shapes, sizes and materials – ranging from the large painted pin-up Venus (Ill. 97), sprawling awkwardly across a massive sea-shell which pointed to her mythical birth from the waves, to miniature dancing bronze figures of the Lares or 'household gods' (Ill. 98) or a little bronze bust of Mercury used to balance a set of weighing-scales. Some were presumably intended to prompt feelings of reverence and awe: the large marble head of Jupiter, for example, found in his temple in the Forum (Ill. 99). Others, such as the boisterous caricatures in the private baths in the House of the Menander (Ill. 51) or some of the more overblown phallic versions of the divine Priapus (Ill. 36), must have been joking parodies. Others again, such as a self-consciously old-fashioned bronze Apollo from the House of Julius Polybius, were no doubt valued as precious *objets d'art*, as much as they were revered as sacred images. Many of the standardised images of Minerva in her long robes and helmet, or Diana in hunting gear, would have seemed safely traditional. Not so the ivory figure of Indian Lakshmi (Ill. 11) or the miniature images of the dog-headed

97. Roman gods were imagined in variety of guises. This Venus, with little Cupid in attendance, seems disconcertingly like a modern pin-up.

98. Bronze figurines of the 'household gods' or Lares, dressed in their characteristic tunics (said to be made of dog-skin) and carrying an offering bowl and brimming cornucopia (horn of plenty).

99. The majestic face of Jupiter. This colossal head was found in the remains of the Temple of Jupiter, Juno and Minerva in the Forum.

Egyptian god Anubis. To some Pompeians these would have seemed at best troublingly exotic, at worst weird and dangerous.

We now tend to take the images of ancient gods too much for granted. We are usually interested to spot the key attribute that will identify the deity concerned (if it's a thunderbolt, it must be Jupiter) and to move on. This is to underestimate the cultural and religious work that these images did in the ancient world. No one then debated, as we might do, whether there existed a divine power in the world. Atheism would have been barely comprehensible as an intellectual or religious position. In fact, apart from among Jews and Christians, the idea that there was only one god, rather than many, would have seemed almost equally eccentric in the first century CE, although it became a commoner view, even among pagans, later. But this did not mean that ancient polytheism was without its disputes and controversies. Romans could disagree violently, not about whether the gods existed (that was a fact rather than a belief), but about what they were like, how the different deities related to one another, and about how, when and why they intervened in the lives of humans. It was perfectly possible to wonder, for example, if the gods really did have a human form (or exactly *how* like humans were they?), or whether they were concerned with the lives of mortals at all. How did they reveal themselves to people? Just how capricious, or benevolent, were they? Friends, or always potential enemies?

In this sense, many of the images of gods and goddesses that Pompeians saw around them in their daily lives were much more meaningful than we assume. Standardised, funny, expensive or exotic, they were also ways of imagining the divine inhabitants of the world in material form. Size, shape and appearance could all matter. A colossal statue, like the vast Jupiter, was not merely a bombastic creation, it was also a way of reflecting on the power of the god, and on how he might be pictured – literally or metaphorically – in physical form. Ancient religion set great store by images.

A religion without the book

The traditional religion of ancient Rome and Italy was unlike most religions of the modern world in many important respects. The fact that there were many gods and that their number was not fixed (more deities might always be discovered at home, or imported from abroad) are only two of the things that make Roman religion so strikingly different from Judaism, Christianity or Islam. It is also the case that there were no tenets of belief that an individual would be expected to hold, no equivalent of the Christian creed and no authoritative sacred texts which laid down doctrine. That did not mean that there was a complete religious free-for-all. There were, no doubt, many more options than in a modern 'religion of the book'. But the crucial fact is that the community's adherence to its religion was demonstrated through action and ritual rather than words. As we shall see shortly, the act of animal sacrifice, at Pompeii as elsewhere, was the most important action of all.

The focus of the religious system was much more on the community as a whole than on its individual members. True, many Pompeian men and women might claim some kind of personal relationship with one or more of the gods. They might detect the influence of the gods on their lives and might turn to them in crises great and small. Many written traces of this survive from the city. In one of the corridors of the theatre, a graffito asks Venus to look kindly on a young couple. 'Methe, slave of Cominia, from Atella, loves Chrestus. May Venus of Pompeii be kind to them and may they live together happily ever after.' Two people in the House of Julius Polybius recorded their vow to the household gods: 'For the well-being, return and success of Caius Julius Philippus, Publius Cornelius Felix and Vitalis, slave of Cuspius here made a vow to the Lares.' This was a standard formula used at all levels of Roman religion, public and private: a vow made to the gods, which would be paid with an offering or sacrifice to them, in the event of the desired outcome. Here, these humble servants must have been praying that one of the masters of the house made it home safely from wherever he had been. Nonetheless, for all the expressions of private devotion that we find, it was the links between religion and the city or the state as a whole that gave Roman religion its distinctive character.

To put it at its simplest, the official line was that the gods protected and supported Rome or, on a smaller scale, Pompeii, so long as they received due worship. If they were neglected, disaster would surely be the result. In these terms – far from the nineteenth-century Christian idea that the eruption of Vesuvius was punishment for the paganism, or for the pagan immorality, of the local populations – the Pompeians themselves would have been much more likely to take the final destruction of their city as a sign that the worship of those pagan gods had not been properly carried out. There was a certain instrumentality in Roman dealings with the gods: 'you scratch the divine back and the gods scratch yours' can sometimes seem to have been the main guiding principle of Roman religion. But we might perhaps better understand it in terms of the *reciprocity* of patronage, honour and benefaction that we have already seen in the relations between the Pompeian elite and the rest of the citizens. One of the ways the inhabitants of Pompeii envisaged their gods was as larger-than-life, and infinitely more powerful, *duoviri*.

Exactly which community the gods belonged to could be a tricky question. Since the Social War, Pompeii's religion was both Roman and Pompeian. As elsewhere in the Roman world, there was a trade-off between the centralising tendencies of Rome and a tremendous degree of local distinctiveness. This meant that what is for us the 'same god' (Minerva, Apollo, Juno or whoever) could actually be significantly different in different towns. The Venus of Pompeii (*Venus Pompeiana*), who was asked to bless the partnership of Methe and her Chrestus, is a good example of this. For Pompeii's Venus had a classic Roman aspect which would be recognisable all over the Roman world and was sometimes associated with her role as the patron goddess of Sulla's colony. But she also had distinctive local Pompeian traits, powers and associations, as well as a compound title, 'Venus Fisica', which may have gone back to the Oscan period (what it means, we honestly do not know for sure). Even more striking divergences are found in religious rituals and festivals. Although there was some overlap between Rome and Pompeii, and although animal sacrifice was found everywhere in the Roman world, many festivals were local events, following a local calendar, according to local custom.

Hand in hand with the basic political axiom which linked the success of the community with its worship of the gods went the structure and character of priesthood. In most cases (though we shall explore some exceptions towards the end of this chapter), priests were not people with a special religious calling, they were not full-time religious officials, and they did not take any pastoral responsibility for the moral and religious needs of a congregation. Priests of the gods were usually the same men as those who conducted the political business of the city. As Cicero, who was himself both a political leader and a priest, put it, 'Among the many things … that our ancestors created and established under divine inspiration, nothing is more renowned than their decision to entrust the worship of the gods and the highest interests of state to the same men.'

The result is that religion is found in several places in Pompeian life where we might not expect it. It is, for example, integrally connected with politics at all levels – so much so that the Roman emperor himself was treated like a god with his own priest. But it is also absent from some areas where we might expect to find it. Most marriages, for example, were not solemnised by any religious ceremony. In fact, a marriage was normally contracted, as the Romans put it, 'by practice':

that is, in our terms, 'by cohabitation'. If you lived together for a year, you were married.

It is against this background that the rest of this chapter looks at the remains of religious life in Pompeii. There is some truth in the old joke which says that archaeologists will label anything 'religious' that they cannot fully understand, whether that is peculiar holes in the ground or phalluses and snakes daubed on the walls. Nonetheless, we shall be trying to identify the places or objects in the city which counted as religious – starting from its main public temples, priests and rituals and ending with the aspect of Pompeian religion that since the eighteenth century has captured the imagination of most visitors, the worship of the Egyptian goddess Isis. But we shall also be wondering what people did and said at the temple or shrine, and even occasionally what might have gone on in their heads when they were there. The most important thing to remember is that the varieties of their response will have been enormous, from cynicism and boredom to piety. Romans were no more unanimous on such things than we are.

City temples

Temples are for us one of the clearest symbols of Roman religion, instantly recognisable with their columns, triangular gables (or 'pediments'), and steps leading up onto the raised platform (or *podium*), from which a visitor might then gain access, through high doors, to the interior of the building and whatever lay within. Romans had a whole repertoire of different kinds of sacred space, ranging from places where a deity was supposed to be present 'in person', as it were, to those from where signs sent by the gods might be observed. We have already come across the traces of an early countryside shrine, or sacred grove, underneath the House of the Etruscan Column (pp. 26–7). And, as we shall see later in this chapter, the final phases of the city included a variety of free-standing altars and other sacred enclosures. But it is the distinctive form of the temple that marks the urban landscape of Pompeii and other Roman towns, much as the parish church is the stamp of religion in an English village.

But if the English village has just a single parish church, Pompeii – as you might expect, given its many gods – had many temples, though by no means one for every god or goddess who might intervene in the lives of its inhabitants. They came in all sizes, in varying degrees of prominence and with very different histories. Some stretched back to the earliest years of the city. The temple of Apollo

100. This nineteenth-century reconstruction shows the Temple of Jupiter, Juno and Minerva, flanked on either side by an arch. It is an accurate drawing, but perhaps gives a rather too grand, monumental and clean impression of the temple and its surroundings.

next to the Forum was established by the sixth century BCE at the latest. So too was the temple of Minerva and Hercules (Ill. 101) in the so-called Triangular Forum (named after the triangular colonnade built around the temple in the first century CE). This, in fact, may long since have been a picturesque ruin at the time of the eruption – though some archaeologists attribute its ruined appearance to the aggressive excavation techniques of earlier generations of diggers (not to mention Allied bombers).

Most of the rest date to the second century BCE or later. In just one case we can reconstruct the precise circumstances of their building. The small Temple of Fortuna Augusta was dedicated to an almost untranslatable combination of the goddess of Good Fortune or Success (Fortuna) and the power of the emperor (the adjective Augusta can confusingly, or conveniently, refer either to the first emperor Augustus himself, or to imperial power more generally – for subsequent emperors used 'Augustus' as part of their titles too). It was funded, according to a surviving inscription, by a local grandee and three-times *duumvir*, Marcus Tullius, and built on his own land, which he donated to the town. He was careful,

101. Looking up to the Temple of Minerva and Hercules, in the Triangular Forum, from outside the town. This imaginative reconstruction (note the solitary charioteer out for a spin) gives a good idea of the gradients and different levels on which Pompeii was built.

102. An early traveller takes a rest – or seizes the chance for some romantic reflection on the passing of time – in the ruins of the tiny Temple of Jupiter Meilichios (or Aesculapius). Even this very small building shows the standard structure of a Roman temple: a room (or *cella*) to house the statue or statues of gods, and an altar outside.

however, that there should be no misunderstanding about exactly how much land he had made over. Behind the temple there was a stone boundary marker, reading 'Private property of Marcus Tullius, son of Marcus'.

Sometimes the gods associated with the temple are easy to identify. The temple in the commanding position at one end of the Forum, for example, can only be that of Jupiter, Juno and Minerva – located in this prime site as in many, if not most, Roman towns (Ill. 100). The goddess Fortuna Augusta is clearly named in the inscription. For several others we are reduced, for better or worse, to conjecture. The vast temple overlooking the sea, next to the Marine Gate, was very likely the Temple of Venus – but there is no firm evidence for this beyond a battered statue and our conviction that there must have been a substantial temple to the colony's patron somewhere in the town. The tiny temple tucked almost out of sight, behind high precinct walls near the theatres, has proved a real puzzle (Ill. 102). Archaeologists have recently returned to the theory of J. J. Winckelmann, the 'Father of Art History', who visited Pompeii in the mid eighteenth century and called this a temple of Aesculapius, the god of healing – again on no firmer evidence than a statue found there which may have depicted the god. Others have called it the Temple of Jupiter Meilichios ('honey sweet' – a title connected with the gods of the underworld). This is on the basis of an inscription which refers to a temple of that name. If it is not the Temple of Meilichios, then that must still be waiting to be found somewhere else in the city (or, as some now think, outside – matching it up with a shrine beyond the city walls). There is, as we shall see again, a domino effect in many of these conjectures – one identification can easily topple another.

The overall design of these temples may be familiar. What went on inside them is much less so and much more surprising. Temples were not places where a congregation of worshippers gathered or where religious rituals were carried out. The essential function of any Greek or Roman temple was to house a statue of a god or goddess. We should not imagine bloody sacrifices carried out in the dark inner room of any of these buildings. These always took place outside in the open air. The temple was the home of a divine image, or 'cult-statue'. The most common Latin word for it, *aedes* rather than *templum*, means simply 'house'.

Yet only rarely would the statue have stood entirely on its own. Many temples acquired a lot of clutter, sometimes very precious clutter. Dedications and offerings to the god or goddess in fulfilment of a vow often ended up here. Someone might, for example, promise a gift to Aesculapius if he got better from his illness – and, on recovery, deposit what he had promised in his temple. Statues and other works of art were often displayed here too. In Rome itself, temples were a favourite place to house rich pieces of booty captured in war, or the authoritative texts of laws inscribed on bronze tablets. And all kinds of other activities might also have gone on around the statue of the god. The Roman senate used the space inside several temples for its own meetings, some of the wealthiest citizens deposited their wills in the Temple of the goddess Vesta, and the basement of the Temple of Saturn served as the Roman state treasury. All these valuables mean that they must have been well-policed by their caretakers (security guards, cleaners and maintenance men rolled into one), firmly locked at night and open to the public only under supervision.

This was the pattern at Pompeii too. The traces are, at first sight, more fleeting than we might hope – whether because, like the Temple of Venus, these temples were in the middle of building works when the eruption came, or because their precious fixtures and fittings made them an obvious target for looters after the eruption (the archaeological remains, after all, being much the same in each case).

Alternatively, of course, their loyal caretakers may have removed some of the more precious objects as they fled the eruption.

But all kinds of telling pieces of evidence do survive. We have already seen the piece of booty from the capture of Corinth in 146 BCE that was put on show in or near the Temple of Apollo. This same temple also displayed a magnificent pair of bronze statues, of Apollo and Diana (only her head now survives) in its piazza, as well as a replica of the strange *omphalos* (that is the 'navel of the earth') which was one of the sacred symbols of Apollo's famous shrine at Delphi – and another example here of Pompeii's wide cultural reach. We even get a hint of the security systems that these temples might use. Still visible along the front façade of the Temple of Fortuna Augusta are the remains of metal railings, which could close the building off (Ill. 103). One leading expert on Pompeii once assured me that these had been a nineteenth-century addition, designed to stop tourists climbing on the monument. That is just what they look like. But they were actually intended to keep ancient Pompeians out.

Even some of the town's most ruined monuments can give us more information on temple life and organisation than we would suspect at first sight, tantalising glimpses of their cult statues and the other riches which once were there, and sometimes unexpected stories of what was going on in Pompeii in 79. A good case in point is the Temple of Jupiter, Juno and Minerva, which at least from the arrival of the Roman colonists housed the trio of deities which defined Pompeii as a Roman town. It is frankly not much to look at now (Ill. 104). Its steps and some sadly truncated columns remain at the front. On top of the podium, the inner room of the temple is still clearly visible, and within it the scant remains of what was once a two-storey internal colonnade. At the far end are the niches which would have displayed the statues of the three gods. In its present state, it is grim and functional. But we get a vivid ancient view of it in one of the small friezes in the House of Caecilius Jucundus (Ill. 5). Although the intention of this sculpture was to demonstrate the damage done by the earthquake (damage from which this temple perhaps never recovered), it also offers us a nice – maybe slightly imaginative – snapshot of the building in its original setting, complete with some of its decoration. The altar stands outside on a platform set into the steps of the temple. On either side of the steps we find an equestrian statue, while behind the altar, by leaving out two of the six columns, the sculptor has been able to show us the doors leading into the inner room and, above, a garland or wreath decorating the pediment.

We have other clues about the building's original appearance and its use. First, the podium on which the temple stands is not solid. It is hollow, and contains a

103. This nineteenth century reconstruction of the Temple of Fortuna Augusta rightly imagines the religious rituals taking place outside the temple and in its portico. The artist has included the metal railings (though not at a height to keep a vandal out) and has brightened up the exterior with festoons. But the crowd of worshippers in front seem implausibly flamboyant.

104. The now rather desolate ruins of the Temple of Jupiter, Juno and Minerva. How dilapidated this end of the Forum was at the time of the eruption is still disputed.

basement room, which you could reach either via some stairs from inside the temple, or through a door at pavement level on the east side. Light was brought into this basement by shafts set into the floor above. This fact alone suggests that the room had a practical use. For why provide lighting if no one was likely ever to go into it? One idea is that it was intended as a store for the surplus dedications from upstairs: whenever the temple caretaker felt that a clearout was needed, he would not throw the pious offerings out, but carefully stash them away in the basement. Another is that it was the city council's treasury or bank vault, just as the treasury at Rome itself was in a temple cellar. Either is possible. But sadly there is no indication that anything was in there at the time of the eruption apart from some assorted pieces of sculpted marble.

There are also clear signs that it was once much more richly decorated than it appears today. The floor was inlaid with geometric patterns of marble (so-called *opus sectile*) and the walls of the inner room were brightly painted. These paint-ings are now faded almost beyond recognition, but they were clearly visible when the building was first excavated in the early nineteenth century and when this temple was one of the star attractions of the site. In fact it was this spot that the poet Shelley chose for his picnic when he visited Pompeii in December 1818. Even if it was originally rather dark – for there is no obvious source of light except the main doorway – the inner room, with colonnade, statues, rich fittings and offerings, must have been an impressive sight. At more than 10 by 15 metres, and with the doors left open so you could see what you were doing, it would have been a place for the local council to meet.

That is, if there was not too much clutter and bric-a-brac getting in the way. The nineteenth-century excavators found a few inscriptions recording dedica-tions for vows fulfilled (including one for the 'well-being' of the emperor Caligula), and the base of a statue put up in honour of a man, Spurius Turranius Proculus Gellianus, who had held various posts in Rome and the town of Lavin-ium. What his connection with Pompeii was, and quite why he was given a statue in this particular place of honour (if this was its original location), we have no idea. The excavators also turned up, in and around the temple, a good haul of bits and pieces of sculpture. As William Gell describes it in the 1830s, giving a nice flavour of the curious assemblage: 'Many fingers of bronze were discovered ... a group representing an old man in a Phrygian cap taking a child by the hand, half a foot high; a woman carrying her infant ... a hand, a finger, and part of a foot, in marble; two feet with sandals; an arm, and many other colossal fragments.'

Standing out amongst all this was a colossal marble torso, which could only have come from the statue of a god, and two striking heads: that colossal bearded marble head of Jupiter himself (Ill. 99), and a smaller female head (Juno or Minerva). These heads have often been thought to be all that is left of the cult statues of the three deities. If so they must have been what we now call 'acrolithic' sculptures (literally 'stone extremities'). This was a favourite ancient method of making huge images that would have been too big, heavy and costly to make out of solid marble, and much, much too costly to make entirely out of bronze. It involved constructing a frame out of wood or metal, covering most of the frame with rich clothing, and using marble just to stand in for the skin of hands, feet and faces. This partly explains why museums of ancient sculpture are now rather over-provided with large marble extremities. It is not only because they break off easily (which they do). It is because hands, feet and heads were often all that was made in marble in the first place.

But a more careful look at these remains produces a strange picture of the Temple of Jupiter, Juno and Minerva at the time of the eruption. For a start the male head and colossal torso cannot possibly belong together. Then there is the puzzle of why these parts of the precious cult images were found just lying around. Perhaps it was the result of an inefficient rescue job as the volcano exploded, or of hurried looting later. But if, as seems more likely in this case, the general disarray in the temple was caused by restoration works in progress (after one or more earthquakes) why was such little care taken with the old statues? Were the authorities really happy that parts of their venerable old images were just scattered on the temple floor? Most curious of all, on the back of the marble torso there is another sculpture in relief, showing three small figures. The marble has obviously been reused. This heroic male chest has, recently we would guess, been carved out of an earlier relief sculpture. All these factors, combined with the haul of other very fragmentary pieces, have made some archaeologists think that in 79 the building was not merely being restored, but it was actually temporarily decommissioned as a temple and was being used as a sculpture depository, workshop and site office. No need to worry about the careless treatment of the old cult statues. What was found here, impressive as some pieces are, were just the spare fragments in the depository.

We cannot now know for sure. But there are intriguing consequences for the little Temple of Aesculapius, and a whole web of possible stories follow. That temple contained three terracotta statues: a full length pair, male and female, plus an instantly recognisable and crudely crafted bust of Minerva. For Winckelmann the male figure was Aesculapius (Ill. 105), which made the female Hygeia, his

105. One of the statues found in the Temple of Jupiter Meilichios: a terracotta image of a god who could equally well be Aesculapius or Jupiter.

daughter and another healing deity – with Minerva thrown in for good measure. But suppose, for a moment, that the Temple of Jupiter, Juno and Minerva really was out of commission at the time of the eruption. Surely the Pompeians would have wanted to lodge its cult images somewhere safe. This trio found in the small temple would make an equally plausible Jupiter, Juno and Minerva. What is against them being those very statues from the Forum, temporarily lodging in the temple down the road?

Well, they are not very grand, and they are made of terracotta not marble. Minerva is only a bust. But in religion, sacred and showy are not always synonymous. Sometimes the most humble objects have the most religious power. Maybe – and it is only maybe – we have been looking in the wrong place for that Jupiter, Juno and Minerva.

Celebrating the gods: in public and private

Carved into an altar also found in the Pompeian Forum is a scene of that most iconic of ancient rituals: animal sacrifice. We see it here in its classic guise, as it

106. The sacrifice of a bull. This altar from the Forum shows – as is usual in Roman art – the preliminaries to the death of the animal, not the kill itself. The social and political hierarchies are made clearly visible, in the contrast between the semi-naked slaves managing the animal and the heavily-draped elite priest, to the left, reciting the prayer.

was described by Roman writers and plastered across the Roman world in thousands of images from coins to triumphal arches. It repays a closer look. For there are details and distinctions that do not immediately strike the modern eye. In the centre is a tripod, serving here as a portable altar. Next to it, the sacrificer, whether a priest or a political official (for both conducted sacrifices on behalf of their community), is reciting the prayer, while pouring an offering of wine and incense. He is wearing a toga, but has pulled part of the material over his head, as was the rule when sacrificing. A musician in the background plays the double pipes, while behind him some attendants (including a child) carry more equipment, including just the kind of shaped bowls and jugs that you can now see filling the cases of the Naples Museum. On the other side of the tripod, the splendid bull is being led to the scene, by three slaves. These are specially dressed for the killing that they will shortly carry out, naked to the waist. One of them is holding an axe ready for the slaughter.

This is, of course, a very idealised image of a sacrifice. It is the equivalent of a commemorative group photograph or rather – given that it was sculpted on the front of a marble altar where sacrifice would actually have taken place – it offered to the participants in the ritual a perfect image of what they were doing. The bull is not only very well behaved, he is also very large. It has been estimated that an animal this size (assuming the human participants were of average height) would have carried some 500 kilos of meat on him. My guess is that real-life sacrifice was usually a less well-ordered occasion, and that the animals were smaller, and less expensive. But even so we can get a sense here of the occasion itself: the noise, the music, the imminent spilling of blood. We see too some of the hierarchical and social conventions of the ritual. The official sacrificer himself stands at the altar, heavily clothed. He speaks the ritual words but he is not going to labour at the kill nor bloody his hands. That dirty work is to be done by slaves, bared for the task. Even (or especially) at ritual moments the divisions of the Roman social order were clearly marked.

What was sacrifice for? It was, in part, an offering to the god. When the animal had been killed its meat was divided. Some of it was consumed by the human participants, some of it was sold off, but some was burnt on the altar – its savour wafting up to heaven as a gift to the gods. It could also provide a way of finding out the divine will. After the kill, experts (*haruspices*) would inspect the entrails of the dead animal for signs from the gods. When Julius Caesar, for example, was sacrificing just before his assassination, the story was that the animal was found to have no heart. A bad omen needless to say – though sceptical Romans pointed out that it was impossible for an animal to live with no heart.

But sacrifice also offered a model of how the world was ordered on a much grander scale. The repeated slaughter *of* animals *by* humans *to* gods was an emblem of the hierarchy of the cosmos, with humans in the middle between the beasts on the one hand and the divine on the other. And the sharing of the meat after the sacrifice, and the communal banqueting that sometimes went with it, reaffirmed the human community and its own internal hierarchies. (There were very few civic handouts in the Roman world that did not reassert social rank by giving more to the rich than the poor – an unsettling reversal of our own assumption that more should go to the needy.) Sacrifice was the closest thing the Roman world had to a creed – a creed in *action*. To reject sacrifice, as the Christians did, was tantamount to rejecting traditional Roman religion. Even vegetarianism was more than a moral or lifestyle choice. By not participating in the consumption of meat, vegetarians put themselves dangerously at odds with the social and cosmic order represented by sacrifice.

We would love to know more of the practical details of sacrifice at Pompeii. How was it funded? How many people actually witnessed it? Did the *duoviri* have *haruspices* on their staff, as is mentioned in the Spanish charter? How many shared in the consumption of the meat, and where did that happen? In Rome on some occasions tables were set up in the Forum. Could that have been done in Pompeii as well? How much of the meat was sold off through the butchers? And was it really the case, as some modern historians have claimed, that all meat ever consumed had been part of a sacrifice? I am not convinced. But if the building known as the *macellum* ('market') was primarily a meat market, then at least it was conveniently close to the main temples of the town.

We would also like to know more about when, and how often, sacrifice was performed. A sacrifice might be offered to a god in payment of a vow or to appease the gods after some disaster. It might mark major events or anniversaries: the accession of an emperor, the anniversary of a temple's foundation, the inauguration of new civic officials or a god's special festival. But exactly how often the distinctive, full-blown animal slaughter took place – rather than the cheaper 'shorthand' of wine, incense and grain, thrown onto the flames of an altar – we can only guess.

Interestingly the sculptor who showed the Temple of Jupiter, Juno and Minerva tottering in the earthquake depicted a sacrifice in progress right next door to it (Ill. 5). It has proved very hard to match up this large and distinctive altar, apparently decorated with the sculpture of a pig, to any monument anywhere in the Forum. But there is no need to read this literally, and certainly no need to suppose that a sacrifice had been in full swing at the very moment of the tremor. Much more likely the sculptor was attempting to capture the kinds of activities that symbolised the life of the town at the moment of its interruption. In the Forum, next to the temple, what else but a large bull being led to slaughter by a man naked to the waist, carrying an axe?

Ancient religious festivals could also be fun. We have very little idea how the participants, in Pompeii or anywhere else, reacted to the slaughter of the sacrificial animals. The poet Horace had some sentimental reflections on the young goat he intended to sacrifice ('his head, swollen with horns, / newly grown, gives promise of love and battles; / in vain …'). But Horace was unlikely to have been typical. And in any case the feasting which followed must surely have been a jolly and celebratory event. Many other ways of honouring the gods involved pleasure for their human worshippers too. We have already looked at shows, theatre and pantomime as part of Pompeian 'Fun and Games'. Very often these were staged as part of a festival with a religious core. Drama in Italy, no less than in Greece, had its roots in religious celebrations. Many early 'theatres' were improvised from the steps of temples, the gods overseeing the performance from within. At Pompeii the Large Theatre is directly linked, by a monumental staircase, to the Triangular Forum and its Temple of Minerva and Hercules – a connection which points to the religious aspect of drama here too.

We happen to know most about Pompeii's festival of the god Apollo. Almost certainly there were festivals of plenty of other gods too. But thanks to the surviving epitaph of Aulus Clodius Flaccus (p. 198) we have a brief order of ceremonies for the 'Games of Apollo' on three occasions when Flaccus, as *duumvir*, was sponsoring the proceedings. We have already discussed some of the range of spectacles he presented: bullfighters, boxers and pantomimes. His epitaph also stresses the 'procession' that was a part of all this. Processions were another distinctive element in ancient religion. Priests, officials of various sorts, clubs and the representatives of particular trades paraded through the streets. Sometimes the images of gods came too, even brought from the temples themselves, or other displays transported on floats or those portable platforms carried shoulder-high. Accompanied by music, by the sprinkling of incense and (if there was a generous sponsor) by presents thrown to the spectators, these festivities put the city, its officials, its representatives and its gods on display – to itself.

By definition, processions are transitory affairs and tracking their progress through the town is difficult. How would anyone be able to reconstruct from any material remains the routes of the London Lord Mayor's procession or of a royal wedding? One theory, as we have already seen, holds that the road which leads from the old temple in the Triangular Forum to the main Forum – largely traffic-free and free of disreputable elements such as bars – was a major processional route in the city, and imagines parades moving between the old religious centre of the Temple of Minerva and Hercules and the new focus in the Temple of Jupiter, Juno and Minerva. It may have been so. But, whichever precise route they took (and that surely must have differed according to the occasion), we have some evidence in sculpture and painting of what the displays might have looked like.

We glimpsed in the last chapter the procession that led to the games in the Amphitheatre. An extraordinary painting from the façade of what was probably a carpenter's shop, just opposite the Bar on the Via di Mercurio, captures the style of display even more vividly. Most of the paintings discovered on the outside of this building have been lost. According to early copies, they featured a trio of gods and goddesses – Mercury (often associated with trade and commerce), Fortuna (for good luck), Minerva (who was regularly the patron of crafts and craftsmanship) – plus Daedalus, the mythical craftsman who most famously built the Labyrinth for King Minos and made the wings which brought about the death of his son Icarus. But luckily one scene was long ago removed to the Naples Museum (Plate 5). It shows another of those portable platforms (or *fercula* in Latin), like the one carrying the model blacksmiths in the Amphitheatre procession. This one is also being carried by four bearers. It must be heavy, for the men use sticks to support themselves, and it appears to be rather more elaborate than the earlier one – with a canopy and a frame decorated with flowers and foliage.

Displayed on the *ferculum* are three groups of model figures. At the back is an image of the goddess Minerva. This part of the painting is badly damaged, but part of her dress and her trademark shield are still visible. In the middle three carpenters are at work, one apparently planing a piece of wood, the other two operating a saw between them. At the front is a much more puzzling scene: a man dressed in a short tunic, with a compass in his hands, stands over a naked man lying in the ground. One attractive theory sees the standing figure as Daedalus again, and this part of the scene therefore as some myth of craftmanship and carpentry. But who is the figure on the ground? Is it a statue that Daedalus has crafted? Or is it his nephew Perdix, whom Daedalus killed in jealous rivalry because the clever lad had invented the compasses and saw? Either way, what we are looking at must be a tableau carried in procession by the carpenters – whether representing this one firm, or the whole carpentry trade in the city. It is rare evidence for what Flaccus' 'procession' at the Games of Apollo might have contained.

Sacrifice of bulls, processions, theatrical performances … all these are rituals on a city-wide scale. What happened in more-local or more-private contexts? There is, in fact, plenty of evidence for the presence of the gods in neighbourhoods of the town and in private houses, large and small. Shrines and altars were set up at many crossroads, and one of the most distinctive and easily recognisable features of Pompeian houses is shrines that we now call by the Latin word *lararium*, shrine of the Lares or household gods (though the term was not used in Latin itself until centuries after the destruction of Pompeii). Some of these are quite elaborate affairs, set up in the atrium or peristyle of large houses. We saw in the House of the Tragic Poet, for example, how the visitor's eye was drawn through the house directly to the shrine on the back wall of the peristyle garden. But many others are much simpler and often placed in the kitchen or service areas. In fact, in the absence of much decoration it can be hard to distinguish an ordinary shelf or niche from one of these simple 'shrines' – and there is a good chance that some of those features confidently labelled *lararium* on modern plans were nothing more than a shelf for normal household equipment.

One of the most impressive of these shrines is in the small atrium of the House of the Vettii (Ill. 107). The painting which covers its back wall includes many of the figures typically found on these *lararia*. To left and right are the Lares themselves, dressed in skimpy tunics and carrying drinking horns and wine buckets.

107. This household shrine or *lararium* from the House of the Vettii is among the most impressive to survive. Above the writhing snake, the Lares themselves (similar to the miniature bronze versions in Ill. 98) stand on either side of a figure in a toga, who may be the head of the household or his 'guardian spirit'.

These mini-gods were often associated with the protection and welfare of the house, or sometimes (when they appear as the 'Lares of the Crossroads') of a local neighbourhood. In one of Plautus' plays a Lar, who appears on stage to speak the prologue, has been responsible for finding a hidden pot of gold in the house. And it was to the Lares that the two members of the household of Caius Julius Philippus made their vow for the master's safe return. But no myths attached to them, as to most other deities, and even the Romans themselves debated their history and exactly what kind of gods they were.

Between the Lares, in the middle of the scene, stands a man dressed in a toga, pulled over his head, as if he were in the act of sacrifice. He is, in fact, scattering incense from a box in his left hand. One would naturally see him as the head of the household (*paterfamilias*), but archaeologists tend – for no very strong reason, so far as I can tell – to refer to him as the *genius*, or the 'guardian spirit' of the head of the household. The difference probably does not matter too much. For,

108. A community of worshippers. It is hard to be certain what kind of religious rituals took place in a Pompeian house. This rough painting seems to suggest some form of communal worship. For next to the large figure of a Lar, we see a group of people, young and old, gathered together around an altar.

in whichever guise, he is making an offering to the Lares. Underneath squirms a splendid snake: a symbol of prosperity, fertility and the protection of the house (or so the usual story goes).

In many cases statuettes of gods and goddesses stood on the ledge or shelf of the *lararium*. Sometimes these depict the Lares themselves, but a much wider range of deities has been found – perhaps giving us a glimpse into the divine favourites of the Pompeians (or at least those rich enough to afford statuettes, mostly in bronze). After the Lares, Mercury is the most popular divine subject, closely followed by the Egyptian gods (whom we shall look at more closely at the end of this chapter), with Venus, Minerva, Jupiter and Hercules, in that order, coming next.

The big question is what ritual, if any, took place at these shrines? We know that offerings were made on the crossroads shrines for the simple reason that on at least one traces of ash and burnt remains have been discovered. These were presumably organised by the 'presidents' and 'attendants' whose names are recorded in a handful of painted lists found close by (p. 211). As for the private houses, one common idea is that the whole household – owners, slaves and other dependants – would gather at the *lararium* regularly, while the *paterfamilias* made an offering to the gods. That may seem unlikely. Not only does it sound much too like the Victorian custom of family prayers, but in some cases the shrine is in such a poky room that it would have been impossible to assemble many of the household around it. All the same, something along those lines does appear to be shown in an unusual painting found right next to the *lararium* of one small house (Ill. 108).

Between two giant Lares, a *paterfamilias* is making an offering at an altar. This is not full-blown animal sacrifice, but it does feature a pipe-player just as on the sacrificial scene from the Forum. Just behind the *paterfamilias* stands his wife, while on the right we see another thirteen people, all of whom, apart from the little boy in front stand in exactly the same position, with their right hand on their chest. Again there are dangers in reading the image too literally. Certainly this crowd could not have fitted into the cramped room where the painting was found. But it must hint at some kind of *lararium* ritual attended by the household in general – and at the formal stance they would have been expected to adopt during the proceedings, the Roman equivalent of 'hands together' for prayer.

As in the case of processions, the problem in reconstructing the religious life of the home is that rituals such as this very rarely leave any archaeological trace, apart from the lucky survival of a bit of ash. Only very occasionally can we detect religious action in the remains we find on the ground. At the back of one house, excavators found a pit filled with rubble and on top a tile marked *FULGUR* (i.e. 'lightning'). Might this have been part of the process of appeasing the gods after a lightning strike? In the recent excavations of the House and Bar of Amarantus, other curious pits were found in the floor, in both the Roman and the pre-Roman phases of occupation on that particular patch of ground. The later ones contained sheep and cockerel bone, as well as charred fig and pine-nuts. The earlier ones included, for example, a newborn piglet, some cereals, whole fruits as well as fig and grape pips. The excavators saw here evidence of sacrifice (some of the piglet's bones were burned, and knife marks suggested that some of it had been eaten), along with offerings of whole fruits and cereal, the remains of which were then ritually buried. This would be, in other words, rare evidence for some kind of religious rites in the home – unless, of course, it is one of those cases where, as the old joke has it, 'religion' is a convenient fall-back for explaining odd features we cannot easily make sense of.

Politics and religion: emperors, attendants and priests

Roman religion was a flexible and expandable system. New gods and goddesses were brought in from abroad. In fact there is a nice parallel to be drawn between the way Romans incorporated ex-slaves into their citizen body and the way they incorporated new gods into their pantheon. But new gods were also recruited from among mortal men: the boundary between humans and gods could occasionally be crossed. According to Roman myth both Hercules and Aesculapius had been born mortals. But it did not stop with myth. Many Roman emperors became gods.

That process was a complex one, and it took different forms in different parts of the Roman world, at different periods and on different occasions. Sometimes the Roman senate would officially declare a Roman emperor a god at his 'death', and would grant him a temple and priests. In some provinces religious worship of the emperor during his lifetime was the central way that loyalty to Rome was expressed. Sometimes the emperor would merely be likened to a god, given honours that were 'equal' to the gods, but not exactly the same. None of this is quite as crude (or silly) as it is often painted. In Rome the division between humans and gods was seen essentially in terms of power. There was almost bound to be a debate about where on that spectrum the all-powerful single ruler of the Roman world belonged. Or, to put it another way: if gods could be treated rather like overblown *duoviri*, then the infinitely more powerful emperor could, or must, be treated as a god. In a nutshell, divine or quasi-divine power was a way of understanding and representing human autocracy.

Emperors and the Roman elite could exploit this religious aspect of imperial power in all kinds of ways. As well as finding the 'imperial cult', as it is now often called, a useful means of channelling the loyalty of provincial communities, the first emperor, Augustus, took care to insert himself into the neighbourhood religious organisations of Rome. The traditional worship of the 'Lares of the crossroads' was refocused onto the 'Lares of the emperor', as an exercise in promoting the loyalty to the imperial regime of those slaves and ex-slaves who were the major participants in these local cults. Yet there was also a degree of quizzical and humorous reflection about the very idea of the emperor being a god. A skit about the doddery old Claudius trying to take his place in heaven (the *Apocolocyntosis*), perhaps written by the philosopher Seneca, is one of the funniest things to survive in Latin. The emperor Vespasian is reputed to have made a deathbed quip at his own expense: 'Dear me,' he said, 'I think I'm turning into a god.'

What impact did divine emperors have on the town of Pompeii? Just as in

Rome the worship of the emperor seeped (or was pushed) into all kinds of traditional forms of religion. The conflation of Fortuna with the power of the emperor
in Marcus Tullius' temple is a typical case of that. In Pompeii we have no direct
evidence that the crossroads cults took on an imperial aspect as they did at Rome.
But a revealing series of inscriptions shows how other traditional deities could
eventually be squeezed out by the presence of the emperor. Somewhere in the
town – we do not know where – there must have been a shrine to the god Mercury
and his mother Maia. What survives of their worship is a number of plaques
recording, with a precise date, dedications made by the officials of the cult, who
were overwhelmingly slaves and ex-slaves. In the earliest of these they record
dedications to (or describe themselves as attendants of) just Mercury and Maia.
Then the emperor Augustus joins them: 'attendants of Augustus, Mercury and
Maia'. After 2 BCE, Augustus completely takes over. There is no mention in any
of the later dedications of the original pair of gods.

There were also entirely new imperial elements brought into local religion,
including new priests. As we have already noted, the major priests of the city
were drawn from the ranks of the elite, part-time officials dealing with the religious business of the state – sometimes, we may guess, conducting sacrifice,
sometimes advising the council on religious decisions and actions. They might be
attached to individual gods, to judge from one reference to a 'priest of Mars'.
Others, since the establishment of the colony, were members of what we might
call priestly 'committees', modelled on the practice of the city of Rome itself. We
know of *augures* who, on the Roman model, would have been concerned, amongst
other things, with signs from the gods. There were also *pontifices*, who were supposed to advise on such things as religious law, the calendar and burial rules.
Women, for once, had a formal role. There were public priestesses of Venus and
of Ceres. Wealthy Eumachia was one such 'public priestess', another was Mamia.
We do not know exactly what their religious duties were. There is some doubt
whether Roman women were actually allowed to conduct sacrifice. But they certainly disposed of considerable cash and sponsored public works. As we have
seen, to judge from a fragmentary inscription, Eumachia's vast development in
the Forum was bordered by another sponsored by Mamia.

To this repertoire was added a priesthood of the reigning emperor, held by
some of the most prominent citizens, including Marcus Holconius Rufus. The
duties must have included sacrificing on important imperial occasions and anniversaries. But it is very likely too that holding the priesthood of the emperor was
a fast-track way to getting noticed by the imperial hierarchy in the capital. Far

below that level, even if they had many other functions in the town, the *Augustales*, as their name suggests, must also have had some responsibilities for the worship of the emperor.

New shrines or temples were built too. As well as the Temple of Fortuna Augusta, there was also a building on the east side of the Forum devoted specifically to the imperial cult. It is from this temple that the altar with its scene of sacrifice comes. And it is, in fact, the altar itself that gives away the connection with the emperor Augustus: the design on its back features two of the honours (the oak wreath and laurels) voted to Augustus by the senate in 29 BCE; and the face of the sacrificer bears more than a passing resemblance to that emperor. It was presumably here that the priests of the imperial cult would conduct their imperial sacrifices.

The overall impression, then, is that the emperor was becoming a bigger and bigger part of the religious world of Pompeii. But perhaps not *quite* such a large part as some modern scholars have claimed. It is predictable perhaps that the more interested archaeologists and historians have become in the Roman imperial cult, the more they have found its physical remains at every turn. Put simply, there is a tendency to find what you are looking for. In Pompeii, this enthusiasm has combined with the lack of much evidence about what several of the buildings on the east side of the Forum were actually for to encourage at least three buildings, or parts of buildings, to be assigned to the worship of the emperor.

In addition to the temple with the altar, there is the building next door, often labelled on no evidence at all 'Imperial cult building' (though the alternative idea that it was a library seems no better to me). Then, at the back of the *macellum*, there is supposed to have been another shrine to the emperor. This view is largely based on the discovery in the early nineteenth century of a marble arm, holding a globe (an imperial figure?) and a pair of statues which some have identified as members of the imperial family – though others (such is the difficulty of putting names to faces) have seen them as a couple of local grandees. As if that were not enough, some imaginative scholars have argued that the lump of concrete at the centre of the piazza was the base of a large altar dedicated to the emperor.

If all this were true, the Forum of Pompeii in 79 CE could only be described as a monument to dynastic and political loyalty, on a scale that would impress the most hard-line, one-party regimes of the modern world. Happily there is hardly a shred of evidence for any of it.

Mighty Isis

Were there Christians in Pompeii? By 79 it is not impossible. But there is no firm evidence for their presence, except for an example of a common Roman word game. This is one of those clever, but almost meaningless, phrases which read exactly the same backwards and forwards. It also turns out to be (almost) an anagram of PATER NOSTER ('OUR FATHER') written twice over, as well as two sets of the letters A and O (like the Christian 'Alpha and Omega'). Some of the later examples of the same game do seem to have Christian connections. This one may too ... or it may not. The charcoal graffito which was said to include the word 'Christiani', but faded almost instantly, is almost certainly a figment of pious imagination. There is stronger evidence for the presence of Jews. No synagogue has been unearthed. But there is at least one inscription in Hebrew, a few possible references to the Jewish bible, including the famous reference to Sodom and Gomorrah (p. 25), and a sprinkling of possibly Jewish names – not to mention that kosher *garum* (p. 24).

There were nonetheless other religious options for the people of Pompeii beyond the traditions we have already looked at. From as early as the second century BCE, there were religions in Italy which offered a very different kind of religious experience. These often involved initiation and the kind of personal emotional commitment that was not a crucial element in traditional religion. They often held out the promise to the initiates of life after death. This again was not an issue of great importance within the traditional structures of religion, where the dead did have some shadowy continuing existence and might receive offerings at their tombs by pious descendants – but it was certainly not a very desirable existence. These religions were commonly served by priests, or occasionally priestesses, who were more or less full-time, had a pastoral role with their followers and – unlike the *augures* and *pontifices* of Pompeii – lived a specially religious life. They might, for example, wear distinctive clothes or be shaven-headed. They often had an origin overseas, or at least defined themselves with recognisably foreign symbols.

It has proved very easy to misrepresent, and to glamorise, these religions. They were not direct precursors of Christianity. Nor did they arise in complete opposition to traditional religion, to provide the emotional and spiritual satisfaction that Jupiter, Apollo and so on did not. Nor were they practised predominantly by women, the poor, the slaves and other disadvantaged groups attracted by the promise of a blissful afterlife to make up for the wretched conditions of the here and now. They were very much part of Roman polytheism, not outside

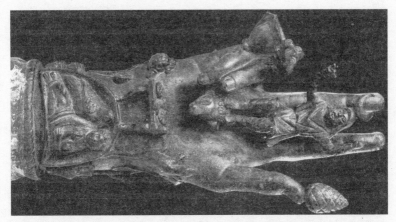

109. Bronze hands, like this one found in Pompeii, are commonly associated with the Eastern god Sabazius. Its meaning and use is uncertain, but it is decorated with symbols of the cult (for example, the pine cone at the end of the thumb). One idea is that these hands were displayed on poles and perhaps carried in procession.

it, even if they had a shifting and sometimes awkward relationship with the authorities of the Roman state. So, for example, the worship of Bacchus (or Dionysos) and the Eastern goddess Cybele (also called the 'Great Mother') had both a civic and a more mystical version. The mystical, initiatory cult of Bacchus was severely restricted by the Roman authorities in 186 BCE, not far short of a total ban. Priests of the Egyptian goddess Isis were on several occasions expelled from Rome, but later Isiac religion received official sponsorship from Roman emperors.

Several of these religions were known, even if not fully organised, at Pompeii. We have already looked at the frescoes in the Villa of the Mysteries which, though baffling and impossible to decode completely, certainly evoke some aspects of the cult of Bacchus, with its revelation of secret objects, and the sense of an ordeal that the initiate must undergo. One house not far from the Amphitheatre turned up various objects connected with the cult of the Eastern deity Sabazius (Ill. 109) – though whether the house was a fully fledged shrine of the god, as is often claimed, is a moot point. But by far the most prominent of these religions at Pompeii was the worship of Isis and other Egyptian deities.

Isis came in many guises, from protector of sailors to the mother of the gods. But one crucial element in her myth was her resurrection of her husband Osiris,

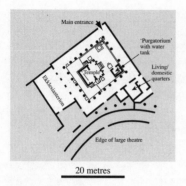

Figure 21. Temple of Isis. Unlike the traditional civic cults of Pompeii, the Temple of Isis included room for a community of worshippers, and probably domestic quarters for the priests.

who had been killed and dismembered by his brother Seth. Isis put his body together again and even went on to become pregnant by him with their child Horus. Hers was a story and a cult that offered hope of life after death. Something of the flavour of the religion for Roman worshippers is captured in the second-century CE novel by Apuleius, *The Golden Ass*. In this, after a series of terrifying adventures, the narrator Lucius is finally initiated into the Isiac cult. He describes the beginning of this process: the ritual washing, the abstinence (no meat or wine), the presents given by other worshippers, the dressing up in new linen. But of course he does not reveal the ultimate secret: 'You may perhaps, attentive reader, ask anxiously what was then said and done. I would tell you if I could; you would find out if you could be told. But your ears and my tongue would be equally punished for such rash curiosity.' But he does go on to make it clear enough that what was promised by the religion was the conquest of death: 'Having reached the boundary of death ... I was borne through all the elements and returned.'

The Temple of Isis at Pompeii is one of the best-preserved, and least looted, buildings in the town (Fig. 21). Tucked into a small site right next to the Large Theatre, which looms above it, it had been recently completely rebuilt and was in full working order in 79 CE. It was hidden from the street by a high curtain wall, broken by a single main entrance up two steps and with a large wooden door. Enough survived of this for the eighteenth-century excavators to see that this door was made in three pieces. Just the central section would have given day-to-day access. It would, presumably, have been thrown wide open on festival occasions.

The door opened into a colonnaded courtyard (Ill. 110). In the centre stood a small temple, with other structures round about and further rooms off the courtyard. The temple was constructed of brick and stone, its outside stuccoed and painted. The walls of the courtyard itself were covered in frescoes. Hardly a spot was left undecorated. Statues were placed around the courtyard and in niches on the temple building itself. We quickly meet here again the old problem of labelling and reconstruction. Archaeologists have examined these remains for centuries, trying to match them up to descriptions given by ancient writers of the rituals and organisation of the cult of Isis, and to name the various parts. So, for example, the large room to the west is usually called by the Greek name *ekklesi- asterion* ('assembly room'), and assumed to be the place where the initiates met. It may have been. But the important thing is to see how this complex differs from the traditional civic temples of the town, and how the different decorations and finds in the different areas may point to different functions.

The first thing to emphasise is that it was not open to public view, and the entrance was not welcoming to all-comers. This was religion for initiates. Sec- ondly the building was catering for more congregational religious use and pos- sibly a resident priest or two. Whether or not the assembly room really was for meetings of the members of the cult, there were places here for people to congre- gate and do things together. There were also a large dining room and a kitchen, and spaces that could be used for sleeping. As we have seen in other places, light- ing was an issue. Fifty-eight terracotta lamps were found in one of the back storerooms.

The precise function of some parts is clear enough. The temple itself origi- nally contained the cult statues of Isis and Osiris. These were not found in place on their podium inside. But an elegant marble head, found in the so-called *ekkle- siasterion* near some other marble extremities (a left hand, a right hand and arm, the front of two feet), may well be the remains of the acrolithic cult statue from the temple. The temple's altar is outside in the courtyard, and opposite it is a small square structure, marking out a sunken pool. Whether or not archaeologists are right to give this the title *purgatorium*, it does very likely relate to the stress on washing and cleansing we find in ancient discussions of Isiac rituals. And not just any water would do. In theory at least the initiates of Isis bathed themselves in water brought specially from the Nile.

Meanwhile, whatever happened there, the decoration of the *ekklesiasterion* and that of the room next door marked them both as different from the rest. There were a few specifically Egyptian religious scenes in the decoration of the court- yard, but much of it seems to have had no particular relevance to the temple's cult or Isiac myth. By contrast, in both these rooms the flavour is decidedly Egyptian.

110. The little Temple of Isis still captures the modern imagination much as it did that of eighteenth-century visitors. Because it was in full working order at the time of the eruption, and not looted in the years that followed, it offers the most vivid picture of a religious centre in the town.

The 'assembly room' originally included at least two large mythological panels. One was a perfect emblem to greet new initiates: it depicts the Greek heroine Io, in flight from the goddess Hera, being welcomed to Egypt by Isis herself (Plate 18). The other room displays paintings of Isiac symbols, of the goddess herself and her rituals. In addition to the fifty-eight lamps, it was full of various pieces of religious equipment and Egyptian memorabilia, from a little sphinx to an iron tripod.

The overall impression is one of cultural mix. Here, for example, standard classical portraits (such as the bronze of mime actor Norbanus Sorex) and sculptures of traditional deities such as Venus rub shoulders with 'real' Egyptian bric-a-brac, such as a fourth-century BCE tablet from Egypt inscribed in hieroglyphs – presumably intended to evoke 'authentic' Egypt. We see this mixture too in the best-preserved image of Isis from the complex (Ill. 111). This statue was made in the first century CE, adopting a Greek style of sculpture of several hundred years earlier. She is hardly Egyptian at all, but for the characteristic rattle or *sistrum* she carries in one hand, and the ankh, or Egyptian cross, she once carried in the other. It is hard to resist the feeling that this cult is treading a fairly safe line between its traditional civic Italian links and its mystical Egyptian 'otherness'. That is the message too from all those Egyptian deities who shared space on the household *lararium* with little models of Lares, or Hercules, or Mercury.

The traditional aspects of the Isiac cult are well illustrated by the inscription above the main entranceway, recording the restoration. It reads: 'Numerius Popidius Celsinus, the son of Popidius, restored with his own money the Temple of Isis, from its foundations, after it had collapsed in the earthquake. On account of his generosity, the decurions co-opted him onto the town council, without fee, although he was only six years old.' There are other signs of this family's benefactions in the temple. Celsinus' father, 'Numerius Popidius Ampliatus, senior' donated a statue of Bacchus. Their names also used to appear in black and white mosaic, along with that of Corelia Celsa (presumably wife and mother) on the floor of the *ekklesiasterion*.

As we have already seen, it looks as if the elder Popidius was using the restoration of this temple to launch his young son into the Pompeian political elite. We do not know for sure that Popidius Ampliatus was an ex-slave and so precluded himself from political advancement in the town, but a man of that name does appear among the 'attendants of Augustus', who were predominantly slaves or ex-slaves. So that seems very likely. What is more interesting though is that restoration of the Temple of Isis so easily counts in the game of benefaction and generosity that characterised civic advancement in Pompeii. Initiatory, foreign and strange, the Isiac cult may have in some respects been. But the bottom line was that it was a public cult, on public land, as plausible a vehicle for social advancement as that of Fortuna Augusta. Isis was one religious option among several for the inhabitants of Pompeii.

In the 1760s, the Temple of Isis was among the first buildings fully excavated on the site. It was a lucky find and it instantly captured the imagination of European travellers. True, a few killjoys found it disappointingly small. But for most it offered double excitement: simultaneously a glimpse of ancient Egypt and of ancient Rome. Exotic and a little bit sinister, it gave Mozart, who visited Pompeii in 1769, ideas for the *Magic Flute*. Fifty years later, it gave Bulwer-Lytton the idea for the nasty conniving villain of his *Last Days*, the Egyptian Arbaces – who was written up with all the predictable racial stereotypes. But it was responsible for even more powerful myths too. For it was the pristine state of the temple, almost

III. A nice illustration of the cultural mix represented by the cult of Isis at Pompeii, straddling the traditions of Egypt, Greece and Rome. This nineteenth-century painting shows a statue of the goddess herself, holding Egyptian symbols. But the figure itself looks back to a recognisably Greek style of sculpture.

undisturbed, that helped to create 'our' myth of Pompeii, a city interrupted in mid-flow.

In fact, the last sacrifice was still burning on the altar here when the pumice started to fall. Or so they said.

CITY OF THE DEAD

Ashes to ashes

Early visitors to the remains of Pompeii entered the city through its cemeteries. We now buy our tickets, maps, guidebooks and bottles of water in a modern 'visitor centre', which could just as well be the entrance to a busy train station as to a buried city. Our eighteenth-century predecessors usually followed one of the ancient roads into the town, lined as they were with imposing and affecting monuments to the dead.

Romans kept the dead out of their towns. There were no city-centre cemeteries or village graveyards, putting the dead in the middle of things. Instead, here at Pompeii just like in Rome itself, the memorials to earlier generations hugged the routes in and out of the town outside the walls. Ancient travellers entered Pompeii past the often imposing residences of those who had lived decades, maybe centuries before. For although cremation was the normal funerary practice during the heyday of Pompeii (at least since the arrival of the Roman colonists in the early first century BCE), this did not discourage extravagant memorials. Tiny urns holding the ashes of the dead were lodged in a whole range of grand designs – in the shape of altars, elegant semi-circular seats or benches, (convenient resting places for the living too), multi-storey constructions with columns and statues of the departed.

For the early tourists this set the tone for their visit. Pompeii was a site of human tragedy, a city of the dead. The tombs they first saw as they started their visit (albeit the memorials of those who, likely as not, had died safely in their beds) offered the prompt to a good deal of reverie on the transience of human existence, and on the inevitabity of death for all of us, high or low. Dust to dust, and – appropriately for Pompeii – ashes to ashes.

But, of course, death and commemoration was anything but equal in ancient Pompeii. The memorials reflected exactly those hierarchies and inequalities that we have seen repeatedly in the life of the town. We already spotted (pp. 2–4) the irony of that little party of unsuccessful fugitives, with some 500 *sesterces* between them, being finally overwhelmed next to the tomb of Marcus Obellius Firmus, aedile and *duumvir*, whose funeral alone had cost ten times that amount. His tomb was typical of the grander designs, though by no means the most splendid: a simple walled enclosure, within which the single urn was buried, with a terracotta pipe installed next to it, to channel offerings made to the dead man by his descendants. Unless they had been convinced by the more optimistic claims of some of the newer religions, most Romans had, it seems, a rather hazy and grey picture of what happened after death. Nonetheless, as here, they might take the trouble to provide some kind of sustenance for their ancestor – though how often the tube was used we do not know.

Other members of the Pompeian elite, both male and female, were commemorated with more flashy monuments than Obellius Firmus. In fact, the tomb of the priestess Eumachia is the biggest so far uncovered, standing high above the road on its own terrace and including – a wry reflection on her gender, as it must now seem – a marble sculpture of Amazons (mythical female warriors), a large seating area and the burial plots of Eumachia herself and some of her relations and dependants. On some, the honours or benefactions of the deceased were displayed in images as well as words. We have already seen (Ill. 72) the *bisellium* or seat of honour carefully carved onto the tomb of the *Augustalis* Caius Calventius Quietus, as proud an assertion of status as any made by the richest aristocratic landowners. Others carry sculptures or paintings of gladiatorial contests – presumably intended to represent those financed by the dead man during his lifetime.

Many of these monuments ended up marked with graffiti of the usual demotic type, or covered with publicity notices for games and shows. Their plain walls must have provided a convenient space for messages and adverts in a prominent roadside location. But it is hard not to suspect that there was also an element of 'getting your own back' at work here. How satisfying it must have been to deface these aggressive memorials to wealth, power and privilege.

Needless to say, the poorer sections of Pompeian society did not enjoy such luxurious final resting places – unless they were among those slaves and ex-slaves lucky enough to be granted space in their masters' monument. For the rest, some

112. Street of tombs. This engraving captures the approach to the city for the early visitors. Entering the city by the Herculaneum Gate, they came face to face with the monuments of death. On the right, just visible is the semi-circular seat which formed the memorial to the priestess Mamia – celebrated by Goethe in his account of a visit to Pompeii.

would have been able to afford a small part of a large communal tomb. The ashes of others ended up in cheap containers inserted directly into the earth, marked with just a simple stone. Even that would have been too good for those at the very bottom of the social pile. At Pompeii, as elsewhere in the Roman world, their bodies were probably unceremoniously dumped or burnt, with not a funeral celebration or permanent marker at all.

Quarrels beyond the grave

It was not only the inequalities of Pompeian life that left their permanent mark in the cemeteries outside the town. Occasionally the quarrels and disputes of the living city extended beyond the grave. In fact, one of the most vivid glimpses of the rough realities of ancient society, a sad story of friendship made and lost, comes from a large tomb outside the Nuceria Gate, located near the monument of Eumachia. It is the memorial of an ex-slave, Publius Vesonius Phileros, who built it well in advance, during his own lifetime, for himself and for two others to share. It is a nice indication of the fluidity of relationships and affections, cutting across the formal hierarchies of Pompeian society. For Phileros built a tomb to

113. The tomb of Publius Vesonius Phileros and his one-time friends. The circumstances remain a mystery, but after this tomb was commissioned, the two men fell out – and ended up in litigation (as the added plaque on the façade explains). What had been intended as a monument to friendship became a 2000-year memorial to a quarrel.

include also the remains of his one time owner, a woman named Vesonia, and his 'friend', a free-born man by the name of Marcus Orfellius Faustus. Full-length statues of all three of them – sadly missing their heads – still look down at the passers-by from a niche on the upper storey of the façade.

Phileros made two adjustments to the monument after it had been completed. He must have become an *Augustalis* late in life, and was proud enough of that status to have added the word to the plaque that had already been inscribed with the names of the threesome. There was not much space left, so *'Augustalis'* appears in smaller letters. The other adjustment involved adding an additional plaque to explain that he had since fallen out with the erstwhile friend, Faustus. It runs:

Stranger, stop a little while if it isn't too much trouble and learn what to avoid. This man that I had hoped was my friend – it was he who produced accusers against me and started a court case. I thank the gods and my innocence that I was freed from all this trouble. May neither the household gods nor the gods below receive the man who lied about our affairs.

The circumstances remain baffling. Why, for example, add this extra notice, rather than simply remove the other man's name from the first plaque and get rid of his statue? And can we be quite sure that the writer was Phileros? Is it not possible that the injured party was not Phileros but Faustus, who attached this notice to the monument built by his one-time friend? But whatever the exact details, it is a rare story of a friendship between two ordinary Pompeians – which ended not just in recriminations, but in the local courts.

Even the memorials to the dead can throw precious light on the Life of a Roman Town.

MAKING A VISIT

A visit to Pompeii almost never disappoints. There are only three pieces of essential equipment: a map of the site (you can get one at the main entrance at the Marine Gate), a bottle of water (a small one is fine, as you can replenish it at one of the many water fountains) and a comfortable pair of sandals or shoes (the streets are rough and a death-trap for any kind of high-heel).

There are three public entrances to the site. The most convenient route is to come by the local Circumvesuviana train, running between Naples and Sorrento, getting off at the station *Pompei scavi – Villa dei Misteri*. You then enter the site by the main entrance, running the gauntlet of guides and souvenir sellers. Make sure you take some official photo ID (passport, drivers' licence or *bona fide* student card) if you want to claim free or reduced entrance to the site. And check the times of the returning trains when you arrive. They run regularly, but (despite a decent, traditional Italian station bar) waiting even half an hour seems a lot longer when you've finished a day on the site.

You can also get into the site by the Amphitheatre or at the Piazza Esedra between the Amphitheatre and the Marine Gate. But, for these entrances, you should travel by a different branch of the Circumvesuviana (going towards Poggiomarino) getting off at *Pompei santuario*, or by the main national (FS) line running north–south, getting off at the *Pompei* station. Unless you have strong reasons to opt for the others, the *Pompei scavi* route is the best option, and has the best bookshop.

You can leave the site (but not enter or re-enter) at the Villa of the Mysteries (below no. 10).

There is a large self-service restaurant and bar near the Forum, where you will find the only lavatories in the main area of the site (free, but you will be much more welcome if you leave 50 cents).

The most enjoyable part of any visit is simply to walk through the streets of the town. Don't spend too much time getting hot in the Forum, which you reach soon after the Marine Gate. There are better things to come. One excellent plan is to walk along the Via dell'Abbondanza – taking in the façades, the bars, the shops and the changing character of the street as you go along. Keep your eyes open for the traffic calming measures, the ways the flow of water is blocked, the holes in the side of the pavement for tying up the animals, etc. And go into any house you find open. Also try to head down any side street where you can escape the other visitors and, cliché as it is, just imagine that you are back in the first century CE.

The site administration is under-funded, and this means that some of the buildings you will want to see will be locked. A few of these may be open through an internet site (*www.arethusa.net*), which allows you to book a timed entrance to a particular house, which will then be un-locked specially. (This usually, but not always, works.) The list which follows represents my top ten of buildings that are regularly open. You will have missed out if you do not see some of these, at least.

1. *The House of the Tragic Poet* (pp. 81–8). Bulwer Lytton's house of Glaucus.
2. *The House of Octavius Quartio* (pp. 110–13). A marvellous garden with water features, and an outdoor *triclinium*.
3. *The House of Marine Venus* (p. 155) Take a look at the sprawling goddess of love.
4. *The Stabian Baths* (pp. 243–6). The easiest place to get an idea of what Roman bathing involved.
5. *The Forum Baths and the Suburban Baths* (pp. 247–50). If you get interested in baths, these make nice comparisons with the Stabian – and the erotic paintings in the Suburban Baths are well worth seeing in their own right.
6. *The brothel.* Cheesy, but … (pp. 237–40)
7. *The Temple of Isis* (pp. 304–8) The best preserved temple on the site
8. *The Amphitheatre* and the *palaestra* next door (pp. 259–64). But remember that it *is* a long way from the Marine Gate to here. You probably need to decide in advance whether you are up for it.

9. *The Fullery of Stephanus* (on the south side of the Via dell'Abbondanza at
   I.6.7). It gives a good idea what a commercial establishment was like.
10. *The Villa of the Mysteries* (pp. 131–4). Even if it has been re-touched, the
   painting is tremendously impressive. It is a good idea to walk to this out
   of town villa as the last port of call on your visit, past the tombs lining the
   route. Then you can exit directly and go back to the station.

Once you have seen Pompeii, if you have time, you should try to make it to
the nearby town of Herculaneum (also on the Circumvesuviana, a few minutes
walk from *Ercolano* station). This has a much smaller excavated area than Pompeii,
but the preservation of some materials (notably wood) is much better, and there
are fewer visitors.

Many of the best finds from both sites are displayed – and even more are in
store, or temporarily closed and not on view – in the Naples Archaeological
Museum in the city centre. This is easy to reach from Metro stops *Piazza Cavour*
or *Museo*. It is closed on Tuesdays, and when last visited had only a small, ill-
stocked café, but better than nothing.

FURTHER READING

The bibliography on Pompeii is vast and multilingual. What follows is inevitably selective. It aims to give pointers to explore further the main topics of the book, and directions to some of the more out-of-the-way material I discuss. Where possible, I have included works easily available in English – but sometimes the best, or the only, accounts are in other languages.

General

There are several recent archaeological handbooks and histories of Pompeii. Particularly useful are: J. Berry, *The Complete Pompeii* (London and New York, 2007); F. Coarelli (ed.), *Pompeii* (New York, 2002), though the translation from the original Italian is dreadful; A. E. Cooley, *Pompeii* (London, 2003); J. J. Dobbins and P. W. Foss (ed.), *The World of Pompeii* (London and New York, 2007); R. Ling, *Pompeii: history, life and afterlife* (Stroud, 2005); P. Zanker, *Pompeii: public and private life* (Cambridge, MA, 1998). These often provide further information on the topics I discuss, and I have not usually referred to them specifically in the bibliography that follows. Many of the ancient documents I quote (whether graffiti on the walls or Pliny's account of the eruption) can be found in A. E. Cooley and M. G. L. Cooley, *Pompeii: a sourcebook* (London and New York, 2004) – though I have provided my own translations of the Latin, which differ slightly from the Cooleys'. I have only given references here to documents not included in this *Sourcebook*.

Exhibition catalogues provide some of the best guides to the city. J. Ward-

Perkins and A. Claridge (ed.), *Pompeii AD79* (Royal Academy of Arts, London, 1976) is still useful. More recent discoveries and up-to-the minute interpretation can be found in A. d'Ambrosio, P. G. Guzzo and M. Mastroberto (ed.), *Storie da un'eruzione: Pompei, Ercolano, Oplontis* (Naples, Museo Archeologico Nazionale, etc., 2003) – which is available as an abridged English exhibition guide, P. G. Guzzo (ed.), *Tales from an Eruption: Pompeii, Herculaneum, Oplontis* (Naples, Museo Archeologico Nazionale, etc., 2003). Also important, and lavishly illustrated, are M. Borriello, A. d'Ambrosio, S. de Caro, P. G. Guzzo (ed.), *Pompei: abitare sotto il Vesuvio* (Ferrara, Palazzo dei Diamanti, 1997) and A. Ciarallo and E. de Carolis (ed.), *Homo Faber: natura, scienza e tecnica nell'antica Pompei* (Naples, Museo Archeologico Nazionale, 1999), translated as *Pompeii: life in a Roman town* (Los Angeles County Museum of Art, 1999). Most recently an important exhibition at the National Gallery of Art in Washington is accompanied by a catalogue edited by C. C. Mattusch, *Pompeii and the Roman Villa: Art and Culture around the Bay of Naples* (Washington DC, 2008).

A useful website is the site hosted by the archaeological authorities at Pompeii itself (www2.pompeiisites.org). This has an English version and you can search for information on all the major buildings, as well as finding news of recent work in the town (occasionally the Italian version is more up-to-date). A good bibliography, research news (at least up to 2007) and links to e-books concerned with Pompeii can be found at: www.pompeiana.org.

Introduction

The discoveries outside the Nola Gate and the Tomb of Obellius Firmus are fully discussed by S. de Caro, 'Scavi nell'area fuori Porta Nola a Pompei', *Cronache Pompeiane* 5 (1979), 61-101. The story of these and other would-be fugitives are featured in *Storie da un'eruzione* (*Tales from an Eruption*), above. Excellent essays on the history of travel and tourism to Pompeii, and on its modern representations in literature and film, are included in V. C. G. Coates and J. L Seydl, *Antiquity Recovered: the legacy of Pompeii and Herculaneum* (Los Angeles, 2007); a lively account is also given by J. Harris, *Pompeii Awakened: a Story of Rediscovery* (London, 2007). Primo Levi's poem (trans. Ruth Feldman) is from his collection, *Ad Ora Incerta* (Milan, 1984).

The stature of ancient Pompeians and other information derived from their skeletons is discussed by M. Henneberg and R. J. Henneberg, in *Homo Faber* (above), pp. 51–3, and 'Reconstructing medical knowledge in ancient Pompeii from the hard evidence of teeth and bones', in J. Renn and G. Castagnetti (ed.), *Homo Faber: studies on nature, technology and science at the time of Pompeii* (Rome, 2002), 169–87. The teeth and other physical characteristics of the group found together in the large house (House of Julius Polybius, IX. 13. 1–3) are the subject of M. Henneberg and R. J. Henneberg, 'Skeletal material from the House of C. Iulius Polybius in Pompei, 79 AD', in A. Ciarallo and E. de Carolis, *La casa di Giulio Polibio: studi interdisciplinari* (Pompeii, 2001), 79–91. A definitive study of the skeletons of Pompeii will be E. Lazer, *Resurrecting Pompeii* (London and New York, 2008). The fisher-boy is discussed by A. Butterworth and R. Laurence, *Pompeii: the living city* (London, 2005), 207. The ancient tooth polishing recipe is given by the Roman pharmacologist, Scribonius Largus (*Compositions*, 60).

Much important recent work has focused on the seismic activity in the region from 62 CE onwards and on the precise stages of the eruption of 79. T. Fröhlich and L. Jacobelli (ed.), *Archäologie und Seismologie: la regione vesuviana dal 62 al 79 DC* (Munich, 1995) is an important collection of essays on these subjects, some in English. For discussion of the exact date of the eruption, see M. Borgongino and G. Stefani, 'Intorno alla data dell'eruzione del 79 d. C.', *Rivista di Studi Pompeiani (RStP)* 10 (1999), 177–215, and G. Stefani, 'La vera data dell'eruzione', *Archeo* 206 (2006), 10–13. Modern scholars have usually (but for no very good reason) followed Tacitus (*Annals* XV, 22) who places the earlier earthquake in 62, rather than Seneca who places it in 63 (*Natural Questions* VI, 1–3). The results of ongoing seismic activity at Herculaneum, with associated changes in the coastline, are being explored by the Herculaneum Conservation Project of the British School at Rome (www.bsr.ac.uk/bsr/sub_arch/BSR_Arch_03Herc.htm)

Wartime bomb damage is the subject of a fine study (with dramatic photographs) by L. Garcia y Garcia, *Danni di guerra a Pompei: una dolorosa vicenda quasi dimenticata* (Rome, 2006). The Africanus graffito from the brothel is (overconfidently) interpreted by J. L. Franklin, 'Games and a Lupanar: prosopography of a neighbourhood in ancient Pompeii', *Classical Journal* 81 (1986), 319–28. The children's doodles are discussed in A. Koloski Ostrow, *The Sarno Bath Complex* (Rome, 1990), 59; and the coin impressions by P. M. Allison and F. B. Sear, *Casa della Caccia Antica* (VII. 4. 48) (Munich, 2002), 83–4. The bed-wetter's graffito can be found at *Corpus Inscriptionum Latinarum* (*CIL*) IV, 4957. For the intestinal parasites whose eggs were found in house VI. 1. 4, see www.archaeology.org/interactive/pompeii/field/5.html

Chapter 1

Useful archaeological discussion of the pre-Roman history and development of Pompeii, includes: J. Berry (ed.), *Unpeeling Pompeii: studies in Region I of Pompeii* (Milan, 1998), 17–25; M. Bonghi Jovino (ed.), *Ricerche a Pompei: l'insula 5 della Regio VI dalle origini al 79 d.C* (Rome, 1984) (the House of the Etruscan Column as the site of a rural shrine, pp. 357–71); P. Carafa, 'What was Pompeii before 200 BC? Excavations in the House of Joseph II, etc', in S. E. Bon and R. Jones (ed.), *Sequence and Space in Pompeii* (Oxford, 1997), 13–31; S. de Caro, 'Nuove indagini sulle fortificazioni di Pompei', *Annali dell'Istituto Universitario Orientale [Napoli]. Sezione di Archeologia e Storia Antica (AION)* 7 (1985), 75–114; M. Fulford and A. Wallace-Hadrill, 'Towards a history of pre-Roman Pompeii: excavations beneath the House of Amarantus (I. 9. 11–12), 1995–8', *Papers of the British School at Rome* 67 (1999), 37–144 (stressing the early origins of the street plan); S. C. Nappo, 'Urban transformation at Pompeii in the late 3rd and early 2nd c. BC', in R. Laurence and A. Wallace-Hadrill (ed.), *Domestic Space in the Roman World: Pompeii and beyond (JRA* suppl., Portsmouth, RI, 1997), 91–120. R. M. Ammerman, 'New Evidence for the Worship of Athena at the Doric temple in Pompeii's Triangular Forum', *Journal of Roman Archaeology (JRA)* 17 (2004), 531–6 conveniently summarises recent early finds from the Temple of Minerva and Hercules. The re-use of the terracotta sculptures in the House of the Golden Bracelet (VI. 17 [ins. occ.]. 42) is discussed and illustrated by E. M. Menotti de Lucia, 'Le terrecotte dell'Insula Occidentalis' in M. Bonghi Jovino, *Artigiani e botteghe nell'Italia preromana: studi sulla coroplastica di area etrusco-laziale-campana* (Rome, 1990), 179–246.

P. Zanker, *Pompeii* (above) has been particularly influential in the study of the town in the second century BCE (and in the early years of the Roman colony). The impact on Pompeii of the war with Hannibal is suggested by, among others, Nappo, 'Urban transformation' (above). The Alexander Mosaic in the House of the Faun (VI.12.2) is the subject of A Cohen, *Alexander Mosaic: stories of victory and defeat* (Cambridge, 1996); F. Zevi, 'Die Casa del Fauno in Pompeji und das Alexandermosaik', *Römische Mitteilungen* 105 (1998) 21–65 considers the house as a whole. For the identification of the spoils of Mummius, see A. Martelli, 'Per una nuova lettura dell'iscrizione Vetter 61 nel contesto del santuario di Apollo a Pompei', *Eutopia* 2 (2002), 71–81. Wider issues of 'Romanisation' in Italy throughout this period are the theme of A. Wallace-Hadrill, *Rome's Cultural Revolution* (Cambridge, 2008).

The siege of Pompeii is documented in F(lavio) and F(erruccio) Russo, *89 A.C. Assedio a Pompei: La dinamica e le tecnologie belliche della conquista sillana di Pompei* (Pompeii, 2005). Cicero's service in the war under Sulla is mentioned by Plutarch, *Life of Cicero* 3 (though he himself suggests in a speech – *Philippic* XII, 11, 27 – that he served under the rival general Pompey). The place of the veterans within the physical layout of the city is discussed by J. Andreau, 'Pompéi: mais où sont les vétérans de Sylla?', *Revue des Etudes Anciennes* 82 (1980), 183–99. F. Zevi, 'Pompei dalla città sannitica alla colonia sillana: Per un' interpretazione dei dati archeologici', in *Les élites municipales de l' Italie péninsulaire des Gracques à Néron* (Rome 1996), 125–38. The dating of the Temple of Jupiter, Juno and Minerva to the early years of the colony is suggested by the Pompeii Forum Project (see J. J. Dobbins, 'The Forum and its dependencies', in *The World of Pompeii* (above), 150–83).

For the political tensions between colonists and the earlier Pompeians, see F. Coarelli, 'Pompei: il foro, le elezioni, e le circoscrizioni elettorali', *AION* new series 7 (2000), 87–114; E. Lo Cascio, 'Pompei dalla città sannitica alla colonia sillana: le vicende istituzionali', in *Les élites municipales*, 111–23; H. Mouritsen, *Elections, Magistrates and Municipal Elite. Studies in Pompeian Epigraphy* (Rome, 1988), 70–89; T. P. Wiseman, 'Cicero, *Pro Sulla* 60–61', *Liverpool Classical Monthly* 2 (1977), 21–2. The survival of Oscan language is discussed by A. E. Cooley, 'The survival of Oscan in Roman Pompeii', in A. E. Cooley (ed.), *Becoming Roman, Writing Latin? Literacy and Epigraphy in the Roman West* (*JRA* suppl., Portsmouth, RI, 2002), 77–86. For the Oscan graffito in the brothel, see *CIL* IV *ad* 2200.

Pompeian *garum* reaching Gaul is documented by B. Liou and R. Marichal, 'Les inscriptions peintes sur l'amphore de l'anse St Gervais à Fos-sur-Mer', *Archaeonautica* 2 (1978), 165. A sceptical view of the image of Spartacus is offered by A. van Hooff, 'Reading the Spartaks fresco without red eyes', in S. T. A. M. Mols and E. M. Moormann, *Omni pede stare: Saggi architettonici e circumvesuviani in memoriam Jos de Waele* (Naples, 2005), 251–6. The connections of Nero and Poppaea with the town underlie much of Butterworth and Laurence, *Pompeii* (above). S. de Caro, in 'La lucerna d'oro di Pompei: un dono di Nerone a Venus Pompeiana', in *I culti della Campania antica : atti del convegno internazionale di studi in ricordo di Nazarena Valenza Mele* (Rome, 1998), 239–44, identifies the very lamp given by 'Nero' to Venus. The satiric graffito about Nero's 'accountant' can be found at *CIL* IV, 8075, and the reference to Suedius Clemens inglorious early career at Tacitus, *Histories* II, 12. The spread and replication of Augustan imagery (such as the images found in Pompeii) is a major theme of P. Zanker, *The Power of Images in the Age of Augustus* (Ann Arbor, 1989).

Chapter 2

A classic (if somewhat lurid) study of Roman filth is A. Scobie, 'Slums, sanitation and mortality in the Roman world', *Klio* 68 (1986), 399–433. The same topic has been treated more recently in X. D Raventos and V. J. A. Remola, *Sordes Urbis: La eliminición de residuos en la ciudad romana* (Roma, 2000), with discussion of Antioch by W. Liebeschuetz (51–61) (the volume is fully reviewed by A. Wilson, 'Detritus, disease and death in the city', *JRA* 15 (2002), 478–84). Juvenal's rant can be found at *Satires* III, 268–77 (trans. P. Green); Suetonius' anecdotes are from his *Life of Vespasian* 5; the admonition to the 'shitter' is *CIL* IV, 6641. The papal visit to Pompeii in 1849 was the subject of an exhibition, with catalogue: *Pio IX a Pompei: memorie e testimonianze di un viaggio* (Naples, 1987).

Street signs and finding the way are the subjects of R. Ling, 'A stranger in town: finding the way in an ancient city', *Greece and Rome* 37 (1990), 204–14. The clusters of bars and the 'hospitality industry' is discussed by S. J. R. Ellis, 'The distribution of bars at Pompeii: archaeological, spatial and viewshed analyses', *JRA* 17 (2004), 371–84. On zoning (or its absence) and deviant behaviour: R. Laurence, *Roman Pompeii: space and society* (2nd ed., London and New York, 2007), esp. 82–101; A. Wallace-Hadrill, 'Public honour and private shame: the urban texture of Pompeii', in T. J. Cornell and K. Lomas (ed.), *Urban Society in Roman Italy* (London, 1995), 39–62. Augustus' quip about going home for lunch is from Quintilian, *Education of the Orator* VI, 3, 63. The 'privatised' street runs between city blocks I. 6 and I. 7.

All aspects of the water supply are discussed in N. de Haan and G. Jansen (ed.), *Cura Aquarum in Campania* (*Bulletin Antieke Beschaving – Annual Papers in Classical Archaeology*, Leiden, 1996). The recent detailed revisions of the chronology of the water supply and aqueduct by C. P. J. Ohlig – *De Aquis Pompeiorum. Das Castellum Aquae in Pompeji: Herkunft, Zuleitung und Verteilung des Wasser* (Nijmegen, 2001) is summarised and reviewed in A. Wilson, 'Water for the Pompeians', *JRA* 19 (2006), 501–8. R. Ling, 'Street fountains and house fronts at Pompeii', in Mols and Moormann, *Omni pede stare* (above), 271–6 discusses the house owner taking advantage of a re-positioned fountain. The interruption of supply on the eve of the eruption is documented by S. C. Nappo, 'L'impianto idrico a Pompei nel 79 d.C.', in *Cura Aquarum*, 37–45.

The ground-breaking study of cart ruts was S. Tsujimura, 'Ruts in Pompeii: the traffic system in the Roman city', *Opuscula Pompeiana* I (1991), 58–86. Elaborate suggestions of the one-way system can be found in E. E. Poehler, 'The circulation of traffic in Pompeii's Regio VI', *JRA* 19 (2006), 53–74. Pavements are discussed by C. Saliou, 'Les trottoirs de Pompéi : une première approche', *Bulletin Antieke Beschaving*, 74 (1999), 161–218. S. C. Nappo, 'Fregio dipinto dal "praedium" di Giulia Felice con rappresentazione del foro di Pompei', *RStP* 3 (1989), 79–96 is a complete publication of the Forum scenes. The Roman law mentioning the upkeep of roads is the 'Table of Heraclea', translated in M. H. Crawford et al. (ed.), *Roman Statutes* (London, 1996) Vol. 1, 355–91. Herodas, *Mime* III describes the 'over the shoulder' flogging (a method alluded to also in Cicero, *Letters to Friends* VII, 25, 1). A translation of Augustus' adjudication of the Cnidian case can be found in M. G. L. Cooley (ed.), *The Age of Augustus* (LACTOR 17, London, 2003), 197–8.

Chapter 3

Almost all recent studies of Pompeian domestic architecture refer back to A. Wallace-Hadrill's classic book, *Houses and Society in Pompeii and Herculaneum* (Princeton, NJ, 1994). Also fundamental, on the use of rooms within the house, is the work of P. M. Allison. Her major study is *Pompeian Households: an analysis of the material culture* (Los Angeles, 2004), supplemented with an excellent 'on-line companion' at www.stoa.org/projects/ph/home. An important collection of essays is Laurence and Wallace-Hadrill (ed.), *Domestic Space in the Roman World* (above).

The House of the Tragic Poet (VI. 8. 5) is beautifully reconstructed by N. Wood, *The House of the Tragic Poet* (London, 1996). The nineteenth-century interested in the house is discussed by S. Hales, 'Re-casting antiquity: Pompeii and the Crystal Palace', *Arion* 14 (2006), 99–133. The garden of the House of Julius Polybius (IX.13.1–3) is described in W. F. Jashemski, *The Gardens of Pompeii, Herculaneum and the villas destroyed by Vesuvius*, Vol 2 (New York, 1993), 240–52; the garden a few doors away (in what is now usually called the House of the Painters at Work, IX. 12) in A. M. Ciarallo, 'The Garden of the "Casa dei Casti Amanti" (Pompeii, Italy)', *Garden History* 21 (1993), 110–16. Petronius' description of the entrance to Trimalchio's house is at *Satyrica* 28–9.

All aspects of The House of the Menander (I. 10. 4) and the neighbouring houses in the block have been exhaustively studied and published by R. Ling and others, in several volumes. Particularly relevant are R. Ling, *The Insula of the Menander at Pompeii, Vol 1, The Structures* (Oxford, 1997) and P. M. Allison, *Vol. 3 The Finds, a contextual study* (Oxford, 2006). G. Stefani (ed.), *Menander: la casa del Menandro di Pompei* (Milan, 2003) is a well illustrated exhibition catalogue, featuring finds from the house. The House of Julius Polybius is the subject of Ciarallo and de Carolis (ed.), *La casa di Giulio Polibio* (above) – which includes an article on the lighting. That house, the House of Venus in a Bikini (I. 11. 6) and the House of the Prince of Naples (VI. 15. 8) are included in Allison's *Pompeian Households*.

The wooden furniture from Herculaneum is discussed by S. T. A. M. Mols, *Wooden Furniture in Herculaneum: form, technique and function* (Amsterdam, 1999). The toilet specialist is G. Jansen, whose work is usefully summarised in G. Jansen, 'Private toilets at Pompei: appearance and operation', in Bon and Jones (ed.), *Sequence and Space* (above), 121–34. Seneca's anecdote about sponges can be found at *Letters* LXX, 20. The detritus from Herculaneum is being analysed as part of the British School at Rome's Herculaneum Conservation Project. The architecture of formal dining, at Pompeii and elsewhere, is discussed in K. M. D. Dunbabin, *The Roman Banquet: images of conviviality* (Cambridge, 2003).

A good introduction to recent work on the Roman family (including special reference to Pompeian material) is B. Rawson and P. Weaver (ed.), *The Roman Family in Italy: status, sentiment, space* (Oxford, 1997). The term 'housefuls' is advocated by A. Wallace-Hadrill. The instititions of patronage are well discussed in A. Wallace-Hadrill (ed.), *Patronage in Ancient Society* (London, 1989). Temporal zoning is suggested by Laurence, *Roman Pompeii* (above), 154–66. The most relevant section of Vitruvius is *On Architecture*, VI, 5; the moans of Martial are from his *Epigrams* X, 100.

Koloski Ostrow, *The Sarno Bath Complex* (above) discusses the layout of the accommodation there. F. Pirson explores the rental properties of the *Insula Arriana Polliana* (VI. 6) and of the Estate of Julia Felix (II. 4. 2) in Laurence and Wallace Hadrill (ed.), *Domestic Space*, 165–81. L. H. Petersen offers a positive account of the House of Octavius Quartio in *The Freedman in Roman Art and Art History* (Cambridge, 2006), 129–36, in contrast to the sniffier approach of Zanker, *Pompeii* (above), 145–56 (who uses the name Loreius Tiburtinus for the house). The most comprehensive published material on the House of Fabius Rufus can be found in M. Aoyagi and U. Pappalardo (ed.), *Pompei (Regiones VI-VII). Insula Occidentalis. Volume I Tokyo-Pompei* (Naples, 2006). Seneca's comments on the baths are in *Letters* LVI. Renting from the first of July is referred to by Petronius, *Satyrica* 38; Trimalchio's insult to his wife is at *Satyrica* 74. Cicero's views on garden features can be found at *On the Laws* II, 2; *Letters to his brother Quintus III, 7, 7; to Atticus*, I, 16, 18. For 'I wish I could be a ring …', see E. Courtney, *Musa Lapidaria: a selection of Latin verse inscriptions* (Atlanta, Georgia, 1995), 82–3.

The most ambitious attempt to tie the houses of Pompeii to particular individuals is that of M. della Corte, *Case ed Abitanti di Pompei* (3rd ed., Naples, 1965), criticised by Mouritsen, *Elections, Magistrates and Municipal Elite* (above), 9–27, and P. M. Allison, 'Placing individuals: Pompeian epigraphy in context', *Journal of Mediterranean Archaeology* 14 (2001), 53–74 (raising doubts on the ownership of the House of the Vettii). The state of the Bar of Amarantus in 79 CE is the subject of J. Berry, 'The conditions of domestic life in Pompeii in AD 79: a case study of Houses 11 and 12, Insula 9, Region 1', *Papers of the British School at Rome* 52 (1997), 103–25; the graffiti from the property is discussed by A. Wallace-Hadrill, 'Scratching the surface: a case study of domestic graffiti at Pompeii', in M. Corbier and J.-P. Guilhembet (ed.), *L'écriture dans la maison romaine* (Paris, forthcoming). Domestic fulleries are explored by M. Flohr, 'The domestic *fullonicae* of Pompeii', in M. Cole, M. Flohr and E. Poehler (ed.), *Pompeii: cultural standards, practical needs* (forthcoming). The door plaque of Lucius Satrius Rufus and its context is described in *Notizie degli Scavi* 1933, 322–3; the crimes of Ladicula and Atimetus are recorded at *CIL* IV, 4776 and 10231.

Chapter 4

The paintings of Pompeii have attracted scholarly attention since the moment of the town's rediscovery. Still useful on all aspects, from technique to mythological images, is R. Ling, *Roman Painting* (Cambridge, 1991). Several books by J. R. Clarke have explored different themes of painting at Pompeii and elsewhere: *Looking at Lovemaking: constructions of sexuality in Roman art, 100 BC – AD 250* (Berkeley etc., 1998); *Art in the Lives of Ordinary Romans: visual representation and non-elite viewers in Italy, 100 BC – AD 315* (Berkeley, etc., 2003); *Looking at Laughter: humor, power and transgression in Roman visual culture, 100 BC – AD 250* (Berkeley etc., 2008). A number of the paintings featured in this chapter (including the 'Judgement of Solomon', various paintings from the House of the Vettii and from the baths in the House of the Menander) are more fully discussed by Clarke.

The paintings (and painters) of the House of the Painters at Work are the subject of a series of articles by its excavator, A. Varone, including a brief article in English, 'New finds in Pompeii. The excavation of two buildings in Via dell'Abbondanza', *Apollo*, July 1993, 8–12. See also 'Scavo lungo via dell'Abbondanza', *RStP* 3 (1989), 231–8; 'Attività dell'Ufficio Scavi 1990', *RStP* 4 (1990), 201–11; 'L'organizzazione del lavoro di una bottega di decoratori: le evidenze dal recente scavo pompeiano lungo via dell'Abbondanza', in E. M. Moormann (ed.), *Mani di pittori e botteghe pittoriche nel mondo romano* (*Mededeelingen van het Nederlands Instituut te Rome* 54 (1995), 124–36. The 'painters' workshop' is discussed by M. Tuffreau-Libre, 'Les pots à couleur de Pompéi: premiers résultats', *RStP* 10 (1999), 63–70. The most determined (if not always convincing) attempt to identify different 'hands' is L. Richardson, *A Catalog of Identifiable Figure Painters of Ancient Pompeii, Herculaneum and Stabiae* (Baltimore, 2000). The entirely implausible identification of a South Italian artist at Fishbourne is suggested by B.W. Cunliffe, *Fishbourne: a Roman palace and its garden* (London, 1971), 117.

Zebra stripe pattern is fully documented by C. C. Goulet, 'The "Zebra Stripe" design: an investigation of Roman wall-painting in the periphery', *RStP* 12–13 (2001–2), 53–94. A complete compendium of the decoration in the House of the Menander is provided by R. Ling and L. Ling, *The Insula of the Menander at Pompeii, Vol 2, The Decorations* (Oxford, 2005). The conservation of the Villa of the Mysteries frieze, and its various modern interpretations, are the subject of B. Bergmann, 'Seeing Women in the Villa of the Mysteries: a modern excavation of the Dionysiac murals', in Coates and Seydl (ed.), *Antiquity Recovered* (above), 230–69.

The classic formulation of the development of the Four Styles is A. Mau, *Geschichte der decorativen Wandmalerei in Pompeji* (Berlin, 1882). Problems with its rigid application are raised by Ling, *Roman Painting* 71 (the 'eclectic' Fourth Style) and Wallace-Hadrill, *Houses and Society* (above), 30 (on the difficulty of distinguishing Third and Fourth Styles). Vitruvius' reactions are from his *On Architecture* VII, 5, 4.

The influence of function on design is a major theme of Wallace-Hadrill, *Houses and Society* (see p. 28 for the remarks on perspective). Cicero's views on unsuitable statuary can be found at *Letters to Friends* VII, 23. Information on the relative cost of pigments is given by Pliny, *Natural History* XXXIII, 118 and XXXV, 30. Vitruvius' 'scribe' is mentioned at *On Architecture* VII, 9, 2.

The significance of particular myths on the walls of Pompeii is usefully discussed by B. Bergmann, 'The Roman House as Memory Theater: the House of the Tragic Poet in Pompeii', *Art Bulletin* 76 (1994), 225–56 and 'The Pregnant Moment: tragic wives in the Roman interior', in N. B. Kampen (ed.), *Sexuality in Ancient Art: near East, Egypt, Greece and, Italy* (New York and Cambridge, 1996), 199–218; and by V. Platt, 'Viewing, Desiring, Believing: confronting the divine in a Pompeian house', *Art History* 25 (2002), 87–112 (on the House of Octavius Quartio).

B. Bergmann, 'Greek masterpieces and Roman recreative fictions', *Harvard Studies in Classical Philology* 97 (1995), 79–120 is a good discussion of the relationship between Greek 'originals' and Roman recreations. The inscription from the façade of the House of Marcus Lucretius Fronto (V.4.a) can be found at *CIL* IV, 6626. 'Amazement' at the painting of the old man and his daughter is recorded by Valerius Maximus, *Memorable Deeds and Sayings* V, 4, ext. 1. Timanthes' Iphigeneia features at Pliny, *Natural History* XXXV, 74 and Cicero, *Orator* 74; Achilles on Skyros at Pliny, *Natural History* XXXV, 134. The story of the Roman lady's reaction to the painting of Hector is told by Plutarch, *Life of Brutus* 23. The graffito referring to the painting of Dirce is noted by E. W. Leach, 'The Punishment of Dirce: a newly discovered painting in the Casa di Giulio Polibio and its significance within the visual tradition', *Römische Mitteilungen* 93 (1986), 157–82. The fifth-century BCE jug is discussed by F. Zevi and M. L. Lazzarini, 'Necrocorinthia a Pompei: un'idria bronzea per le gare di Argo', *Prospettiva* 53–6 (1988–9). 33–49.

Chapter 5

An up-to-date starting point for debates on the ancient economy is W. Scheidel, I. Morris and R. Saller (ed.), *The Cambridge Economic History of the Greco-Roman World* (Cambridge, 2007) – with references to the evidence from the Greenland icecap. A very 'primitive' model of the Pompeian economy itself can be found in W. Jongman, *The Economy and Society of Pompeii* (Amsterdam, 1988), with a powerful critique by N. Purcell, in *Classical Review* 40 (1990), 111–16.

The estate of the Lucretii Valentes is the subject of M. De' Spagnolis Conticello, 'Sul rinvenimento della villa e del monumento funerario dei Lucretii Valentes', *RStP* 6 (1993–4), 147–66. The Villa of the Mosaic Columns is discussed by V. Kockel and B. F. Weber, 'Die Villa delle Colonne a Mosaico in Pompeji', *Römische Mitteilungen* 90 (1983), 51–89 (with *Notizie degli Scavi* 1923, 277 for the fourteen person leg iron). S. de Caro, *La villa rustica in località Villa Regina a Boscoreale* (Rome, 1994) is the major publication of the small holding near Boscoreale (fully reviewed by R. Ling, '*Villae Rusticae at Boscoreale*', *JRA* 9 (1996), 344–50). Estimates of surplus production in the territory of Pompeii (plus the reference to 'the old story') are given by Purcell, in *Classical Review* 1990. Pompeii's wine trade is discussed by A. Tchernia, 'Il vino: produzione e commercio', in F. Zevi (ed.) *Pompei 79: raccolta di studi per il decimonono centenario dell'eruzione vesuviana* (Naples, 1979), 87–96 and relevant material from the

House of the Menander is illustrated in Stefani (ed.), *Menander* (above), 210–23. The *amphorae* in the House of Amarantus are documented in Berry, 'The conditions of domestic life' (above). The cargo of pottery table ware is the subject of D. Atkinson, 'A hoard of Samian Ware from Pompeii', *Journal of Roman Studies* 4 (1914), 27–64. The vineyard near the Amphitheatre is documented by Jashemski, *Gardens of Pompeii* (Vol. 2) (above), 89–90; commercial cultivation more generally within the town itself is discussed in the first volume of *Gardens of Pompeii* (New York, 1979), especially 201–88. Commercial flower growing is documented by M. Robinson, 'Evidence for garden cultivation and the use of bedding-out plants in the peristyle garden of the House of the Greek Epigrams (V. I. 18i) at Pompeii', *Opuscula Romana* 31–2 (2006–7), 155–9. Pompeian cabbages and onions are mentioned by Pliny, *Natural History* XIX, 139–41; Columella, *On Agriculture* X, 135; XII, 10, 1. The problem of metal working is briefly addressed by W. V. Harris, in Scheidel, Morris and Saller (ed.), *Cambridge Economic History*, 532; and in greater detail, and more optimistically, by B. Gralfs, *Metalverarbeitende Produktionsstätten in Pompeji* (Oxford, 1988)

The excavations of the bakery in the House of the Chaste Lovers are described by A. Varone, 'New findings' and 'Scavo lungo Via dell'Abbondanza' (above). The inscriptions from the property are published by Varone, 'Iscrizioni parietarie inedite da Pompei', in G. Paci (ed.) *EPIGRAPHAI: miscellenea epigraphica in onore di Lidio Gasperini* (Tivoli, 2000), vol. 2, 1071–93. The animal skeletons and their housing are assessed by A. Genovese and T. Cocca, 'Internal organization of an equine stable at Pompeii', *Anthropozoologica* 31 (2000), 119–23; and, through the mitochrondrial DNA, by M. Sica et al. 'Analysis of Five Ancient Equine Skeletons by Mitochondrial DNA sequencing', *Ancient Biomolecules* 4 (2002), 179–84. A survey of Pompeian bakeries is offered by B. J. Mayeske, 'Bakers, bakeshops and bread: a social and economic study', in *Pompeii and the Vesuvian Landscape* (Smithsonian Institution, Washington DC, 1979), 39–58.

J. Andreau, *Les affaires de Monsieur Jucundus* (Rome, 1974) is the major study of the Jucundus tablets. The hierarchy of the witness lists is a major theme of Jongman, *Pompeii*. A low estimate of levels of literacy is made by W. V. Harris, *Ancient Literacy* (Cambridge, MA, 1989). Against this, Wallace-Hadrill, 'Scratching the Surface' (above) stresses the importance of everyday reading and writing in trade and craftwork.

Garum has almost become the modern scholarly monopoly of R. I. Curtis, who discusses the mosaics of Umbricius Scaurus in 'A Personalised Floor Mosaic from Pompeii', *American Journal of Archaeology* 88 (1984), 557–66; the shop in

'The *Garum* shop of Pompeii', *Cronache Pompeiane* 5 (1979), 5–23; and the trade more generally in 'In Defense of Garum;', *Classical Journal* 78 (1983), 232–40.

Chapter 6

The political life of Pompeii (and the character of the electoral notices) is the subject of Mouritsen, *Elections, magistrates and municipal elite* (above). A comprehensive list of known Pompeian families, their members and their political office holding is provided by P. Castrén, *Ordo populusque Pompeianus. Polity and society in Roman Pompeii* (Rome, 1975) – still valuable for its data, despite some of its dubious theories about a 'crisis' at Pompeii in the reign of the emperor Claudius. J. L. Franklin, *Pompeii. The Electoral Programmata, Campaigns and Politics, AD 71–79* (Rome, 1980) attempts to reconstruct the electoral campaigns of the last years of the town's life. His book probably overstated the lack of competition in local elections, and contributed to Jongman's view, in *Pompeii* (above), that elections were in practice in the control of the *ordo*. This is challenged by H. Mouritsen, 'A note on Pompeian epigraphy and social structure,' *Classica et Mediaevalia* 41 (1990), 131–49 – who also challenges the view of particular 'disorder' in the politics of the town after the earthquake in 'Order and Disorder in Later Pompeian Politics', in *Les élites municipales* (above), 139–44. The voting system and districts of Pompeii, as well as the lay-out of the Forum, are discussed by Coarelli, 'Pompei: il foro' (above). The recommendation for Bruttius Balbus is *CIL* IV, 3702; the wake-up call to Trebius and Soterichus is *CIL* IV, 7632.

The role of women in election campaigns is discussed by F. S. Bernstein, 'Pompeian Women and the Programmata', in R. I Curtis (ed.), *Studia Pompeiana et classica in honor of Wilhelmina F. Jashemski* (New Rochelle, NY, 1988), Vol. 1, 1–18 and L Savunen, 'Women and elections in Pompeii', in R. Hawley and B. Levick, *Women in Antiquity: new assessments* (London, 1995), 194–203. The poster of Taedia Secunda is *CIL* IV, 7469; the recommendations of the 'bar maids' are *CIL* IV, 7862, 7863, 7864, 7866, 7873.

The classic study of the culture of benefaction in the classical world is P. Veyne, *Bread and Circuses: historical sociology and political pluralism* (London, 1990). R. P. Duncan-Jones, 'Who paid for public buildings in Roman cities', in his *Structure and Scale in the Roman Economy* (Cambridge, 1990), 174–84 includes material relevant to, if not about, Pompeii (including the role of the financial contributions made by local officials when they entered office). Daily routines are discussed by Laurence, *Roman Pompeii* (above), 154–66. The Spanish charter can be found at Crawford et al. (ed.), *Roman Statutes*, vol 1, 393–454. The graffito on the *accensus* is *CIL* IV, 1882.

The career of Marcus Holconius Rufus is discussed by J. H. D'Arms, 'Pompeii and Rome in the Augustan Age and beyond: the eminence of the Gens Holconia', in Curtis (ed.), *Studia Pompeiana et classica*, vol. 1, 51–73. His statue is the subject of P. Zanker, 'Das Bildnis des M. Holconius Rufus'. *Archäologischer Anzeiger* 1989, 349–61, and his building projects (including their specifically Augustan character) are prominently featured in Zanker's *Pompeii* (above). The position of 'military tribune by popular demand' is mentioned by Suetonius, *Life of Augustus* 46.

Local organisations in Pompeii are discussed by W. van Andringa, 'Autels de carrefour, organisation vicinale et rapports de voisinage à Pompéi', *RStP* 11 (2000), 47–86. The role of the *Augustales* in the wider imperial context is the subject of S. E. Ostrow, 'The Augustales in the Augustan scheme', in K. A. Raaflaub and M. Toher, *Between Republic and Empire: Interpretations of Augustus and his Principate* (Berkeley etc., 1990), 364–79 – who also discusses their history in the Bay of Naples in 'Augustales along the Bay of Naples: a case for their early growth', *Historia* 34 (1985), 64–101. The elusive evidence from Pompeii is introduced by Petersen, *The Freedman* (above), 57–83 (with a discussion of the rebuilding of the temple of Isis by Numerius Popidius Celsinus, pp. 52–3). The idea of the Eumachia building being a cloth workers hall was strongly advocated by W. O. Moeller, *The Wool Trade of Ancient Pompeii* (Leiden, 1976); the possibility that it was used as a slave market is floated by E. Fentress, 'On the block: *catastae*, *chalcidica* and *cryptae* in early imperial Italy', *JRA* 18 (2005), 220–34.

Chapter 7

Roman dining in general has been the subject of many recent studies. In addition to Dunbabin, *The Roman Banquet* (above), a good collection of esssays, exploring various aspects of dining is W. J. Slater, *Dining in a Classical Context* (Ann Arbor, 1991). Pompeian images of drinking and dining in the House of the Chaste Lovers (IX. 12. 6) and elsewhere are discussed by Clarke, *Art in the Lives of Ordinary Romans,* (above), 228–33 (focussing on how far the paintings represent distinctively Greek conventions of drinking and eating) and M. B. Roller, *Dining Posture in Ancient Rome: bodies, values and status* (Princeton, NJ, 2006), 45–84 and 139–53. The House of the Menander treasure is catalogued in K. S. Painter,

The Insula of the Menander at Pompeii, Vol. 4, The Silver Treasure (Oxford, 2001). The connections between death and dining are explored by K. Dunbabin, 'Sic erimus cuncti ... The skeleton in Graeco-Roman Art', *Jahrbuch des deutschen archäologischen Instituts* 101 (1986), 185–255, and summarised in *The Roman Banquet*. The tomb painting of silver is from the (widely illustrated) tomb of Vestorius Primus. The bronze statue from the House of Julius Polybius is illustrated in d'Ambrosio, Guzzo and Mastroberto, *Storie da un'eruzione* (above), 424 and in Boriello et al., *Pompei: abitare sotto il Vesuvio* (above), 231. The nutrition of the poor is well discussed by P. Garnsey, *Food and Society in Classical Antiquity* (Cambridge, 1999). For animal bones from the House of the Vestals, see www. archaeology.org/interactive/pompeii/field/5.html. The dormouse jar is described by Varro, *On Agriculture* III, 15. A dormouse recipe is given by Apicius, *On Cookery*, VII, 9; his 'casserole of anchovy without the anchovy' is described at IV, 2, 12. Trimalchio's banquet features in Petronius' *Satyrica*, 26–78; Elagabalus' dinners in *Scriptores Historiae Augustae*, *Life of Elagabalus* 19, 25. Plutarch's *Table Talk* is a mine of curious information on Greek and Roman dining customs. Pliny's dining arrangements are described in *Letters* V, 6.

Pompeian bars and their menus are surveyed by S. J. R. Ellis, 'The Pompeian Bar: archaeology and the role of food and drink outlets in an ancient community', *Food and History* 2 (2004), 41–58, J. Packer, 'Inns at Pompeii: a short survey', *Cronache Pompeiane* 4 (1978), 5–53. An exhibition in 2005 gathered together most of the finds from the bar on the Via dell' Abbondanza, published as *Cibi e sapori a Pompei e dintorni* (Naples, 2005), 115–28 (with an excellent discussion). The paintings in the Inn of Salvius and in the Bar in the Via di Mercurio are featured in Clarke, *Art in the Lives of Ordinary Romans* (above), 160–70, 134–6 and in *Looking at Laughter* (above), 205–9. Horace's remarks are at *Epistles* I, 14, 21–2, Juvenal's at *Satires* VIII, 171–6. The legislation of Nero and Vespasian is recorded at Dio Cassius, *Histories* LXII, 14, 2; LXV, 10, 3. Pliny's discussion of Falernian is at *Natural History* XIV, 62.

Different aspects of Roman sexuality are helpfully explored in C. Edwards, *The Politics of Immorality in Ancient Rome* (Cambridge, 1993), M. B. Skinner, *Sexuality in Greek and Roman Culture* (Oxford, 2005), C. Williams, *Roman Homosexuality: ideologies of masculinity in classical antiquity* (Oxford, 1999). Different approaches to the 'brothel problem' are taken by T. McGinn, 'Pompeian brothels and social history', in *Pompeian brothels, Pompeii's Ancient History, Mirrors and Mysteries, Art and Nature at Oplontis, & the Herculaneum 'Basilica'* (*JRA* supp., Portsmouth, RI, 2002) 7–46 and, more cautiously, Wallace-Hadrill, 'Public honour and private shame' (above). Wider aspects of Roman prostitution are discussed by T. McGinn, *The Economy of Prostitution in the Roman World: a study of social history and the brothel* (Ann Arbor, 2004). Detailed studies of the 'purpose-built' brothel and its graffiti, include A. Varone, 'Organizzazione e sfruttamento della prostituzione servile: l'esempio del lupanare di Pompei', in A. Buonopane and T. Cenerini (ed.) *Donna e lavoro nella documentazione epigrafica* (Faenza, 2003), 193–215 and an enterprising website from Stanford University, traumwerk.stanford.edu:3455/SeeingThePast/345. The Roman tombstone to the dutiful wife is M. R. Lefkowitz and M. B. Fant, *Women's Life in Greece and Rome* (London, 1982), no. 134. The bracelet given by master to slave is illustrated and discussed in d'Ambrosio, Guzzo and Mastroberto (ed.), *Storie da un'eruzione*, 470, 473–8. Praestina's lack of affection for Marcellus is displayed at *CIL* IV, 7679.

A good introduction to modern work on the history, archaeology and culture of Roman bathing is *Roman baths and bathing : proceedings of the First International Conference on Roman Baths* (*JRA* supp., Portsmouth, RI, 1999). G. G. Fagan, *Bathing in Public in the Roman World* (Ann Arbor, 1999) and J. Toner, *Leisure and Ancient Rome* (Oxford, 1995), 53–64 are both excellent on different aspects of the ancient sociology of bathing (the quip about the 'hole in the ozone layer' is Toner's). F. Yegül, *Baths and Bathing in Classical Antiquity* (Cambridge, MA, 1992) surveys the structure of Roman baths, empire wide (including detailed descriptions of the remains at Pompeii). The definitive publication of the Suburban Baths is L. Jacobelli, *La pitture erotiche delle terme suburbane di Pompei* (Rome, 1995), with useful discussion by Clarke, *Looking at Laughter* (above), 194–204 and 209–12.

The tombstone hailing 'wine, sex and baths' can be found at *CIL* VI, 15258; the text from Turkey, on a spoon, is *CIL* III, 12274c. The story of Augustus' mother is told by Suetonius, *Life of Augustus* 94; Martial's squib about the hernia is *Epigrams* XII, 83; the nasty flogging is described at Aulus Gellius, *Attic Nights* X, 3; Hadrian's canny generosity is the subject of an anecdote in the *Scriptores Historiae Augustae, Life of Hadrian* 17. For the unhygienic aspects, see Martial, *Epigrams* II, 42 and Celsus, *On Medicine* V, 26, 28d (though in general Celsus is upbeat about the curative properties of baths). The dual role of the bath manager is mentioned in the *Digest of Justinian* III, 2, 4, 2.

Chapter 8

Gambling is discussed by N. Purcell, 'Literate Games: Roman urban society and the game of *alea*', *Past and Present* 147 (1995), 3–37 and J. Toner, *Leisure* (above), 89–101. The snorting noise is mentioned by Ammianus Marcellinus, *Histories* XIV, 6.

The range of Roman theatre is discussed by R. C. Beacham, *The Roman Theatre and its Audience* (London, 1991). C. Edwards, *The Politics of Immorality* (above), 98–136 explores the moral ambiguity of 'theatrical culture'. Mime and pantomime are the theme of E. Fantham, 'Mime: the missing link in Roman literary history', *Classical World* 82 (1989), 153–63 (whence the nice remark about the 'Swedish masseuses') and of E. Hall and R. Wyles (ed.), *New Directions in Ancient Pantomime* (Oxford, 2008). The career and portraits of Caius Norbanus Sorex are discussed by M. G. Granino Cecere, 'Nemi: l'erma di C. Norbanus Sorex', *Rendiconti della Pontificia Accademia Romana di Archeologia* 61 (1988–9), 131–51. J. L. Franklin, 'Pantomimists at Pompeii: Actius Anicetus and his troup', *American Journal of Philology* 108 (1987), 95–107 tries to piece together a pantomimist's company and its fan-club.

The structure of the Amphitheatre at Pompeii is clearly discussed by D. L. Bomgardner, *The Story of the Roman Amphitheatre* (London and New York, 2000), 39–54 and K. Welch, *The Roman Amphitheatre from its origins to the Colosseum* (Cambridge, 2007), 192–8. The Pompeian evidence for gladiatorial spectacle and organisation is gathered together and well illustrated in L. Jacobelli, *Gladiators at Pompeii* (Rome, 2003). K. Hopkins and M. Beard, *The Colosseum* (London, 2005) cast a slightly sceptical eye on the frequency and lavishness of ordinary gladiatorial shows, especially those outside Rome itself – a view which is reflected here. B. Maiuri, 'Rilievo gladiatorio di Pompei', *Rendiconti dell' Accademia Nazionale dei Lincei (scienze morali etc.)*, Series 8, Vol. 2 (1947) 491–510 carefully dissects the relief showing procession, gladiatorial combat and animal fights. The classic passage from Juvenal about the lady and the gladiator is *Satires* VI, 82–113.

Chapter 9

The title of this chapter is taken from K. Hopkins, *A World Full of Gods: pagans, Jews and Christians in the Roman empire* (London, 1999), which includes an attempt by two imaginary modern time-travellers, returning to the ancient world, to make sense of Pompeian culture and (especially) its religion. The general approach adopted in this chapter (including the model of sacrifice, and of 'foreign' cults) inevitably owes a good deal to that of M. Beard, J. North and S. Price, *Religions of Rome* (Cambridge, 1998), where many of the religious themes raised here can be followed up. The second volume (*A Sourcebook*) contains most of the ancient literary texts I have quoted or referred to. J. Scheid, *Introduction to Roman Religion* (Edinburgh, 2003) is also very useful. Horace evokes sacrifice at *Odes* III, 13.

An excellent overview of the evidence and bibliography for all the various cults, shrines and temples in Pompeii is offered by L. Barnabei, 'I culti di Pompei: Raccolta critica della documentazione', in *Contributi di Archeologia Vesuviana* III (Rome, 2007), 11–88. On the new identification of the Temple of Jupiter Meilichios, F. Marcatelli, 'Il tempio di Escalapio a Pompei', in *Contributi di Archeologia Vesuviana* II (Rome, 2006), 9–76. The sculpture within the Temple of Jupiter, Juno and Minerva is usefully discussed by H.G. Martin, *Römische Tempelkultbilder: eine archäologische Untersuchung zur späten Republik* (Rome, 1987), 222–4. A different view of Pompeian Venus is offered by J. B. Rives, 'Venus Genetrix outside Rome', *Phoenix* 48 (1994) 294–6. The *ferculum* of the carpenters is discussed by Clarke, *Art in the Lives of Ordinary Romans* (above), 85–7.

Household religion and the Lares are discussed by P. Foss, 'Watchful Lares. Roman household organization and the rituals of cooking and eating', in Laurence and Wallace-Hadrill (ed.), *Domestic Space in the Roman World* (above), 196–218. *Lararia* are catalogued by G. K. Boyce. *Corpus of the Lararia of Pompeii* (Rome, 1937), and more recently their paintings are included in T. Fröhlich, *Lararien- und Fassadenbilder in den Vesuvstädten. Untersuchungen zur 'volkstümlichen' pompejanischen Malerei* (Mainz, 1991). The 'Fulgur' tile is discused by A. Maiuri, '"Fulgur conditum" o della scoperta di un bidental a Pompei', *Rendiconti dell'Accademia di Archeologia, Lettere e Belle Arti, Napoli*, 21 (1941), 55–72. The 'offerings' at the House of Amarantus are noted by M. Fulford and A. Wallace-Hadrill, 'The House of Amarantus at Pompeii (I. 9. 11–12): an interim report on survey and excavations in 1995–6', *RStP* 7 (1995–96), 77–113. The practices of ancient household religion more generally, including Rome, are the subject of J. Bodel and S. Olyan (ed.), *Household and Family Religion in Antiquity* (Oxford, 2008).

The implausible concentration of buildings connected with the imperial cult in many modern reconstructions of the Forum is dissected by I. Gradel, *Emperor Worship and Roman Religion* (Oxford, 2002), 103–8. Other useful essays (though sometimes too eager to see traces of the imperial cult where few or none exist) are contained in A. Small (ed.), *Subject and ruler: the cult of the ruling power in clasical antiquity* (*JRA* supp., Portsmouth , RI, 1996).

R. E Witt, *Isis in the Graeco-Roman World* (London, 1971) is still a useful introduction to the history of Isis in the Roman Empire. The temple of Isis was the subject of a major exhibition in the early 1990s, published as *Alla ricerca di Iside: analisi, studi e restauri dell'Iseo pompeiano nel Museo di Napoli* (Naples, 1992). Also relevant is E. A. Arslan (ed.) *Iside: il mito, il mistero, la magia* (Milan, 1997).

Epilogue

I. Morris, *Death-ritual and social structure in classical antiquity* (Cambridge, 1992) is an overview of burial practice in Greece and Rome. *Pompei oltre la vita: nuove testimonianze dalle necropoli* (Pompeii, 1998) is the catalogue of an exhibition on Pompeian tombs. Petersen, *The Freedman* (above), 60–83 discusses tombs of freedmen. On tombs as houses (and the case of Phileros), see A. Wallace-Hadrill, 'Housing the dead: the tomb as house in Roman Italy', in L. Brink and D. Green (ed.) *Commemorating the Dead. Texts and Artifacts in Context*, (Berlin and New York, 2008), 39–77. The inscription from the tomb of Phileros has been re-examined by E. Rodriguez-Almeida, in *Topografia e vita romana: da Augusto a Costantino* (Rome, 2001), 91–103.

ACKNOWLEDGEMENTS

Pompeii is a wonderful place to visit and study. My own work there has been helped at every stage by the staff of the Soprintendenza Archeologica di Pompei (under Pietro Giovanni Guzzo), who go out of their way to assist visiting scholars; and, in particular, I have learnt a great deal about Pompeii, both ancient and modern, from Mattia Buondonno. Maria Pia Malvezzi and Andrew Wallace-Hadrill of the British School at Rome have also done an enormous amount to make possible the research that lies behind this book. Visits to Pompeii were made more enjoyable by Zoe and Raphael Cormack – and, of course, by Robin Cormack, whose eagle-eyes and Pompeian expertise helped me to see even more on the site than I ever expected. Some of the sharpest observations in the book I owe to him.

Many friends at home and abroad have helped my work in all kinds of ways. I am especially grateful to Rebecca Benefiel, John Clarke, Louise Guron, Edith Hall, Henry Hurst (and the students of his Pompeii class in 2008), Bradley Letwin, Michael Larvey, Roger Ling, Martin Millett, Clare Pettitt, Mark Robinson and Nicholas Wood (for his marvellous reconstructions of the House of the Tragic Poet). Discussions with Andrew Wallace-Hadrill have provided some of the most memorable, funny, and instructive moments in getting to know Pompeii.

Part of the book was written while I was Visiting Scholar at the Getty Villa in Los Angeles, where I was able to draw on the expertise of Ken Lapatin and Claire Lyons, and the able assistance of Kristina Meinking. As always the staff and colleagues in the Faculty of Classics and the Classical Faculty Library (under Lyn

Bailey) have helped in more ways than they know; so too has the team at Profile Books – Claire Beaumont, Peter Carson, Penny Daniel, Andrew Franklin, Kate Griffin, Ruth Killick.

Chapter 9 would have much less to say if it were not for the conversations about Roman religion (and much else) that I have enjoyed with Simon Price over the last thirty years, since we first met in Cambridge in 1978. This book is for Simon.

LIST OF FIGURES

LIST OF ILLUSTRATIONS

Abbreviations:
MANN – National Archaeological Museum, Naples
SAP – Soprintendenza Archeologica di Pompei

Colour plates

1 Mosaic of musicians, from the Villa of Cicero (MANN 9985). Photo courtesy of Corbis.
2 Orpheus from the House of Orpheus, V. Loria in F. and F. Niccolini, *Le Case ed I Monumenti di Pompei* (Naples, 1854-96).
3 Painting of Nero (?) as Apollo from Moregine. Photo courtesy of Foglia Fotografica.
4 Reconstruction of street frontage on the Via dell'Abbondanza, V. Spinazzola, *Pompei alla luce degli scavi nuovi di Via dell'Abbondanza* (Rome, 1953), Tavole III.
5 Carpenters' procession, MANN 8991. Photo, M. Larvey.
6 Gambling scene from the Bar on the Via di Mercurio. Photo, R. Cormack.
7 Forum scene from *Praedia* of Julia Felix, MANN 9068. Photo courtesy of Corbis.
8 Model of the House of the Tragic Poet, N. Wood.
9 Detail of model of the House of the Tragic Poet, N. Wood.
10 Painting from west wall of the *triclinium* in the Bakery of the House of the Chaste Lovers. Photo, M. Larvey.

Illustrations

In addition to the credits noted above, the following illustrations are reproduced with the authorisation of the Italian Ministero per I Beni e le Attività Culturali:

Soprintendenza Archeologica di Pompei: Colour plates 6, 10. Illustrations 2, 8, 12, 15, 17, 19, 20, 30, 33, 35, 36, 38, 43, 52, 57, 66, 75, 79, 86, 104, 108. Museo Archeologico Nazionale di Napoli: Colour plates 5, 12, 13, 15, 22. Illustrations 1, 3, 7, 11, 16, 46, 49, 56, 62, 68, 71, 73, 74, 93, 95, 98, 99, 105. Soprintendenza Archeologica di Napoli: Colour plate 23.

While every effort has been made to contact copyright-holders of illustrations, the author and publishers would be grateful for information about any illustrations where they have been unable to trace them, and would be glad to make amendments in further editions.

INDEX